THE ORAL HISTORY OF MODERN ARCHITECTURE

Interviews with the Greatest Architects of the Twentieth Century

John Peter

THE ORAL HISTORY OF

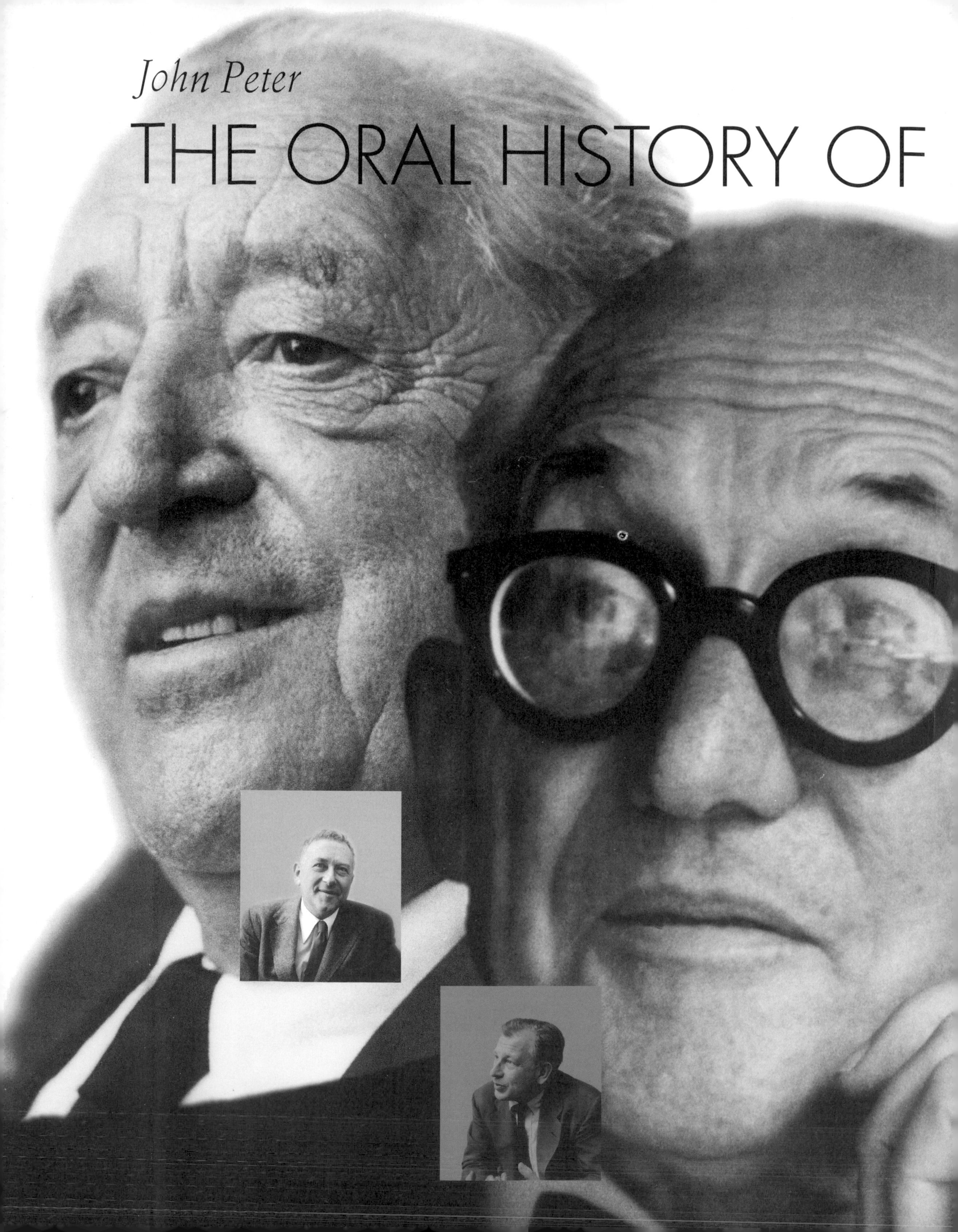

Interviews with the Greatest Architects of the Twentieth Century

MODERN ARCHITECTURE

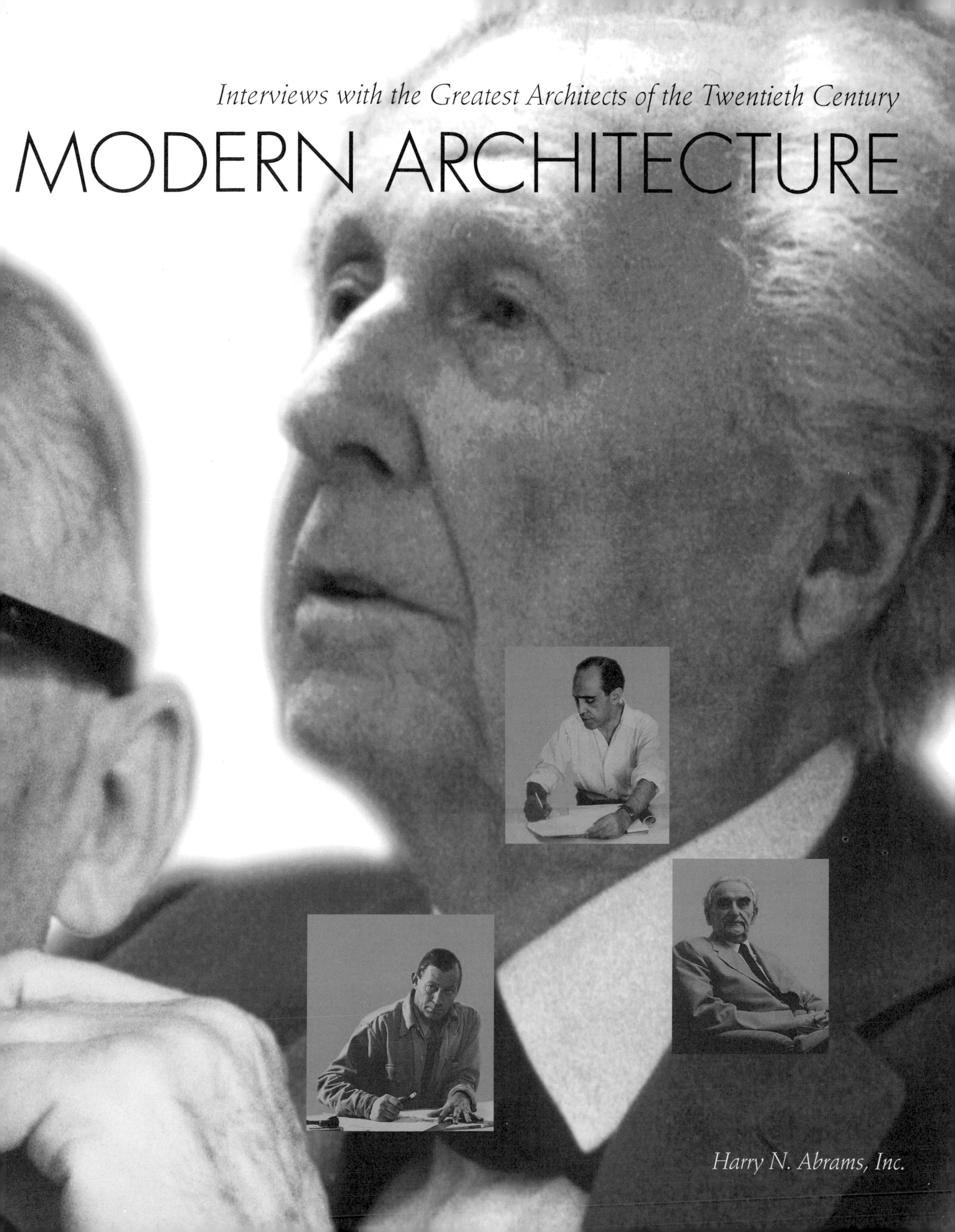

Harry N. Abrams, Inc.

CONTENTS

to my wife, Anna, and my children,
Laurie, Wendy, Sarah, Molly

Editor: Diana Murphy
Designer: Robert McKee

Library of Congress Cataloging-in-Publication Data

Peter, John, 1917-
The oral history of modern architecture: interviews with the greatest architects of the twentieth century / John Peter.
p. cm.
Includes bibliographical references and index.
ISBN 0-8109-3669-0
1. Architects—Interviews. 2. Architecture, Modern—20th century.
I. Title.
NA680.P375 1994
724' .6—dc20

Published in 1994 by Harry N. Abrams, Incorporated, New York
A Times Mirror Company

Additional copyright notices are on p. 314.
Printed and bound in the United States

Title page: left to right, Ludwig Mies van der Rohe, Le Corbusier, Frank Lloyd Wright; inset, Marcel Breuer, Eero Saarinen, Alvar Aalto, Oscar Niemeyer, Richard Neutra

Preface

"THIS IS THE STORY OF MODERN ARCHITECTURE IN THE RECORDED WORDS OF THOSE WHO CREATED IT."

Oral history is not new. In the earliest ages of mankind all history was oral history. Yet oral history as we know it today developed only in recent times with the introduction of sound-recording equipment. The early recordings in *The Oral History of Modern Architecture* were made on a bulky Wollensak, a reel-to-reel tape machine that was optimistically described as portable.

Only recently has oral history been recognized as a valid form of history. If, as historian William Moss suggests, "the discipline of history is a means by which we may keep from kidding ourselves about what has happened," it follows that audio recordings are a highly qualified source of history. Like the shards from an archaeological dig, oral history is a kind of artifact from which we can help reconstruct a period of the past.

When I embarked on the *Oral History* project, in the early 1950s, it was not only because of my special interest in architecture, but also because architecture, which involves politics, planning, finance, engineering, and construction, lags behind the other fine arts. By that time the founders of modern painting and sculpture had died. However, many of the early masters of modern architecture were still alive, and by a circumstance of history a number were residing in the United States. I did not set out to write a book. I wanted to capture the architects' voices before they were lost.

I began by visiting the office of historian Allan Nevins, who had very recently established an oral history program at Columbia University in New York. I found that the program's mission was to prepare written documents for historical research. Once transcribed, the tapes were erased for reuse. To this day still, far and away the bulk of oral history represents invaluable social research undertaken by historians to record the less-privileged members of society who had no voice in past history. The emphasis has been on providing written documents for historians, and less attention has been paid to the audio aspect. Since I viewed the audio record as the raison d'être of my undertaking, I set out on my own.

I made the first tape in 1953 and the last in 1989. In all, my colleagues and I recorded, in their homes and offices, over seventy architects and architectural engineers who practiced during the period of the International Style, which may be defined roughly as the 1920s through the 1960s. The original tapes of *The Oral History of Modern Architecture* represent an archival document. Only a portion of the total recordings are utilized in this work.

The architects were selected on the basis of several criteria. They were voted the most significant modern architects living at that time in a poll we made of over one hundred American architects. This list was cross-checked by citation frequency in the leading international books and journals of modern architecture. From these sources, we made a serious attempt at a consensus regarding the architects to be recorded, and we traveled the world to achieve it. Fortunately for this history, a number of them were driven by World War II to the United States, such as Walter Gropius, Ludwig Mies van der Rohe, Marcel Breuer, L. L. Rado, José Luis Sert, and Antonin Raymond. We did tape more architects born in America than in any other nation. A few of the individuals we had selected, like the Brazilian planner Lucio Costa and the Swedish architect Gunnar Asplund, were unavailable for an interview. Some, like Alvar Aalto and Pier Luigi Nervi, by inclination and the pressure of work, gave us less time than we might have wished. On account of a mechanical failure, the material from the session with Le Corbusier is briefer and less satisfactory than I would have liked. It is the sole case where I have taken the liberty of including in the book some words transcribed from another audio source. However, the audio selection of Le Corbusier is taken from our visit with him. We recorded a number of architects in their native tongue. Some who could speak English preferred their own language, to be more precise. For this book and compact disc their remarks have been translated, but on the disc I have also included some in the original language.

The present book, in company with the recording on compact disc, is an effort to create an appropriate oral history format. Like early modern architecture itself, it is marked by enthusiasm for the new and suffers from lack of precedent. It endeavors to tell the story of modern architecture in the living words of the individuals who created it. While avoiding the lexicon and form of academic research, my colleagues and I have made every effort to create a document that is thorough and precise.

With an oral history there looms always the large question of whether the people who created the works under discussion are the best judges of what they accomplished. Are the players the best judges of the game? Most people would respond along with historians that a more objective and accurate appraisal can be made by outside authorities with both independence and perspective. There are, indeed, many books on modern architecture written from the outside by highly qualified authorities. Ours represents an effort to do something different—to tell the early story from the inside. What the founders of modern architecture thought and said they were doing is essential to a real understanding of what they did. It is true that many of these pioneers wrote their own books and lectured about their ideas. Le Corbusier's publications may well have been more influential than his built work. Others, such as Gropius, have frequently been described as propagandists. One of the activities of the Bauhaus was book publishing. Frank Lloyd Wright told me, "My father was a preacher and I'm a preacher, too." This work seeks to provide the living words of not only the founders, but also other contemporary architects, less renowned, who provide important insights into those people and their times. Such is the very loam of history.

As in all history, one period overlaps another. Indeed, Gothic cathedrals are still being built in the United States today. Modern architecture has its roots in the architecture of the past. There is a long and familiar list of early architects and builders who sought the new forms of modern architecture. They receive less emphasis in this work than they deserve quite simply because they were no longer alive when I began making the recordings. Fortunately, in the cases of H. P. Berlage, Peter Behrens, Tony Garnier, Adolf Loos, Auguste Perret, Eliel Saarinen, Louis Sullivan, Henri van de Velde, and Otto Wagner, we were able to tape some observations of people who knew them. These are included in the book.

In the pages that follow, the observations of most of the architects interviewed are included in the introduction or are grouped under the headings Technology, Society, and Art, so-named for three important forces that shaped modern architecture. In Great Works the architects respond to my request to name individual buildings that were especially influential to them and to explain the reasons for their choices. Some preferred instead to name architects for their entire body of work. It is no surprise that three architects—Frank Lloyd Wright, Le Corbusier, and Mies—were overwhelmingly considered the most outstanding and influential. More-extended thoughts and ideas of ten highly significant contributors to the field—Wright, Le Corbusier, Mies, Gropius, Eero Saarinen, Louis Kahn, Philip Johnson, Oscar Niemeyer, Sert, and I. M. Pei—are featured in individual sections. In Assessments architects comment on modern architecture and its potential for the future. The accompanying CD presents excerpts from the recorded conversations with sixteen architects: the ten mentioned above, along with Alvar Aalto, Breuer, Pier Luigi Nervi, Richard Neutra, J. J. P. Oud, and Kenzo Tange.

Not surprisingly, a distinctive print format for oral history has not yet evolved. Books of recorded interviews generally follow a question-and-answer format in traditional magazine style. In designing this book, we have sought to create an oral format responding to the special nature of the material. For example, informal photographs of the architects taken at the time of the interviews are a prominent part of the work in emphasizing the fact that this is a personal oral history. This, despite Wright's assurance to his wife, Olgivanna, when we were taking pictures, "You'd be surprised how little photographs show." Accompanying the text are illustrations and captions selected to supplement and enrich it.

Just as we have learned that early civilizations did not exist in worlds apart and that ideas traveled across the ancient continents and daunting oceans, we know that ideas move with far more amazing speed across our modern world. As the American architect Eero Saarinen, son of the Finn Eliel Saarinen, observed, "My father admitted that Sullivan's Transportation Building in the Chicago Fair influenced him greatly when he designed the railroad station in Helsinki. Of course, everybody in the whole world is aware of everybody else in architecture."

It is perhaps only natural that today we might assume these architects knew the work of certain other architects, movements, or even distant periods or civilizations. We may even suspect that they did know them but deliberately disavowed this knowledge in self-justification or in the cause of a pure, clear doctrine. There is frequently a wide discrepancy between their words and their works. Nevertheless, the tapes have recorded what they said or chose to say. In fact, on hearing their actual voices one cannot help but be struck by the sincerity of and dedication to their beliefs. For the most part it would seem both cynical and cavalier to doubt whether they were telling the truth as they perceived it.

Unquestionably, the best way to know architecture is to experience it. I have visited and revisited a good number of the recognized great works of modern architecture. There is nothing like living for a time at Taliesin or attending a beautifully sung high mass at Ronchamp to appreciate them. With this in mind, I have provided a Visitor's Guide at the back of the book, which lists the addresses of many important works of modern architecture open to the public.

It well may be argued that hearing about architecture is the least valuable way to understand and appreciate it. However, there is something uniquely convincing and moving in hearing the spoken words of these people, with the individual timbre, pronunciation, and emphasis that no other medium can surpass. It is history alive. An oral history book perhaps demands more of the reader then a regular history book. Like all conversations, oral history is discursive. Within limits I sought to channel the recording sessions, but it is the wandering observation and anecdote that give the *Oral History* its documentary interest and sense of life. There is a significant and distinctive quality to the spontaneity of thoughts expressed in speech. The reader will also be asked to put up with a certain amount of repetition. A good deal of overlap appeared in the comments of the architects. I have deleted much of it in compiling the book, but have left enough to demonstrate the universality of experiences and ideas that coalesced into modern architecture.

The term modern architecture, as used in this project, refers to the predominant trends of a forty-year period. As historian Henry-Russell Hitchcock wrote, "No better name than 'modern' has yet been found for what has come to be the characteristic architecture of the twentieth century throughout the western world. . . ." It is the important task of scholars to explore the diversity within modern architecture, as with architecture of the Gothic, Baroque, and other periods. The *Oral History* is a witness to some of this plurality.

There remains the difficult task of determining when modern architecture began. For the purposes of this work, we have somewhat arbitrarily considered it in relation to the publication of two books. The first was written by Henry-Russell Hitchcock and Philip Johnson to accompany a 1932 exhibition at The Museum of Modern Art, New York. Entitled *The International Style,* it baptized modern architecture. Johnson said to me, "Nineteen twenty-three is what I call the magic year, the annus mirabile, that is, the year from which the historians, I am absolutely certain, will date this style."

With equally arbitrary logic we have considered the publication of *Complexity and Contradiction in Architecture* by Robert Venturi thirty-four years later as heralding what is described as Post-Modern architecture. Although in continuing to develop the oral history document we have, to date, interviewed others and reinterviewed some of the original architects, we have, with the exceptions of Niemeyer and Pei, who referred to their early works in subsequent interviews, confined our book to observations made before 1966. Throughout the book, the year of the interview has been placed in the margin by the quotation.

We can now say of modern architecture what Winston Churchill said of the Battle of Britain, "It is not the beginning of the end, but it is the end of the beginning." In the real world and in the real world of architecture, things are not even as tidy as this. In my conversation with Walter Gropius, he warned, "The irrepressible urge of critics to classify contemporary movements which are still in flux, putting each neatly in a coffin with a style label on it, has increased the widespread confusion in understanding the dynamic forces of the new movement in architecture and planning." The *Oral History* includes Frank Lloyd Wright, who was working before this century began, as well as architects designing in the International Style who may be practicing when the century ends. The time chart on pages 306–07 shows the overlapping life spans of the architects in the book.

There are so many people and organizations to whom I am indebted for this work that I have named them on a separate page later in the book. However, I cannot fail here to mention Pat Del Grosso, who has served as director of The Oral History of Modern Architecture Project for the last seven years. It would be difficult for me to imagine a more dedicated and stimulating colleague. With suggestions and admonitions, she has contributed immensely to this effort.

Although the book begins with some background to the modern movement and closes with appraisals, the emphasis is on living history at the time it occurred rather than as viewed today in hindsight. In the *Oral History* read, see, and hear the creators of modern architecture, judge them and their works for yourself.

Introduction

"LIKE TRUE REVOLUTIONARIES THEY WERE INSPIRED BY A PURE VISION WHICH THEY PRACTICED WITH DEDICATED ENTHUSIASM."

Modern architecture was a revolution. It destroyed the existing Beaux-Arts regime and replaced it with a new order. The face of the earth would never be the same. The architects came from such places as Richland Center, Wisconsin; La Chaux-de-Fonds, Switzerland; Aachen, Germany; Pécs, Hungary; Barcelona, Spain; Rio de Janeiro, Brazil; Kuortane, Finland; and Imahara, Japan. Like true revolutionaries they were inspired by a pure vision, which they preached and practiced with dedicated enthusiasm as well as frequent intolerance.

All revolutions are rooted in the past. In perspective, modern architecture can be viewed in the flow of history, but more specifically as the result of the cataclysmic changes that took place in the nineteenth century. Architecture is a product of its time or "not of the time but of the epoch," as the master architect Ludwig Mies van der Rohe put it. Without attempting to assign priorities to these changes as they affected architecture, it is nonetheless clear that they occurred in three areas of contemporary life and culture: technology, society, and art.

As the twentieth century dawned, architecture was clearly overdue for a change. The nineteenth-century Beaux-Arts style was out of joint with the times. Frequent observations in the Oral History *tapes express the widespread recognition that the vitality had drained from the Beaux-Arts. It had calcified into traditional forms, essentially decorative, which were no longer relevant to the new age.*

Mies van der Rohe remembers:
When I was, maybe, sixteen years old I worked in the stucco business. In the morning we had to do a quarter of a full-size ceiling in Louis Quatorze, in the afternoon, one in the Renaissance. We went through all these periods, chestnut ornaments and so on. I got so much of it that I couldn't be impressed anymore with these things.

Another characteristic observation was that of the Mexican architect Juan O'Gorman:
The architectural school I went to was an academic school where they taught us on the basis of the Beaux-Arts. The Greek orders were the order of the day. Everything was that. If you made a secondary school it had two stories. Therefore there were two orders and so on and so on. It was the usual Beaux-Arts academic stuff and that, of course, was piled on in such a way that we became completely bored with it.

The American architect Eliot Noyes recounts his youthful feelings:
Eclecticism was the thing that was going on around us. Harvard was building only old-fashioned stuff. Yale was going up Harkness Gothic. "Thanks to Mr. Harkness for his expensive Gothic darkness," is a line out of a Harvard song. Harvard, I thought, was luckier because at least it had the big-window style of the Georgian.

I entered Harvard architectural school, where they were to give us the tools that we would need. This, it turned out, was still under Jean-Jacques Hafner, a wonderful old Frenchman who had hardly ever built anything in his life, but who was still in the old Beaux-Arts tradition.

My first problem was a Doric gateway. I ran across this drawing the other day in the basement here. It is the kind of gate around the Harvard Yard that says, "Enter and Grow in Wisdom," or "Plato," "Aristotle," "Socrates" across the pediment. I find that my own mood at the time was very nicely expressed by the inscription on mine, which reads, "Ad Absurdum," cut into the stone.

Well, the next problem I was given was an Ionic temple to a great French actress. This was beginning to seem a little silly.

All the drawings were done in Chinese ink. Do you remember Chinese ink? You used to grind it in the pot and you'd drip it so that you could get all the sediment out. Then you'd take one drop of it with some water and then you'd run a wash. You'd run another wash and after about ten washes you'd gotten it down so that you could see that it was a gray there. This is the way all these renderings were done. You built it up and it made these beautiful transparent drawings. It gave you a marvelous exercise in using brushes and all this stuff.

But by the time my second problem came around, I wanted to use watercolor. Well, this was heresy. I, however, did do it in watercolor—a sort of gray-green terrible wash—but it was on this Ionic temple. I wasn't doing very well with these things, really.

The next one was supposed to be Corinthian. I remember, at about this time, I observed some advanced class which was working on a problem which was a palace for an exiled monarch. Isn't that marvelous? A palace for an exiled monarch! Here we are, 1933 or something or other, facing the world, a whole new generation trying to solve its problems.

By this time we'd identified all the books in the library where you'd got the proper proportions for Corinthian, Doric, and Ionic, and you realized that this was the way architects have been trained for a long, long time in this country. Every school, I think, was like this. It was the beginning of a real period of restlessness for me.

Antonin Raymond recalls when he was a student in Czechoslovakia:
It was around 1906, 1907, 1908, you see. In our discussions in the society of the architecture students, the Czech architecture magazines, one of them was called *Smer,* which meant "direction," was already modern and introduced us to Frank Lloyd Wright. You see, because about that time Wasmuth in Berlin published the first book on Frank Lloyd Wright, the small one, I don't know if you ever saw it. And then the big portfolio came out in 1908, while I was still at school, you see, and it had a

tremendous influence on us. Then I also began to long to go to the country which created Frank Lloyd Wright, because I felt that Europe was finished. Everything was finished.

However, Minoru Yamasaki and a number of others later found things to admire in the Beaux-Arts training:
During the period that I was in school, the Beaux-Arts system was a predominant system in the United States and modern architecture was hardly thought of. To me, at that time, modern architecture meant battered walls and simple lines, but I did not have an understanding of modern architecture as such.

At that time we all disliked the Beaux-Arts system. I suppose because everyone dislikes the thing at hand more than anything else. But, also, because we realized that there was something completely false about the Beaux-Arts.

However, looking back on it now, I'm rather glad that I had this kind of background because one of the needs that we are just beginning to understand is the development of feeling for proportion, for refinement and detail. I think that we learned much more about that from the Beaux-Arts than we did from the Bauhaus.

Partly because of the reaction from this overrefined architecture that they were doing, we abandoned completely the idea of the fine details or proportion and only people like Mies really held fort on that.

It was the new science, with its offspring, technology, placing a premium on function that proved to be a principal lever in bringing down the Beaux-Arts tradition. One interpretation of the importance of function in architecture was the emphasis on structure. As early as the mid-1800s, Eugène-Emanuel Viollet-le-Duc, the restorer of ancient French châteaux, concluded that everything in a building had to have not only a reason, but a structural reason.

It was, perhaps, an inevitable consequence of the priority given to structure that engineers, in this new age of science, produced some of the seminal works of modern architecture. In London in 1851, Joseph Paxton created an enormous iron and glass exhibition hall christened the Crystal Palace. It consisted of 123 standardized units. Erected in just six months, it covered one-third of a mile in Hyde Park. In New York in 1869, John August Roebling pioneered a use of steel, suspending the Brooklyn Bridge from great cables to span the East River. In Paris in 1889, Gustave Eiffel erected the unprecedented 984-foot tower of prefabricated iron parts that bears his name. These three pioneering structures are also the ones most-often mentioned in the Oral History *recordings.*

The architect and structural engineer Eduardo Catalano observed:
The building that was done one hundred years ago but, I feel, is contemporary in spirit and concept is Paxton's Crystal Palace. I am very interested in that building. I think the building really puts all the present philosophies of design into effect, like standardization, demountability, modular coordination, lightness, and so on. . . . Also, it has a wonderful design that is very well related to the atmosphere of Hyde Park. So it is not only the building as a piece itself, but it's related to the environment.

Frank Lloyd Wright told me that he admired all three men—Paxton, Roebling, and Eiffel—but said that the Eiffel Tower could have been made of wood because the material was used in compression, whereas Roebling employed steel in tension.

Regarding tension, Buckminster Fuller had this comment:
I point out to you that the augmentation in man's technical advantage over our a priori environment lies strictly in the history of the improvement of the tensile strengths of the various alloys. . . . At the present moment, the inventory of tensile abilities has been so augmented that we're now ready to do a bridge twice the size of Golden Gate. This isn't because men are more daring, it is simply that there is higher ability.

Neither Paxton, Roebling, nor Eiffel were architects, they were engineers. As Louis Sullivan remarked in his book Kindergarten Chats, *"The engineers were the only men who could face a problem squarely." Their works were outstanding, but not unique in the early nineteenth century. Smaller iron and glass structures like Paxton's had been built for botanical gardens. Bridges, most notably the early British railway bridges of Thomas Telford, George Stephenson, Robert Stephenson, and Isambard Kingdom Brunel, were the very symbols of the new age. In the 1889 Paris Exhibition, Eiffel's tower was complemented by the Palais des Machines. Designed by the architect Ferdinand Dutert and the engineer Victor Contamin, it had great arched ribs of steel that rested on huge hinged joints.*

In their 1932 book The International Style, *Henry-Russell Hitchcock and Philip Johnson singled out structure as the first principle of the new style. They cited the fact that the modern building is constructed with a supporting skeleton and screening walls, as distinct from traditional construction, in which masonry walls were both the supports and the protection from the weather. The authors cited as other characteristics of the International Style regularity and the use of standardized parts, as well as the absence of applied ornament and the emphasis on surfacing materials.*

As Mies van der Rohe observed:
I saw that the structural elements are important to show with simplicity. It was a more objective architecture.

However, function was interpreted in terms not only of structure, but also of performance. The invention of the steam engine, pioneered by the Scotsman James Watt, marks for many the beginning of the Industrial Revolution. The functional efficiency of the machine was widely admired by early modern architects. Machines function and buildings should function. This was a restricted interpretation of function, but it was a clear one. Sullivan's dictum, "Form follows function," became one of the rallying cries of the revolution. Interpreted even more narrowly than he intended, it led to a reexamination of both the needs and the purposes of architecture.

Eero Saarinen remarked:
In a way function became one of the gimmicks, one of the sales gimmicks, of modern

architecture, but it was a sort of Frankenstein that was created. Architects began to believe that through the function, this Frankenstein would come up with the architecture. So they sat around and waited for him to produce, but he didn't.

Le Corbusier's dramatic definition, "A house is a machine for living in," was a characteristic overstatement of the period. Its impact and durability, however, rest not only on the fact that it was an insightful way of looking at a house. It was a dramatic declaration of architecture's practical aspects. Le Corbusier's view was and is entirely of our modern age and no other. It has the excitement of radical, revolutionary times.

Along with functional efficiency, the technology of the machine implied economic efficiency. The machine would make architecture less expensive. This premise was to prove deceptive in some celebrated instances where innovative architects exceeded budgets. Yet what is frequently lost sight of is that modern architecture is dramatically more cost efficient. While this fact may dismay some enthusiasts and disappoint some critics, a fundamental reason for the success of modern architecture is that in the modern world it is, by and large, cheaper.

The products of the new technology—steel beams and cables, reinforced concrete, and plastic—changed the way buildings were designed and built. Units mass-produced in factories and assembled with modern machinery on the site save both time and money. Perhaps most important of all, they save labor. All of this is still true today, despite the fact that our buildings contain sophisticated equipment for heating, cooling, lighting, communications, and security unimagined in earlier times.

Focusing, as most architectural books do and as the Oral History does, on the outstanding examples of the art of architecture, one might lose sight of the billions of modern buildings throughout the world. The truth is that except in undeveloped societies, it is today prohibitively difficult and expensive to build in any style other than modern.

In addition to inspiring an emphasis on structure and efficiency in architecture, the machine had direct effects on the aesthetics of buildings. For example, Le Corbusier not only propagated in his writings functional comparison between architecture and such modern machines as the ocean liner and the airplane, he also applied the appearance of these machines in his own architectural designs.

The machine aesthetic was an important influence in the development of modern design, but it was not the only one. Modern art—both painting and sculpture—also inspired architectural design. For instance, Le Corbusier divided his time fairly equally between art and architecture. His drawings and paintings are generally admired, but it was the style of his architectural drawings that was widely adopted as the rendering style of modern architecture.

The Dutch art movement De Stijl also had an important aesthetic impact on early modern architecture. Founded in 1917, the De Stijl group of artists and architects was loosely organized around the magazine of the same name. Central to the movement's development were the radical theories of color and space evolved by the painter Piet Mondrian. De Stijl embraced not only painting and architecture but also furniture, graphics, and typography. Painter-turned-architect Theo van Doesburg, architect J. J. P. Oud, and designer Gerrit

Rietveld applied the theories to buildings. De Stijl's simple abstract shapes and brilliant primary colors expressed the desire to wipe art and architecture clean of the past by using formal elements that could be understood universally.

Oud noted:
Mondrian was, in my opinion, looking for a clear, bright world. He tried to make, in simple forms, proportions and color the strongest values in art. And that's the same thing that I try to do in architecture.

A less direct, but perhaps more important influence on modern architecture was that of traditional Japanese architecture. Elements of this style were translated and transmitted by the residential open plans of the American architect Frank Lloyd Wright, although he resolutely denies he was influenced by Japanese architecture. Wright told me, "I didn't even see the Japanese building at the Chicago World's Fair." The 1910 Wasmuth publication of Wright's work in Germany had an explosive effect. The free-flowing spatial continuity destroyed the classical box room.

The ideas of modern architecture run back to European philosophic and scientific traditions. Mies was fond of quoting the medieval philosopher Thomas Aquinas. Richard Neutra refers to the German physiologist Wilhelm Wundt. More proximate roots can be found in the socioeconomic theories of Karl Marx and Friedrich Engels. Socialism defined the ideological climate of the early 1900s. Its interpretation of social justice provided the sense of moral imperative that characterized the entire modern architectural and design revolution.

Another frequently cited early source of modern architecture is the English Arts and Crafts movement, initiated by William Morris in 1861. He argued that machines were devaluing aesthetic quality and destroying traditional craftsmanship. He sought a new social order by restoring craftsmanship into industrial society.

In the climate of Germany such ideas took a different turn. The machine came to be viewed as an elaborate and versatile new tool in the hands of the craftspeople. In 1907 artisans, industrialists, and architects joined together in Munich to form the Deutsche Werkbund, maintaining that it was more ethical for craftspeople to design mass-produced products for the public than unique objects of art for the wealthy.

Ideas have consequence, but the true measure of architecture must be buildings—buildings built. As early as the last decade of the nineteenth century many of these ideas were simmering into building. In Brussels in 1897 the Belgian architect Victor Horta dramatized the new materials in the Maison du Peuple with its curved iron and glass facade. During the same years another Belgian, Henri van de Velde, urged the creation of a new architecture that incorporated the new industrial materials into the Art Nouveau style. He realized it in his design of the Werkbund Theater in Cologne.

The Swiss architect Alfred Roth remembers:
Henri van de Velde was living in Switzerland during the last ten years of his life. I met him very frequently. It was a wonderful time for me to stay with a man of his

importance and greatness of spirit, having been at the beginning of the modern movement. So, naturally, I had discussions with him and he said some wonderful things. Something which I will never forget is: "Art comes only out there where things are done with love."

In 1887, with equal dedication, the Scotsman Charles Rennie Mackintosh designed the School of Art in Glasgow with a vigor that was later recognized as a mark of modern architecture. The same year the Dutch architect Hendrik Petrus Berlage combined brick and iron with straightforward respect for the materials in his Amsterdam Stock Exchange Building.

Oud spoke of Berlage:
I was friends and connected with the Berlage family. So I had the privilege of meeting and talking now and then with Berlage. I admired his works, his buildings, and his building principles. In the beginning I tried to follow the latter, and, later, I strove after enlargement of his principles and came to ideas of my own. This did not really lead to conclusions other than the ones to which he came. I think that part of his principle was to build honestly. Not to build with adornments and so on, but to build exactly out of construction. That was what interested me in Berlage very much. It may be that I admire more what he did after his convictions than what he showed. I don't think what he did is all beautiful. He also made ugly things, but the things were true. It was the first time you saw a true architecture. That was what interested me so much, you see.

As early as 1895 Louis Sullivan designed the Guaranty Building of Buffalo with the strong vertical style that became characteristic of the American skyscraper. Frank Lloyd Wright observed, "Lieber Meister was a poet. He was the type we don't have now." The Frenchman Auguste Perret pioneered the use of reinforced concrete in buildings like the Church of Notre-Dame in Le Raincy, near Paris.

The Swiss architect Marc Saugey makes the point that:
Perret was extremely helpful in paving the way for contemporary architecture, and around 1910, without a doubt, his influence was enormous. I worked as a draftsman at Perret's and saw the utility of his work. Perret always said, "Reinforced concrete exists. I build in reinforced concrete."

But I think Perret failed to free himself in time from the classical education he received at the École des Beaux-Arts in Paris. He was always held back by wanting to give too conventional a plasticity to reinforced concrete. He still worked with the pedestal, the capital, the architrave. One feels, in all his buildings, he did not escape enough from his bonds.

Today, with Nervi, for example, we see how one can exploit reinforced concrete in a plastic way without resorting to these old solutions which date back to the use of stone.

Perret struggled against later contemporary architects, in particular against Le Corbusier. I think he was afflicted with the same malady as that suffered by certain revolutionaries toward the end of their lives.

Saugey had this to say about another reinforced-concrete pioneer, Tony Garnier:
When I had the pleasure of having conversations with Tony Garnier, one of the major modern French architects, he told me, as he would to a friend, "Remember that when one has a clear idea, whatever the size of a project, the project can be drawn on a metro ticket. If you are not capable of expressing your idea on a tiny scrap of paper, well then, your idea is not yet defined. Therefore do not begin to draw yet, continue searching."

In Vienna in the early twentieth century, the Austrian architect Otto Wagner was widely recognized for work that included the Post Office Savings Bank. In the Post Office and other buildings, he employed modern materials in a manner that reflected his classical training. Richard Neutra said, "As to his architecture it is probably the European equivalent to what Frank Lloyd Wright did here or Sullivan before him." Meanwhile the uncompromising Adolf Loos, who maintained that ornament was a sin, went largely unheralded.

The Austrian born American architect Victor Gruen recalls:
A person who impressed me very much was Adolf Loos. Adolf Loos not only built, but he also wrote. He was probably one of the clearest thinkers and strongest attackers on everything which seemed to him old-fashioned. I believe many young people were very excited by what he had to say. I always remember that he used to show us a beautiful, British-made suitcase and say, "This is design."

Shortly before that there was a great excitement about the first big building which Loos erected in Vienna. It was built opposite the Hofburg, which is a castle of the Austrian kaiser. Inasmuch as that was before the revolution, the kaiser got terribly upset because he said he couldn't look at such a building without eyebrows. So Loos had to put eyebrows on it. He did it in the form of little flowerpots which hung below each window. Loos had a tough fight. I was so excited about him that I was very deeply moved when he died.

In fact, I wrote his obituary for one of the leading Viennese newspapers. I always felt because of his philosophical approach to architecture, because of his clear thinking and his attacking spirit, he was one of the most important contributors to modern architecture. It is probably true that the man has not built as much as others, but he had made his contribution to the direction of modern architecture by his writings, by his speaking, and by his fighting.

Actually, this man not only fought the classicism and the imitation of the Renaissance, but at the time when everybody else was engaged in inventing a new style, Art Nouveau, he fought Art Nouveau with the same kind of energy and disgust as he fought the Renaissance. He made his friends very unhappy, but he said it didn't make any more sense to put these silly flowers on the buildings than it did to put architraves in a classical order.

At the beginning of the new century, in 1909, the German architect Peter Behrens designed the influential Berlin Turbine Factory for the electrical firm Allgemeine Elektrizitäts-Gesellshaft. With its reinforced concrete and huge glazed side-walls, it signaled the emergence of a new architecture. Walter Gropius, Mies van der Rohe, and Le Corbusier worked in his office.

Van de Velde, Berlage, Sullivan, Perret, Garnier, Wagner, Loos, Behrens, and others we have just mentioned are the precursors who bring us up to the first generation of architects in the Oral History. *Every age has its turning point—a new way of perceiving the world. Though the founders of modern architecture do not hesitate, in the* Oral History, *to acknowledge their debts to the people and ideas of the past, they proclaimed themselves revolutionaries. They utilized the popular nomenclature of the proletarian revolution in propagandizing their doctrines. Manifestos, pamphlets, books, and speeches announced the advent of a new style. However, the bulk of this early vocabulary is absent from our recorded document, which was made when the movement and the participants had matured. Yet the basic concepts and convictions had not changed, nor had the enthusiasm for the cause diminished. This gives the first-person account its sense of living history.*

TECHNOLOGY

The Industrial Revolution changed the way people thought about building. The new technology, defined as industrial or applied science, produced a multiplying array of new machines and materials. The American superstrategist of technology Buckminster Fuller enthusiastically put it to me this way: "I want to make mankind a success through design."

Function has always been a part of architecture. Buildings were always expected to work. In his ten-book treatise On Architecture, *the Roman architect Vitruvius enumerates the qualities that define architecture: beauty, convenience, and durability. The latter two of these are functional. Early modern architecture redefined function in the image of that prototype creation of the*

"IN THE CASE OF ARCHITECTURE, TO LIKE OR DISLIKE IS NOT SIMPLY A MATTER OF TASTE. WE HAVE TO CHOOSE MATERIAL ACCORDING TO REALITIES."

new age, the machine. This concept was reinforced by the new functional building types—factories, plants, offices, and airports—demanded by the machine age. It is a challenge even to conceive of nuclear power plants or rocket-launching platforms in any style of the past.

Today it is sometimes difficult to grasp the dimension of physical changes wrought by modern architecture. One has only to compare photos of, say, Paris at the time the Oral History *begins with a city like Hong Kong in the 1960s to appreciate the scale of the technological revolution. Modern architects recognized the arrival of the new technological era, but they were divided on adapting to it.*

OLYMPIC STADIUM, CITY UNIVERSITY OF CARACAS.
Carlos Villanueva. Caracas, Venezuela. 1950

TOWN HALL. *Willem Dudok. Hilversum, the Netherlands. 1930. Combining the abstract De Stijl concepts with traditional Dutch building materials, Dudok designed an early milestone of the modern style.*

WILLEM DUDOK: 1961

It is, needless to say, that efficient construction is the first requisite of good architecture. But don't let us be so foolish as to identify this and to expect that correct construction will automatically lead to good architecture. Construction is a means, so important a means, that without it no architecture is possible, just as poetry is not imaginable without language.

Why should only visible construction be considered as honest work? An idea which, when I was young, was ventilated by many architects, has never become clear to me. It is neither necessary nor important that construction should always be visible. Such is not even the case in nature. No one would deny the efficiency or the beauty of the human body because the skeleton is not outwardly visible. One senses its presence, although it is hidden from view.

Nor do I see why one should not be allowed to cover a good reinforced-concrete construction with material of finer color and texture. I like to cover a reinforced-concrete skeleton in a building by fine enamels, for instance, that can be seen from the outside. Why not? You have to. They have to serve different purposes. Reinforced-concrete structure for the strength of the building, but the outer wall has to resist climatic influences as well, and it has quite a different function. You may cover the construction by other materials of a nicer texture or a fine color. Why not? I like to make use of enameled materials, plates and tiles.

I detest the color of concrete. It quickly becomes very dirty. I am a man who doesn't like that my buildings are weathering. I don't like that. If I begin a building I have in mind the color scheme of the building and I want it to stay that way. For instance, the same way that our great Grecian architects were proud when they were dying that they could say, "My building looks as if I built it yesterday. It stands as fresh as I built it at the time." You see what I mean? Now, if you see the reinforced-concrete building, oh, it is to weep.

Look here, you must not make unnatural constructions. You must make quite logical constructions. But it is not necessary that you can see that. You must feel that it is in the building. You will feel the construction if you see the building from the outside. You must feel the composition. I certainly want us to build in an efficient and uncomplicated way so that full justice is done to the character of the material used and to the method of the construction. But, after all, it is not the construction which is the essential, but space. Man is served by space.

ELIOT NOYES: 1957

This business about the function was a very crystal clear thing in my mind. It was very clear to me as a guide when I latched on to it. The function is the clue. We scrutinized hard for the function and this became the clue to form. Then came the arguments, you know the drafting room arguments at school. "Okay, I'm going to put a vase out in front of my driveway on a pedestal and it's 'function' too. Its function is to give me pleasure as I come into the house." Now this immediate distortion of what was to me a very crystal clear thing was very bad. We used to have real battles about it.

It seems to me that the nice thing about the idea of function was that you could knock off this vase argument, and say that is exactly what it does not mean, and that function, as we're talking about it, is the function of the machine, the efficiency, the right relationship of parts. As that was our clue; it really took us quite a ways.

The appeal of it was that so many of the buildings that we were inhabiting—houses, classrooms, dormitories—function so badly in this so clear sense. You know, okay, let's solve that one thing and we're off to the glorious future. We didn't realize that this was still too limiting for really good architecture, great architecture, ever to come out of it, but it sure was a good clue. It really was.

FRANK LLOYD WRIGHT: 1955

Workmanship and design are one thing. Good workmanship has to have a good design because the design is in the nature of the workmanship. You can't separate workmanship from design. This organic architecture I'm representing and preaching and trying to build is based upon what? The machine as a tool. Craftsmanship, the thing the machine can do exceedingly well, made beautiful—that is what it is all about.

Now I have bones in my system. This hand is full of bones, isn't it? And what are the bones for? To activate the form, aren't they? Now if I take the bones out, and say the bones are this hand, is that true? It's only an element designed to activate the very form which has its uses, its purposes, and its expression. Now the International Style is just that foolish. It has left out what is beauty and what is human.

Form follows function, certainly. But who the hell cares? It's the form and the function, not reducing that to some scientific analysis, that will separate it and take it all apart. We want it together. We want the poetry of the thing.

R. BUCKMINSTER FULLER: 1964

You have to know about the difference between my kind of undertaking and the world of something that is called architecture. You can see how the architects like me.

I seem to be producing things that are akin to them. I always had a purpose, I had to produce higher and higher performance per pound. I'll find a Mies, incidentally with perfect integrity, I'm not charging that at all, but he said, "Less is more," but he's talking about that really aesthetically, not the way I'm talking about actual by weight.

When the university asked me what I wanted to call my work here they made me research professor. I gave them my title as generalized design science exploration.

Ford Motor Company was the first to come to me in an emergency on their need for their rotunda dome. They were getting ready for the fiftieth anniversary of the Ford Motor Company. Young Henry Ford was intent on doing something his grandfather would like. He said his grandfather had said for years he would like to have the rotunda court domed over. They were not getting anywhere near the use of the rotunda they should have been. He thought it would be fine to build that dome. But he didn't think about that until it was relatively late, about three-quarters of a year to go to the opening. Then he asked his engineers to arrange it.

FORD ROTUNDA. *R. Buckminster Fuller. Dearborn, Michigan. 1953. Erected in thirty days on an existing building, Fuller's first geodesic dome of aluminum and plastic was a celebrated structural breakthrough.*

They found that the rotunda building which Ford had had out at the Chicago World's Fair was made of very light steel framing, not meant to be a permanent building at all. But old Henry had liked it so much he had it moved from Chicago to Dearborn and had it re-erected. So the structure wasn't anywhere nearly heavy enough to carry a conventional dome. They said they'd have to beef the building up to carry the weight of a conventional dome. Young Henry was intent about this. He had a cousin, another Ford, and he knew about my work. He was a typical one of these students who'd run into me and he told his cousin, Henry, that he thought that possibly I could do it.

So Ford Motor Company came to me and I was given the job, but the Ford engineers were so skeptical about it that they really battled me all the way through that job. I had to work very, very hard on it, and I did get it done a month ahead of time and for a relatively small amount of money. I had erected it on a vast hydraulic lift. We had finally let the dome down on the roof and removed the scaffolding and there was a great celebration.

It was great and the chief engineer of the Ford Motor Company came to me and said, "I'm going to not only congratulate you, but I'm going to shock you. I hate to tell you, but we were so certain that your dome wouldn't work and that you wouldn't get it up that we let a contract to a wrecker to remove the unfinished work to get it out of the way." They had twenty-five million dollars all invested in the TV shows and all the things that were going to go on this fiftieth anniversary. If the building was going to fall down they wanted to get this junk out of the way. So, he said, "We were retaining him on an emergency basis" and, he said, "We've actually paid him more than we're paying you to build it."

The rise of modern architecture was due in large part to the development of new materials: processed materials such as steel and glass; composites, including concrete reinforced with steel; synthetic plastics; and veneers of every sort. All of these were not new. Steel was made from iron about one thousand years ago in India and unsurpassed Japanese steel swords were forged in A.D. *800. But steel only replaced iron in architecture at the begin-*

ning of this century. The origins of glass are lost in antiquity. There are glass beads dating back to 2500 B.C. *Although glass had been used for windows since Roman times, processed sheet-glass came only with the industrial age. The Romans used concrete, but the modern reinforcement with steel initiated its true structural use.*

Modern architecture was characterized not only by the materials, but also by architects' forthright attitudes toward them. As Ludwig Mies van der Rohe said, "A girder is nothing to be ashamed of."

J. J. P. Oud

J.J.P. OUD: 1961

My favorite building material is concrete protected by the covering with bricks. For the bricks I prefer great bricks in bright colors. For the greater part, white, with now and then a door, a gutter, or something like that in strong, pure color. This gives a gay and cheerful effect. I like a joyful architecture just as I like a joyful mankind. Architecture can help to bring forth the latter. It is a wonderful thing to be a good architect.

ERNESTO ROGERS: 1961

I think that material is only means. I don't think, therefore, that there are only good or bad means. There are good ends and bad ends. If you are able to use brick you can do a masterpiece as the Robie House by Wright. If you are Mies van der Rohe you will use steel fundamentally. If you are Corbusier you will use concrete. I think the three examples there offer all the conventional possibility for everyone. Of course, there are some congenialities for some artists.

MARC SAUGEY: 1961

I think new solutions are arising in technology. We were speaking last night of Nervi's idea. In contrast to nature, he feels we are still using far too much material in building and that the structural approach to building will certainly give way to an enveloping support system, as is found in nature with leaves, with conch shells, or other shells.

Among these technological developments, furthermore, one must keep in mind the new materials in this area with all of the plastics and other artificial materials. We are also merely at the beginning. I think that within a few years we will be seeing infinitely more significant industrialization and prefab solutions which will enable us to build far more quickly. There is, incidentally, a whole form of architecture that is being ignored and that is the architecture of light. A building today must not be seen only in daylight. People today live at night all the time and a building must be conceived also in terms of artificial light.

PAUL RUDOLPH: 1960

Mies van der Rohe has made most eloquent the steel frame in this country, and it's really difficult to see how that can be carried further. However, the precast, pretension, reinforced-concrete member potentials has hardly been touched. Europe has done much more in this field than we have. If one were to make a prognostication, one would say that the aesthetics of precast, reinforced concrete will lead us to an architecture which depends on the play of light and shadow, as opposed to the architecture which depends basically, for its aesthetic values, on reflections which come from a curtain wall.

Now this does not mean to say that the curtain wall is no longer meaningful as a dress for the steel cage. It does have meaning. But it's just that it's not the only way to do it. One of the things that we all long for is much more plasticity or depth in the treatment of the exterior of our buildings. This, I feel, will come to a large degree through manipulation of reinforced precast concrete.

BRUCE GOFF: 1956

The material that I think of immediately is the new type of plastic that is being developed for structure, which is supposed to reduce the weight of the building by ninety percent and that would also tend toward this lighter, more athletic feeling that we're striving to arrive at. However, I wouldn't say that's the only one. There are many, many other possibilities. Plastics have many promising potentials, but much of it is still experimental and not able to be used yet.

The metals, of course, are right in there with them on that. I think aluminum, structurally, hasn't been explored yet to do things that would seem to offer more than, say, steel or other heavier metals.

FORD HOUSE. *Bruce Goff. Aurora, Illinois. 1949. Goff designed this characteristically unorthodox residence around a sunken central kitchen and dining area. A studio is located above, on a cantilevered balcony, and the house is sheltered by a circular shingled dome.*

EDUARDO CATALANO: 1956

The aircraft industry always claims—they don't claim, but we claim—that they use aluminum in the correct way. I don't think they do. There are two ways of using metals. One is by using linear elements where you can individualize, which is compression, which is tension, and so on. A very simple way to calculate the structure. Then there is another way, that is dealing with thin shells or skins. Very seldom do you find, in the aircraft industry, airplanes that have been approached from that three-dimensional point of view in terms of the skin behavior or thin-shell behavior. So, I feel, the only reason we always say that the aircraft industry is so much advanced is to create some interest in the architecture, not to tout the aircraft industry more than anything else.

If you see things that were well done in Germany thirty years ago in terms of thin shells with reinforced concrete, from the structural point of view, they are far, far superior to many of the airplanes designed. The problem, to me, more than a material itself, is how the material is used.

You have the case, of course, of reinforced concrete. Reinforced concrete is an idea that has been used for many, many years. Every time people find new applications of the material, the material is the same, but the application is different. If a clear statement is lacking I think then that the whole result is very weak. In the structure of Mies's building you see the elements of support. You see slabs, columns, and so on. Those elements are holding floors, supporting loads, and so on. Now this is a very simplified way of building structure and is not very rich in itself.

The matter of honesty is an intellectual approach. I mean, sometimes it is better not to be honest. I think that everybody tries to show naked things for honesty. Sometimes we have to put on a dress. This is my idea. One of my greatest difficulties with the students is that they are playing too much with ideas that are intellectual, but not emotional in any way. It's the idea of putting one thing that is separate from the next one just because they are independent in function. Sometimes it is better to unify them. When the element has richness in itself and really is the dominant element, then it is all right to expose it. But sometimes it is not. There is something else besides that structure, so it is better to send that structure into the background.

VICTOR GRUEN: 1957

Victor Gruen

I feel quite strongly that the all-glass facade is in the long run really no solution. It lifts borrowed glory. It does not give the effect of light and shadow which we are used to connecting with an architectural appearance. It reflects and the reflections are interesting. To a large degree the most beautiful part of the architecture of these all-glass cubes are the old buildings which are around it and which you see mirrored in the glass. If you would put a glass building on a plane without these old-fashioned buildings, the building would be rather hard to take. Yet I believe that glass buildings definitely have their merit, especially in an office building, which basically has no individuality to offer because hundreds of people will be there only during their work time and go home at night.

We have certain problems to overcome with these glass buildings because the load which is imposed on the air-conditioning and heating system is a greater one. Obviously, we have some glare problems witnessed by the fact that you usually see all the venetian blinds and the curtains drawn.

I believe a wonderful use of an all-glass facade is the Manufacturers Trust Bank, the New York bank by Skidmore, Owings, and Merrill, because there double function is fulfilled. A strong promotional function is at the same time ideally taken care of as the lighting of the interior. The whole bank has become a shop window and everybody knows what's going on inside the spaciousness created, which is an impressive one. So we always have to ask ourselves in those cases: Is what we are doing worthwhile? Does it fit the particular use which this building is supposed to serve, or are we

MANUFACTURERS HANOVER TRUST BUILDING. *Gordon Bunshaft for Skidmore, Owings, and Merrill. New York City. 1953. This four-story glass box, with the vault in the show window on busy Fifth Avenue, challenged traditional classical bank architecture with a "money shop" concept.*

just translating something which we have once dreamt about as a technical achievement to use where it does not have its place?

MARIO SALVADORI: 1957

In America we have a very large vocabulary of expression. We have a variety of materials, a variety of traditions. We are eclectic. Now, I find that the artists who have produced the greatest creations, first of all, use a single language, and, secondly, gave themselves artificial limitations in which to work. Think of Dante working out the *Divine Comedy* with iambic rhythms, which seem impossible. Just by putting yourself into a straitjacket you seem to be able to produce the great creations, if you've got it in you, of course. Now, in America, we are so free that this has become a great danger.

The only material that I know of is concrete. I think it is a wonderful material. But that is the only one I would know how to work with. However, with concrete you can actually do anything you like. Because I like a certain freedom of form. Now I can say freedom and that is a very dangerous word, particularly in forms. If you are free, you can sketch the form. A sketched form is not a structural form. So there are certain limitations which go back to earth pull and other things.

I think that concrete has not really been used yet. I think we are just at the beginning of it because, so far, concrete has been used by contractors. It has been used by engineers who were trained in designing steel structures. It's only the last, maybe, twenty years, that concrete has been used even slightly in a creative fashion. I, for one, don't think Le Corbusier has yet conquered this. I think there are two men who know, Maillart and Nervi. Nervi, of course, has gone further than Maillart. We really just know the ABCs of concrete.

"THE ENGINEER SHOULD THEN FREE HIMSELF FROM THE FORMS DICTATED BY THE TRADITIONS OF OLDER BUILDING MATERIALS, SO THAT IN COMPLETE FREEDOM AND BY CONCEIVING THE PROBLEM AS A WHOLE, IT WOULD USE THE MATERIAL TO ITS ULTIMATE. PERHAPS THEN WE WOULD ARRIVE AT A NEW STYLE, AS IN AUTOMOTIVE AND AIRCRAFT CONSTRUCTION, AS BEAUTIFUL AND, IN THE SAME WAY, DETERMINED BY THE NATURE OF THE MATERIAL."

Robert Maillart

PIER LUIGI NERVI: 1961

A good architect is someone capable of seeing the main problems of a design, capable of examining with serenity the various possible solutions, and who finally has a thorough grasp of the technical means necessary to accomplish his project.

I like reinforced concrete because in it we find all the static, plastic, and structural characteristics of all other materials and, at the same time, it offers almost unlimited and not yet explored possibilities.

LOUIS KAHN: 1961

The materials are beautiful today. Concrete is a marvelous material. It's stone that can span with guts. It's just stone and steel. Stone that can understand. I like certain things. I like brick. I like stone. I like all these materials. . . . I got to like concrete. I sort of moderately like steel, you see.

PHILIP JOHNSON: 1955

It's American prosperity that influences our attitude toward materials. I'm sure that our buildings have twice too much steel in them because it's safer. The engineer gets paid just the same, even more, and the building certainly would stand up then. No one has used steel even to its full advantage of letting it sway. A tall building sways a foot. Let it sway three feet and lighten your steel thereby and get a more interesting building. That's what I mean by people not stressing anything.

You take one example where we have done it. That is the George Washington Bridge, where we've carried the tension principle in steel as far as it can be done. The result is the most beautiful structure in this part of the world.

Now the engineers did carry it too far in the Tacoma Bridge and it fell down. More power to the engineers. The nave of Beauvais fell down, too, but that doesn't mean that the Gothic architects were wrong to stress stone to the pinnacle of its ability. That daring, I feel, is lacking in American engineers, but even more in American architects.

1963

Stone is real somehow. Concrete never can be real. The way to handle concrete, I suppose, since I've never handled it much, is the way Corbusier does it with great, deep shadows, extraordinarily rough, enormous overhangs, and deep cuts in black and white in a brutal fashion. Of course, I'm under the influence of Le Corbusier, as we all are these days.

As much as I admire Corbusier, my last visit to the Marseilles building was quite a shock because of the ugliness of the rough materials. The extraordinarily bad lighting also affected me to such a degree, probably more than other people. I had to struggle to enjoy the forms.

But for concrete that gets delicate . . . Nervi is a plaster ceiling man to me. Of course, he's the greatest ceiling decorator of our time.

JOSÉ MIGUEL GALIA: 1955

I believe that concrete is a material that has tremendous possibilities ahead of it. But at present it has its weaknesses, which are the limitations of the methods of calculation regarding structure. The day when these are solved, we'll be able to make use of the fluidity which concrete possesses at the time it is being shaped.

HARUMI HOUSING. *Kunio Mayekawa. Tokyo. 1957. This massive ten-story public housing scheme, with its splayed footings, is a bold example of Mayekawa's distinctive modern style. It is located on an island in Tokyo Bay.*

KUNIO MAYEKAWA: 1962

If we work in Japan, whether we like it or not, we cannot help making ferroconcrete buildings. As you know, in Japan, architecture should be planned under the special conditions to protect against earthquakes. Whether I like it or not, I have used concrete for a long time. I think I have gradually developed an affection or some affinity for it. Technical development has, in effect, changed architecture and, in some cases, the changes have resulted in dehumanizing our lives and environment. I think modern architecture is now facing such great difficulties that it is having a bad effect on human life.

KENZO TANGE: 1962

In the case of architecture, to like or dislike is not simply a matter of taste. We have to choose material according to realities. As far as Japan is concerned, concrete is currently the most favorable and basic material. It is cheaper than iron and is capable of making freer forms.

For the past few years, the realities in Japan have rapidly changed and the labor cost has been expensive in comparison with material cost. We have to use prefab material and its method. I think we have to use concrete in the direction of industrialization.

In the past, I wanted to use steel for my works, but under the circumstances in Japan it was too early to do that. I felt I could not fully express or make forms that I wanted. Therefore, I have heavily depended on concrete for my design. However, recently the circumstances have changed. The technology of manufacturing or handling steel has advanced and also labor costs have become comparatively higher. This

SPORTS CENTER. *Kenzo Tange. Takamatsu, Japan. 1962. This impressive reinforced-concrete structure reflects Tange's determination to consider the Japanese architectural tradition solely as an inspiration in creating a new architectural order.*

is favorable in terms of the improvement of our lives. It has become difficult for us to design freely with concrete. But I think it is possible that concrete will still be used more than steel.

AFFONSO EDUARDO REIDY: 1955

Affonso Eduardo Reidy

We can't deny that steel-reinforced concrete, because of its ability to be molded, seems to be the material of preference. Steel establishes a certain rigidity in the actual design whereas steel-reinforced concrete gives the architect much more freedom of creativity. I think basically what one should strive to do is to take advantage of each material for its function, color, texture, and form. Whenever possible, take advantage of the material as it is, trying to preserve, as much as possible, its original state.

I don't know why, but here, in Brazil, it is easier to construct than to conserve. Maybe it's a question of mental attitude. The problem is more severe in public service on government works than in private initiatives. In public service, all the jobs are done through funds which are allocated on a budget from the city or the state. When a job is approved and credit is extended for its construction, payments are usually parceled out every year. The credit is not very difficult to get. But when the administration is solicited for money for maintenance or conservation, these funds are cut and reduced in such a way that the funds available are not enough to do anything. What happens is premature aging of the buildings, which look like very old structures within a few years. They begin to deteriorate because of the paint that's missing to protect the iron. The iron corrodes and the wood rots. In other words, there is a series of damages that occur due to the lack of maintenance.

MARCELO ROBERTO: 1955

Maintenance is a problem here, in Brazil, due to a number of adverse factors and particularly because there is a lack of care. We create something, then we drop it and do it over rather than preserve the older efforts. South Americans, in general, and Brazilians, in particular, do not like antiques. They don't care for tradition. They'd rather let something fall apart and build another one. Maybe that's the right approach.

Of course, here we use concrete because it's easier. But that doesn't mean that we don't use other materials. I have worked with wood, stone, steel. There isn't any material that can't be used. When we work with wood or we work with stone, what we turn out is not very different from what we do with concrete or steel. The spirit of the work remains the same. I don't think the choice of material plays an important part.

ALFRED ROTH: 1961

I do not belong to this group of modern architects who prefer rough concrete. I do not like that. This house, in which I'm living, it's of concrete outside. Its outer wall is made of reinforced concrete plus insulation inside. I did not like it. It seemed cheap. I plastered the whole thing. See my neighbor here, his house is made of rough concrete. To make it well and to solve all the details with windows, it will cost you more than plastering, which solves the problem. Therefore, I do not like Le Corbusier's ideal too much or his theory of rough concrete. Here in Europe, especially here, in Switzerland, among the younger generation they are a little bit blind with these things. Rough concrete has become extremely popular.

Naturally, I can use rough concrete if it suits my purpose. For instance, the retaining walls here of my house are of rough concrete. Or in the school we just started a couple of weeks ago, it's a large school for the city of Zürich. I will have rough concrete of a nice, smooth finish, for all the outside of this school, the retaining walls, stairs, and so forth, but not on the main buildings. I think we cannot go back to lower cultural states. We are in the twentieth century, but maybe for some it's more romantic, more exciting to give the impression we are living in earlier ages.

CARLOS VILLANUEVA: 1955

I like simple materials that for their crude sincerity allow me to defy the stupid vanity of exhibitionism. Among them, I am particularly fond of concrete, symbol of the construction progress of a whole century, submissive and strong as an elephant, monumental like stone, humble like brick.

L.L. RADO: 1956

If we go back to past periods of architecture, we can see that certain materials were used. They had certain inherent qualities. For instance, when they used stone or brick, especially stone, it was a natural material and there was a certain affinity between that natural material and the surroundings that was directly related to nature. Now I think our big problem today is how to use our new materials that apply to metals and synthetic materials that are not natural materials. Stone and, naturally, wood are close to nature and their use is somehow governed by conserving the natural character of the material. When we come to metals and synthetic materials, there I think we still have a long way to go. I think one aspect where modern architecture somehow did not grow up yet is the aspect of aging gracefully.

OLYMPIC STADIUM, CITY UNIVERSITY OF CARACAS.
Carlos Villanueva. Caracas, Venezuela. 1950. The stadium is the culmination of Villanueva's plan for University City. Its most dramatic element is the boldly cantilevered concrete shell, which elegantly covers the great grandstand.

The old masterpieces, even buildings that don't go back to the Gothic or Baroque, but say are one hundred or two hundred years old, there we see that materials that were used aged. They weathered and it didn't harm the appearance. On the contrary, it enhanced their appearance. That goes for stone, that goes for wood. It goes even for some metals, for instance, copper. You have very beautiful copper roofs and they age. They oxidize and get green. You have, for instance, some beautiful examples of Baroque copper roofs where that aging has mellowed down the material and really enhanced the architecture.

Now, with our new materials, I think we haven't found a way of detailing and finishing where that happens. There are some outstanding examples of modern architecture where the design is very good. When they were new they photographed beautifully and after ten years they look shabby. It will take a long time to develop certain rules or certain principles. As I said, with natural materials we have a certain guide. That means the rules of nature. With metals and synthetic materials, it's much more difficult. Some materials also have an apparent inherent quality. For instance, take bronze. In sculpture that's the material mostly used for casting. It has a certain inherent quality. We have to find how to bring out that certain inherent quality of the new materials. Those are things that almost touch certain mysteries in nature. We need to discover those mysteries, that makes certain materials thick, beautiful, stronger. It's not only the strength, it's not only the durability, but it's the appearance and maintenance that is part of it.

Today's materials it seems always have to be polished and somehow maintained like a kitchen sink to be beautiful. That in a way is not a natural thing. The old materials like stone and wood had a certain affinity with nature and nature wasn't fighting them. It appears to me that nature seems to fight our new materials. There isn't that affinity. It will take time to discover how to find that proper relationship.

JUAN O'GORMAN: 1955

In relation to materials, I'll tell you one thing which I one time asked the Mexican painter Diego Rivera. I said, "Why is it that we, in general, prefer stone and wood to these modern plastics, which are very wonderful materials to use? As a matter of fact, some of them are extremely good materials." He answered something which perhaps comes through from his Indian consciousness: "The human species has lived with stone and wood and earth many more years than with plastics, and therefore perhaps that is the reason why those materials appeal to us more as aesthetically beautiful than the plastics."

Juan O'Gorman

PAUL WEIDLINGER: 1956

Broadly speaking, there are no drawbacks to any material, as long as you recognize them. Drawbacks are only with architects and engineers, never with the materials. The people have the drawbacks and not the materials.

In many ways, machines have been a critical factor in the development of modern architecture. In ancient times, the availability of materials was limited by transport. Modern

NATIONAL LIBRARY, UNIVERSITY OF MEXICO. *Juan O'Gorman. Mexico City. 1952. Rising from a low block, this slab with twelve floors of book stacks displays architect/painter O'Gorman's remarkable mosaic, executed in rough native minerals.*

architects accept distribution of building materials as a given. Scores of powerful machines make modern construction both possible and economical. In addition, machines are a part of buildings themselves. The skyscraper was made possible by the development of the elevator by the American civil engineer E.G. Otis. He installed the first safety elevator in 1857. Of the mechanical systems—electrical, plumbing, heating, and air-conditioning—it was of the latter that the architects I interviewed most frequently spoke.

PHILIP WILL JR.: 1956

In designing buildings, basically what we are doing is creating environment. The greatest step made recently in controlling environment is the invention and development of air-conditioning. Its impact on planning is really only beginning to be felt. We can feel it in our own work. We are now going into new plans and building types in schools. These would be impossible without air-conditioning. While such planning creates problems, it solves many that have been troubling educators. But that added means of controlling environment threads its way through almost all building types, and its effects are only beginning to be felt.

HEATHCOTE ELEMENTARY SCHOOL. *Philip Will Jr. with Lawrence Perkins. Scarsdale, New York. 1953. With classrooms clustered around a core housing common rooms such as the library and auditorium, this school pioneered a plan and a noninstitutional look that were adapted in countless schools elsewhere.*

I would say thirty-five or forty percent of one's budget that you spend on mechanical equipment, in the next two decades, we will find ways of making more meaningful. This, for me, becomes much more the element which becomes really sculptural. It gives the possibility of a really great play of light and shadow. Why should all our multistory buildings just mysteriously be air-conditioned? I think you might really express this fact. This obviously could lead to a kind of mechanical exhibitionism, just as we have gone through a stage and are still in a stage of a kind of structural exhibitionism.

You know, this thirty-five or forty percent that one spends on those things, one used to spend that on painting, sculpture, and adornment. You couldn't sell anyone on that now. We have to be more comfortable. But it's just possible that we get the real manipulation of light and shadow by this very means. The fact is, the advent of air-conditioning has not been faced in terms of architectural design. We mysteriously air-condition and heat our buildings as a matter of fact. Beautiful structures are evolved, but then they are rendered like Swiss cheese by all the duct work and so forth. Now then, the integration of those two is really interesting.

I don't know whether you know our Blue Cross-Blue Shield Building in Boston, a multistory building which is now on its way up. We've made an effort to make the mechanical system into something more meaningful than just keeping you hot or keeping you cool or keeping you dehumidified, or whatever it is. For instance, in this building the support, of course, comes from the bottom. But the mechanical system is like a great octopus coming from the top and encircles the whole building. The hot air and the cold air and the returns are outside the columns, and then the horizontal branches are clearly shown. So that this becomes like a great vine encircling the whole building.

BLUE CROSS-BLUE SHIELD BUILDING. *Paul Rudolph with Anderson, Beckwith, and Haible. Boston. 1960. Air-conditioning ducts and structural columns are incorporated in the verticals of the gridded precast-concrete facade.*

The machine and the control of the climate, of course, are here to stay. The Industrial Revolution has affected architecture in industrialization structure. It is meaningful. The whole prefabricated movement, one cannot deny. But I present the thesis that the machine should serve us, not dictate to us; that the air-conditioned building in Boston does not have to be the same as the air-conditioned building in San Francisco; that the scales of these two cities are quite different and the way the people live are really very different. You could even use the same prefabricated parts, but that the building can take on overtones of the individual area. That's easier said than done. I don't mean to say that regionalism is the only determinant of architectural form, and I certainly don't mean to deny the whole Industrial Revolution.

The optimistic hopes for prefabrication inspired by the machine have been partly fulfilled and partly frustrated. Many of the elements of buildings today are manufactured off-site; prefabricated components have transformed a surprising amount of site work into a job of assembly. These components range from structural parts and wall and window units to mechanicals for plumbing, heating, and air-conditioning. However, due to costs and the dictates of codes and unions, a great deal of construction remains on-site. Private homes in the United States are typical of this large number of possibilities. They run from prefabricated houses and residential trailers made in factories to development and custom homes built on-location.

MAX BILL: 1961

I think in a certain way good design-prefabrication will change many things. But I think that is very difficult. The prefabrication must be done in the way that it has many possibilities. These many possibilities, that's the question for prefabrication. We always thought it would go very quickly. But it didn't go so quickly as we thought. I agree completely with prefabrication, but prefabrication becomes in a certain way a religion, a mystique. Prefabrication in one way is a real technical problem and in another way is a human problem. It is a problem of flexibility.

SCHOOL OF DESIGN. *Max Bill. Ulm, Germany. 1955. Designed in the Bauhaus tradition, this technical school for architecture, industrial design, and visual communication sited on a hill is a simple and efficient complex.*

We've always erected prefabricated buildings. All my buildings are done with prefabricated elements. But even in the structure, which could be prefabricated, you may have to do a building in a certain way. For example, this Design Institute building I did in Ulm. There I had, first, a completely prefabricated building, but we did not have money to do a prefabricated building. We had to do a concrete building as cheaply as possible. It could have been the cheapest possibility to prefabricate this building, but it was not possible because prefabrication needs a certain technical level and volume.

SAUGEY: 1961

Despite what we are very often told today, especially by builders and suppliers, that prefabrication and industrialization prevents you from being free and imposes very strict limits on the art of building, I think we will follow a completely different path. Once the initial crisis in prefabrication is past, we will see infinitely greater flexibility in the production. The architect will be given much more freedom in order to draw nearer to one of the architect's goals, which is liberation through housing and the art of construction, and not imposing limitations upon those using the buildings.

WALTER GROPIUS: 1955

Beginning with the sixties of the last century, the great invention in steel—the real steel for buildings, which didn't exist before—and the reinforced concrete, which was invented by Gardner, brought completely new viewpoints. We can make large spans today, whereas the old building was made of a brick or stone wall with cut-outs for the windows. We can now build a skeleton and have a skin around it. That is a completely different approach. That makes us much freer because we can make the openings where we want because the structural part is the skeleton and not the wall as it had been before. So we are much freer in the development of our plans and all the details of the building on account of these great inventions.

Of course, in line with that comes the big movement toward prefabrication. Prefabrication will be the future. I am rather proud that in 1910 I had written something on this. In my opinion, prefabrication was not a sudden revolution so that everybody would live in exactly the same house. It is a slow evolutionary process, taking one thing after the other out of the hands of the craftsmen and letting it go through the machine, so that one day we come to the result that we can buy, on the market, competitive parts of the same dimensions, to be used, at will, by the architect to make the whole design out of these component parts. Whether we take bricks or stone for the design units, we can also take these ready-made parts by industry.

I found recently that this type of prefabrication has penetrated further into the skyscraper buildings than into residential buildings. You take a building like Lever Brothers, where eighty-five to ninety percent of the whole building was component parts ready-made in a factory, brought to the site, and assembled there. So from the development of a building, we come to an assembly process where most of the work is done in the stationary workshop and then the part brought to the site to be assembled there.

People are afraid that we will get into too great a conformity of everything, which is not true because the natural competition of the market will bring such a variety of these parts. Even when they follow the same dimensions, which is a necessary thing, we have enough variety to choose from. Also, the architect will not be thrown out of the market because assembling a house from existing component parts is just as difficult as assembling it from bricks. In spite of the machine and the multiplication quality of the machine, we have more at our disposal in types today than we have had in the craft's time.

I am not at all afraid of too great unification by industry in the country. We will have a great variety of parts and, I think, if certain common denominators of parts go through the whole, it is only an advantage. We will avoid the terrible hodgepodge we have today when we go to a street scene where everything is different, instead of keeping it in a more restrained attitude.

It is not only the technical problems, for instance, it is the financing. It is really a vicious circle. I went through that myself. I had patents with Konrad Wachsmann of the General Panel Corporation. We didn't get congenial merchants. So the factory didn't succeed. But the main drawback was the financial methods, because when you get your FHA money it comes back in six or eight months. Whereas when you have a factory and warehouse, the prefabricated units go through in a few hours. The factory is choked in a jiffy if you cannot dispose of them fast enough. So you have to have the market in order to get it through, but you cannot get the market before you have the house. This is the most difficult thing. If the government doesn't have specific financing methods for prefabrication, it will still go slower and slower.

You see, it takes a long time until this development comes about. I never expected prefabrication to be a sudden breakthrough, throwing others out of the market. It is a slow, continuous process and when you open a Sweet's Catalog you will find that a great part is already available coming from the industry. My only point is that the architect didn't take part in that enough. He left it too much to the engineer to develop these parts. He should go into the industry and develop them.

It will definitely go. After many prefabrication systems and factories failed, there are still a few going on. I think it will be more a general fabrication of parts of a house than one factory making the whole house. The house is composed of so many different parts that we have to assemble it from many factories, not only from one.

Pietro Belluschi

PIETRO BELLUSCHI: 1956

Having things built in a factory at the very lowest cost and assembled on the site is perhaps the largest, the greatest contribution to architecture and to forms of modern architecture. I think that plastic and aluminum and other materials of that kind which lend themselves to be worked, just like the automobile can be formed to a press, offer the greatest opportunity and the greatest change in the future. We really cannot afford to use bricks laid one by one by extremely highly paid workers. We cannot afford to have absolute systems now that wages are going up. Therefore, we will be forced, simply by economics, to use the materials which lend themselves to, let's call it, prefabrication, that much-abused word, from which people expected so much some time ago and a lot of people have been disappointed. But actually we are on our way and we see it all around us and we can't really change the course of events because it is a direct result of our industrial skill.

EQUITABLE SAVINGS AND LOAN ASSOCIATION BUILDING. *Pietro Belluschi. Portland, Oregon. 1948. This structure was recognized as a pioneering work, both for its sleek reinforced-concrete frame, tinted glass, and aluminum cladding, and as the first sealed, air-conditioned building in the United States.*

RALPH RAPSON: 1959

There have been tremendous technological strides. It seems to me that we're obviously going to have one of the trends of the future be the greater and greater use of industrialization as applied to the building picture, and this naturally means prefabrication. Now, whether it's prefabrication of the individual parts you assemble and put together or prefabrication as a total thing, I wouldn't know, but I think that both of these things will happen.

It's certainly going to happen in the residential field. I'm sure that we'll go on for many years with the idea of the individual structure. This seems to be something of an American illusion—a desire so that we're going to have the individual house with us. I would hope that we will stop squandering our natural resources in land and have a little greater respect for our total environment. Perhaps we will begin to think in housing and in other buildings in terms of the total space more and that this might mean row houses or group houses. Not that I think we should rule out the individual home for sure. The individual house can certainly be with us even though it may be part of a large complex whether in rows or strung out horizontally.

CHARLES GOODMAN: 1956

Of course, the technical development that interests me most, and I suppose every industrialist in the country, is automation. I think that's going to have the greatest significance in technical development because it is self-correcting. Anybody who has anything to do with an industrial process knows what that means. Housing mass-production has had a weakness in the past. Its tolerances have worn off. In other words, if you have the same set of dies and jigs and so on, those jigs don't always remain perfect, which means constant personal checking unless you have an automatic checking system. The development of automation to its fullest will do that. To me that is the greatest contribution of automation, the self-correcting process which cheapens the process automatically and, as an end result, gives the buyer a lower-cost product.

The reason, of course, that I mentioned automation is because that to me is what eventually is going to make prefabrication a force so great that I don't see how anybody will even consider doing a conventional domestic building anymore. Of course, you are talking to somebody who feels this is the only way to build domestic architecture even though, as you know, we still do many, many individual homes and subdivisions in the conventional manner. However, these subdivisions we have industrialized to an extremely high degree even though it is a single project.

When you are talking about prefabrication, you are talking about something that has characteristics so similar to the automobile industry that it isn't funny. The thing that originally retarded the purchase of automobiles and, note, I am not just talking about the assembly line, which everybody uses as the parallel, because prefabrication in domestic architecture has a system of prefabrication, or will have, which will have no relation to the automobile assembly line at all. It's a different kind of assembly line.

When automobiles were first produced, their cost was prohibitive and the thing that made them common was, one, the assembly line and, two, the financing system. The assembly line would have been worthless without the financing system. Right now in domestic architecture we have what you might call a kind of assembly system which contributes to lower costs, but we do not have a financing system worth the name. It's still the Dark Ages. As far as industrial architecture and commercial, we have had prefabrication for some time. After all, when you do an office building, what is it? It's a series of parts. Certainly prefabrication is nothing new there. It's here.

CARL KOCH: 1956

The off-site building of components, larger and larger parts of the structures, is the most interesting, significant change that is taking place. I think what gets me going in the whole housing field now is the way things can be put together and the tremendous facilities we have for improving construction, production, and materials, rather than the individual results of any one of these at the present time.

We are moving in the direction of having our buildings and building groups in effective relationship between up-to-date technical methods and construction systems. I think we are beginning to get away from what, in a great deal of modern architecture, is almost a worshipping of the machine itself, but not using it as an

EASTGATE APARTMENTS. *Carl Koch with William Hoskins Brown, Robert Woods Kennedy, Vernon De Mars, and Ralph Rapson. Cambridge, Massachusetts. 1950. Koch designed this twelve-story building along the Charles River to include a community room, penthouse laundry, and retail space. Each of the two hundred sixty-one apartments has a balcony or terrace.*

effective tool at all. Doing a great deal of very painful and expensive hand-labor to try to make it look as though it came out of a machine at the end. I think it's just as ridiculous, don't you, to make a plaster wall that looks as though it was a sheet of steel.

Gordon Bunshaft

GORDON BUNSHAFT: 1956

It seems to me that the greatest change that is occurring in this country is that buildings are no longer being built to last five hundred years. They're no longer monuments that are built and that the interior purposes change with each generation such as some of the structures in Paris and London. Today the economics of our civilization and the increasing requirements of comfort demanded by the people are making buildings obsolete in twenty to twenty-five years. This change, I think, is going to have a basic effect eventually on the structure and on the design theories of architecture.

In other words, the Detroit automobile industry, with new models, is being felt, at least in New York City. Especially where a building is torn down twenty years after it is built, primarily because of economic analysis of the site and the need for the latest mechanical gadgets such as air-conditioning, better elevators, lighting, etc.

There, of course, is also another reason for it, an economic and social one. The large apartments in these buildings were built primarily for people who had servants. Today servants are a disappearing race. The architecture must be designed to suit our needs today. I don't know whether this is a good direction and whether it is a national one or international one, but it is an indication of something happening.

As far as the technical aspects of development, there is no question that we must develop a method of building these buildings precisely, lightly, and quickly, and this, of course, leads to prefabrication. Today buildings are primarily being built as they were forty years ago. The skins are different, but the basic construction is the same. Tons of cement, tons of water, tons of sand, tons of brick, moved up and down structures, the same old way they did when they built the Woolworth Building. The building industry, as a whole, not just the architectural aspect of it, is a slow-moving device and it is full of trades, unions, guilds, and what not. These move very slowly. There is another small detail called building codes. These things also move slowly. But eventually we will have prefabricated, light constructed, rapidly constructed, clean buildings.

LEVER HOUSE. *Gordon Bunshaft for Skidmore, Owings, and Merrill. New York City. 1952. One of the most influential early modern office buildings, this eighteen-story blue-green glass tower sits atop a wider single floor; the whole is raised on stainless-steel-faced pillars, leaving most of the Park Avenue site open to pedestrians.*

SOCIETY

Architecture has always been a social art. It is the most public of the fine arts. The realization of a building demands the coordinated activities of many people in the fields of politics, planning, design, finance, and construction, and the result affects the entire community.

The heightened social awareness of the post–World War I era gave modern architecture its special sense of broad social mission. Socialism, in its multiple forms, was not just a background to modern architecture; it was

"THERE EXISTS PRACTICALLY NO CULTURE IN THE WORLD WHERE IT'S ONLY UTILITY THAT COMMANDS, BUT IT SHOULD BE RELATED TO SOME KIND OF HUMAN SERVICE."

a critical motivating force. The desire among architects to make life better for people was genuine and compelling—so compelling that it inspired a missionary zeal, with the accompanying sense of rectitude. Architecture developed a new morality. The architectural historian Sigfried Giedion maintained, "Contemporary architecture takes its start in a moral problem." The new architecture, contrasting itself with the Beaux-Arts, claimed to be true, healthy, and honest.

OTANIEMI INSTITUTE OF TECHNOLOGY. *Alvar Aalto. Otaniemi, Finland. 1961*

EDUARDO CATALANO: 1956

We are too concerned with technical developments. Social developments and social structures are more important than concrete structure. I would put social structure in the first position to affect building design.

OSCAR NIEMEYER: 1956

Socialism will simplify architecture. It will deal with big human problems, which will lead to the solution to problems of collectivity.

ERNESTO ROGERS: 1961

Once I said that the form is the conclusion. I would say in more general terms that architecture also is a conclusion. It's not a separate activity of man. It's an activity which rises from historical context and, if I may say so, a social context. The form, therefore, is a result of different premises. All architecture is the result of different premises. It is, when it is finalized, something that we can consider autonomous, but that doesn't mean that it is really detached. It means that it is included.

OTANIEMI INSTITUTE OF TECHNOLOGY. *Alvar Aalto. Otaniemi, Finland. 1961. Sited in a wooded park on a high hill, the auditorium and laboratories, as well as other units of this brick, granite, and marble complex, are designed so they can be expanded without disturbing the whole.*

Oswaldo Bratke

ALVAR AALTO: 1961

I don't think that architectural form always should be practical or so. There exists practically no culture in the world where it's only utility that commands, but it should be related to some kind of human service. I have a feeling that form just for itself is not quite a religion for a human being. It has to have some relation. I view my forms from other points of view, too.

OSWALDO BRATKE: 1956

I tend to believe that technical developments are less responsible for the transformation of life and constructions than social changes. After thousands of years, the dominant materials in most parts of the world are wood, brick, and clay tiles. I believe that new forms appeared which are made possible because of new materials and more

MORUMBI CHILDREN'S HOSPITAL. *Oswaldo Bratke. São Paulo, Brazil. 1951. Reflecting Bratke's lifelong social concerns, this hospital of simple design and low-maintenance materials has homelike interiors and rooms for parents to stay with their children.*

sophisticated techniques. However, the important aspect is the function and this is motivated by social structure. Certainly, reinforced concrete was very responsible for changes in architecture in the last decades. But it was the social structure that characterized medieval, nineteenth-century, as well as contemporary architecture.

GIO PONTI: 1961

In the past, the architect built grand buildings for princes, kings, and emperors. Today the architect contributes to a prediction for the future and is no longer a man of the court. Today our philosophy is to be independent, to study the future of humanity through city planning and its issues and to be the first to instill it. Le Corbusier, for example, is a precursor as Neutra was a precursor for schools. Gropius was a great precursor and teacher. All of today's architecture works together with and also gives rise to social developments.

KENZO TANGE: 1962

It is always impossible to think about technological things or technological advance separately from social advance. Accordingly, we cannot take out technological things only. We have to think simultaneously as to how the social change affects architecture. Therefore, I think it is easier to understand if we think of it on the basis of the two axes.

First, as the technology of manufacturing and building things, including air-conditioning, is further advanced, a lot of changes will naturally occur. On the other hand, communication technology will change rapidly. This will, I think, totally change the social structure. If I say "social structure," it may seem to be too abstract. But communication is the technology of creating the relation between man and man, man and thing, or thing and thing. So, I feel that the social structure will be changed a great deal. I think perhaps it will greatly affect architecture. The connection of one architecture to another, one architecture to a bigger architectural group, or to an urban community structure, will be greatly changed. It will depend on the nature of communication.

PIRELLI TOWER. *Gio Ponti. Milan, Italy. 1958. Tapering side walls accentuate the slenderness of this elegant thirty-three-story tower, in which Ponti and engineer Pier Luigi Nervi departed from the standard rectangular modern office block.*

It is a future problem for us architects to give a careful look at the relation between one architectural element and another, or architecture and the city. In other words, because each architectural element performs its function in the entire city, it is the era in which we can hardly design simply individual architecture. In this sense, there emerges the problem of spatial mobility. We have to think about architecture within the limits of this spatial mobility.

An appropriate example related to communication is automobiles. I think that automobiles affect more things than their own function. Speaking extremely, space exists for communication and the automobile plays a role of connecting one thing to another. Accordingly, if we use the role of communication for the inside or outside space of architecture, a new way of thinking about architecture and the city will be developed. Therefore, I think communication technology or the change in social structure through it will considerably change future architecture.

Social change is very closely related to the technological change, although I cannot say it comes chiefly from technological change. At present, the technology of manufacturing or building things has developed a great deal. The absolute number in terms of national production has become very large. More than twenty percent out of the total national production in Japan went to the construction field. The rate of five percent in the past has grown to twenty percent. Thus this overwhelming amount of construction has led to the rapid growth of the physical environment of society. On the other hand, close to the remaining eighty percent out of the absolute number of large production went to consumption. So the absolute number of consumption became large. The growth in consumption means that things disappear faster. The more rapidly physical environment structure develops and grows, the faster old minor elements disappear and change to new ones. It means time-wise mobility has been intensified. This is one of the characteristics. If we do not invent some kind of architecture to cope with this phenomenon, architecture itself will be left behind.

When we think about architecture, we have to think about it in a condition that is moving in time and space. I do not deny functionalism, but I think we should overcome the static way of thinking that exists in functionalism. As both architecture and the city are the places where people live and work, their basic premise is, of course, for people. This remains the same as before. The modern cosmopolitan society admits individual's free will, but society is an organism. This should be influenced and reflected in the physical forms of architecture and the city.

RICHARD NEUTRA: 1955

I have, of course, no doubt that the most precious of all materials is the human material which has been studied as an object, recommended as an object of study by many philosophers for the last ten thousand years. Probably before this thing was put into writing, this recommendation already held true when people have been interested in human beings. On the other hand, while it looks so gray of age, this recommendation, it is extremely green and new if you consider the thousands of papers published in various systematic scientific journals relating the observations and laboratory work and experimentation which distinguishes our time much more than that of Aristotle.

Richard Neutra

I don't want to smear Aristotle here by any means, but I think that we had made some progress in recognizing what makes organisms tick. We know very much more about organic life and we know very much more about human organisms in particular. So that this is perhaps the most novel development to be considered if we speak of housing life, and after all, architecture always does so. Even if you have a power station in which you are producing millions of kilowatts, but only five people are working, the five people are the deciding factor on how to design that station.

Now I think, therefore, it is the study of human responses and all the sensorial endowment of a human organism and then what goes on in the central area, how is this being stereoscopically composed and works together is the great novelty of our time. It is very often in conflict with technical developments, which have their own law and their own sequence.

The common denominator, the factor which will help us to find principles of regulating all this into a real order, is evidently: What can human beings take? What is the biologically bearable? What is the biologically wholesome? We never will overcome that. This is absolutely what we don't want to overcome, we want to further.

The architect who really designs for a human being has to know a great deal more than just the five canons of Vitruvius.

MAX BILL: 1961

What influenced all my thinking in doing architecture is always the human need. The social background, the personal, the individual background with the individual need of things, the relation between need and form, need and design. I think everything needs to be in the right place so that human need can function. I think architecture should never be self-expression, never ambition, something like exhibitionism, so-called original or individualistic ideas.

While building has always been a group effort, it was the social climate of modern architecture that emphasized the egalitarianism of the design team. Walter Gropius was its most articulate advocate.

W ALTER G ROPIUS: 1956

We have to learn teamwork from the bottom up. The field we have to see today is so large that it is impossible in one head to have everything. There is a mechanics to teamwork which we have to study. I think it is a definite necessity as building and architecture comes more and more to the field of planning.

ENRICO PERESSUTTI: 1956

Sometimes teamwork is when you have worked together like Rogers and myself for so many years. There certainly are some jobs which will have more influence on one of us. Statistically, I would say, we are even. Our works reflect the whole of our work and our teamwork. Working on the same shape and the same problem, our own ideas change and are modified by the thought of the other, by what the other can see better than I can and vice versa. It is difficult to say if it is an advantage or not. It is an advantage if the collaborator goes on the same stream. We have our own criticism but, as I say, the best result of the collaboration is when the ideas of one or the other become one and the same thing. Naturally, then we know that this thing is the right one.

Personally, I'm very proud of our teamwork because I think it shows two things. One, a moral possibility to work in teams which is not very usual. Secondly, I think it corresponds as Gropius said to certain necessities of our present cultural conditions. Of course, there are some dangers. I think it is very difficult in life to be a bachelor or to be married. It's always a problem.

PIER LUIGI NERVI: 1961

Pier Luigi Nervi

Beautiful, unlimited, full of unlimited possibilities, provided that architects come closer to the technical and static aspects of architecture. Or provided that architects form the habit of studying their projects in teams composed of architects, engineers, and developers. It is an extremely important collaboration because the architect could have a creative role in the overall design, whereas the engineer must help him immediately, from the first draft, to establish and define the static and structural possibilities of the architect's conception. In this way certain dangers would be eliminated. For example, those of developing projects which turn out to be impossible to build, or may only be built with great difficulties and technical complications, which are not economical and also bring something unnatural to the final architectonic result.

RUDOLF STEIGER: 1961

Teamwork seems to me, on the basis of my rather long experience, an important condition for the development of architecture, because the possibility exists to master the wide field of architecture better by means of teamwork. However, it must be said that teamwork should not be a specialization. It should not mean, he does the architecture, he does the technical things, he does that, etc. That is not teamwork in my understanding of it, that is a combination based on specialists in the same office.

Teamwork should be work by equally educated and equally capable people. It should be such that one can replace the other completely. Only then will teamwork have reciprocal value. Otherwise the most important thing will be missing, that is, mutual criticism. Among specialists there is no mutual criticism, but among architects with the same training—though one may, of course, follow one direction more in his development according to his nature—but among such architects there is a discussion.

We have teamwork examples, I, with Haefeli, [Werner] Moser, my son, etc. One goes in the morning, orders a color sample. In the afternoon the other turns up and takes the sample off. We work so closely together that it is as though one were doing it. With my son, the way it works, he corrects a plan and I continue with the corrections. The next day he continues to correct, and all this without our speaking to each other. It is done in the same spirit. Teamwork is of value only if mental coordination is possible. A team composed from the outside, as it is often unfortunately done here, when someone does not know which architect should be entrusted with what, that is absolute nonsense. Artificially formed working groups mean enormous expenditure of energy, while teams originating in a natural way, that is an enormous advantage.

A friendly exchange that was fairly important—I was a member of the CIAM Council with Gropius and Le Corbusier, van Eesteren, Giedion, van den Broek, and others. These were always very interesting meetings. We always met in the rue de Sèvres, 25, at Le Corbusier's. There were discussions about all kinds of things, but basically less about architecture. For example, formal matters, more general things of urban construction, publicity, how the group should be developed.

Of course, immediately two groups formed. That was in CIAM from the very beginning, there were two very separate groups and I think it is this way at the present as well. One group was more the Dutch, Nordics, Swedes, and Swiss, who wanted to reach a more systematic, documented basis, and on the other side there was Corbusier and later Sert, who stressed the publicity more. And as long as there was a good equilibrium, CIAM was productive and had its emanations.

From these discussions something always emerged, sometimes they became quite vehement. I recall altercations between Mart Stam and Corbusier and between Hans Schmidt and Corbusier with Moser. These were very vehement discussions which were very productive, so to speak, because they corrected each other dialectically. Later, unfortunately, the propaganda aspect was emphasized too much and that was the reason many forces or, rather, many colleagues, lost interest in CIAM because they did not value the propaganda aspect that highly. It is very interesting that as soon as something has lost its equilibrium it more or less lapses into inactivity. I deeply regret that these meetings are no longer held, that we no longer get together and many have withdrawn.

At the time of the Industrial Revolution there were an estimated 720 million people in the world. By 1920 the number had risen to roughly 1.8 billion. This totally unprecedented population explosion made a new architectural solution imperative. It was only natural that given the social climate of the period, the focus of the new architecture worldwide was on housing.

LOGIS ET LOISIRS. *L'Architecture d'Aujourd'hui, Boulogne-sur-Seine, France. 1938. The report of the fifth CIAM congress held in Paris in 1937 on urbanism was typical in tone of the publications that carried on the revolutionary dialogue of the modern movement.*

The early and influential showcase of modern architecture, the 1927 Weissenhof exhibition in Stuttgart, consisted entirely of housing. It featured thirty-three residential units, which ranged from single-family units to apartment blocks, designed by Ludwig Mies van der Rohe, Le Corbusier, Gropius, J. J. P. Oud, Peter Behrens, Bruno Taut, and others.

PEDREGULHO ESTATE. *Affonso Eduardo Reidy. Rio de Janeiro, Brazil. 1952. This twelve-acre residential neighborhood, which includes a school, playground, health center, laundry, and shopping center, is a singular social achievement. A mammoth, curving seven-story apartment building follows the contour of the hilltop site.*

AFFONSO EDUARDO REIDY: 1955

It's not only because it's an inclination; circumstances brought me to this housing sector. It's a sector that I always loved. I truly consider it to be the most important area of architecture. It attracted me as an architect to seek a solution to the housing problem in the best possible way. I have worked in this sector for almost ten years now. I'm more convinced of the need for architects to become more involved in this area to improve the living condition primarily of those of lesser financial means.

JOSÉ MIGUEL GALIA: 1955

I believe that the population explosion in the world and our country, Venezuela, which creates the need to properly house and serve a vastly greater number of people than was the case in the past, will provoke or cause a change in construction methods in order to simplify them.

José Miguel Galia

ELIOT NOYES: 1957

I think every time there is any social change, if you can identify it immediately, it has an effect on architecture. Talking rather small scale ones compared to the history of the world, let's say, I'm thinking of the fact that in the thirties, after and during the Depression, the lack of money had an effect on architecture in the need for maximum economy. You know, conspicuous economy was a sort of principle by which we had to design.

I was going to contrast it with the fact that while there we were looking for aesthetic virtues in our poverty; we had the necessity for economy and we were making a virtue out of it. This was a good thing and I think it's still quite valid. Now, suddenly, prosperity is upon us everywhere and this is having, I think, quite an effect on design and the richness, the lushness of design sort of still within a disciplined framework than we ever would have had without ever having gone through the other period.

This is kind of balancing, an alternating rhythm of some sort that comes and goes. I don't think there's any doubt that every time you get a change of economic status for a country or a period, it has an immediate effect on the way buildings look and what happens in their design. Of course, it's the same thing with new forms of transportation and suburbia. It's a constantly changing thing. I just don't think that anybody can predict it. I would simply say that you can't have a social change without it having an immediate effect on architecture.

The social impulse in modern architecture is nowhere more evident than in city planning. Declaring that the town plans of the past were no longer relevant to the spirit of the new age, the architects of the modern movement proclaimed a design dogma of collective well-being. They proposed nothing less than to change people's lives through architecture. A manifestation of this goal is the remarkable number of ideal city plans produced between the 1920s and the 1940s. They range from Frank Lloyd Wright's semiagrarian Broadacre City to Le Corbusier's visionary designs—Ville Contemporaine, Ville Radieuse, and Plan Voisin—and his ill-fated plans for the cities of Pessac, Algiers, Antwerp, and Saint-Dié. In accepting the American Institute of Architects Medal of Honor, Le Corbusier said, "I have a little paper in my pocket which contains all the defeats in my life. It was the greatest part of my activity."

BROADACRE CITY, MODEL. *Frank Lloyd Wright. 1935. In this unrealized design for a self-contained community living in a rural democracy, Wright brought many of his ideas and ideals together.*

MARCEL BREUER: 1956

Marcel Breuer

I think the greatest change will be social changes that will probably influence architecture the strongest. While we design today's buildings, we feel we should design at least streets, but probably districts. Of course, to design districts or streets is another type of financing, another type of client, than we deal with today.

The greatest future possibilities in architecture lay in city planning. I do not mean city planning is architecture, but architecture's solutions of city planning. In other words, solutions which are large-scale solutions. That, of course, requires also social changes or anyway some new methods of financing, of owning properties.

Some beginning was done, let us say, in projects like Stuyvesant Town. I don't think that the project is a very good project, but it has an outstanding feature in that it takes the whole district together. I wish that planning would have been better and

UNESCO HEADQUARTERS. *Marcel Breuer with Pier Luigi Nervi and Bernard Zehrfuss. Paris. 1958. Designed by an international team of architects and engineers, this eight-story, Y-shaped building with a curving facade on tapered columns is an impressive headquarters for the United Nations' cultural and educational activities.*

the architecture would have been better. But I see that this type of planning on still a larger scale gives a completely new element to architecture. For instance, Saarinen's project at General Motors is a very good example of large-scale planning because, actually, each building is not anymore a building, but a part of a much bigger composition.

We won't speak about buildings, but about spaces between buildings. We will speak about squares and streets as the form of architecture. The negative form, the space, will be the form of architecture and not the blocks and the masses. Masses as architectural form of expression will stop, more or less.

PETER COOPER VILLAGE-STUYVESANT TOWN. *Irwin Chanin and Gilmore Clarke. New York City. 1946. The huge Metropolitan Life Company complex, comprising one hundred ten buildings with 11,251 apartments as well as playgrounds and landscaping, lacks architectural distinction but is a remarkably successful example of urban housing.*

W I L L E M D U D O K : 1961

I think that we must take a wider view of the subject and that we must not apply it to the building, but rather to the towns and villages as a whole. For society requires quite a different development of city planning not only owing to the enormous increase of population, but especially owing to the totally changed character of the traffic.

In the middle of the previous century, the railway and the industrial development created the millions in cities. At that time, concentration was perfectly normal. But literally all inventions after the railway do not point to concentration, but to decentralization. The motorcar, telegraph, telephone, radio, television create a mutual human contact in unlimited distances. The fast traffic created by the automobile has made the big towns, which were not intended for it, practically useless. They hardly serve their purpose. Although people live close together they can hardly reach one another. The towns no longer answer their original purpose. This they prove, for they show more and more, by a flight out of the center.

The only solution is a reasonable spreading in medium and smaller towns with excellent mutual communications and a healthy contact of the inhabitants with the surrounding country. Added to this, the architectural future is not so much for the separate building as for the town, the village, as a whole.

We see that already in the housing on the large scale after the last world war. Never has the housing of the people been studied so seriously as in our day, both in regards to housing types and the grouping of the housing. This is certainly a gain. But more is necessary to come to city planning, which is an art. This requires an ideal cooperation between the gifted architect–city planner and the architects for the different buildings—a voluntary subordination and a great confidence in the authorities. It is very much the question of whether the future society will be able to reach such a cultural height. Although in entirely new towns such as some satellite towns near London, we are now witnessing a development in the above-mentioned direction.

To a certain extent, there existed in the Baroque more favorable conditions for this art of the building of entire city parts. We still take a great delight in some very fine examples of that period. Meanwhile, it would take me too much time to develop these ideas for the future. After all, we are not prophets. I prefer to look about in the fascinating life of our own time.

ROEHAMPTON ESTATE. *London County Council. London. 1953. This London public authority created an outstanding postwar, low-cost housing development with an adept mix of high and low concrete slab buildings on a hilly park site.*

R A L P H R A P S O N : 1960

For me, architecture is a total of things, a total environment. We're interested in the total man, first, of course, then we're interested in the complete environment. In a way, I think this doesn't mean that every architect becomes a planner as such, but I think he must have this interest, this desire for completeness and total building and total environment.

One of the places where architecture is wrong today—maybe it will be more proper to say what's wrong with culture today—in our headlong rush to conquer the unknown and the acquiring of scientific knowledge is that the culture has lagged far behind. This is certainly one of the places where we as people have troubles. As Einstein once said, "Perfection of means and confusion of aims," seems to be a characteristic of our society. I think this is in a sense true of architecture.

The technical know-how, the scientific advantage, the technological developments are here. They give us the means, the ability to create a truly superior environment, but, by and large, we do not have this. I suppose we can close the gap between technology and our ability to absorb it. This is where we as architects and the art of architecture come in. We must never forget that it is an art. This is a kind of broad expression, but I suppose it means that we are dealing with humanity. We must always keep in mind the needs of man. We must understand him in relation to everything we do in relation to the structure and the material.

MARC SAUGEY: 1961

The architect must have a much broader approach to his vocation than his profession requires. The architect, especially in modern society, has a very large role to play because often the direction of an architect's concepts has a bearing in important ways on questions which have real-life significance. Depending on the designs, the results can have enormous practical implications on social issues or even political issues, sanitation issues, traffic issues.

I believe the architect must also be an urbanist. While one could imagine in days gone by great architects who conceived of buildings in isolation, today we've gone way beyond that. The architect must go beyond the idea of a beautiful bulk or mass which does the job, which works, and which may even be very beautiful; the architect must go further: he orders space. Therefore, he must concern himself almost more with the voids and spaces, both interior and exterior. Consequently, when he attacks these spaces, he attacks at the same time almost districts of a town or of the countryside. And in so doing he becomes an urbanist.

This is the definition of an architect. It is, first, a man of ideas, whose personality is given to the improvement of human relations, and then to beauty, comfort, the ease and improvement of life, for populations and for all mankind.

Alfred Roth

ALFRED ROTH: 1961

Naturally, the evolution of technology is going on very fast. New things will come, but we should not believe that these new things will solve our problems. The big problem is not on the level of technology. It is on the level of humanity, of sociology, of the human being. That's the real basis to build up. All the rest, all that produces technology and science, that has to serve. We architects have to make a sum of these things. More important, first of all for city planning, regional planning, country planning, but also for designing flats, groups of flats, civic centers, all these things.

Multiple dwellings have a social purpose. For example, I found it not decent to build an individual house for myself on this wonderful ground. Straight from the beginning I have this idea, I do not want that this house is just only for myself. I want to give it a sort of social purpose. Let's build in some students' rooms. You know we have such a need for students' rooms here in Zürich. It's a very big, big problem.

Just at the moment, we are working together with my colleagues of the school, on a new big students' home at the Institute of Technology for twelve hundred people. It will become a student center to live in because we have nothing of that type in this town. The students' dwelling problem has reached a very critical point, you know. I'm going on firmly in this direction of designing such model things.

Then, as you know, I have always been very interested in school buildings and educational problems. For instance, I built my first school in your country, you know, near St. Louis. I had the wonderful chance to build a school in association with Helmut [Hentrich] and Yamasaki.

I claim the historic privilege to have contributed to the start of modern school design in this country. When I came back from America, it was 1953, I produced here in Zürich a large exhibition on school design. The exhibition was visited by people from the whole country. From the small villages they came to learn from this exhibition. That was really the beginning of a new trend, a real good trend in school design which was certainly true.

In recognition for what I did for schools in this country, the city of Zürich gave me this commission to build our school here. They gave me full freedom for designing that school. It's a large center. It's a first. We are now building the first part, which is a primary school. Then will come a second part, which is a secondary school. There will be a third part that will be a youth activity center. They are rooms for young people, adult young people to use in their spare time connected with school. That's something which Zürich is very much sponsoring today.

So, for me, the happy development of architecture depends much more upon establishing the programs given by human needs. We always have to reconsider these prob-

FELLOWSHIP HOUSE, INSTITUTE OF ZÜRICH.
Alfred Roth. Zürich, Switzerland. 1961. This student dormitory, part of Roth's progressive plan and advanced designs for the Institute, reflects his strong belief in education as a means of human and cultural emancipation.

lems, the needs of man. We have not reached the end of doing this research. We will never reach the end of the research of the real needs of man. That's first of all questions—knowing man's need better and then only the question of form or construction and materials and details. Unfortunately, today quite a number of architects are in somewhat an abstract way looking for new trends and formalistic principles.

WOLFSBURG CHURCH. *Alvar Aalto. Wolfsburg, Germany. 1959. This church with its dramatic belfry dominates the center of the parish, which includes administration buildings, vicarages, club rooms, and facilities for young people.*

AALTO: 1961

We can take a secondary function as main background for architecture. Let's say we could do that this way. An electrical system works well, that's not enough. . . . The main function is that the human being is growing up in some good way.

I had, for a few weeks ago, in Wolfsburg, I build there the cultural center—which means all things, libraries, concert halls, and that sort of thing, the center of the town—the director of the city told me that we have to build up a counter-power to the monotony of the industrial work. This can't be done without architecture. That's the great problem of modern architecture, we have to build up the life which saves the human being who does from morning to night only monotonical work.

Technical things will change the way buildings are built slowly, but I think the system of society, the way people are educated and the way they work, change it more. I don't mean politically social developments, but what slowly happens in the human being. Let's say today we civilize everybody. It's an enormous change in the society in contrast to the few aristocrats before. If I should say my final words, I should say that one of the great problems for an architect today is to save the human being—to make individualism of collectivism.

MARCELO ROBERTO: 1955

Technical factors are not as important as the spirit of the times. I believe what is precisely the most important is the spirit prevailing over the particular point in time. I'm one of those who believe in and like to refer to the medieval period. In the Middle Ages, the architecture of pointed arches and flying buttresses predated the era when the advantages of cupolas and all that sort of thing became apparent. The Gothic arch and the flying buttress were needed to express the spirit of the times, so they were created.

Nowadays the same is true. If we need a certain type of material or technology to express ourselves, we create them. It doesn't work the other way around. No technical innovation or invention is going to change the spirit of the architecture or the urban development of the times. On the contrary, I believe that the spirit of the times requiring a particular type of architecture or of city planning to express itself, calls for the discovery or development of certain techniques or inventions.

Without a doubt I believe that it is precisely the number of people, this desperate increase in the birth rate, that will compel the use of much more intelligent procedures than those used at present. Right now the whole world could use a series of inventions and processes that are very well known and could result in highly interesting creations. Unfortunately, certain factors, backwardness, the cult of sameness, and the like keep those solutions from being used. I think that the very thing that is happening now will become increasingly widespread, that is, the spiraling population and rising number of businesses will compel the use of these procedures.

Hence, what may appear to be bad at first blush might be beneficial for architects because it will give us a series of opportunities that we cannot attain at present, for we are always faced with that conservative attitude that rejects innovations and insists on following the same old ways. The exuberant process now taking place is going to force a change in those methods. That can be simply fabulous for us architects if we manage to be in the vanguard of the movement.

LUDWIG MIES VAN DER ROHE: 1955

I think the social developments, the spread of the cities and the increase in population—I think that changed really nearly everything, not always for the best. But change it did. There is no question about that. Spread out. There are no cities, in fact, anymore. It just goes on like a forest. That is the reason why we cannot have the old cities anymore. It is gone forever, you know, the planned city and so on. I think we should think about means that we have to live in the jungle and maybe we do better by that.

ART

"MY AESTHETIC CONVICTION WAS DIRECTED BY THE REVOLUTION RISING IN THE FREE ARTS LIKE CUBISM, FUTURISM, AND SO ON."

Architecture is one of the fine arts. The Brazilian architect Oscar Niemeyer characterized it as "something beautiful which can overcome prejudice." We must admit that in the end, the architects in the Oral History, along with many others, did not gain renown because of their mastery of technology or their social values, but because of their admired aesthetics. Modern

architecture had an early and important relationship with modern art. It has been observed that never in history has architecture been so influenced by painting. The aesthetic aspects of the new architecture were the subject of frequent comment by the architects we interviewed.

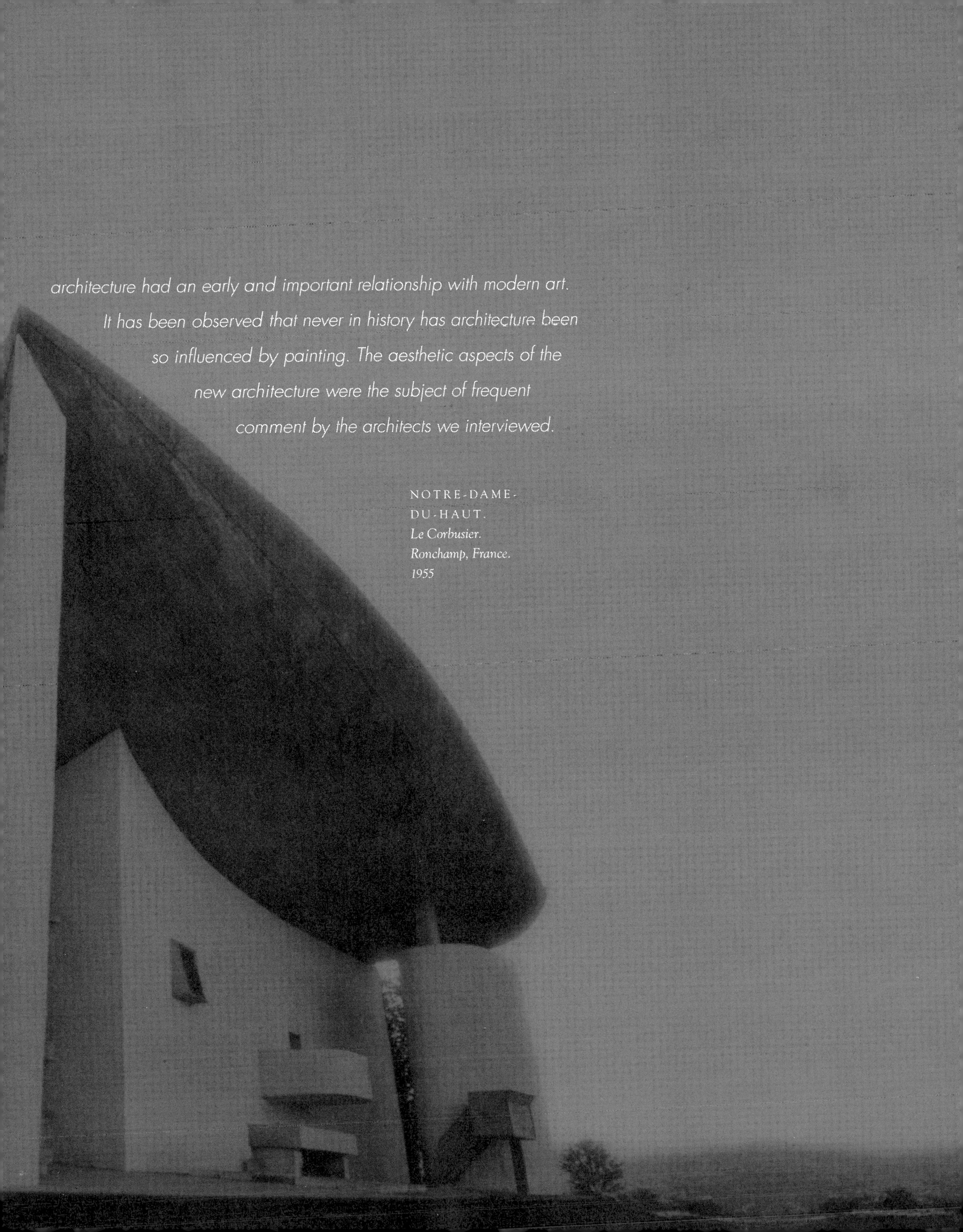

NOTRE-DAME-DU-HAUT.
Le Corbusier.
Ronchamp, France.
1955

HOOK OF HOLLAND HOUSING. *J. J. P. Oud. Hook of Holland, the Netherlands. 1927. This building secured Holland's place in the early modern movement. Oud unified the sixteen attached apartments with a long, horizontal first-floor balcony and shops at the rounded terminals.*

J. J. P. OUD: 1961

In this first time of growth my aesthetic conviction was directed by the revolution rising in the free arts like Cubism, Futurism, and so on. In a peculiar way there was a congruence with the art of practical insight which [was carried out] by . . . the ideas of Berlage and Muthesius.

So I got, of course, from these predecessors also aesthetic impulses, a total vision of the future of architecture as art in building. It was enlarged especially by the experiments of the free arts. It was spurred and brightened by the ideas of Mondrian and his work. What Mondrian did in painting I tried to do in a similar way in architecture. He tried to make, in simple forms, proportions and color, the strongest values in art. I tried to find what was the real necessity of a work or building. What people want, not what they like to have, not what they wanted for ornament or for show, but what they wanted in the practical life. And that is partly the same as what Mondrian did. Mondrian tried to find out nature, the essential things, what for him were the essential forms. I try in architecture to find what for me is the essential form in architecture. And that has, like I say, some congruence.

This is what happened in technology. We admire very much technology and the value of mechanical things like tools and electrical apparatus. . . . I should like to transform them into architecture, but with emotional value added to it. And this emotional value I found especially in modern painting.

What interested me in Cubistic architecture too was that it did not give the illustration of nature, but especially what was behind nature. And what is behind nature is to me the same as what I look for behind architecture. The inner value of the thing. . . . For me the inner value of architecture is one of the first things that interest me.

In the beginning, in the time of Mondrian, they didn't like bright colors at all. No, because in Holland we always have clouds and moist in the air, we want more soft colors. I, too, sought this always, but it is proven that it is very possible to make things more clear and give them more color, and as soon as we had the courage to do it, most people went to do it.

MAX BILL: 1961

Frank Lloyd Wright, at that time, was a romantic who couldn't give us anything. We had a very strong feeling against all this Art Nouveau and he had been classed with it. My mind changed very much afterwards. At that time I had been much closer to the Russian movement, the Constructivists, Loos, and after that Oud and the Dutch.

In the beginning, I always had a very great respect for Constructivism and for all these things, but I didn't like them. I felt a need to go their way, but I had been too close to the Bauhaus people, Klee, Kandinsky, Schlemmer, Moholy, even Albers, that I accepted really the work of the others in this first time. But afterwards, I became a very good friend of all these people as well as a very good friend of Mondrian and of Vantongerloo. I am still a very good friend of Vantongerloo. We meet often. So as a youngster, I became a collaborator of this movement.

However, the theory that art influences architecture, I don't like that theory at all. I think aesthetically artwork is something independent. It has its own function and every clear work can influence another work. I don't like this confusion between architecture and sculpture and painting which is on the way for a few years.

Architecture is something more than the art of good building and good construction. Architecture is also more than the logical organization of the spaces which are required by a building program. However much one may aim at the straightforward solution of the demands of the program, there are always various possibilities for the architect. This means that function, however important an aspect of architecture it may be, is likewise not the determining factor.

What causes architecture to rise to an art above construction and above spatial organization? In my opinion, it is this: Just as the human mind derives beauty from reason, and sound in poetry and music, it also recognizes beauty in proportions of spaces in architecture. Building only becomes art when it is made sublime by beautiful and harmonious space proportions which ingeniously express the character and cultural significance of the building. Architectural art has really one means, proportion, the proportion of spaces and building masses in both form and color.

Max Bill

LE CORBUSIER: 1961

I've always been attracted to the creative, whatever form it takes, and particularly when applied to man in his environment. One has sympathy for man in his environment. I found in painting the means to develop this feeling. It's a fascinating means, but perilous.

I have a great weakness for being seduced by visual things. I have eyes for everything that is visual—drawing, painting, sculpture, architecture. It is all one thing. It is symphonic. Architecture requires certain intellectual ideas. Painting and sculpture, too, but they have more immediate physical possibilities. Sometimes it's my hand that works before my mind because of its habits, its possibilities. It's extraordinary. The human hand is wonderful.

I like beautiful things. I have a sense for volumes and colors. I claim the right to do painting and sculpture as well as architecture. If it bothers people they can stay home. They needn't bother to look. But, if by chance, at my age of seventy-five, people ask me, "Show us a little of what you've done." People can come and see. They shouldn't be jealous. They should leave me alone.

I have been very busy, terribly busy. The last paintings of these recent years are all dated Christmas, New Year's, Pentecost, July 14th, all long weekends. Each one was three days. For example, I have three of them ready which I prepared for August, then there are months and months when I do not have the time. I have boxes of colors which are here and I am going to make some time for them right away.

ALFRED ROTH: 1961

I met Mondrian and that was the second very important step in my life. The first was Le Corbusier and then Mondrian.

I met Mondrian in a very curious way. I was in Holland from Paris, invited to give a talk on Le Corbusier. My first talk I gave to an architecture association for the modern group of Holland. Then they showed me around Amsterdam and showed me some modern buildings. They showed me this modern building designed by Oud, one of his very early houses. The owner had a painting by Mondrian. This painting was somewhat damaged. Somebody had put their dirty fingers on it. This man asked me to take the painting back to Paris and to ask Mondrian to repair it. He wrapped the painting in a piece of paper, I took it to Paris and strangely enough I had it a few days, maybe weeks, in my studio. I did not even look at it. I was not so interested in Mondrian at that time.

Well then, I had to go to visit him and I was told to write him at least a postcard to announce my visit. He did not like visitors to just drop in. So I wrote him a postcard that I shall come a given day. At that time I went to his office, to his studio. I knocked on the door and there was Mondrian, who was a very shy man. He very kindly greeted me and asked me to come in. Then I entered his studio and that was something.

NOTRE-DAME-DU-HAUT. *Le Corbusier. Ronchamp, France. 1955. The sculptured forms and spaces of this chapel—the curving white walls, randomly placed and oddly shaped windows, and bold projecting roof—created a most inspiring statement in modern religious architecture.*

That was heaven! His studio was decorated, that's the right word, with his color elements. The whole studio—red, blue, yellow—in a wonderful rhythmic way. It was a space that had no limits, no dimensions. It was simply music. Pow! I was completely, what do you say, enthusiastic about it. Through the space I met Mondrian, not his painting. But then, naturally, I became very much interested in his painting and was enthusiastic about his painting.

When I was there Le Corbusier never visited the place, I'm absolutely sure and Mondrian never met him. He did not like Le Corbusier's work too much. Mondrian was with the Dutch movement of the style of right angles. Le Corbusier was too romantic for him. He didn't like it. There was no connection at all. But then I frequently visited Mondrian. We became really good friends. I understood his art, that was a second step in my artistic development.

One of Mondrian's ideas was to produce a type of art which could be understood by all people of the world regardless of their cultural background. Be it a Japanese or an American or a South American or a Negro, they still have an understanding of these strong colors—blue, red, yellow—the straight line, and the right angle. The right angle is the invention of man, the symbol of man. So he produced a type of art which is somewhat detached from local conditions, from a regional climate. He compared this type of art with a film produced by Charlie Chaplin. Charlie Chaplin, who is understood universally. That's what he wanted to do.

I became enthusiastic about his work and I visited him very frequently. Le Corbusier was always choking a little bit when I went to Mondrian. "You're always visiting this strange painter. This painter who knows just red and blue, yellow and white. He just uses straight lines and right angles. That's no art. That's a very primitive way of putting things together." At that period, that was Le Corbusier's feeling, but later on he changed that completely.

I would basically say there are two aspects of art. One aspect concerns the art produced as individual works, the easel painting, or the piece of sculpture. Most of these are somewhere in a museum, private houses, or in a square. The other aspect is the problem of the integration of works of art into architecture. First of all, there should be a deep need for that integration. A deep need which is beyond the desire of the artist. Many architects and many artists today agree, let's try this synthesis, but that's one part of the problem. There should be a deeper need within, I would say.

Is our period in a deeper sense willing to accept such a synthesis? Is it necessary in a deeper sense? I would say, yes, there is a deeper need. First of all, generally speaking, our period today, the general trend is toward a better integration of everything in life, whether it is science, whether it is technology, whether it is sociology, whether it is art.

WILLEM DUDOK: 1961

I always saw a big difference between painting and architecture. I know Mondrian personally. What you are presented with a painting of Mondrian, is this. Like this here and here. I just drew it. Here is a little "p" for Piet Mondrian. That was the whole painting. There are certain proportions of this line. But these are values which we use in our architecture as a means, but as a picture it has for me no value. It is not interesting enough.

The Baroque period is a great period in art. It is always looked upon as if it was a denigration. But, in my opinion, it was a beautiful game of space. There is an enormous difference between the Baroque buildings and the modern buildings because in a modern way we use the finishing of the space, the enclosure of a space, only in a secondary way, mostly to enclose. The simpler you do it, the more expressive the space is. Whereas in the Baroque, the walls and all sort of halls attract your attention.

Willem Dudok

Forty years ago there was a man, a great man, Loos—Adolf Loos—who believed that ornament is a crime. I am not at all of that opinion because I think ornament is so elementary in the human desire. I once said that ornament is the condensed joy of life.

In the earliest times in architecture, there was no architecture which was not at the same time ornamented. Even the very primitive make the ornament in their simple houses. That proves that you can't say that ornament is a crime, not at all. I also want ornament. But I want it in a limited way. I want it in an economical way. I can imagine, for instance, a fine room where the architecture leads the attention to one special wall. That wall is decorated, whereas the other walls are very simply done. That, in the economy, you can have great expression. You know, Goethe said, "In the limitation, the master shows himself." That you can also apply, in my opinion, to the applied arts.

It is difficult to find a good cooperating mind in sculpture or in painting. You must not apply those arts if they were not meant to be in the architecture from the very beginning. If you have not considered the applied arts, then you make an architecture which is finished in itself. When a thing of art is finished, it can't have another thing.

For instance, the theater in Utrecht has a big wall. I meant, from the very beginning, to have a sculpture in a certain place on that wall, a golden figure before a big wall. I can't imagine that building without that ornament. It must be one whole.

LOUIS KAHN: 1961

An individual style must be subservient to something which is true to a way of life. The style itself can be your way of expressing something. But if it is completely out of context, with a way of life, then I believe that it doesn't have enough. No one else can take it and expand from it.

In other words, if I produce an instrument which I only can use, it will not be of very great importance. But if I produce an ax, you see, then immediately the forests need it. Now the style, my own individual style, is the way I shape the handle. My tendency is to look at the laws of nature in such a way that I make a good rule which makes my ax somehow better than the other fellow's. My style may be adopted as being good style, but the general way of life which it is part of must be part of the making of it.

ERNESTO ROGERS: 1961

I would say that beauty is a goal. It's not a premise. It's an achievement. I'm speaking of our contemporary way of doing architecture. Maybe it wasn't so in earlier times, but anyhow, for us, beauty is a conclusion. It's never a priori. Therefore, when I say an architect needs culture and imagination, I don't know where culture and imagination will end up. I mean in which shape. The shape is the synthetic connection of the many components of his personality.

ANTONIN RAYMOND: 1962

An architect is principally an artist. A Japanese will love nature, real nature, not only this world and animals, trees, landscape, and so on, but the whole world, the cosmos, you see. He's interested in the order of the universe. He believes that an artist is a man who can reveal to the people a glimpse into the order of the universe. I agree with him. That's the only function of an artist, to give the human being a glimpse into the order of the universe, to make him feel one with the order, with the supreme order of things. He's a profound philosopher, otherwise he's got nothing to say, nothing to offer. His facility to draw or to do things is against him, not for him. You can hire a good draftsman for twenty dollars a week. All that means nothing. What really means something is his profound understanding of the problems of the society with respect to the understanding of the order of the universe, why things are beautiful or unbeautiful.

For instance, from my experience, I claim that beauty is absolute. Now when I say that to an American, he will not agree, he will argue. He will say, how do you know it's beautiful, how'd you find out, how do you know what I like, the only thing that's beautiful is what I like. Well, that is not so. Beauty is absolute. That is, it would exist if the human being is here or not, and it's awfully difficult for a Westerner to understand. If you live long enough in the Orient you will begin to understand, but for a Westerner it's almost impossible.

Antonin Raymond

READER'S DIGEST BUILDING. *Antonin Raymond with L.L. Rado. Tokyo. 1951. Considered the masterpiece of Raymond's Japanese career, this two-story office building combined modern American materials and technical innovations with traditional Japanese wood construction.*

Alvar Aalto

ALVAR AALTO: 1961

From my maternal side I have come from an artistic family, not professional artists, but it was mostly forestry science—about nine forester scientists on this line. But I think the Finnish forests give us some of our artistic and human approach to life.

EDWARD DURELL STONE: 1963

I have this belief that great architecture will give everyone, the man in the street, the uneducated man, the uninformed man, an exhilaration. He'll be thrilled by it. The idea that architecture is something that can only be appreciated by a minuscule minority of precious initiates is all wrong. I think anybody would agree that Chartres is a beautiful thing. I think everybody really is thrilled with the interior of Grand Central Station. I think great architecture, people should sense and feel.

UNITED STATES EMBASSY. *Edward Durell Stone. New Delhi, India. 1954. In this strikingly modern rectangular building, with the overhanging roof supported on thin gold-leafed steel columns, Stone combined the simplicity of a classical Greek temple with the rich grilles of a Muslim shrine.*

AFFONSO EDUARDO REIDY: 1956

Today it is common to hear that architecture is a big sculpture. I don't hold that opinion. I think that architecture has an aesthetic aspect, but it's not essential to architecture. I believe more that architecture is closely linked to a spatial concept than to the aesthetic element of a sculpture.

Architecture today has no place for the kind of reasoning used twenty years ago, which followed a rigid principle of rationality and functionality. You can in no way forget that architecture has its utilitarian side. It exists to serve a purpose. Now it's not enough that it serve this purpose. It is necessary that the function and the technology—the external and internal spaces—are the basic objects the architect searches for. Evidently this space, from my point of view, should be assimilated within an architectural effort. This is an effort which does not necessarily have to take the form of elementary geometry. It can be any form that disciplines space. I don't think architecture has to be limited to the freedom of spatial conception. As I see it, the free plan is the basic element of modern architecture and the problem of space, which is fundamental, needs some architectural discipline of space. The volume will call into play the qualities of sculpture to architecture. The sculptural aspect emerges with the volume and contains the space, which defines architecture.

MARIO SALVADORI: 1957

The fact is that nowadays it's very fashionable to talk about architecture as being sculpture. You have to sculpt this and sculpt that. It is an idea in which I do not believe. I believe that in all of our activities, quantity is not just an addition of numbers, like two and two is four, and four and four is eight, but if you add eight and eight and get sixteen and you go on and on, you get to numbers so large that their quality is different from the two you started from. This is very unorthodox in mathematics, so don't quote me to my friend the mathematician.

It seems to me that the moment you take a piece of sculpture, which has certain dimensions which are more or less on the human scale, usually they are smaller, but may be as large as a human being. Then you blow them up and you have an actual building, a big structure. You have an entirely different factor and this is not just a highbrow idea, this has got to do with gravity. In a sculpture, gravity has nothing to do with the form, the appearance, the meaning; but in a structural creation, you have to be able to withstand the wind and other factors, but essentially it is gravitation that counts. So, in going from small to large, you should abandon the idea that you are sculpting. You are doing something which is very funny. You are fighting against gravitation and that is what lies behind all the difficulties.

Of course, like in a bullfight it is not enough to kill the bull, you have to kill him in a very elegant fashion. In killing gravity it is not enough to kill it, that is very simple. You just make it very, very strong and it will stand. But if you do it elegantly then you get a good result, a beautiful result, an architectural result. Not only that, it becomes beautiful architecture. I don't believe that it makes any sense at all to look for beauty. In this I wholeheartedly agree with my friend Luigi Nervi.

May I tell you a little story about him? You know that he and I went around for months delivering lectures. He lectured and I translated. After a month, I didn't know whether I was Mario Salvadori or Luigi Nervi. I was completely gone. One night at a regular lecture, he threw on the screen his beautiful Turin Exhibition Hall. He looked at it and I said, "Well, what do you want to say?" He said nothing but, "Let's go on." I couldn't help it. I turned around and I told the public, "Mr. Nervi says that he has nothing to say about this. I feel compelled to say that this is one of the most beautiful structures ever designed and built. That in particular this idea of what I call the fan, the four-pronged fan that brings the various arches into the buttresses, is one of the most superb realizations of truth in structures and beauty in structures." And the public applauded.

So Nervi got very mad and demanded in Italian, "What in the hell did you say?" I told him and then he mumbled in Italian, "This is ridiculous. That's the only thing you can do anyway." So I translated that, they laughed. He said, "What did you say?"

EXHIBITION HALL.
Pier Luigi Nervi. Turin, Italy. 1948. Bold prefabricated reinforced-concrete sections, some glazed for light, form the famous shell covering the vast exhibition area.

because he doesn't understand a word, you see. I told him what I just translated was what you told me. So he really became mad and said, "Look, Mario, what would you have done but that?" He felt that it was unavoidable. It was obvious.

I believe that the time you hit upon the right solution which is obvious, which just comes to you because there is nothing else you can do, then you get the beautiful solution, the structurally correct solution, the economical solution, from the point of sound mechanics and everything else.

MCGREGOR MEMORIAL COMMUNITY CONFERENCE CENTER, WAYNE STATE UNIVERSITY. *Minoru Yamasaki. Detroit, Michigan. 1955. With its reflecting pools, travertine walls, and jewellike glass central hall, this university conference hall is a fine example of Yamasaki's belief that in addition to exhibiting good planning and detailing, a building should create an emotional experience.*

MINORU YAMASAKI: 1960

I think architecture is not merely an exterior, physical problem, a shape. It has to be derived and grow from the needs of man. It can't be a superimposed form to the whim of the sculptor. One can't fit the people who use the building into it in any fashion the architect desires just to suit the exterior appearance. I'm afraid that Corbu is more of a sculptor and not an architect in that sense. Consequently, though he is certainly one of stature and has great influence on modern architecture because of the understanding of the plasticity of the material with which he works, and the fact that architecture can be a very dynamic thing with the technological background, I still feel that his approach is purely sculptural.

The art of architecture had long been related to the other fine arts, painting and sculpture. Rejecting the decorative elements of the past, modern architects altered this relationship in favor of a revolutionary purity. They expressed this change in their observations on color, ornament, and art. They favored the honest colors of natural materials but also frequently adopted the vivid primary colors of modern painting.

VICTOR GRUEN: 1957

I think that nearly all color combinations have their great decorative value and can be used in interiors in various combinations. Color is everything, including white, black, and gray. I knew somebody who said he liked all colors as long as they were gray. We should not be limited to white, black, and gray as a neutralizing background to nature, to trees, to flowers, to the blue sky as the most satisfactory colors which we can give to architecture. I do feel that if handled with great skill and with a certain amount of judgment, a color in architecture can play a very great role and can be very desirable. It also depends on the region and the type of environment. We could use more colors besides black, white, and gray, beige and dark brown, as we are using now.

NOYES HOUSE. *Eliot Noyes. New Canaan, Connecticut. 1954. In his own house, Noyes employed the natural materials of the region and placed two units facing a central patio under one roof.*

I believe in everything which is temporary; like an exhibition, we should be much more daring. We can afford to be much more daring because we are not exposed for a long period to the objects which we observe, but a quick impression is to be gained. There color can play a tremendously important part. It is strange that people who even start out with the use of color in their design seem to lose courage when it comes to execution.

ELIOT NOYES: 1957

I like the idea of putting color into architecture, but every time I've tried to do it I've suddenly backed away again. I did a laboratory for IBM where I was all set to put in colored porcelain enamel panels in the spandrels. Then I thought, five years from now I'm going to come and look at that color and think, oh brother, I'm sick of that color. So I backed off and did two shades of alternating grays.

Now in this house and in other architecture that I've done, mostly, I have tended to let the materials take their own color, or do something like staining cypress, which I don't consider a sin to the material, to bring out or dramatize the grain or refine the natural quality and then to introduce color through Matisse rugs, red Calder mobiles, you know, accessories and furnishings. I feel more assured doing this than I do introducing color into the building. Marcel Breuer does this work marvelously. It's funny, I haven't found in my own buildings the place where I could do it. I think it's maybe partly the artistry of it.

I think the color in Eero Saarinen's General Motors Technical Center buildings is probably stunning. I haven't seen them. It seems to me that it not only takes incredible courage on the part of a guy like Eero to do this, but incredible salesmanship. My experience with big companies is that you may start out to sell such an idea, but about the time the first five color-glazed bricks show up, there are forty executives or their wives who begin to cast doubt. You know, "Does it have to be that bright? Couldn't it be sort of a pastel tone? I've always liked dusty red." You know, this kind of thing. I'm sure it would've been coming at Eero from all sides. It takes considerable guts to stand there and say, "No, it's this and this and this. I know I'm right, and you have to go along with me." Somehow he does this and this is terrific.

GORDON BUNSHAFT: 1956

Color in buildings is a very difficult and sometimes a dangerous thing to do. I'm a firm believer of the theory that was written in a book a long time ago called *Form and Color*. The theory of this book is that if surfaces of a structure are extremely smooth and do not have their own shades and shadows, which in a sense is color, then it is justifiable to have color as an excitement.

That is explained, for example, in the interior of Santa Sophia in Constantinople, where the forms are all very smooth and plastic and the color is the accent. In contrast, for example, to a Renaissance structure full of pilasters, cornices, and things that are full of shades and shadows, which give a sense of color, and to put brilliant color in that destroys the structural expression of these elements.

In other words, in Saarinen's General Motors Technical Center his color is only on areas that are extremely simple and are closing end-walls or elements like that of a building. In the pattern surfaces of the building, where the glass and the spandrels and the mullions create a rich pattern of shades and shadows, you will notice that he has kept that practically colorless or very neutral.

ENRICO PERESSUTTI: 1955

I think that color in architecture is a very important element. I just came back from Mexico two days ago. I must say that the first important impression I had down in Mexico, against the fact that here in the northern part of America there is less color, was about the color they use there, which makes architecture deep and really connected with nature and giving much more pleasure.

Enrico Peressutti

EDGARDO CONTINI: 1956

Historically, architecture has always been made of the proper use of mass, composition, and color. So the moment you take color away from architecture, you take one of its essential components. But that doesn't mean that color can be artificially applied. It's the difference between tinting a black and white picture or having a color picture. Color has to come out of the very nature of the material and the very choice of the materials.

WALTER GROPIUS: 1964

We have eyes given to us by nature, but we have to learn to see. What is color and what is the meaning of color? For instance, I can say, as an architect, I have to build a hall. This must be right in materials, in space, in all these things. But the appearance of that space has to be done with different things. When you sit in this room and have the ceiling in matte black, it comes down on us. When I make it in glossy black it goes away. When the wall there is lemon yellow, it attacks me and comes to me. When it is dark blue, it goes away from me. So it appears to be something different from what in measurement it is. With the tricks of the artist I can change the appearance of this space. I must know these things because they are based on certain facts about seeing, of our psychology, of biological facts, and so on.

JOSÉ LUIS SERT: 1960

I have a certain approach to color that perhaps came to me through my friends the painters, people like Léger and Miró. We very often have long conversations on color and the use of color. I generally like—that's a personal approach, of course—to use bright, pure colors in certain spots accentuating certain parts of the building. But the predominating color is a more neutral color, like white or gray or whatever color comes to me, because of the type of building. I mean, it comes from the materials, the nature of the materials and the surroundings. But I do like to use very strong color accents.

MARIO CIAMPI: 1956

I feel that something very significant happened to me in South America about five years ago. I remember that when I arrived there I stopped and called on Oscar Niemeyer, the architect, because I always had a very high regard for his work. There was a certain quality about his work which set it apart from the work we are normally accustomed to seeing and appreciating in our country.

I remember when I called on him this day in Rio de Janeiro, after a short chat he said to me, "Well, come along now. I want you to meet a man who is going to work on this project with me." Together we called on a very well known South American artist called Portinari. Now many people in this country may not have heard of Portinari. The thing that impressed me at the time was that Mr. Niemeyer wasn't just designing a building in terms of his ability to express architecture, but to bring into architecture other values which he felt were very significant. He impressed on me very definitely how important it is to include the arts in architecture. That architecture wasn't merely the expression of a solution to meet the material needs of people, but that architecture was something that you admire, live with and that it influences your way of life. The incorporation of the arts such as painting, sculpture, and the work of other crafts in the embellishment of a building is equally as important and, perhaps, more vital to people than just a good solution or the use of good building construction.

CHURCH OF THE MIRACULOUS VIRGIN. *Félix Candela with Enrique de la Mora. Mexico City. 1953. The thin shell vaults of the church dramatically display Candela's superb skill with reinforced concrete.*

FÉLIX CANDELA: 1961

It's very difficult to use sculpture or painting in a building just to apply the sculpture or the painting to a building, you see. It must be a general conception. I mean you must be at the same time an architect, maybe a sculptor, because painting is difficult to integrate into a building. I think a sculpture goes more easily with architecture. Then, there have been several periods in history, perhaps not too many, in which sculpture has been integrated with the architecture. The Gothic is one of the most important times, and also, in the work of Gaudí.

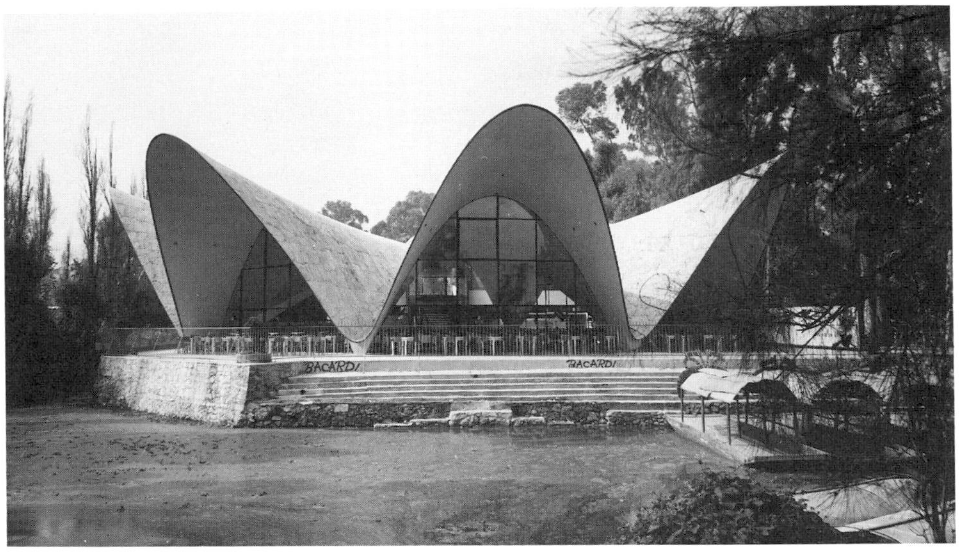

XOCHIMILCO RESTAURANT. *Félix Candela and Joaquín Ordonez. Xochimilco, Mexico. 1958. Candela's restaurant, with its soaring reinforced-concrete hyperbolic paraboloids, sits like a huge waterlily in the floating gardens of Xochimilco.*

HELMUT HENTRICH: 1961

I think it's all art, actually. Even the smallest detail should be art. You see, a whole building consists of small things. It's an assembly of small things. So if the small things are not good, the whole thing is not good.

PAUL RUDOLPH: 1960

A building should be meaningful from no matter what distance you look at it, if you are quickly flying over it or riding by it in a vehicle. It should have a certain diagrammatic quality which can be read. You can see it at a glance. If you approach it by foot, it has to have additional layers of meaning. You have to see things which you haven't seen before. As you come closer in traditional architecture, the meaningfulness of the building is maintained by the introduction of moldings and capitals on the columns and so forth.

We, of course, have knocked all of that out and in a sense have not found anything to replace it. It's one reason why grilles tend to be satisfying, up to a certain point anyway, because it does give this play of light and shadow and maintains one's interest as one comes really close to the building. It has to do with how architecture is read and from what distance. We know well how to make diagrammatic buildings, which are meaningful from a great distance. But quite often they fall apart when one approaches them more closely.

I might add that the screens that we used [on the Jewett Arts Center] at Wellesley College were introduced not only to keep the light and control the glare, but to help relate it to the earlier buildings, which had very, very delicate moldings, as small as a quarter of an inch sometimes. The sense of the reduction of the scale was eloquently maintained in the earlier buildings. We wanted in some way to do the same thing in that building.

Another example of this is that clusters of columns were used rather than a single column. From a distance the cluster looks as a single column. But as you approach it, it is seen that it is really a cluster of columns. Of course, this is a page directly out of Gothic architecture. When the great revolution in architecture came, which had

PHOENIX-RHEINROH BUILDING. *Helmut Hentrich and Hubert Petschnigg. Düsseldorf, Germany. 1957. An example of postwar rebuilding, this slim modern curtain-walled administration building was designed to take advantage of the light and view of the adjacent city park.*

Paul Rudolph

validity, we threw out much. We are slowly now sifting and putting back in some things which then didn't seem to have so much validity.

I think that architects are interested in juxtaposing works of art to their buildings. But I do not believe that any architect has found the satisfactory way of really integrating works of art with a building. I really believe that the painters and the sculptors are on quite different wavelengths from the architects. I am not saying that we are right or wrong. I am just saying that their concerns are vastly different from ours. Part of the difficulty is one of scale. The painters and the sculptors make everything too small and these things are lost. That's perhaps not necessarily their fault, because sculptors, especially, do not have the opportunity to make things of sufficient scale. I believe that it's going to be fundamentally up to the architect to find a way of reintroducing painting and sculpture. There is the desire, but there is not the knowledge how to go about this.

The art of landscape architecture is almost completely lost. It is only the large commercial firms that can afford a fountain, or think they can afford a fountain. I'm not saying this is right or wrong, but it is part of the spirit of the times. It may be that the municipality or the governmental agencies will become more potent in the sense of the city as a whole and its beautification. Architects will give lip service to this, but architects are not the people who really bring this into being. They, only in a sense, are the tool by which the people's desire becomes manifest. It is noteworthy, of course, that in Italy the first thing they did after the war was turn on the fountains. It would have been the last thing we would have done if we had any fountains to turn on.

A mistake hurts the whole future of commissioning big art for buildings. We didn't do right in Seagram's. But at least what you do see inside is the big Picasso tapestry, big as all hell. You see it and it's good. When you enter the Four Seasons restaurant down below, you see one or two big enough things.

I am into water and light. Anything that moves, anything that makes a focal point, anything that is existing in time. I always wanted fountains at Seagram's and not sculpture. Mies and I never agreed on that. I originally designed a system, but when it came to one million dollars to put it in and $600,000 a year to maintain it, it got, shall we say, pushed out because Mies was against it. I was the one who always pushed for fountains. Mies wanted to do the sculpture himself until he found he couldn't. I never wanted sculpture. I think the noise, the accidental spray, the lights, the fact that it's living is what interests me. I feel about it the way I do about processionals. It's an emotional feeling that's in space—the way to decorate that space to enhance it, that is unique.

That's one reason I like Saint Peter's. Yes, one reason. But, of course, there isn't the volume that will fill a square as this fireplace fills this room. You see, to me, if neither the fountain nor the fireplace is going, I have a sense of loss. At Saint Peter's the fountains are like pieces of sculpture, sweet little things, like a lamp. I'm talking about something that fills the room with its energy and flicker. It exists in time. Perhaps, to me, it takes the place of decoration, the same as the light does.

See, the lighting in this house takes the place of an awful lot of architecture. It's why I use candles so much in this house—a moving light, flicker—why I've used flares in the pavilion, and fire in this house. The fire is not only a warmth, it touches so many senses, the fire and the flicker. The heat the fireplace gives you. Water gives you the noise, flicker, and light. This is the depth and deepening of architecture which formerly could be given by the handcrafts of decoration which we are no longer able and maybe we don't want. It's a matter of time. I do feel that you have to introduce the fourth dimension into architecture. Times change. That is one thing that my "wallpaper" does in this Glass House, it changes as the light of the day changes. It changes as the wind and as the seasons. So, we're adding, instead of a beautiful decor—let's say, like a Rococo, which I of course love—we have the seasons changing through glass walls.

Now water is the same. It always changes. It's a sequential thing, much as the processional changes in architecture as you walk through it. I think that with our severe restrictions that were caused by the lack of craft, that we have to substitute enrichments of other kinds, which can be done in time, light, heat, and cold.

You see, it's very cooling in a hot day to come up to Seagram's now. When they're up full height, the crashing of the water is just sensually cool. People sit there attracted to the cooling. As you are in the winter when I keep my house cool. It's so that you walk over to the fireplace, get warm, come back, get cool and go over and get warm again. It adds movement of all kinds to architecture.

GROPIUS: 1964

I am somewhat disappointed that what I call the science of design hasn't been developed more. Men like Albers put something new into it. Kepes here in MIT put something into it, but not enough, you know. To really find out more about the designs of objects, of our seeing, and so on, we can learn something new every day. The more the individual who is an artist knows about these things, the better he can build his own ideas. I'm of the opinion that this is not only a preparation which should be given to the art students, but I believe that it is essential and imperative to build it into the whole school system from the nursery on.

A designer or an artist who creates something needs the response of the people. The response of the people is not there if the man is not educated for it. In this country, it is still very much apart. Among very many people art is still considered a standard of luxury which is used and bought when there is some extra money. It is not a thing which is constitutionally in the life of the people, such as a necessity. In all times of great culture, it was absolutely basic to the whole population. This can be done only by education.

We are outstandingly backward. Several countries in Europe have made arrangements that in public buildings the government gives a definite percentage for artwork automatically. We haven't got that yet. It's a good thing because then art is not dependent on this or that man who may be too vulnerable when he makes this decision, but it is an institution so that everyone has the right to use so much money for art in public buildings. I think this would be very good to have that. But I wouldn't like to call it adornment, because it should be a part of the whole.

I will give you an example. I was asked to design the Federal Office Building, which now will be called the Kennedy Building, here in Boston. It's under construction. I wanted to arrange it so I could work with artists in the beginning, so that the architect and the artist conceive it together. I asked the government whether they could give me some fee for these artists to work with me. They said, no, we cannot do it. Only when we have gone out for bids and there is some extra money left, then we will give you money to buy some artwork. Then it becomes an adornment and added on instead of part of the whole conception.

Minoru Yamasaki

YAMASAKI: 1960

The other thing that I have been interested in is that I believe that buildings should have ornament. But I think that the ornament cannot be man-made, rather carved by hand. It can't be handicraft because obviously this is solving nothing. We can't have handicraft ornament on our buildings today. If we do, we are just being somewhat sentimental and proving nothing. But if we can produce really lovely ornaments through the machine, machine-made ornament, we are proving something because then again another element in architecture becomes a part of our technological building. It's really an important part of a technological building.

Also, I believe that ornament, as such, just plastered to the face of the building, isn't good. It has to arise from the need. So, consequently, if the screen to shut out the sun from the building can add richness to the building, then it answers a need.

NORTHLAND SHOPPING CENTER. *Victor Gruen. Detroit, Michigan. 1954. Incorporating many of the ideas of modern town planning, including plazas and parking, with those of the traditional village marketplace, Gruen created this pioneering and influential shopping mall.*

Consequently, it's an integral part of the building. It still is part of our heritage and part of our education from the masters, from Mies, Wright, and Corbu, that the elements we put into the building must be integral with the building or must be a necessary and important part of the building. In other words, we can't do the Baroque yet. And I hope we don't.

GRUEN: 1957

When it comes to ornament, it's like asking whether there should be more love in the world. I'm all for romance when it comes naturally. Any faked and artificially brought on romance we call necking or flirting and I believe they're much less enjoyable things than the proper, real romantic love. The seeking for ornament just because one feels, by God, we have to get it back, is one which will end up in very artificial expressions. I believe very often what happens in those cases is that the architect says to himself, well, I have to stiffen the material and, also, I feel that it is about time that we get some ornament. Let's combine the useful with the beautiful. If it fits with the purpose of the building, if it creates a spiritual enrichment of the building, then it is in order. It is again in character of our times that the place for such is very rarely to be found.

EERO SAARINEN: 1956

In many ways I seem to believe that in architecture every problem is a specific problem, specific for answering the client's functional needs, specific for answering its environmental needs, and specific also for capturing the spirit of that particular function. Therefore, I find it harder and harder to generalize. I feel . . . perhaps too much generalization is being made by architects and architectural firms. Therefore, while I have used color, maybe . . . made a stronger statement in color in relation to architecture than anybody else I can think of at the moment, still there are architectural problems where maybe color shouldn't be used. There's some places I am definitely not using colors just because it's not in the nature of the problem.

As a civilization of architects, or as a profession of architects, we are partly new and partly old. Some of the ideas are partly old. What we have to be very careful about is when we think of art that we define our rules.

I like, for instance, the way Calder went at it designing another piece of sculpture for the General Motors Technical Center. There was enough hardware there as it is, but instead he designed a water ballet, moving jets of water which will create an interest. It will be like a symphony in water. I think this can be a marvelous thing.

I think also another good example is the screen that Harry Bertoia designed three years ago for the restaurant, where the problem was a semiarchitectural problem of making a transparent screen. It is very difficult because sculptors are not really used to facing the practical world. Also it's not always easy to convince the clients that money should be spent for these things. Fortunately, my wife, Aline, knows so much more than I can ever hope to know about the whole artist world. Much with her advice, I've gotten to the right artists for several projects where I was working with artists.

We're working on several right now. The Stuart Davis mural for the dining room for Drake University, which the Cowles Foundation gave, which is, I think, a really marvelous thing. I think one of Stuart Davis's best things. It's a mural about thirty-two feet long.

Then in the MIT chapel, there's the screen which Bertoia did and, more important than that, the spire or the ironwork, which has not yet been placed there. It will be thirty-two feet high on top of the chapel that Roszak has worked on. This was a project which I, frankly, began by asking the question, is this architecture or is this sculpture? I worked quite hard on that, made several models, and many in the office made models, and gradually we came to a form. We didn't want to go out to the sculptor before we had matured our thoughts about it. But then there came a point where one realized that in certain things the sculptor is more sensitive and can give more to a project than the architect, who is trained for a different thing. So then we gave the whole thing to Roszak. He went through the same searching process and came out with what I think will be a marvelous bell tower.

You know there was a time when we didn't even talk about texture, much less ornament. Then we began to talk about texture. With texture, I mean the texture of a wall. For instance, the texture of a glass wall that mullions and the glass give it, or the texture of a wall with the windows and the wall in between the depth facade. The moment you start talking about texture, you're already on your way toward ornament. In other words, you're willing to have ornament, but you don't know how to get it. You can't just dig up some old acanthus leaves and put them there. I'm sorry, I

CHAPEL, MASSACHUSETTS INSTITUTE OF TECHNOLOGY. *Eero Saarinen. Cambridge. 1953. This red brick cylinder punctuated with arches and encircled by a water-filled moat creates an unusually moving, nondenominational religious atmosphere.*

think ornament, in our time, will come as it always has come, from the accentuation of structure. I mean starting with the structure and then the playing up of it beyond the necessity of the structure. With a willingness to have this texture which it creates, we will have ornament.

In the London Embassy we tried enormous amounts of ornaments and grilles and tried to justify them. Finally we ended up with fairly simple grilles, quite a simple fence and a fairly simple cornice line, but this was after discarding hundreds of different variations. But I'm not saying that we won't go farther than that. We're on the road to ornament, yes.

1958

Some friend of ours took a psychoanalyst to General Motors and then while there he made the remark, "You know, the architect is really the only one of the arts which is not at war with society in our time." In other times the painters, the Rubenses and the other Renaissance painters, they were not at war with society. But today the painters are. What's good about their statements is that they are at war with society and that's fine. But I think the statement is true that the architect is essentially not at war with society.

GREAT WORKS

"I THINK WE HAVE THESE THREE GREAT FORCES THAT ARE WITH US EVERY TIME WE THINK ABOUT ARCHITECTURE. THERE IS WRIGHT AND HIS LIFE WORK; THERE IS CORBU AND HIS LIFE WORK; AND THERE IS MIES AND HIS."

FALLINGWATER.
Frank Lloyd Wright. Bear Run, Pennsylvania. 1935

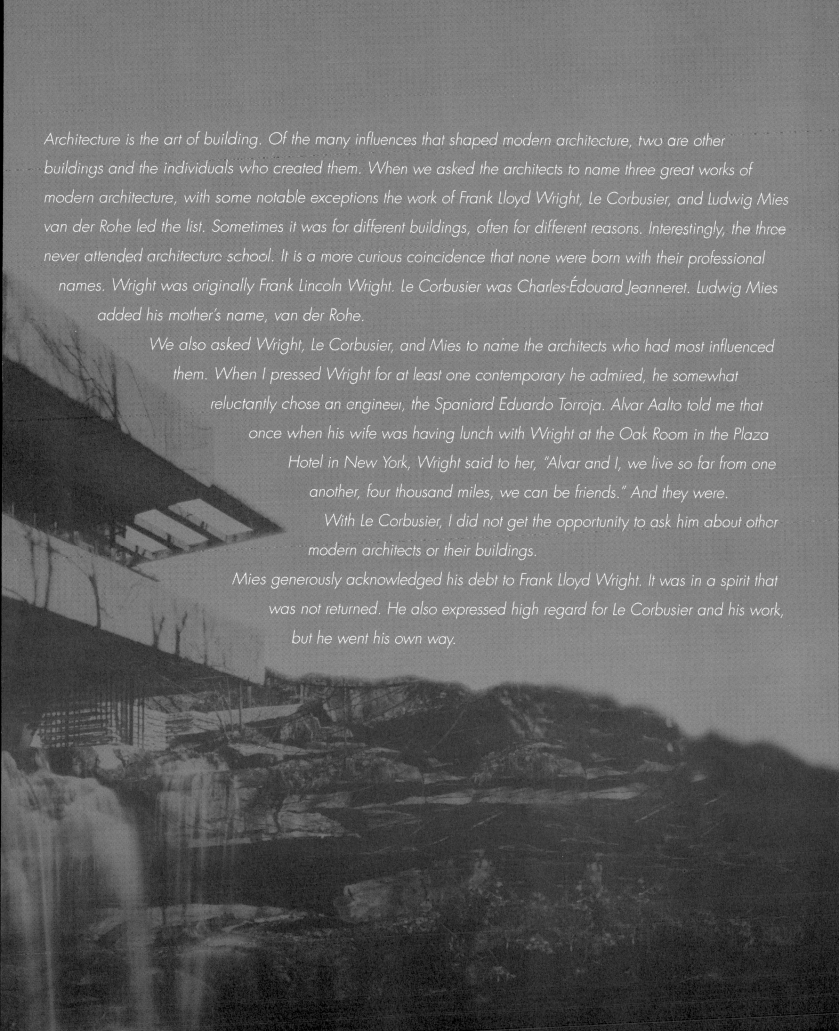

Architecture is the art of building. Of the many influences that shaped modern architecture, two are other buildings and the individuals who created them. When we asked the architects to name three great works of modern architecture, with some notable exceptions the work of Frank Lloyd Wright, Le Corbusier, and Ludwig Mies van der Rohe led the list. Sometimes it was for different buildings, often for different reasons. Interestingly, the three never attended architecture school. It is a more curious coincidence that none were born with their professional names. Wright was originally Frank Lincoln Wright. Le Corbusier was Charles-Édouard Jeanneret. Ludwig Mies added his mother's name, van der Rohe.

We also asked Wright, Le Corbusier, and Mies to name the architects who had most influenced them. When I pressed Wright for at least one contemporary he admired, he somewhat reluctantly chose an engineer, the Spaniard Eduardo Torroja. Alvar Aalto told me that once when his wife was having lunch with Wright at the Oak Room in the Plaza Hotel in New York, Wright said to her, "Alvar and I, we live so far from one another, four thousand miles, we can be friends." And they were.

With Le Corbusier, I did not get the opportunity to ask him about other modern architects or their buildings.

Mies generously acknowledged his debt to Frank Lloyd Wright. It was in a spirit that was not returned. He also expressed high regard for Le Corbusier and his work, but he went his own way.

UNITÉ D'HABITATION. *Le Corbusier. Marseilles, France. 1947. This complex for a self-contained community of sixteen hundred provides sun-shaded apartments, a central shopping street, and a rooftop nursery school, pool, solarium, and running track. The huge concrete slab is raised off the ground on massive pillars.*

PHILIP JOHNSON: 1955

Three great works and why? Well, I prefer to name three that I know rather than ones I don't know. I'd rather take buildings that I'm very familiar with that have given me a special inspiration as to further design, let's say. And I would pick the three as the Marseilles apartments of Le Corbusier, Taliesin West of Wright, and the 860 Lake Shore Drive towers of Mies van der Rohe.

Now, the first, the Marseilles apartments. Why? Because he carries as far as possible aesthetic experimentation in the modern style. The modern style of architecture is one in which we emphasize the weightlessness, the lightness, the inherent characteristic of skeleton construction. Corbusier has carried that much further than anyone else by holding the building up on great expressive hands, almost expressionistic, but they are regularly spaced. They keep the basic rhythm, the boom-boom-boom of the base rhythm that's required in any building, that they make this massive building float and keep light, which is the essence of modern.

Then above it he has a reticulation. He's carried his glass back, not to make this eternal flat-skin effect that all modern buildings in New York seem to get by trying to keep the outer walls thin for economic reasons. He has pushed them way back, twenty feet sometimes, to keep the hollow honeycomblike effect of the entire building.

And then, thirdly and most important, he has carried the sculptural effects on the roof materials to such a degree that if you were just to consider it large sculpture it would still count. It does seem to me that there is no contradiction between architecture and sculpture. An architect has a perfect right to make sculptural forms out of his needs, as Corbusier does out of his chimneys, to make an expressive unity to bind the whole composition together against the sky. Too many modern people have neglected the sky. It makes for shadows, for delight, for contrast that you can't get any other way.

Taliesin West, of course, is quite a different matter. Frank Lloyd Wright belongs to the ages. There, I think, the essence of his house is the human element, the procession through the building. I once counted the turns that you make when you approach the building until you get into what he calls the cove, the holy of holies, where you finally sit down with the high priest. And the number of turns, I think, was forty-five. Now he is playing with you as you walk through that space. He stops your car, as any good architect should, two or three hundred feet from the entrance. It doesn't rain enough to make any difference. Then you start down the steps, up the steps, to the left, to the right, down the long, very long pergola and you turn to the right to get out under that famous prow. And you take those few steps down onto the magnificent view that's been concealed from you for two or three hundred feet of walking. Then you see Arizona stretched out as he meant it to you.

And then you turn and go into the little tent room where—the man, of course, understands light better than anybody in the world—and he has this tent light that trickles, filters down through into this private room. Before he opens any flaps you are just bathed in this canvas light. Then when he opens the flap onto the little secret garden, you say, I can't, there are no more surprises, there can't be any more unfolding of spaces, but there are. And you get into this private courtyard with the green grass and the falling water, which I notice he's just changed. He now has a series of round circular paths surrounding the seats.

Then you finally get into the cove and just when you're used to Frank Lloyd Wright's six-foot ceiling, it has a fourteen-foot ceiling and the fireplace runs the full length of the building. There are no windows, all of a sudden, and no canvas. You're entirely enclosed in the middle of this experience. And by the time you get there you realize that you've been handled, and petted, and twisted much as a symphony will caress you, or an opera, until you get to the crisis. That, perhaps, is not even architecture in the same sense that the Corbusier building is, but they both have something to tell later architects.

Then the third building, 860 Lake Shore Drive, is quite different. There is a master builder at work, as the other two don't know anything about building, you might say, to exaggerate slightly. Mies knows all about building. He knows before he puts a line to paper how it's going to look. But he also knows what's possible . . . and what you have to admit is going to have to be put in the building before you do it. And then he realizes more than that. He realizes what civilization we're in. You can't repeat Marseilles. Who is going to be able to build something of the processional incredibleness of Taliesin West? But everyone can, and mostly does, build apartment houses. And the patterns which he has developed for sheathing the skeleton building is the

TALIESIN WEST. *Frank Lloyd Wright. Scottsdale, Arizona. 1938. Wright designed the winter headquarters for the Taliesin Fellowship with a solid concrete and desert stone base topped by wood framing and tentlike canvas in a superb handling of space and light.*

860–880 LAKE SHORE DRIVE APARTMENTS. *Ludwig Mies van der Rohe. Chicago. 1951. Mies's first masterpiece in the United States, these two apartment towers of glass in black steel frames are set at right angles to each other to optimize the spectacular views of the city and Lake Michigan.*

first, yes, it certainly is the first step in this economic problem–cum–architectural problem since Sullivan, who first used verticality to organize multistory buildings.

It's amazing to realize that the multistory building is quite a new problem in architecture. Sullivan was the first to grapple with it. Richardson only built buildings five or six stories high that were still blown-up one-story houses. That warehouse, the Marshall Field warehouse, is a one-story building, but the Wainwright is a skyscraper. And the Wainwright thesis of the base, the vertical columns—the pilasters almost—and the heavy cornice, have been copied ever since because it is the logical way to sheathe a multistory building; if it goes up it's with vertical emphasis.

Mies, of course, doesn't know this. He's never seen any Sullivan work. It's a pure accident, but it isn't an accident because the problem is the same that Mies solved in the technique of our day what Sullivan solved in the technique of his. And that is a basic pattern from which it is extremely difficult to diverge. Many of us have tried. I say, now look, I just mustn't have those exposed mullions that create that wonderful impression of 860, but the more you try to make a building cheap, which you have to do in today's economy and socio-setup, the more you try to make it expressive, the closer to 860 you're going to end up.

Just as in Mies's newest building in New York, the Seagram tower, the projected mullions, although made of a different material, serve exactly the same purpose. They create a separate plane out from the plane of the glass, which adds so much to the interest of the building in that it doesn't become a blank glassy box. What you really see is the surface of the projected mullions, unless you are looking directly onto the building. The effect is that of a bronze building, not a glass building. These mullions, of course, are merely an extension of a functional and necessary part of the building. You have to have wind bracing, so you are perfectly legitimate. You have to have spandrels to exaggerate or pull out or push in or play with those two elements, the spandrel and the mullion. As a matter of fact, the building is a plaid. The Carson, Pirie & Scott building is a plaid that emphasizes the horizontal. The Wainwright Building is a plaid that emphasizes the vertical. Mies's building emphasizes the vertical.

The trouble with glass boxes is that they have to have a superimposed pattern. And it is the duty of the great architect to impose one so simply and so logically, or pseudologically, from the nature of the building itself that it will have a beauty, well, almost inherent. It's the slight pulling away from the absolute necessities that is the art of that building. It may be . . . and that building may be much more important in history, you see, than the other two for the simple reason that it's in line.

You might use the analogy of the Palladian style which Nowicki used on Mies, that Palladio may not have been Michelangelo, although they were contemporaries, slightly. Palladio was younger, but Palladio so vernacularized the problems of his late Baroque time that his name became synonymous with architecture for three hundred years.

Now, it's a question if Taliesin West will ever be a beacon for younger generations, but there is absolutely no question at all, because it's already being done, that Mies's basic solution for tall buildings will be used. How it will be diverged from will be interesting, but that it will form the basis, and I know it is for a great number of us, that we can't anymore try to think of how you do a multistory, and I mean repeated stories, not a pyramidal composition, but a repeated-story building, which is of the essence of the problem of architecture today, as the church was in the Middle Ages. You cannot start designing that without pulling off from 860 Lake Shore Drive, and that seems to me to make it rather basic among today's buildings.

Carlos Villanueva

CARLOS VILLANUEVA: 1955

I consider that the three greatest works of modern architecture are: first, the Villa Savoye by Le Corbusier, for its significance in the return to volume; second, the Barcelona Pavilion by Mies van der Rohe, for its renovation of monumental, universal space; third, Taliesin West of Frank Lloyd Wright, for its reemphasis of individual, intimate space.

VILLA SAVOYE. *Le Corbusier with Pierre Jeanneret. Poissy-sur-Seine, France. 1929. A residential masterpiece, this white concrete box floating on twelve slender pillars employed many of Le Corbusier's early architectural principles and elements, such as open planning and flat roofs that served as terraces.*

GERMAN PAVILION, INTERNATIONAL EXPOSITION. *Ludwig Mies van der Rohe. Barcelona, Spain. 1929. Designed for ceremonial purposes, this pavilion was not a conventional building but a composition of horizontal and vertical planes that eloquently expressed Mies's concepts of open, flowing spaces.*

I. M. PEI: 1955

Wright's contribution has been tremendous in our field. The most representative building—well, let's say, Taliesin West. Let's use that as the building. I consider that a very important building because it shows, to me anyway, more effectively than any building he has done, the interrelationship between light and space. It also shows more conclusively than any building he has done really the richness that you can get from natural materials. I consider that a very important piece of work.

Then, of course, you cannot omit Marseilles, the apartment which perhaps more than any building by Corbusier expresses so very fully the perfect integration or synthesis of architecture, sculpture, and painting. I would consider that a very important piece of work. Certainly it is most representative of that man.

Then, the third one, well, Lake Shore Drive, perhaps. That is important because it is probably the most appropriate expression, architecturally speaking, of the American way of building. Our mechanized society, the way we produce, the way we construct seems to have the most perfect expression in that one building, regardless of its other technical defects. As an expression, I think, that building has tremendous significance and I don't expect that there will be many changes from that for a long time to come. This may very well form the classical tradition, the return to the classical tradition.

I think the importance of Mies's work lies in that it's trying to get to the essence of things. As such, of course, it is very difficult to improve over the essence, you see. Undoubtedly, there will be a great deal of variation in the use of materials, in the proportions, in the scale, and so on. But, I think, as an expression of skin, let's use that as an expression, for that type of building, I think that is probably a very, very excellent piece of work.

ENRICO PERESSUTTI: 1956

To talk about a work is very difficult because you cannot detach it from the man who did it. So more than one work, I admire the man that did it because I can also understand the faults this man had. It is not right to take one building out of the whole work of a man because even the faults show the changes in his work. They show the humanity of the man that did it.

I think that one of the most important expressions in modern architecture, which I visited many times, is an experiment that was done by Le Corbusier in Marseilles. This building he calls Unité d'Habitation. It seems to me that the building also has some difficulties, for many reasons which I won't mention here. It seems to me that this building is one of the most important experiments done in modern architecture, trying to resolve the housing problem of our society, as it is today. With his particular vernacular, Le Corbusier tried to resolve these problems in the best architectural way. By architectural I mean from all the points of view, from the technical possibilities to the spiritual expressions.

FALLINGWATER. *Frank Lloyd Wright. Bear Run, Pennsylvania. 1935. At the age of sixty-nine, Wright reclaimed the world's attention with Fallingwater, the most widely known house in modern architecture. The great reinforced-concrete slabs cantilever out of the solid rock over a tumbling stream.*

The second building, one of the most important expressions in modern architecture, I think, is the Fallingwater house by Frank Lloyd Wright near Pittsburgh. I arrived there, through the woods of thin trees. I was going along trying to find the house among these vertical trees. Once, and very slightly, I saw in the fog the horizontal lines of the house. Then coming closer to the house on one side, I saw better these horizontal lines. On the other side, once again, I saw the vertical expression of the falling water. This, I think, is one of the most important and the best expressions of Frank Lloyd Wright's artistic sense. He understands and expresses the surroundings so well, the site and the nature around the house. I think that Frank Lloyd Wright has the most important sense of nature of almost all modern architects. I admired him very much for this, but I must be sincere. I must say that I cannot agree with the forms he creates in the house, the decoration.

The third building—it's a recent one—is a house that Mies van der Rohe built for Mrs. Farnsworth near Chicago. I think this is the most advanced expression of Mies van der Rohe, who, of course, is a poet, I would say the abstract poet of our times in architecture. Because of that I admire him very much.

FARNSWORTH HOUSE.
Ludwig Mies van der Rohe. Plano, Illinois. 1950. Divided only by an elegantly sheathed service core and cabinets, this one-room glass house with a raised travertine floor and flat roof is suspended beautifully on eight white enameled steel columns.

But, again, I must say, that life with all its variety, unfortunately, or, fortunately, needs much more than that. One needs to leave a newspaper on the floor without thinking that this newspaper spoils everything in the house. It is life and we need architecture for life, not for poetry.

When you try to resolve problems of life from just a few points of view and not from all of them, you are limited. There are limitations found in the different architectures of Le Corbusier, Frank Lloyd Wright, and Mies van der Rohe. They are, of

TUGENDHAT HOUSE.
Ludwig Mies van der Rohe. Brno, Czech Republic. 1930. This house is built on a steep slope. The sober one-story street side offers little clue to the rear—a glass-enclosed double story overlooking a garden and superb city view. The free-flowing interior made the house one of the most influential examples of modern architecture.

course, limited because of the limitations that the architect started with in the beginning. They can be different types of limitations that may affect the architecture. For instance, the main limitation in the Le Corbusier building in Marseilles was an economical one. It is my belief, and I think also Le Corbusier's belief, that the best house for a family would be a house next to the ground, where people can really live. They can have their own garden, their own trees, their own vegetables to grow; they can touch the ground. This would be a human way of living.

PHILIP WILL JR.: 1956

I have a feeling that architecture has been divided into two mainstreams. I'm talking now in terms of design character. One we might call the classic and one the romantic. The classic implies a kind of structural order, a repetitive quality, a certain dignity which is derived from that kind of order. The other kind is a more naturalistic, in some respects a more relaxed, a more emotional architecture and is usually more closely related to its place of being than the classic, which in many respects is almost interchangeable as far as geography is concerned.

ROBIE HOUSE. *Frank Lloyd Wright. Chicago. 1906. This horizontal residence of Roman brick, lined with long, decklike balconies, is one of the most influential of Wright's early houses.*

I have thought of two examples of that which have certainly had a major influence on architectural design. One would be Mies van der Rohe's Tugendhat House, or if you wanted another example of his work, you might equally pick the Barcelona Pavilion. The influence of that on younger architects has been tremendous. I think it has served to introduce a new kind of order in composition and architectural design.

Probably the major exponent of the romantic school, although he would deny it, of course, is Frank Lloyd Wright. If one would take a single example of his work we might settle on the Robie House, which again has influenced generations of architects.

NATIONAL PENSIONS INSTITUTE. *Alvar Aalto. Helsinki, Finland. 1950. Aalto's beautiful building of warm brick in a natural setting manifests the appealing human qualities he brought to the pure International Style.*

GIO PONTI: 1961

Frank Lloyd Wright is a genius. It's destiny to be a genius, particularly if one lives past ninety, like Titian. In my opinion, Niemeyer belongs to that race of genius, but he hasn't yet had the chance to show himself at his utmost in spite of his already great works. There is always something fragile about Niemeyer's work.

ALFRED ROTH: 1961

I like Alvar Aalto's works very much. His social insurance company in Helsinki, one of his recent works, is a wonderful piece of architecture and so full of ideas, true ideas, not the sort of false originality. He's such a genuine man. Aalto's a very wonderful combination of the great artist, a great talent, a highly cultivated man, and a very human man. We are very good friends. It's so easy to be with him, such a wonderful comrade, so absolutely free from all this business of publicity and so forth.

I have a great admiration for Frank Lloyd Wright. I am not directly influenced by Frank Lloyd Wright. I like his houses very much. The famous Hollyhock House comes to my mind in Palo Alto [sic]. It's a wonderful house. I also like his Johnson Wax factory in Racine. Fallingwater is a little bit too dramatic for me. I prefer more restrained houses.

BARNSDALL "HOLLYHOCK" HOUSE. *Frank Lloyd Wright. Los Angeles. 1917. The hollyhock motif and shape of this important early concrete residence suggest a Mayan temple, but the interior is a distinctly new Wrightian vernacular.*

I must frankly say that I also have some admiration for Richard Neutra's work. Neutra today has been extremely faithful to his principles. He has not changed. He has developed himself, but he has not changed his basic attitude toward architecture and his concepts. I especially like his Tremaine House, which I saw. That's a wonderful piece of architecture. Some of his houses may be a little bit too fashionable, you know, but I like people who stay faithful to their principles. That's what we have to do today.

RICHARD NEUTRA: 1955

At the earliest age it was Otto Wagner, who was a contemporary of Louis Sullivan. Sullivan at that time I didn't know. But Wagner was the man who, and I've been rereading some of his writings, which by the way I say rereading, I never read them. I read him now because his granddaughter and son-in-law have been starting to write to me from Vienna recently. All of a sudden they heard about me and they think that I am one of the men who continues his work and they have been sending me interesting family papers and also some reprints of some things he wrote in 1890 and I am just stunned by the modernism of his thinking. I have no doubt that as far as literature is concerned that what he wrote at that time and what he proposed to the city council of Vienna is probably more up to date than anything which was written at that time.

He built all the railway stations of the city railway of Vienna and the subway stations. There was a belt line where it was possible to pay five cents and travel the whole day, never leave, just go around. I did that. And this was a great instruction in architecture because I was just looking at these stations from below and then I was looking at them also from above. It was a fairly low tuition, as you can see, and very instructive. This man had a great influence on me and I decided at that time that I would become an architect. He was a very revolutionary man. He started as a renaissance architect or in the style of eclecticism of that age, but he became gradually, and in a most interesting development, a person who completely divorced himself from all stylistic canons.

"EACH NEW STYLE EMERGED FROM THE ONE PRECEDING IT, SO THAT NEW CONSTRUCTION, NEW MATERIALS, NEW HUMAN TASKS AND VIEWS CALLED FORTH A CHANGE OR RECONSTITUTION OF EXISTING FORMS. . . . GREAT SOCIAL CHANGES HAVE ALWAYS GIVEN BIRTH TO NEW STYLES."

Otto Wagner

TREMAINE HOUSE. *Richard Neutra. Los Angeles, California. 1929. This early modern house was a breakthrough residential use of prefabricated light steel frames, reinforced-concrete walls, and wide glass windows.*

I had a chance to watch this and some fight about this developed in the newspapers. He was very much attacked by all the people who had to make jokes about him and he happened to be a very independent man financially and so he went on with his development. Most of it, fortunately, happened after he had already got a very leading position, holding the chair for the most important school at the Academy in Vienna, so that he couldn't be easily dislocated. He had a tremendous influence on a generation of students and on the world. He became very well known also in this country, but that has been forgotten now. Well, so much about Wagner.

"We already possess the style of our time. It may be found wherever the artist, that means any member of that association, hasn't yet stuck his nose in. . . . Can it be denied that our leather goods are in the style of our time? And our cutlery and glassware?! And our bathtubs and American wash-basins?! And our tools and machines?! And everything—I repeat everything—which the artists haven't got their hands on yet!"

Adolf Loos

The next man who played a great role in my life as an architect was Adolf Loos, who was a great admirer of Wagner, but his influence on me was of a very different nature. He never was a great architect in the sense of plan preparation. As a matter of fact, he prided himself not to draw plans. He was thinking to use work on paper and to use a 4-H pencil, as Wagner would do, was just denaturing the task of an architect.

As a matter of fact, he slowly brought me around to the idea—although he never used these expressions—that architecture was not a paper affair, but that it had something to do with human life and that it was danger to use scales. It was danger to use pencils. It was danger to use paper. That these were, of course, conveniences to the execution and realization of the executing crew and, perhaps, as such, necessary. Also, he even doubted that. But it was danger to become a paper architect.

Loos had a great influence on me to bring me to this country. He had been in America during the Chicago World's Fair and spent two years here utterly fruitless and utterly without any trace of success. His American story was not a success story, but the contrary. It was a story of a most passionate but unhappy love. He loved this country and he fitted it evidently very badly. He never proceeded far to get a job than to be the night-shift dishwasher in a second-rate hotel, although he couldn't find, even to save his life, a job as a draftsman. He tried everything. He advertised in newspapers that he was an expert in heraldry because there were some people in Manhattan who wanted to have some letterheads made. He told me much about America and what America was to him. He probably has been the greatest influence on me to bring me to this country, much later, but it stuck with me. He liked me very much and considered me his favorite pupil. He gave me presents and I am sorry that I don't have the books which he gave me with beautiful inscriptions. I think about a week before he died he wrote one postal card to me, but he was already quite mentally disturbed. He died, I think, in an institution.

MINISTRY OF EDUCATION AND HEALTH. *Lucio Costa, Oscar Niemeyer, Affonso Eduardo Reidy, Carlos Leão, Jorge Moreira, and Ermani Vasconcelos; Le Corbusier, consultant. Rio de Janeiro, Brazil. 1943. The uninterrupted, sun-shaded window walls made this sixteen-story office slab with auditorium and exhibition halls one of the most renowned examples of modern architecture in South America.*

TOMÁS SANABRIA: 1955

I would say that one of the works that made a great impression upon me, for its scope and influence in the terminology of contemporary architecture, is the building of the Ministry of Education by Lucio Costa and Oscar Niemeyer with Le Corbusier as consultant in Rio de Janeiro. What impressed me most was to see how that group of professionals solved the problem in such an excellent, direct, and honest way.

Another building I saw recently that I would like to mention is the City Hall in Tokyo by Tange, which impressed me for the fine conception of spaces, how well they are bound to the exterior environment and to the lively atmosphere of the Japanese city.

JUAN O'GORMAN: 1955

In modern architecture I would consider Gaudí, the Catalan architect of Barcelona, the greatest architect of our times in spite of the fact that his architecture has more the talent of the sculptor and the painter than of the architect. But, of course, I consider him a great, great architect. The fundamental greatness of Gaudí, I would say, in the Sagrada Familia of Barcelona, consists in the incredible fact of his having been able to bring into existence the combination of the Spanish Gothic with the Baroque and to have created with those two a very personal and a very individual form of expression which only Gaudí has. Then, after him, the other great architect is Wright in the United States.

OLYMPIC STADIUM. *Augusto Perez Palacios with Raúl Salinas Moro and Jorge Bravo Jimenez. Mexico City. 1951. Dug into the ground with curved concrete retaining walls and finished with lava facings, this modern sports stadium recalls the splendor of Aztec construction.*

The three greatest works of architecture are, one, the Sagrada Familia in Barcelona of Gaudí, which, of course, is unfinished, but what is there is sufficient to know what it would be to have it finished. The other one, I would say, would be the house of the Kaufmanns at Bear Run or Fallingwater of Wright's, and the third, not to repeat another thing of Gaudí or Wright, I would say the stadium of University City in Mexico. I consider those three perhaps the most important things. I include the stadium of the University City because I want to include something in Mexico.

I also think the works of Le Corbusier are some of the greatest works of modern architecture as much for the buildings constructed as those which he didn't get built. He is like Picasso, a man full of imagination who isn't stuck in any doctrine. He does exactly as he pleases, the Marseilles building, the Ronchamp church. That church has a freer approach, which is the approach I prefer, making things with the greatest freedom of form, without concern whether the form is based on professional reasoning. He did it only because he thought it was beautiful.

ERNESTO ROGERS: 1955

To me the four makers of modern architecture are Le Corbusier, Wright, Gropius, and Mies van der Rohe. Immediately after in importance is Alvar Aalto, who, I think, is a kind of medium between the generation of the masters and our generation.

But your question is which buildings. What impresses me more now is the Monastery of La Tourette by Le Corbusier, which I think is a fantastic example of the present. The subject of the monastery is unimportant because today a monastery is absolutely unimportant to most of humanity. It is very important for the few persons who live there, but if you go into this building, which is a masterpiece, you have the feeling of going into a very old monument. You feel at ease. You feel the building is part of yourself and you are part of it, not as a monk, but as a man. When you observe the many parts and whole of this building you will see that nothing of the building was done before. Nothing is an imitation. Nothing is a copy. Nothing is directly related to the shape of the forms of early architecture. Therefore, only the essence of this building is connected with the essence of good architecture, historical architecture. I think to be able to make up a synthesis like that, a kind of continuity which carries on into the future, that is really the game of architecture. That, I think, is the future. Perhaps it's not the future, but it is the hope for a good architecture in the future.

PERESSUTTI: 1961

Le Corbusier I admire the most, almost everything of his, but I can also see the limits that he had. Again for Mies van der Rohe, there are some works which I admire very much, but I can see more limits than in Le Corbusier. Frank Lloyd Wright I admire very much again, but I see also the other part of the Fallingwater. It's a wonderful house, but I can see many details that I don't like at all.

RUDOLF STEIGER: 1961

I know only a few single buildings well. There is Ronchamp, which made an impression on me, less as architecture than as sculpture. It is, let us say, sculpture, and I would most like to buy the little plaster model of Ronchamp, as a sculpture.

Then there are the buildings by Wright, which I appreciate very much. My son was there and brought a lot of material back because I value Wright as one of the greatest architects of his epoch, as a true design engineer and an architect.

There are the English buildings, which I also know only from publications, the new postwar city housing projects, which are interesting.

BRUCE GOFF: 1955

The three greatest works in modern architecture, in my way of thinking, and by modern I suppose you mean recent because all architecture has been modern when it was done. If we say architecture since 1900 up to now, in the last fifty years, I would have to name three buildings. Two of them have never been built and the third isn't even finished.

The first one I would have to name is the Holy Family Cathedral in Barcelona by Gaudí. It's a very great conception and probably the most tremendous architectural conception of our time even though the building is not finished. Gaudí estimated it would take at least three hundred years to finish it. He said that it was the last great Gothic cathedral. Still, there is something very prophetic in a way that we haven't

PALACE OF THE SOVIETS, MODEL. *Le Corbusier. 1931. This modern Constructivist design, with its auditorium roof suspended from a freestanding parabolic arch, was rejected as the Soviets shifted to proletarian architecture based on classical models.*

even caught on to yet. I think it's great because like all great architecture, it's expressive of its purpose, its material, and reasons for being and still it transcends all of these into a spiritual quality that is woefully lacking in almost all contemporary work, where the emphasis is on material things rather than other values.

The second building that I would have wished had been built, is one, if it had been, would have been one of the great achievements of our time, was Corbusier's Palace of the Soviets. It was a magnificent scheme. It's too bad that it was not understood by the people that it was done for because it would have symbolized something new in government work in architecture for great numbers of people. Certainly, structurally it was daring and interesting. I don't know of any design that has the feeling of lightness and sinewy strength, almost insectlike strength, that this design has. At the same time it transcends all that and becomes a very poetic expression of a government building.

HUNTINGTON HARTFORD COUNTRY CLUB PROJECT. *Frank Lloyd Wright. Hollywood Hills, California. 1947. Wright cantilevered several saucer-shaped platforms containing restaurants, gardens, and pools at different heights on a soaring trapezoidal base in this unrealized California country club.*

The third example, naturally, we would have to have one by Frank Lloyd Wright. Of all of his, the one I admire the most is probably the design for the Hollywood Club. That one seems to me to reach way out. It is remarkable that an architect with the tremendous wealth of experience could be so young, so daring, and imaginative at this stage of his life, to do a building so exciting and so forward looking as that building. I think it is forward looking because it seems to take off from the ground. It's prophetic of what we might expect in the not too distant future, when architecture will free itself from the ground more.

Arne Jacobsen

ARNE JACOBSEN: 1957

I would almost count Philip Johnson's house as being one of the most important works and the one that has meant the most for architecture. But Le Corbusier's chapel at Ronchamp is, in any case, the building that has made the greatest impression on me. In a certain sense it is such an intimate composition of the three disciplines—the art of painting, the art of sculpture, and architecture—that it attains such a high level that almost no other building has ever reached.

WILLEM DUDOK: 1961

I was a guest of Frank Lloyd Wright in 1953. He had an influence on me—more by his free way of his floor plans than on his details. We were very much impressed by his free way of doing things, his poetic solution. For instance, the Midway Gardens made a great impression on me. I thought it very nice. I prefer that over his later work.

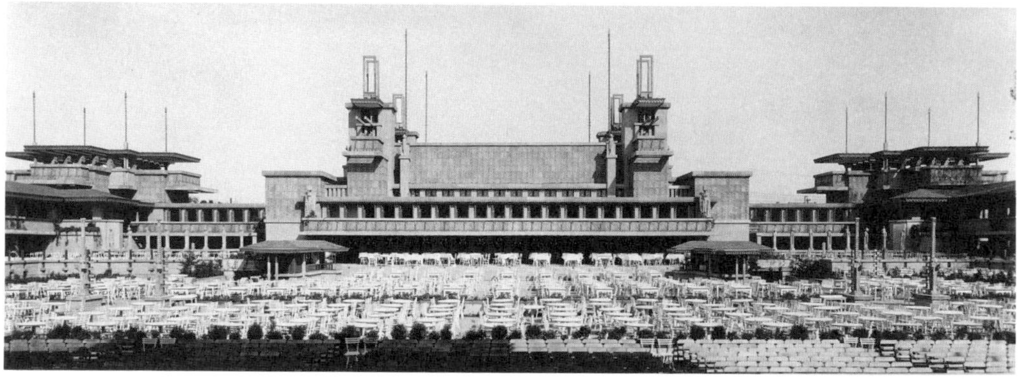

MIDWAY GARDENS. *Frank Lloyd Wright. Chicago. 1913. Enclosing an entire city block, this extraordinary pleasure palace of brick and ornate concrete was destroyed after the enactment of prohibition.*

VICTOR GRUEN: 1957

I believe that Rockefeller Center is an important experience in architecture, not because of its architectural detailing, but because it was the first time a large complex of buildings was created which established relations between the buildings, spaces between the buildings, and created unity. This is probably the only little island of a real cityscape within the large area of New York.

Many people wouldn't say that this is architecture, but I believe it is. The Tennessee Valley Authority, the TVA, dams show that architecture is not just buildings. That it is a creation of any man-made venture in that it can be created with drama, with an integrity, and with beauty.

The third one is just because I spent a weekend there and therefore experienced it, the Fallingwater house of Frank Lloyd Wright. I had seen it before in pictures, which I didn't quite trust because it looked a little bit like a tour de force. But living in it for three or four days, I felt strongly attached to it. I felt immediately at home. I was impressed by its livability and by the genius which went into creating new vistas, interior and exterior impressions, and by being a place of delight, of structural daring and obviously, also, of usefulness.

EDUARDO CATALANO: 1956

I don't know if you want to deal with buildings or to use the word architecture in a broad sense. You find here in America one example, the TVA. The TVA has a great social implication and a tremendous scale. I think that this has to be considered. As a planning problem I think it is wonderful. It is one of the best things that America did in the last fifty years.

PONTI: 1961

Among examples from the past, I was very influenced by Palladio's architecture. Of present-day architecture, something that comes to mind immediately is Ronchamp because it is an extraordinary representation of an extraordinary man, Le Corbusier. I say the man because my expression is independent. He is the greatest man whose thinking has influenced me and everyone. Oftentimes I enjoy observing the presence of a man more than I do architectural laws.

The work of Niemeyer helped me understand many things. I am not interested in Frank Lloyd Wright's architecture although I consider Frank Lloyd Wright a great genius. I'm interested in him as a person as manifested in the architecture. Concerning Mies van der Rohe, I like most the Barcelona Pavilion, built when Mies van der Rohe was more of an aesthete. Le Corbusier is a precursor, Gropius a teacher, Alvar Aalto an artist.

CARL KOCH: 1957

I think we're between the beginnings of modern architecture and its fruition. What's happening now is a necessary stage but not a particularly satisfying one in terms of actual buildings.

The Barcelona Pavilion of Mies van der Rohe says so much more than anything he has done since then that that would be the one of the buildings I would pick. Of Frank Lloyd Wright's work, who is certainly one of the biggest influences on architecture today, I would pick a building, perhaps Taliesin in Wisconsin or one of his earlier ones much more definitely than one of the more recent ones. Using Frank Lloyd Wright as the romance, and Mies as the simplicity out of chaos.

Now for the humanity in architecture, which I think perhaps is the most important of the three, I am completely stumped trying to get a specific building. I keep thinking about the City Hall in Stockholm. That's really a hodgepodge of all kinds of things, and perhaps that's one reason I keep going back to it.

TALIESIN III. *Frank Lloyd Wright. Spring Green, Wisconsin. 1925–59. Wright's remarkable home, built of native limestone and wood with plaster surfacing, is named Taliesin, Welsh for shining brow. Fittingly, the house clings to the side of a hill, on ancestral land high above the left bank of the Wisconsin River.*

SWISS PAVILION, UNIVERSITY CITY. *Le Corbusier. Paris. 1932. Elevated on sculptured concrete piers, this cantilevered residence hall for some fifty students was Le Corbusier's first major public building.*

Certainly the Scandinavian tradition and growth is, to me, a very important influence. I think they are the only people who are really practicing the precepts of democracy as it applies to architecture. I was there fifteen years ago the first time and have been back three or four times since. Somehow or other their buildings, as a group, seem to weather much better than ours. It's the only place that the passage of that many years has done so little harm to the buildings, and they are so much more a part of the life of the people. I haven't been able to put my finger on any one building or even on a person or anything too specific, but the city of Stockholm is the one thing I would point to. It's a city which is alive today, which isn't depending on buildings of many, many years ago. We always talk about the Piazza San Marco, but that's dead as far as today is concerned. It was completed many years ago and people are still using it, which is fine, but it isn't saying anything for what we are doing today. Stockholm is saying very effectively that democracy works, that the people are intelligent, are civilized, and do know what they want. There are darned few places in the world where you can say that, or get that feeling at all.

GORDON BUNSHAFT: 1956

I consider, of the buildings that I've seen and studied, that Mies van der Rohe's glass towers—the apartment buildings in Chicago on the lake, 860 Lake Shore Drive—are the best structures in the United States.

The building that expresses concrete to me and is very important in its influence and expression of concrete. It has a dramatic setting and is a dramatic building. I would put second Le Corbusier's Marseilles apartments.

The third structure, one of the few buildings that is still beautiful and was built thirty years or so ago, is Le Corbusier's Student Dormitory Pavilion at the International University in Paris for the Swiss government. I think that is a magnificent expression of basic concrete structure with a superimposed structure of light steel. It has probably had one of the greatest influences on modern architecture in the world. That plus the work of Mies van der Rohe.

KENZO TANGE: 1961

I appreciate most highly Corbusier's works. I also highly appreciate Mies's works, but as he has set limits to his work, I think no one can develop it further. Therefore, I appreciate Mies because he has approached the ultimate goal on one line. I do not know in what way it will be developed after this point. It might be impossible. In this connection, Corbusier still continues to walk freely, leaving various possibilities. As a teacher of architecture, I highly appreciate Gropius. All of them are our great teachers and I respect them very much. But, as a friend, I most appreciate Saarinen.

Kenzo Tange

ELIOT NOYES: 1957

Honestly, in modern architecture, there are only two that hit me at once, that really shook me in a way. One was the Savoye House, by Le Corbusier, which I went to see three or four years ago in its present state. Apart from that I know it in its original state only through drawings and pictures. The other was the Taliesin West of Wright, which I also only saw when it was fairly new, not yet finished by any means. But he took us around it in about 1941. It just shattered me. Now those two things, I think, are my two nominations in modern architecture. I've got a large range of buildings that I think are terrific, but somehow those two have had something special for me. They're quite different. I think that the building that shook me most apart from that was the Parthenon. Those three buildings, which really you can hardly mention in the same sentence and make sense, but in each case I had a real reaction to these three.

The Savoye House, I was prepared to have a reaction because I had been so impressed by it all the way through school, just as a published thing. When I got there, walking through this crazy, ruined building, walking around it, seeing the hay sticking out of the second-floor porch, walking into the living room, the kitchen and so on, to see how, in 1930, here was where it started. Here he'd done this, which we've all been using ever since. The chimney with the stack that goes up. Detail after detail after detail, more than I had realized, are still there in a kind of ruined state. The incredible inventiveness of this guy, at that one moment, in this one building is just beyond belief. It really is fantastic still. This is an extraordinary building. It stands there in that meadow, a ruin, with the greatest authority, almost like the Parthenon, another ruin. It has a similar kind of authority.

I met Madame Savoye there by chance. I talked to her in my best French and listened to her describe how this place had been. Where the poppies had been and how the orchards had been. You could see her sort of begin to relive the thing. She suddenly told me how her husband and sons had no interest in it. How it had been so badly treated by the Germans during the war, and yet there it stands. A terrific experience to see.

Taliesin was the same thing, truly. First of all, I was absolutely enchanted by the sequence of spaces, by the unfamiliar materials, by the canvas, by the cockeyed shapes, by the flats, by the wood, by the stone, by the way the light came through, the whole marvelous flow of space, from open to shut, from big to tiny, and from huge fireplaces to little nooks and peeks through slots and great boulders and the color in the desert concrete, an absolute masterpiece. I think that's the one of his buildings that has moved me the most.

The first one of his that showed me that there was something in Wright that could mean things to us is the Kaufmann house, Fallingwater. In school, this was the tip-off to a lot of us that it wasn't all this California Mayan decorated stuff. Here was this guy who was doing a brand new thing which suddenly did mean something to us. Even though we had sort of given our allegiance to Corbu for a while. Suddenly Wright began to come back into focus with that. I suppose it was these great white panels, the boulders and the cantilevers. It was clear, it was easy to understand. It was more modern. But Taliesin was the building that I thought was the best.

I haven't got this feeling of architectural triumph about any of Mies's buildings, I honestly haven't. I have seen the apartments in Lake Shore Drive and the concrete ones, the Promontory. I haven't seen much Mies. I saw the IIT college. The Seagram's might be outstanding, but I have to wait for judgment on that.

HELMUT HENTRICH: 1961

I like the work of Eero Saarinen very much. In Detroit, the Technical Center for General Motors is a marvelous, outstanding job. I think the Seagram Building by Mies van der Rohe in New York is outstanding, but I also like very much the Lever building and that's the United States. I like very much the church of Le Corbusier in Ronchamp, which is very, very important. Then, naturally, also the work of Arne Jacobsen, his furnishings, his details, and also his architecture. I like Wright, all the things he made before the First World War, the big houses near Chicago. What I

ROW HOUSES. *Arne Jacobsen. Søholm, Denmark. 1950. The textured natural materials and the imaginative play of the roofs of these row houses represent a picturesque departure from Jacobsen's sleek International Style.*

don't like as much is the museum in New York, the Guggenheim. It doesn't fit in at all between these high buildings. If it had been built in the park it would be excellent.

RALPH RAPSON: 1959

We, at the University of Minnesota Department of Architecture, have often been accused of being a Mies school. I suppose partly because it's relatively simple. The students are quite often looking for formal methods they can apply to their own solution. This is much easier than the highly virtuoso kind of thing of Wright. I'm not talking about his principles but his vernacular. Maybe this is also true of Corbu although not quite so much so.

In my own work, I suppose in the earlier days, I went through the Wright influence. I suppose it was just about the first, Wright and Sullivan. Then I discovered Corbu and his writings, particularly his thoughts on the larger planning influenced me a great deal. Then a little later Mies came in as a principle of stronger order.

Another one, I think, of course, is Gropius. I suppose education-wise he has been the strongest influence on me. I think more than any other individual he has elevated, shaped, and brought stature to architectural education. Incidentally, while I admire Mies tremendously as an architect, I do not admire him as an educator. Another person I've admired is Marcel Breuer as a person and as a designer. This shows up, I'm sure, a good deal in my work.

I find it rather difficult to name any three buildings. Certainly, I would have to include Frank Lloyd Wright's work in the residential field. The interesting, exciting space that he has achieved in his works, oh, you could name them by the hundreds. Without question the two Taliesin groups are great demonstrations of his mastery of space, his ability to surprise, compose, change, and model space.

Then the Barcelona Pavilion by Mies. I remember it as a great articulation of space and perfection of use of material and details. My own personal development has been extremely influenced in some ways by Mies's latter work of the Chicago apartments. The highly almost abstract quality of these buildings to me is extremely emotional and exciting. I somehow or other cannot quite accept the fact that they're not necessarily the complete answer to the need.

The third one would have to be a work of Le Corbusier. Perhaps here I would pick not Corbu's own building, but the Ministry of Education building in Rio, where he was a consultant, as a building demonstrating his principles, his plastic sculptural quality, the mastery of forms, interior and exterior space.

AFFONSO EDUARDO REIDY: 1955

I believe that three architects have substantially influenced my work. These architects are Le Corbusier, Mies van der Rohe, and Walter Gropius, each contributing an element.

For example, I consider Gropius to have influenced my work greatly by awakening in me an interest in social problems, which at the time were neglected. Mainly it brought up the problem of housing which, until the time I started working, was very disorganized here in Brazil. I had a background for this kind of work because the problem had been reduced to looking to build inexpensive housing without considering that housing is only one element in a group of other services which would give people all the comforts and facilities they need for life in a community. Gropius gave me a great deal of information on this topic.

I greatly admire the work of Mies. It may seem contradictory to admire both Mies and Le Corbusier, who represent two completely different approaches. I don't think there is any incompatibility between the two, although they have completely different personalities. The work of Mies through purity, precision, and the spatial concept it possesses provokes admiration in me.

I think that Le Corbusier has an extraordinary creative power. I consider him to be a true genius, a creative spirit. I remember well a quote of his I heard which is the absolute truth: "I am an invention machine." I thought this definition to be very true in the case of Le Corbusier, who, in fact, is constantly creating and inventing things. He has a tremendous creative spirit and an artistic sense which is truly notable.

One thing that I consider of great importance to modern architecture, not for its volume, but for what it presents of external beauty, its solution that is almost doctrine: the works of Le Corbusier. They have a purity of form, magnificent structure, and purity of realization. Another work that influenced me greatly was the Seagram Building for its purity of execution, fine details, selection of materials, and extraordinary perfection. There are so many works that I could cite.

PAUL SCHWEIKHER: 1960

I think the Seagram Building is a great building. Look at Le Corbusier's buildings at Chandigarh or d'Habitation in Marseilles—these are great buildings.

I agree with anyone who says that a building must belong to its time. I'm sure that it's hard for an artist or architect or anyone to express in his work the people with whom he lives and the time in which he lives. What I think is meant by a building belonging to its time is that it will use the methods and materials that belong to its time.

MINORU YAMASAKI: 1960

I don't think that modern architecture has developed to the point where we can pick out a masterpiece like Chartres, or the Doges Palace, or the Katsura Palace in Japan, or any isolated example. I think that this is still to come. I think possibly my own classification of the most important works would be this. Wright's houses, for instance, are to me a masterpiece of modern architecture. I would like three buildings of Mies: 860 Lake Shore Drive, Crown Hall, and Seagram's. Seagram's being in the sense that culmination is a masterpiece. Together they are a body of really wonderful work.

Although I admire Corbu, I haven't seen all his buildings. I've only seen the one at Chandigarh. I can't say that I was overwhelmed by Chandigarh. I feel that Corbu, though a magnificent artist, really sort of a tremendously creative guy as a sculptor rather than an architect. In a sense, he's not an architect in the same way that Wright is an architect or Mies is an architect.

SECRETARIAT AND ASSEMBLY BUILDING. *Le Corbusier with Pierre Jeanneret, Maxwell Fry, and Jane Drew. Chandigarh, India. 1952–57. The huge Secretariat building, with it sculptured forms and sun-controlled louvers, dominates Le Corbusier's plan for the new capital of Punjab.*

PAUL RUDOLPH: 1960

I feel that Le Corbusier's Villa Savoye demonstrated the sense of continuity of the unfolding space in an admirable way. It also stated eloquently Le Corbusier's feeling about man's relationship to nature, which has proved to be prophetic.

I think that Mies van der Rohe's 860 Lake Shore Drive apartment houses in Chicago elevated the steel frame for the first time to the heights of great art, and because the steel cage is very American, such a building could be built only in the United States. It has true significance. It must be noted, incidentally, that the steel frame is not what is actually shown, but only symbols of the structure are shown. Symbols of structure have been used ever since the beginning of time, and I don't know why all of a sudden there's anything wrong with it.

I think that Taliesin West by Wright is a truly significant building because of the sequence of space which he has managed to achieve as well as the relationship to the site, the whole use of materials, the juxtaposition of the compression of the stonework and the flying quality of the trusses and beams, the light coming through the canvas, the manipulation of the natural light. The manipulation of natural light tends to have escaped the whole International Style. Wright was born with how to do this. But the International Style said, "Let's have light and air." Parallel with that came a lot of glare. As a matter of fact, it took Le Corbusier twenty years to build buildings which didn't have glare in them. He knows how to do that beautifully now. As a matter of fact, I think that's part of the whole impulse of postwar buildings.

MARTÍN VEGAS AND JOSÉ MIGUEL GALIA 1955

We agree that for us the three most significant works would be the Barcelona Pavilion by Mies van der Rohe, the Swiss Pavilion by Le Corbusier in the Cité Universitaire in Paris, and the Robie House in Chicago by Frank Lloyd Wright.

GALIA: 1955

The Robie House was made in 1906. I think it contains all the special elements, all the special concepts and the correct use of materials which are still valid now. You can visit the Robie House today and it continues to be a piece of first-quality architecture, while in all other countries all architects were doing Victorian architecture.

I can also mention, although they are not architectural works, they are still works by architects and it may be of value to mention them, the Barcelona chair and the Eames chair. They are works by architects and I believe them extremely important.

"A GREAT EPOCH HAS BEGUN. THERE EXISTS A NEW SPIRIT. INDUSTRY, OVERWHELMING US LIKE A FLOOD WHICH ROLLS ON TOWARDS ITS DESTINED ENDS, HAS FURNISHED US WITH NEW TOOLS ADAPTED TO THIS NEW EPOCH, ANIMATED BY THE NEW SPIRIT."

Le Corbusier

MARIO CIAMPI: 1956

I have always tended to look at great work not in terms of the actual work that has been completed, but more on the forces which have created the great works, that is, the architects—those great men who are responsible for the great works we have today. The thing that makes for human progress today in the field of architecture is not a building, but the force, the imagination, and the philosophy which directed this work to its completion. As a result of that, I think of men like Mies van der Rohe, Frank Lloyd Wright, and Le Corbusier perhaps as three of the greatest men who are living today who have done more for modern architecture than anyone else.

Take Mies van der Rohe, for example. It's hard to say that his Tugendhat House in Czechoslovakia is more handsome than the Pavilion building he built in the Barcelona Exposition. In my opinion, there are concepts in both cases which are constantly the same and parallel in thinking. This expression of attenuated construction, a certain lightness in character, the use of large expanses of glass, the use of solid form and transparent form together, the use of color and good materials to make an overall living environment which is attractive, refreshing, handsome, and new.

To go on to Frank Lloyd Wright, take his Fallingwater house at Bear Run with its great cantilevers which overhang this waterfall, or take his Johnson's Wax Laboratory multistory building, or take his Imperial Hotel in Tokyo—it would be very difficult for me to say which is the better because in each case they serve a specific function. But, nevertheless, in each of these you find the thinking, the imagination, and the creative forces of the individual which are continuous, constant, and express themselves in very much the same way.

Take the work of Le Corbusier, look at his Villa Savoye at Poissy in France, take his Swiss Pavilion in Paris at the Cité Universitaire, or his apartment house in Marseilles. There, again, you find that there is a quality and a character in the work and the expression of the individual which is unique and at the same time extremely progressive. When you read his books and analyze what he's thinking, you recognize there is a great force behind architecture that is a great stimulant. To take what he has to offer and try to implement it, as well as give it your own personal expression, is the opportunity and the responsibility of every architect.

Marc Saugey

MARC SAUGEY: 1960

Among the works that impress me there is Le Corbusier's housing project in Marseilles, which is a key moment in architecture. Still, I think there are other things

BAKER HOUSE, MASSACHUSETTS INSTITUTE OF TECHNOLOGY. *Alvar Aalto with Perry, Shaw, Hapburn, and Dean. Cambridge. 1949. The sweeping curve of the rough brick dormitory creates a variety of floor plans for student rooms and increases the number with a view of the Charles River.*

that have made more of an impression on me. I have found Aalto's work extremely interesting and extremely worthwhile. I like Aalto a great deal precisely because of his conception of architecture. The way he carries his projects through to completion. The materials he uses are all perfectly adapted to the atmosphere in which he is building. The university campus building he made at MIT in the U.S. is also worthwhile because the conditions were similar to those in his own country. Though, personally, I feel this building does not do enough for the student. I think a building plays a major role in the educational process. In that area, I'm not sure he had as much success as at home.

I think Mies van der Rohe was one of the most powerful men in contemporary architecture. His theories being very similar to Le Corbusier's. He was, with Le Corbusier, one of the great captains of contemporary architecture. Setting aside the merits that are well known, that is, a perfect clarity in his structures, in his way of expressing volume, he provided a very firm underpinning for teaching, and for many architects, to avoid rushing too quickly into a certain modern pretentiousness. At the present time, we are passing out of the danger zone of such a modern pretentiousness. These past few years I was very afraid that thanks to the extraordinary freedom we were given by new materials and projects, we were rapidly approaching architectural forms that would have quickly led to a Jugendstil, a neo-style, an ornamental, pâtisserie style in modern architecture. Thanks to his kind of rigor, Mies van der Rohe was one of the underpinnings that prevented architecture from spilling over in the wrong direction.

Frank Lloyd Wright, to me, was also an extremely helpful and interesting point in architecture because of his concept of the organization of space. He always said that architecture should be organic. In this he was never outdone by Le Corbusier, who also favored organic architecture, albeit founded perhaps on different philosophical grounds. Wright was extremely helpful to me at a certain point. He was a kind of role model in building. His organization of interior spaces, his linkage of the interior and exterior space, is extremely interesting. His way of using materials. That sense of freedom he creates, all the while remaining completely rigorous in the conception of his plan and the application of his program. This feeling of freedom that he gave in his creations showed all contemporary architects how they could liberate themselves from the insistent paradigm of the old "room." He smashed the box and showed us how to be inside and outside at the same time. In this, the work of Wright is extremely helpful. Furthermore, one must not lose sight of the power of his work.

EERO SAARINEN: 1956

I'd rather speak about influences than buildings. I think we have these sort of three great forces that are with us every time we think about architecture. There is Wright and his life work; there is Corbu and his life work; and there is Mies and his. I think the specific jobs or the specific buildings, one has to take one of these as a symbol. I've asked that several times in talking with students. I've asked how they define the influences of these, and I remember one of the best answers I got was that Wright started it all, Corbu gave it form, and Mies gave it control.

Now it can be that it's deeper and richer than that, but I feel, for instance, that Wright's, and let me just talk about these three. Wright started it all. Wright has given us the greatest inspiration about use of space, has also shown us the plastic form of architecture, architecture in relation to nature, architecture in relation to the material, and to a certain degree to structure, and he has shown us also the dramatization of architecture, which I think is a very important thing. Now I think we're at a period of architecture when those that . . . you know, some try to in their work be influenced by him directly. I could never do that and I think that's wrong. His influence on you I think is, and on one is and should be much more, not through the form itself but through the philosophy, the principles, and maybe the enthusiasm behind his forms, and I think it may well be that fifty years from now we will feel him stronger amongst us than right now. We live too close to him now. That is the way I look at Wright and I think of Wright as the greatest living architect.

Well, I might add one little thing to that, that so much of Wright's forms are really of quite a different era. The young architect and the student who isn't aware of that sort of thing slides right into that and wrongly so. But, boy, don't ever underestimate Wright.

Now Corbu gave it form. You know, he is the bible of the form of modern architecture because his books are like the sketches of Leonardo da Vinci, and Gropius rightly refers to him as the Leonardo da Vinci of our time. This terrific inventiveness that he can almost take any theme, any little need that manifests itself, and make it by dramatization and emphasis of that make a whole architecture out of it and in that way he sort of finds form more or less in the functional. But don't think of him as one that finds the form alone in the functional because basically it's in his heart, and buildings like Marseilles are to me very, very strong influences. Here for twenty or thirty years we've made thinner and thinner sticks, and so forth, more or less, on the basis of Corbu. Then he comes along and makes sort of an elephantine, strong, massive building like that and a complete reversal of a trend and he's the most unpredictable. Well, he's the Leonardo in architecture or the Picasso in architecture, just a terrifically inventive person.

To me personally the interesting lessons I get from him are that every problem has its own solution, and architecture is not just a mold or a formula to be found, but it's a whole way of thinking, and also the plastic form that he brings in in relation to the geometric form or to the crystalline form are all, you know, fields that we haven't begun to explore yet. I might just say that I feel some of the people that have taken him too directly and just gone on with that have done it a little bit insincerely. In other words, plastic form is not . . . you know, sculpture is fine but don't ever forget structure. And that is where Mies, the third great influence, comes in.

I'll dwell on Corbu a moment longer. So much of Corbu's architecture was really arrived at from the painting, from the Cubist painting world, that in his work the structural quality of the building is not emphasized and when imitated, often forgotten. But with Mies, who came here late in life, absorbed America during the war years, and then bloomed into really a great number of buildings, I mean his work bloomed into a great number of buildings, and all with this very, very strong, Spartan, almost religious belief in structure. I see it, almost a continuation of the Gothic—Viollet-le-Duc, Berlage, Sullivan, Mies. And just the principle that . . . and the belief that structure is the important thing that influences structures. That the use of a building can change but the structure always stays.

Now again, with Mies, there are many ways of being influenced by him. Many have said that General Motors is the project where I have been most influenced by him. I would say that I have been most influenced by Mies in the MIT Auditorium, not by his form but by his principles. Whether you use concrete or steel or whether you use a box or a dome, those are details, but the principle of making structure the dominant element in architecture and letting the functional ones fit in and be controlled by the structural ones, to a degree, is a Mies principle.

I really wouldn't dare to think this way because everybody is supposed to think that everything is pretty much the same way. I wouldn't dare to except for Corbu. Corbu who just shows by his life work these many directions, many things that one could experiment with, and then also Wright, who hasn't really been integrated into architecture yet. I think that's the wisest statement I've said today. I think Wright's contribution has not yet been integrated into modern architecture.

"IT IS DESIRABLE TO SHOW AT THE OUTSET THAT IT IS IMPOSSIBLE TO SEPARATE THE FORM OF THE ARCHITECTURE OF THE THIRTEENTH CENTURY FROM ITS STRUCTURE; EVERY MEMBER OF THIS ARCHITECTURE IS THE RESULT OF A NECESSITY OF THAT STRUCTURE, AS IN THE VEGETABLE AND THE ANIMAL KINGDOM THERE IS NOT A FORM OR A PROCESS THAT IS NOT PRODUCED BY A NECESSITY OF THE ORGANISM: AMID THE MULTITUDE OF GENERA, SPECIES, AND VARIETIES, THE BOTANIST AND THE ANATOMIST ARE NOT MISTAKEN AS REGARDS THE FUNCTION."

Eugène-Emanuel Viollet-le-Duc

Frank Lloyd Wright

"THE SPACE VALUES OF THE BUILDING PRESERVED, ENLARGED, EXPANDED, PRESENTED MAKES AN ENTIRELY NEW ARCHITECTURE."

Frank Lloyd Wright was such an astounding public figure that neither his appearance nor his manner needs introduction. His photogenic look was the work of both personal vanity and a sense of the dramatic. When I asked him about clothes, he replied, "Observe the terminals, John, the head, the hands, and the feet. They are the most important parts." He designed himself with the same distinctive imagination as his buildings.

No other architect, certainly no other modern architect, lived in the style of Frank Lloyd Wright. He designed and built, with his students, two remarkable residences on extensive estates. They were, of course, architectural schools—or as the state of Wisconsin declared over his vociferous objections, an architectural business—but he lived in them like a monarch. He shared many of the rejections of the bohemian artist, but he never lived like one.

Despite the behavior and unabashed reference to his genius, Wright possessed a surprisingly clear-eyed view of himself. A humorist has been defined as a person with such a firm grasp of reality that he or she makes fun of the deviations. Wright had a ready laugh and a healthy sense of American humor. For example, he told me, "I went down to New Canaan the other day. I'm building a house there for a man named Wayward. It's a

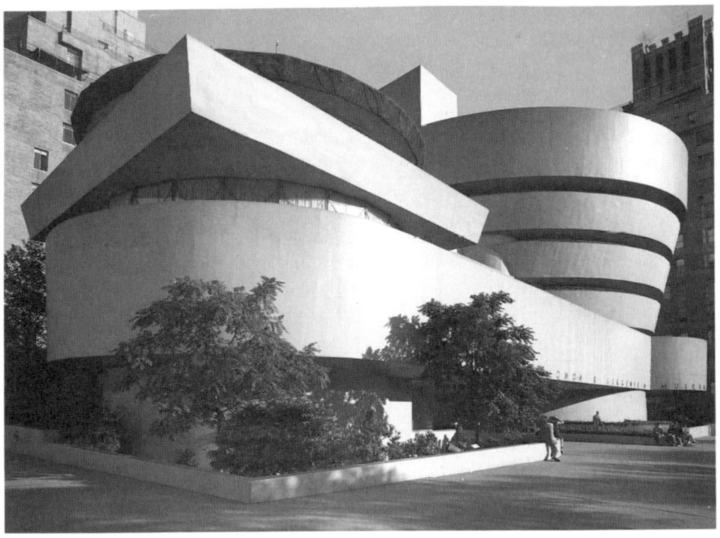

SOLOMON R. GUGGENHEIM MUSEUM. *Frank Lloyd Wright. New York City. 1956. Designed as a continuous spiraling ramp, the striking rounded concrete form of this celebrated museum was intended to contrast dramatically with the square architecture of the city.*

good name for one of my clients." It didn't matter that the man's name was actually Rayward.

Wright was one of those people of whom everybody he met had a story. Much of what he said he had said or written before. Frequently, among the different versions it was difficult to sort out the truth. I once asked him about the often-told story about Wingspread, the Herbert F. Johnson house. Apparently, it started to rain during a housewarming party and the roof began to leak. An infuriated Johnson phoned Wright demanding what he should do as water was falling on him while he sat with his guests at the dining table. Wright replied, "Move your chair." Wright later said to me, "It isn't true, but it makes a good story. Let it stand."

I visited Wright in a number of places but made the bulk of these recordings over the course of a week spent at Taliesin. Both from a distance and close up, the man lived up to the legend. He told me, "They think I'm arrogant, pretentious, jealous, envious, and all the rest, but I have only one great desire: to see America with an architecture of its own."

Wright's own words are followed by some firsthand observations by the architect Antonin Raymond, who worked with him on the Imperial Hotel in Japan.

1957

FRANK LLOYD WRIGHT: Well, how it began is right there in that little round picture.

JOHN PETER: *That's your mother?*

F.L.W.: Yes, she was a kindergarten teacher for me. Set me down at the kindergarten table when I was six, and she wanted an architect for a son. Why I do not know. But she was a teacher, and around my room in which I was born were nine, simply framed with maple, the six—no, nine—of the English cathedrals engraved by Timothy Coles. That's what I saw in the cradle. Then she was determined that I was to be an architect and all down the line everything was so focused on that, that I never had any idea that there was anything else. I didn't know there was anything but architecture.

And so kindergarten training by Froebel and, of course, the scientific, German, thoroughgoing mind of Friedrich Froebel should be the foundation of almost every education of today.

ROMEO AND JULIET WINDMILL. *Frank Lloyd Wright. Spring Green, Wisconsin. 1896. The embracing diamond and octagon construction of the windmill prompted Wright to name it after Shakespeare's lovers.*

1955

Friedrich Froebel was not a scientist. He was a humanist of the highest degree. He ought to be brought back and put into schools here throughout the nation. It would be a good start toward art and religion. Friedrich Froebel believed that no child should be allowed to draw from nature, that is, to look at the surface of things and boondoggle. He should be taught the elemental forms behind all that really went to make it what it is to look at. So here was the square, and here was the triangle, and here was the circle. Then you gave those a third dimension and you got the cube, and you got the tetrahedron, and you got the sphere. Now, there were subordinate forms to be developed from all those. They had little hooks put into them. You'd hang them up, revolve them, and get subordinate forms. Then he gave you this plaited map in color you wove in patterns. You got color. You got weaving. You got form on an elemental basis. And once you got that into your system it could never be taken away from you. You never can take the feeling of those maple forms out of my fingers. You never can take out of my mind the effects of those colors. Here is a whole little box of sixty-thirty blocks, red, scarlet on one side and white on the other. You dumped them out on the table and you made patterns with them.

My mother was a teacher. She was teaching in Platteville Academy when she met my father, who was a circuit rider teaching music and preaching. My father's family was a preacher family going way back. My grandfather was a preacher here and a hatter and a preacher in Wales. Oh, yes, the Welsh strain is very strong. My mother's family were teachers and preachers, too. I'm the only one that has broken the line of not being a preacher way back to the days of the English Reformation, all preachers. So it is.

My mother was a disciple of Theodore Parker. She was very advanced in her views. And in her home the curtains were net and hung straight at the sides instead of being tied back with bows. She had polished maple floors. And on those maple floors, a friend of hers, Mrs. Davis, helped her get colored rugs from India, woven with polychrome on the rugs. The pictures, instead of having the usual frames of that day, were all narrow, polished wooden maple bands.

And when she wanted flowers she cut them with the stems long, and always preferred glass that would show the stems and set them in the water separately by themselves—and I grew up in that.

And my father, of course, was a musician and a preacher, and music and all that environment was my babyhood. I used to go to sleep listening to my father playing Beethoven's sonatas on the pianoforte. So I had all that in my system as a natural.

J.P.: *I was reading about your Lloyd-Jones windmill, Romeo and Juliet, how the doubters looked out every morning to see if it had fallen.*
F.L.W.: It's still there. Forty-five years old. The doubters've gone long ago. The last one disappeared fifteen years ago.

J.P.: *How much of this land here did you know in your own youth?*
F.L.W.: Well, all of it belonged to my uncles. Everything you see. My mother sent me here when I was eleven to work with my uncle James. She saw me as we came back from Boston where my father had a pastorate, I was becoming a sort of Little Lord Fauntleroy, long hair in ringlets she used to curl on her fingers. She saw her man-child getting to be rather refined. So she sent me up here to my uncle, and I never had shoes on nor a hat from the time I was eleven until I was seventeen. It was very far west. It was rich virgin soil. It was just being broken. My grandfather came here when the Indians were here. He'd have tobacco out on his porch step for them and they'd bring venison, lay it on the step, and take the tobacco. Daniel Webster was a great speculator in western lands and he owned this place down here that I now own part of it. Of course, this was to him the wild and wooly. The Sioux Indians were here then.

Down at the bridgehead, where we're building the restaurant, you can pick up Indian arrows there. You can go around and dig them up. That was an Indian ford, where they used to cross the river.

I walk around all over the place and drive around every afternoon. It's the most beautiful region you ever saw in your life. I've seen most of the beautiful regions of the world and none more beautiful than here.

But what would bring me back, anyway, was that I used to squeeze so much of this whole valley between my toes, barefooted. My whole youth is woven in with this place. Of course, the hired men now have a couple of the farms that belonged to my uncles I haven't been able to get back.

J.P.: *How much land do you have now?*
F.L.W.: Four thousand two hundred acres. Five miles of the riverfront.

J.P.: *When it came time for you to go to school, you went to engineering school.*
F.L.W.: We were poor and we couldn't afford an architectural school. There was none. So impatiently I went through nearly four years of engineering school. I had three months left to go and decided after all that engineering was only rudimentary, undeveloped architecture. And I struck out for Chicago on my own, unbeknown to anybody, including my mother, and tramped the streets there for a couple of days till I found a place with Silsbee and stayed with him a year studying residence architecture. He was the leading residence architect at that time in Chicago.

So after that year with Silsbee it became apparent that Sullivan was looking for somebody to do the drawings for the interior of the Auditorium building. He needed an assistant and one of the boys there told him about me. So he told Bill Corfs to ask me to come to see him, and I went. Then he asked me for some drawings. So I was busy making them—I made a lot of them. I made some of his ornament turned into Gothic and took them along, and he glanced at them all until he came to those and he said, "What are these, Wright?" I said, "Well, I thought we could turn it into Gothic to see how easy it is," and he was offended. But he saw the virtue, I was a good draftsman and had a good touch. He said, "Wright, you'll do. You've got a good touch. How much do you want?" Well, the answer was I'd been getting eighteen dollars a week. So, I said twenty-five. And he smiled and he said, "Well, we'll fix that as we go along." I could have asked for fifty and got it.

J.P.: *Did you talk to Dankmar Adler at that time, too?*
F.L.W.: No, I was hired by Louis Sullivan.

J.P.: *What was the relationship there?*
F.L.W.: Adler was the big chief. He was the big engineering architect with advanced ideas of architecture and was really a strong pillar of the AIA at the time, one of the advanced thinkers and performers. He did the Central Music Hall, he did the Exposition Building on the lakefront; he did any number of loft buildings for his clientele of that time. He took Sullivan in as a young, inexperienced member from the Beaux-Arts who had worked around in offices a little and took him in as a partner, believing in his genius.

Adler believed in Sullivan's genius as most people believe in God. And anything that Sullivan wanted he got. And Sullivan, of course, knew very little of the practical side of architecture. That he learned from one of the best masters he could have had, Dankmar Adler. And of course, the two men played in together like thumb and little finger, or thumb and forefinger—Adler the thumb, Sullivan the forefinger. That was a relationship between the two men.

1955

J.P.: *Did Sullivan give you any advice?*
F.L.W.: Well, Lieber Meister was in himself advice. He didn't have to give me any advice. He was advice. Just working with him, and being with him.

J.P.: *What about his own writings, the* Kindergarten Chats*?*
F.L.W.: Well, I was never much interested in those. He read me one of his things one time. He called it "Inspiration." It was one of the early things he wrote. I thought it was kind of a baying at the moon. I never thought he could write very well. But, of course, he could, and did. But his writing never impressed me. That isn't where I got him.

It is poetry. We don't have poets anymore. Show me a poet in the realm of architecture. Where is one? Show me a poet anywhere—in the realm of literature—where is one?

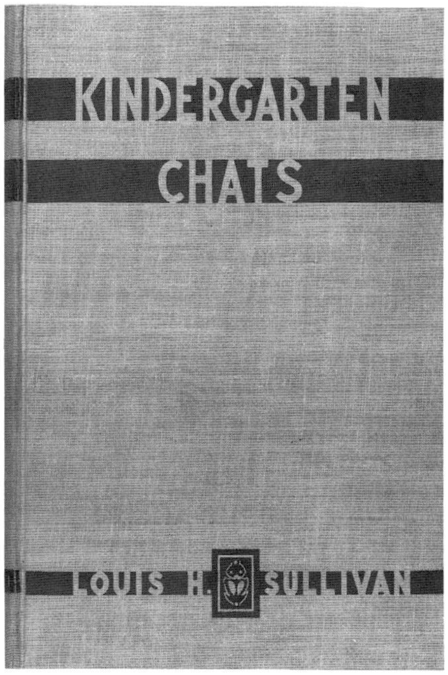

KINDERGARTEN CHATS. Louis Sullivan. Scarab Fraternity Press, Lawrence, Kansas. 1934. Sullivan, the pioneer of the skyscraper and Frank Lloyd Wright's "Lieber Meister," wrote these elementary essays in 1918 "to liberate the mind from the serfdom of tradition." Published later in book form, they made an influential contribution to modern architecture.

1957

I came in and Sullivan adopted me. He was so nice to me when he was insulting to all the rest of the office, and always had been, that they turned on me. I had to fight for my place there.

Sullivan said to me that after I'd been there the first week I got awfully lonesome. George Elmslie was one of the boys, a minister's son like me. There were five ministers' sons including Silsbee in that office. So when Sullivan said to me, "Wright, get somebody in here under you, because if something should happen to you after I've got you going, I won't have anybody." So I got George to come over. George stayed with me during the time I was there in my office as understudy. George was my understudy and I was Sullivan's. After I left, of course, he had George. Then in his decadent period, when he was no longer fit, George carried on for him.

I had thirty under me. I had charge of the planning and designing end of the office. Paul Mueller had charge of the engineering end and the field. He was Adler's man and I was Sullivan's.

You see, in that office, at that day, I was at one end of the drafting room, Paul Mueller was at the other. Adler was right next to the outer office. Sullivan's room was right next to mine and the door opened from mine into his room. Where I sat drawing, I always saw him.

J.P.: *On your own though, you've never had that sort of engineering-architect relationship.*
F.L.W.: No, but I had got a lot of engineering sense. I still felt that engineering was only the undeveloped, rudimentary side of architecture. To my mind they were practically one, except that I used an engineer in the way an engineer uses a slide rule. I used him for calculating. But I never used an engineer for designing. The schemes were always mine. I got, more or less, assistance from engineering as we went along.

J.P.: *How did you start to do more of the residential work that was in Sullivan's office?*

F.L.W.: That was because I'd spent a year with Silsbee, the best house-designer in the region. Sullivan had never built a house and didn't want to. Adler couldn't take them for his clients because they clogged up the machinery, and it took as much of his trouble and work to do a $25,000 house as it would a $250,000 office building.

J.P.: *Which is probably still true today.*
F.L.W.: Oh, yes, sure it is. Every residence we do, we do at a financial sacrifice unless it runs to over $250,000 or $100,000.

I did them on time. All the houses that came to Adler and Sullivan by way of their clientele, they couldn't avoid taking, they'd turned them over to me to do at home nights. I would do the plans for extra labor and bring them down into the office for execution.

J.P.: *But they were built under the name of . . .*
F.L.W.: Adler and Sullivan. Adler had done a few before that, and Sullivan had done the fronts for them. They were all fanciful, early Beaux-Arts Sullivan.

J.P.: *Were the plans that you were doing then very much like the plans of the period?*
F.L.W.: They were, but the plans that I did began to change. I had a sense of a house that I got from Silsbee, which was fluid and better than the average one at the time. Of course, I used that.

J.P.: *You say fluid but you didn't say open plan?*
F.L.W.: None of that was born at this time. It was born about 1893 after the Winslow House was built and the Williams House. I began about 1895 or 1896 on the open plan, several years after I'd been building the improved plan of the period.

The Winslow House had the idea of shelter that I have continued ever since. One of the greatest things of greatest importance in the building was a sense of shelter. The Winslow House had that. And the Winslow House still clung a little to the Sullivanian type of ornamentation on the frieze. But still it was going away at that time. But it was about until . . . the Coonley House was an instance, as many designs of the period were, of the individualized—what we called the "zoned" house, where the dining room is a unit, where the living room is a unit, where the bedrooms are units, and where they're all connected gracefully together around and according to environment.

WINSLOW HOUSE. *Frank Lloyd Wright. River Forest, Illinois. 1893. His first independent commission after leaving Adler and Sullivan, the Winslow House has a number of abiding Wrightian characteristics, such as the broad overhanging eaves.*

COONLEY HOUSE. *Frank Lloyd Wright. Riverside, Illinois. 1908. This home introduced Wright's influential zoned plan. It is recognized as a masterpiece of his Prairie houses.*

The Robie House, that was about 1909. From 1903 and '04 to 1909 was the developing of the open plan and the "zoned plan."

J.P.: *And the "zoned plan"—two different things?*
F.L.W.: They were off the same stem. They were related. Before that houses were all pseudo-Colonial. Architecture was then pseudo-Colonial or pseudo-English, which is Colonial.

J.P.: *Was it the Japanese influence that created the open plan?*
F.L.W.: There never was any Japanese influence. But what I did see was a Japanese print. The Japanese print by Hokusai and Hiroshige. I saw the first ones the year of the World's Fair. I bought some of the prints from a man named Sirocco from the Central Music Hall art store he ran there. I took them home, and was so delighted and fascinated by them, not because of the architecture but because of the phase of art they represented, which confirmed everything I was doing. Confirmed my thought and feeling so thoroughly that I made up my mind when I got a chance, had a little money, got a little rest, and in 1906 I went to Japan. After the building of the Larkin Building and the Martin House—Mrs. Martin had so worn me out that I had to commit suicide or go somewhere. So I went to Japan, where I wanted to study the print. I went to collect prints.

Japan produced tremendously great artists during that period. We call it now the Momoyama Period, the early part of it. The Ukiyo-e was the later part of the Momoyama. That's when these great fellows gave to the world what they gave. The simplifications that they made in painting influenced the printers who came later. That was the beginning of the pure Japanese school. It grew out of Chinese art. The Chinese principles were, of course, inherent in it. All that is Japanese in culture grew out of Chinese art the way a plant or a flower will grow out of leaf mold. So it is basically Chinese. For that reason the Chinese always look down on the Japanese, because they imitated.

I later became the chief procurer of Japanese prints while I was building the Imperial Hotel in Japan. I secured prints for Howard Mansfield, treasurer of the Metropolitan, for Chicago Art Institute, for the Spauldings especially. The Spauldings sent me over $200,000 when I was in Japan to buy prints for them. I made

LARKIN COMPANY BUILDING. *Frank Lloyd Wright. Buffalo, New York. 1903. Demolished in 1950, this mail order company office building with its central open workspace pioneered early "air-conditioning" and the use of plate glass and metal furnishings.*

FRANK LLOYD WRIGHT
at Taliesin, Spring Green, Wisconsin, 1955

the collection that is now in the Fine Arts Museum [Boston]. It was largely made by myself. There were only a few acquisitions otherwise.

J.P.: *Was this a new thing at that time?*
F.L.W.: No, it was practically finished. The French and Germans had practically eaten it up. It wasn't so new here, either, because there had been collectors before. There was Cookin of Chicago, Moss of Evanston, Chandler of Evanston. Oh, there were a great number of them.

J.P.: *Even then you were not interested in their architecture?*
F.L.W.: No. I didn't care anything about their architecture. Their architecture never got to me and hasn't got to me yet because I had everything that they have. All they had then and all they have now confirmed what I was doing. But what I did find in the print was the gospel of elimination. Here they are on the wall there. I keep them with me.

I am a disciple of Hokusai, Hiroshige, and the Ukiyo-e School, and so far as the Japanese architecture is concerned, I never got a thing from it. And that's true. Now whether they believe it or not I don't care. But the Japanese influence architecturally to me was mere confirmation.

When they sent a committee around the world to find an architect to be the Emperor's Kenchikaho [High Builder], they came to Germany. At that time they heard of me in Germany. Now, if they had come to America they never would have heard of me. So when they got to America they came straight out to me at Oak Park and saw those buildings around there already built. There were about twenty-five or thirty of them at that time. They said, "Well, this is not Japanese, but it would look very well in Japan." So they hired me to build a Japanese hotel.

"MOLD CLAY INTO A VESSEL;
FROM ITS NOT-BEING (IN THE VESSEL'S HOLLOW)
ARISES THE UTILITY OF THE VESSEL.
CUT OUT DOORS AND WINDOWS IN THE HOUSE (WALL),
FROM THEIR NOT-BEING (EMPTY SPACE) ARISES THE UTILITY OF THE HOUSE.
THEREFORE BY THE EXISTENCE OF THINGS WE PROFIT.
AND BY THE NON-EXISTENCE OF THINGS WE ARE SERVED."

Lao-tse

J.P.: *Probably that was because in a sense there was a relationship.*
F.L.W.: There is a relationship that goes back to nature and I was going back to the nature that the Japanese had gone back to throughout their civilization, centuries before I was born. Just as the Mayan went back to nature. That was another great influence in my life, Mayan architecture, Peruvian, Inca, Toltec. When I was a youngster all I wanted was to go down there and help dig up that great civilization.

I got this little book by Okakura Kakuzo from our Japanese ambassador and I read it. It was a translation of Lao-tse. I read there, in so many words: the reality of the building does not consist in the walls and the roof, but in the space that has to be lived in. There was a statement exactly five hundred years before Jesus. Here I'd been trying to build it and thought I was a prophet.

J.P.: *That is the statement people quote about modern architecture now.*
F.L.W.: Well, that's where it came from. It never existed until I did it. I've been the one that advocated it. When they talk that language it isn't theirs.

The space values of the building preserved, enlarged, expanded, presented, makes an entirely new architecture and Unity Temple is the first expression of it. That is my

UNITY TEMPLE. *Frank Lloyd Wright. Oak Park, Illinois. 1906. In America's first important poured-concrete structure, Wright broke with ecclesiastical architectural traditions. The building is divided into connected religious and social sections.*

contribution to modern architecture. And that, to me, is modern architecture. Here's the plan, you see. Now there are the features. These are really what might have been walls and they aren't walls. Now come the stairways in the corner, which are features, separate features. There's the plan. Now this is all open above. These are really features set against space, as though to leave it all open and expanded above. There was where the interior space became the reality of the building. And that preceded what I had learned from Lao-tse.

What I learned always has been confirmation. Like the Japanese print, that was confirmation. I was unconscious of Lao-tse. But when I read him I came down like a sail. I thought, my God, I'm no prophet. That's five hundred years before Jesus. Then I began to think, well, trying to build up again, after all, he didn't build it. I was building it. I said the truth is eternal. It doesn't belong to Lao-tse. He perceived it as something. I not only perceived it, but I built it, which he didn't do. So I don't owe it to Lao-tse, I went to the eternal verities. It's all nature study.

J.P.: *When was the concept of the Taliesin Foundation developed?*
F.L.W.: It was developed with Mrs. Wright, when we had no money. I had no work, of course, and didn't expect to get any because I was getting a worm's-eye view of society. So we thought if we could make buildings we could make architects. That was the way it began. We sent out a little circular in 1932, and twenty-six boys walked up the front steps from all over the country.

Alden Dow was one of the first ones to come up, and there were dozens of others now practicing architecture and doing very well. So that's how what we call "the Fellowship" started. It's now twenty-five years old. We ought to have a quarter centennial—quarto centenniale.

J.P.: *How many of these buildings were here at that time?*
F.L.W.: None. Nineteen eleven I built the first house. The one you're sitting in is the third. Two were destroyed by fire, one, a terrific tragedy. The second, no loss of life, but a loss of about $90,000 worth—oh, more than that—$190,000 worth of works of art I brought from Japan.

HILLSIDE HOME SCHOOL. *Frank Lloyd Wright. Spring Green, Wisconsin. 1902. Wright departed from traditional educational-building styles in designing this pioneering coeducational boarding school for his aunts, Jane and Nell Lloyd Jones.*

Hillside was my aunts'. We went to work to make that ready. That was the first work of the Fellowship, to ready those buildings. They were virtually being destroyed. Water was coming in. Vandals had marked on the walls and they were wrecks. We had to bring the whole thing back including this burned-down portion. We had to create the Foundation out of practically nothing except the studio back there and the stable. That's all that was left. We had the farm then. It was a heavy burden.

1955

J.P.: *You established the Foundation—an institution.*
F.L.W.: No, I'm not an institution. I'm just a business. The judges in their decision referred to my "design business." That's how good the judges were. I was conducting a design business under the guise of a school. It's the law. The law today, of course, has been finagled and juggled and pulled apart and put together again by lawyers until it sheds no light whatever. It knows neither justice nor mercy. That's the law.

1957

J.P.: *Your talents were being neglected. Why?*
F.L.W.: Well, I was living here on this hill with a woman who I had not married and could not marry because my wife wouldn't give me a divorce, and that was wicked. I was persistent. I wouldn't give in to them. I said I had a right to live. You read it in the *Autobiography*, it's all told there.

I was distinctly on the off side of every tenet, morally, which they held. Ethically it was something else. But they are incompetent where ethical judgment is concerned. I don't think in our nation today any issue could be decided on its ethical import. It would have to be tainted by morals which are after all only customs. Morals are customs. Ethics are principles—fundamentals.

J.P.: *How much of this house was in the original plan?*
F.L.W.: This tower was in the original plan. That addition was put on it afterward. All this has disappeared twice except that. That's all that's left.

J.P.: *What about the Johnson Wax tower, which wasn't in the original plan? Was there always a conception of a tower there?*
F.L.W.: No, there wasn't. There was no tower conceived at first, but they now say it looks so natural in relation to the whole that I always had it in my mind. Probably after the thing had matured the addition would be better made than if I'd made it in the first place.

Same man, same thoughts, same circumstance, but enriched by experience. The taproot foundation wasn't there with a spine in the center and the cantilevers running out. That's the same principle as the Mile High. So is the Price Tower. Those two things are twentieth-century architecture. You can't call twentieth-century architecture this old steel post-and-beam framing when we've got the rod and the tendon and the flesh of concrete to build from the inside out. That was when the twentieth century was born.

J.P.: *What about an engineer like Nervi?*
F.L.W.: Well, Nervi is twentieth century. Maillart, the Swiss bridge engineer, was twentieth century. There have been, I imagine, other architects, but we don't know their work.

J.P.: *What about Gaudí?*
F.L.W.: No. You mean that mud pie he created there with cement? Sweeney wrote a disquisition on Gaudí that someday he ought to be sorry for. James Johnson Sweeney, the one I'm up against in the Guggenheim Museum. He's the curator. He was against everything that Mr. Guggenheim stood for and left behind him. The situation is extremely immoral, I say.

J.P.: *In the Johnson Wax, though, you also pioneered the column, like the . . .*
F.L.W.: That was the whole struggle with the building commission of Wisconsin and we won out. After that they haven't wanted to come again.

H.C. PRICE TOWER. *Frank Lloyd Wright. Bartlesville, Oklahoma. 1952. The spectacular nineteen-story office and residential tower with a "tap-root" foundation is Wright's only built skyscraper.*

JOHNSON WAX COMPANY BUILDINGS. *Frank Lloyd Wright. Racine, Wisconsin. 1936, 1946. With their streamlined walls of brick and glass, the renowned administration building and research tower, built a decade apart, were designed with ideas that remain innovative today.*

JOHNSON WAX COMPANY ADMINISTRATION BUILDING, INTERIOR. *Frank Lloyd Wright. Racine, Wisconsin. 1936. Wright exhibited his engineering skill in the design for the slender "lily pad" piers. With them he created one of the great light-filled office spaces.*

It was very new. Reinforced-concrete column that raised the compression of the concrete to 12,000 pounds from 3,500 pounds. And also, it took a load that they allowed us only seven feet for the height of the column. We built it twenty-three and then couldn't break it down.

The codes in New York are just as silly. The codes in New York have made the Guggenheim building there that we're building cost at least a million dollars more than they needed to have cost if they'd let us do it our way. The New York people have never experimented outside of the old steel column and plate girder. The code of New York City was made ten years before yesterday and knows neither justice nor mercy. It worked out that we've had to redesign the whole fabrication of the building. We built the Johnson building with cold-drawn steel mesh, diamond mesh, because you get out of it reinforcement in not only two ways, but in depth as well. They'd never heard of it here so they wouldn't allow us to use it.

J.P.: *The building in Wisconsin had only been standing twenty years.*
F.L.W.: Fifteen years. Then we're using it in Price Tower. So we use it in all our work, but they'd never used it down there. So that was the thing we ran up against first of all. We had to throw away all our calculations and use flat bars so we had to redraw every structural drawing we had. Why? They had never had any experience with the latest thing in construction, reinforcement with a third dimension. They were still in two dimensions. Well, we've done all this just to please them, you see.

The Guggenheim is going up to second-floor level above the street, and is proving to be of great challenge to all New York, because it's the first time that in New York a modern, twentieth-century building has been built. All the buildings in New York are nineteenth-century buildings in the sense of the old, engineer's bridge-construction. They are all boxed frames, built from the outside in and the Museum is built from the inside out, and the concrete is the building. All those other buildings are faced with something. This thing is integral. You feel it when you go to see the building. It looks solid, and the other stuff all looks pasteboard and cracker box.

J.P.: *When you say organic, what is meant? I read a definition in Mr. Sullivan's* Kindergarten *book. Did he use the word organic?*

F. L.W.: Oh yes, he did and I always did. But not in the same sense. When he said organic, he meant more or less according to a plant growing when he made the ornament and designed it, you see. But it never entered into his thought of construction, because he wasn't a constructor.

In my case it was integral, vital. It was the nature of the thing, whatever it was. It was the way you built. The materials you used. The way you used them, all that. The materials are all alike to the Lieber Meister.

J. P.: *When he said, "Form follows function," . . .*
F. L.W.: Well, he never lived up to it, because he didn't live long enough. He might have. He admired immensely what I was doing, and he said to me, "Frank"—this was no more than several weeks before he died—several months before he died—"Frank," he said, "I never could have done what you've done. But you never could have done what you've done if it hadn't been for me."

Organic means, with me, that form and function are one. That lifts it into the realm of the spirit. Whereas the other might hang in a butcher shop. When I say function I actually mean essence—essential to integration of the character of the thing. It means something coming out from the inside according to principle.

As a matter of fact, when I use the word nature, I notice that I don't use it as most other people use it that I talk to. Because to me nature is the very form of what we call God. The only form we'll ever see of God, you might say, and be true poetically. That nature is the only body of God you'll ever see.

I told Carl Sandburg that in an interview and I said, "Carl, what about that? What do you call that?" "Well, Frank," he said, "I call that poetry." That is what I mean by nature.

I have always fought, and I am still fighting, a divorce of man from the elements of nature that he belongs to. That he has been fashioned according to. I never wanted him to be separated from the elements that constitute the body of his universe.

J. P.: *In your houses you've always featured natural materials, fireplaces and so forth.*
F. L.W.: I love the fire. I love to see that element. I love to feel that I am using it, that I have access to it, or control of it. I can use it as a feature of an architectural ensemble—water the same, the fountain. You open the windows and here's the shade of the building, which is a great, luxurious element. Shelter is essential. Shade is a luxury.

J. P.: *How do you feel about the new materials?*
F. L.W.: I'm not opposed to any material, modern or ancient. Architecture is in the nature of materials. There is no reason why materials shouldn't go into plastics. Steel is a plastic. Glass is a plastic. All modern materials are in the nature of a plastic. I don't see any reason why aluminum shouldn't be just as good as steel in the course of time and just as useful perhaps because it's light. It has properties that steel lacks, but it also lacks properties that steel has. All these materials have their own future, but it takes an architect with a depth of insight to know what to do with them.

"I COULD NOW START ON THE COURSE OF PRACTICAL EXPERIMENTATIONS I LONG HAD IN MIND, WHICH WAS TO MAKE AN ARCHITECTURE BASED ON WELL-DEFINED UTILITARIAN NEEDS—THAT ALL PRACTICAL DEMANDS OF UTILITY SHOULD BE PARAMOUNT AS A BASIS OF PLANNING AND DESIGN; THAT NO ARCHITECTURAL DICTUM, OR TRADITION, OR SUPERSTITION, OR HABIT SHOULD STAND IN THE WAY. . . . THIS MEANT THAT I WOULD PUT TO THE TEST A FORMULA I HAD EVOLVED THROUGH LONG CONTEMPLATION OF LIVING THINGS, NAMELY THAT *FORM FOLLOWS FUNCTION*, WHICH WOULD MEAN IN PRACTICE THAT ARCHITECTURE MIGHT AGAIN BECOME A LIVING ART IF THIS FORMULA WERE ADHERED TO."

Louis Sullivan

IMPERIAL HOTEL. *Frank Lloyd Wright. Tokyo. 1915. Wright's most famous building abroad combined advanced engineering with richly ornamented architectural forms.*

That's equally true with the materials like steel and concrete. You can get a plastic structure now—that's what saved the earthquake—was the application to that problem of steel in tension. The rod that you could pull on. First time you got a building that you can pull on. An earthquake can't do anything with a building you can pull on. It can just roll it around. It's the same principle that Roebling used on the bridge, except in a very different way.

It's the principle of nature. It's working in the tree. The tree stands on its root and puts out its branches. There you have the cantilever. I used to go through here and see these paths of the cyclones. They used to be quite frequent here. Certain trees would be standing up, bent over but standing. The others would be flat with the root system up like your hand from the ground. I wondered what it was and I found out that it was the taproot. So that started me thinking. I got out of it the taproot system of foundation.

Now almost all these things like the stability of the Imperial Hotel astonishing the world for the simple idea of a building on which you could pull. And the cantilever system is apparent in everything you see around here that I ever did.

MILE HIGH PROJECT. *Frank Lloyd Wright. Chicago. 1956. This drawing shows Wright's tap-root foundation and compares the scale of Mile High with the largest Egyptian pyramid, the Eiffel Tower, and the Empire State Building.*

Opposite: MILE HIGH PROJECT. *Frank Lloyd Wright. Chicago. 1956. Wright's plans for tall buildings, the 1929 St. Marks in the Bowery tower and his 1952 Price Tower in Bartlesville, Oklahoma, reached visionary heights in this spectacular 528-story skyscraper.*

They're twentieth-century architecture. As distinguished from nineteenth-century, which is the old bridge engineers, post-and-beam construction riveted together from the outside in. There you have the nineteenth-century structure of Adler and Sullivan and my early work, too, sometimes. The Eiffel Tower and all the rest of it. But now comes the twentieth-century construction that made the Mile High possible. With this construction the Mile High is possible.

1955

The Usonian Automatic is lightness combined with strength. It's a three-inch steel block reinforced with steel in the joints. It's a perfect wedding of steel and various types of insulated concrete, or concrete insulation. Insulation is another factor that we have to deal with in building.

J.P.: *Does air-conditioning influence your thinking?*
F.L.W.: I think that air-conditioning, like glass, like all these new things, is abused, misunderstood. I think air-conditioning has killed more people probably than almost anything else and will continue to do so. It has now reached the point where man is to be separated from his climate. How long he'll last on that basis is yet to be seen.

J.P.: *On the other hand, you introduced radiant or Korean heating.*
F.L.W.: That is natural heating, gravity heat, natural heat. Heat from the ground up. Heat rises, water descends. Heat is the elimination of weight. Water is the accumulation of weight. The two are opposed and when you're sitting on a floor-heated surface, you're warm, your feet are warm. You can open the windows no matter how cold it is and feel comfortable. That's a natural thing. That is organic heat. The Romans had it. It's a modification of the Roman hypocaust.

I built a house not long ago and one of the experts came in. They always show up and talk to the client. He told him that he would lose so much of that heat going down underneath, and got him to put an insulated surface under the broken stone to keep the heat from going down. He was an expert. Now an expert is a man who has stopped thinking. He knows and you can't tell him anything. So he is lost. But that was the expert's view of floor heating. I had the pleasure of firing seven of them when I built the Imperial Hotel. Some of the most distinguished in the country.

That was the first use by an American or a Westerner. The Easterners had used it. The baron had it in his house when he entertained me, the old Korean hypocaust. I was so comfortable after I had suffered so much in that climate that I made up my mind. I went back and dropped the ceilings of the bathrooms in the Imperial Hotel and the Cutler-Hammer unit had just appeared, where you could put an electric unit exposed. We put it in there in the space between the two. The bathrooms were warm and the tubs were built in the floor and they were warm. People went in, there were no radiators and nothing artificial, but they were all comfortable, and warm tile floor, bare feet, comfortable, tub warm. You'd get into a warm tub, sit down on a warm water-closet, and use a washbowl warm. That was the beginning.

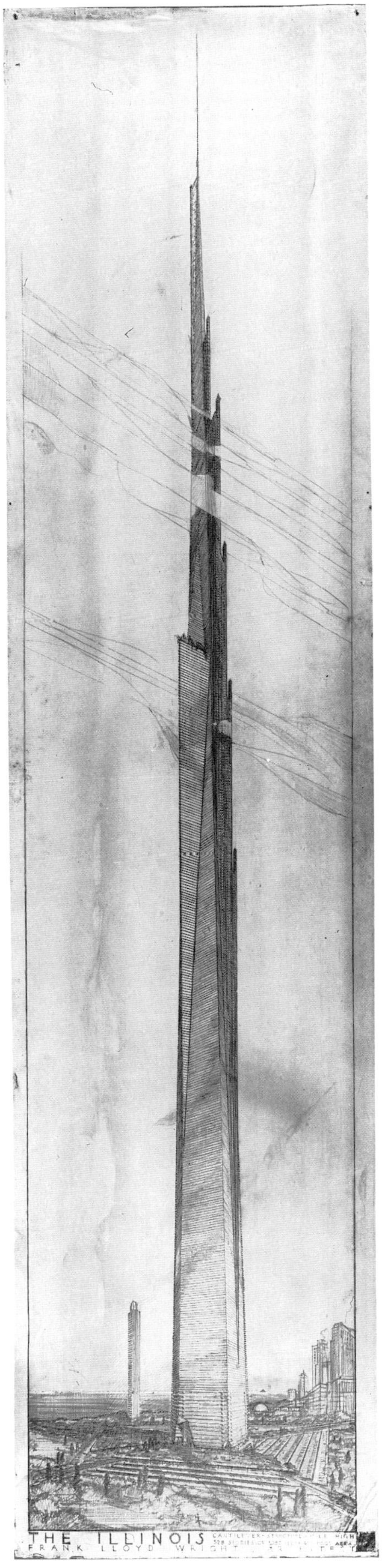

We've been sold down the river by science. Everything scientific. Got a tool box, magnificently filled with tools and never learned how to use one of them. That's the trouble. Have a man come into your home and you want something done. He has all the tools that ever were for doing it. Then he makes a botch of the job because he doesn't know how.

If we'd learn to use the materials we've got, then we'd be entitled to new ones. But you can't keep on using the new ones as fast as they come in and neglect the old ones.

1957

J.P.: *So there's no opposition between your concept of architecture and science?*

F.L.W.: On the contrary, it's a means to the utilization for human benefit of the sciences. The sciences cannot benefit human beings, really, until creative art takes them up and shows how to use them according to human quality and interests.

The scientist has walked in and so bewildered and confused the poor genus *Homo* that he doesn't know which end he's standing on now. He hasn't produced the inspirational means by which this could be a blessing. It is likely to prove in the end a curse.

J.P.: *I'm interested in the prefabricated house you designed.*

F.L.W.: That's on the same stem, from which all these other things have flowered. And with practically the same purpose, which is to create a better environment within the reach of the upper-middle third of our American people—it's not for the lower class yet. I'm going to do one that is for them eventually, but this is for the upper-middle third.

J.P.: *Is it real Frank Lloyd Wright architecture?*

F.L.W.: In the main, yes. But so are almost all the other houses now being built in the country. I doubt if you could ever differentiate much from the principles that they are using in these now common to what I, myself, am doing.

J.P.: *You mean the open plan, radiant heating, the inside-outside plan?*

MARSHALL ERDMAN COMPANY HOUSE. *Frank Lloyd Wright. Madison, Wisconsin. 1956. The van Tamelen residence is one model of Wright's many efforts in lower-cost prefabricated housing.*

F.L.W.: Yes, and the style they use, the details they use, and the appearances they promote. So this is in the same strain. Only this has had benefit of clergy and the others are illegitimate. That's all.

J.P.: *But, with the benefit of the clergy, does a person get the same as a Frank Lloyd Wright . . . ?*
F.L.W.: No, he doesn't get the quality—he gets many of the substantial virtues and advantages. But if he wants quality and wants a distinguished home of his own as a work of art, which is what we're able to give him, that's something else. That cannot be done this way.

A work of art means, of course, individual character, carried to the nth power insofar as it can be in order to perfect it. This is just a roughing out and more or less still the skeleton of what it might be if it were a special creation by ourselves. The fundamental virtues of the residential architecture which I have promoted and given to the country are there in the skeleton.

J.P.: *For instance, you don't have the usual hall but a gallery.*
F.L.W.: That's in every house I built almost. It's a storage wall and a charming little promenade. It's open to the living room and to the bedrooms. I put sculpture and books and things in it so that it's an attractive thing.

The idea of all these houses I build is not to create a containment, to allow nearly everything to come together in a fluid sense as a complete whole. That's all in the handling of space. Space is regarded in one of these houses of mine as the reality of the building. That's the thing, to expand, extend, and preserve. So that you get that sense of spaciousness wherever you are in the house. You are never cut off. It enters into the proportion of the building and the way you handle the details and everything about it. One thing unfolds into another, and they all develop each other.

J.P.: *The new-type bridge you once mentioned. Do you think in Baghdad, you'll get a chance to . . .*
F.L.W.: Well, they're building it in Baghdad, I think. I proposed it to them, and they seemed to like it. It's almost too good to be true, but I believe it's true. As far as I can see.

J.P.: *This will be an entity within itself, I understand. It's out on an island?*
F.L.W.: Yes, well, no, it's tied in. It's integrated with the city and related to the whole. I have tried to put some poetry into the thing because we are going back to the source of civilization. So we are memorializing the Garden of Eden, Adam and Eve, Harun al-Rashid, and all the tales of the *Arabian Nights*. They're all woven into this thing.

I have an idea we can work the ziggurat in and have an enormous circular development, not too high, absorbing the traffic. Then build on that the various buildings of the university. The bridge and the cultural buildings, the art institute, the Garden of Eden, the cars are all absorbed into the scheme by way of the ziggurat. Everywhere

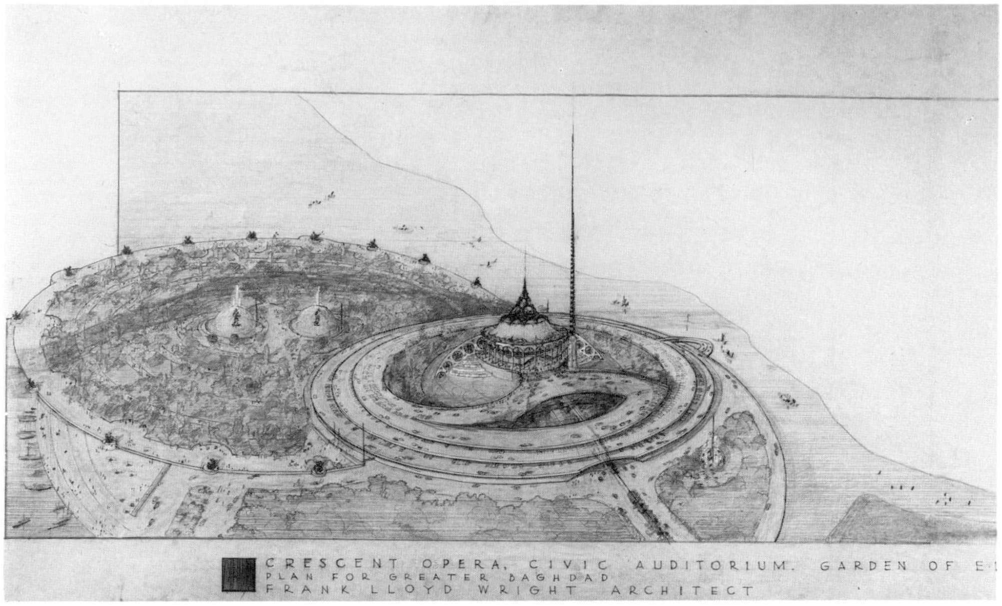

PLAN FOR BAGHDAD.
Frank Lloyd Wright. Iraq. 1957. This aerial perspective rendering of the unrealized plan for greater Baghdad shows the proposed opera house and gardens at the upper right, with the university left of center.

you don't see any cars. They're swallowed up and you get out and walk in. The ziggurat is only three times around and not very high. You can drive up and deposit your load at the entrance, and then park going down.

The traffic problem is a factor that we must reckon with. I don't think we ought to build anything as important as a new Baghdad that doesn't start with what's necessary in that direction. I think it would be silly to spend millions now to perpetuate a great error, or not an error so much as it is a deficit. You see, every building scheme today starts with some sensible disposition of the motorcar. I begin with the motorcar in all these schemes.

J.P.: *Actually, what you sometimes hear is Frank Lloyd Wright doesn't take into consideration the new ways people live.*
F.L.W.: I've never heard that. That's entirely foreign to the whole process. It's exactly the center line of everything done.

I proposed a new city which has got to be built. It's inevitable. The motorcar and the various other implements, improvements, like television, telephone, light, make the present city uninhabitable. You can't retain it no matter how hard you try. Of course, it's an exploitation at the present moment by way of the realtor. He's trying to squeeze the last drop out of it before it is thrown away.

That's the situation now and that's what I saw when I wrote the little book called *When Democracy Builds*. That's Broadacre City, you can see the model over there. It was first exhibited at Rockefeller Center in New York in 1932, I think it was, or 1933. We sent it around to different places in the country. It went to Washington, to Pittsburgh, I don't know where else. But they regarded it as communistic. They so misinterpreted it that we took it home and put it there and waited. If the agronomy of the nation were to be harmoniously fused with the industrialism of the nation, then we'd have what I call Broadacre City.

Henry Ford had an idea of the ribbon development, where there is one single stream of traffic and you located yourself to the right or the left of it. The agriculture was in behind the ribbon on each side. It wasn't a city plan.

J.P.: *Are Greenbelt and some of those developments related?*
F.L.W.: No, I don't think so. They're only suburban. Now you can't make suburbia anything very desirable. It's only an expedient, only an escape. It isn't an arrival. They haven't yet thought it out. The only thought on the subject that I've ever seen was my own.

J.P.: *More people probably ask your advice on architecture than any other person on earth.*
F.L.W.: You know where the advice is wanted now? It is very encouraging. It's the only encouraging note in this whole architectural scene, otherwise it's discouraging, I would say. It's from the teenagers in high school. Not a week passes that one letter doesn't come, usually two, last week three, from students—children, you know—in high school. "Dear Mr. Wright: We've chosen you for our thesis. Can you kindly send us some helpful material?" That shows that fifteen years from now when they are married and when they have homes, when they build, American architecture is going to come into being. I'm only pessimistic concerning the present fellows on the bandwagon, that's all.

J.P.: *In other words, you're not pessimistic about the future.*
F.L.W.: No, oh no. If I were I would commit suicide. I would not have anything to live for. When you get pessimistic concerning the future, the thing that you love, why then you're done. It's not the future I'm worried about. It's the present.

J.P.: *People associate optimism with youth.*
F.L.W.: Young is nothing but a circumstance. You can't do anything about that. I have lots of young people all around me. But youth is a quality. Sometimes young people have it. They lose it very soon often. But if you have that quality of youth, it never leaves you. It's your immortality. Now, try and get it, try and keep it. I guess that once you have it you never lose it.

Look behind you there. You've seen those things? That's a collection of tributes from the world at large. That's one, John, I value very highly. This is the medal that Dante coveted and never got because of political shenanigans—the de'Medici medal. You see the fleur-de-lis on it of France? They took it from Italy. So that's a very great honor. There's only one in the country. That's one from Britain in 1941. That's the one incorruptible honor in the world. That makes me an honorary member of the royal household for life. It's pure gold. Lift it. It's not alloy.

J.P.: *But this is the Royal Institute of British Architects.*
F.L.W.: But conferred by the majesty with the honor carried with it of being an honorary member of the royal household for life, when I'm in London. I've never flattered them. That's one of the things that makes the medal worth having. When you go out in the studio you can see all the citations. There are thirty-two of those.

Look out and see what you see. Do you see anything discordant? This is the hilltop. We call it Taliesin because it's a brow on the hill, you see. We didn't build it on the hill. The brow is still there. That's what Taliesin means—"shining brow"—in Welsh.

J.P.: *Have you visited Wales?*
F.L.W.: Yes, Mrs. Wright and I went last September and, see that red hood hanging on the door? That's the Welsh honorarium from the Welsh university. My old grandfather must be greatly pleased.

J.P.: *Do you feel the Welsh strain in you?*
F.L.W.: Oh, very much. The West has been materialist, and the East is of the spirit. The relationship between West and East is just that relationship. What the West represents in their art is poison, utterly detrimental to the East.

That's the tragedy now in Iraq. They have all this German, English, French architects in there, along with this one from America, the only one that really has any feeling for the East.

J.P.: *How do you have a feeling for the East? You are an American.*
F.L.W.: I'm Welsh and the Welsh would have a great feeling for the spirit of the East. The Welsh were a spiritual people. They came from King Arthur. The Round Table was one of their official institutions. They were the original Britons. When you speak of the British you speak of the Welsh. Some of them got stranded over there on the French coast, and they called them the Britons. Those are Welsh. They are a poetic people, and musical. Poets say the name "Taliesin" here was taken from one of the British poets of King Arthur's Round Table. He sang the glories of fine art, and the only one they ever had that did.

J.P.: *Is it like your feeling for the Japanese, when you found confirmation in the writings of the Chinese philosophers?*
F.L.W.: The Chinese philosophers and the Mabinogion, the writings of the ancient Welsh, the same sentiments. Here's a Welsh definition of a genius that comes down from King Arthur's Round Table. I read it in the Mabinogion, a series of triads in which the wisdom of the Welsh comes down in threes—one, two, three.

A genius is a man who has an eye to see nature.

A genius is a man who has a heart to feel nature.

A genius is a man who has the courage to follow nature.

Beat that if you can.

J.P.: *What about the three symbols that they had, and "Truth against the world"?*
F.L.W.: Well, that was the same thing. That is the same sentiment that the "Truth against the world" is, this sense of nature as opposed to all of the other forces that exist. The symbol is the inverted rays of the rising sun—always in threes.

1955

J.P.: *If you were to pick some of your own works that you think have been or will be most influential, what would they be?*

F.L.W.: I'm not interested in that phase of it at all. I have no favorite child, I have no favorite building, and I have no masterpiece. You have to take my work as a whole, and it's either a masterpiece or it isn't. There is no one thing in it. There's no taking it apart. There it is.

ANTONIN RAYMOND ON FRANK LLOYD WRIGHT

1962

While I was in Frank's office, in 1916, one day there arrived a Japanese gentleman with his wife, both beautifully dressed in beautiful Japanese clothes. He was the manager of the Imperial Hotel, the old one. Aisaku Hayashi, a highly cultured person who really knew Oriental arts and Western arts, invited Frank to come to Japan. That was 1916 or 1915. Frank took his son David, who is here now with him, to Japan at that time to try to get the job.

I had started my own office and there was nothing to do. There was complete depression right after the war, not even a storefront to design, not a thing. When one day Frank Lloyd drops into the office and he says, "Antonin, I have $40,000 in my pocket, let's go to Tokyo and build that hotel." You can imagine what joy! We left everything right there and then. I went to Wisconsin with him and then we got across the continent. At that time it took almost a week to Seattle. We got on a Japanese boat and arrived here in Yokohama on the 31st of December 1919.

IMPERIAL HOTEL. *Frank Lloyd Wright. Tokyo. 1915. Carved lava stonework enriched the bold modern forms of this renowned Japanese hotel.*

It was really the most amazing occurrence. You see, there is kind of a fate involved in all my life. First, the interest in the Japanese during the Russo-Japanese War. My interest in Frank Lloyd Wright, which was the reason why I came to the United States. Then coming to Frank Lloyd Wright in Wisconsin, finding all those Japanese things there, wonderful prints and all kind of sculpture and art objects. They weren't very high art, more decorative than really beautiful, except his prints, they were very good.

Anyhow, we arrived here. Japan was a country out of a different world. You have no idea. You might still find parts of Japan like that, tucked away in the mountains or in the seashore or in some really remote places. Between Yokohoma and Tokyo were only fishing villages, beautiful fishing villages all along the shore. Of course, there was no paved road or straight road, just meandering road. Everybody was in Japanese clothes. There was no such thing as foreign clothes. We arrived here in Tokyo, which was a very beautiful Oriental city, full of wonderful houses, gardens, and temples—a really beautiful Oriental city. Tokyo at that time already, I think, had about two or three million inhabitants, but it was really just a conglomeration of villages. The old Imperial Hotel was a little bit of a hotel. Well, there we were. We started working right away on this thing. Started the foundations. A German builder, Mueller, came from Chicago. It was a very rainy season, a tremendous amount of water. The first word that this German, Mueller, learned in Japanese was water, *misu*, you see, that goddamn misu. He had to do the foundations.

Frank always wanted something new, you know. He bought augers, which you use for sinking telephone poles. They were just invented about that time. Somebody sold him about a dozen. He took them over to Japan, thinking, I will drill holes, fill it with concrete, and I will have piles, you see. He brought those and poor Mueller had to use them. He dug with those things to make a hole. The moment he did, it filled with water. He put in concrete and, of course, the concrete didn't form. That's why I say it's a floating foundation all right. That floating foundation business is just a purely journalistic expression. It doesn't exist. It's perfect nonsense. It's just not so. Wright was a very imaginative person and really did marvelous things.

Then Frank became ill and had to go back and came back again. The Americans here particularly became very, very critical of his work. They could only see something like the Waldorf-Astoria and they created kind of a mistrust in Baron Okakura and in the Imperial Hotel company. You know, of course, Frank would put up a thing and take it down, as he did very often. He had the courage and complete disregard for any commercial interest whatsoever. The Okakura people became more and more distrustful. They didn't know just where they were. The thing cost two or three times as much as it originally was supposed to cost. It took longer.

It's very interesting. Frank had no artistic influence on Japan whatsoever, none whatsoever. Technologically, yes. You see, the Imperial Hotel is the really first complete building with insular form-work. Very ingeniously Frank used hollow tile inside for insulation and special brick keyed in on the outside. He was really a great genius in that matter.

Today, the hotel is practically destroyed. Whatever was left then after the earthquake, it suffered. Also the big building in the rear, the roof was bombed and burned out. The U.S. Army, the brass lived there during the occupation and they finished that hotel. They destroyed a lot of things. The army shoots everything that moves and paints everything that doesn't. So they painted even that stone, you know. They wanted it to look like Leavenworth. They meant well. They wanted to make it sanitary. That oilstone looked unsanitary. They had to paint it white. Then, the heating, they put in steam heat. They put in those phony lights and I don't know what.

It once had all kind of a cozy atmosphere of a home. Frank always did that, very romantic, extremely romantic. Well that's all gone. If you knew it the way we knew it. We designed so many things. That big room up there really was very interesting.

No contractor, no trade knew anything about Western building. They didn't know much but they were marvelous craftsmen. How they ever carved that stone with Frank standing right over them and I, with full-sized drawings. It was fantastic. Although they worked for about forty cents a day, eight hours, it still became very expensive. You can imagine.

There were no plumbers in Japan at all. You couldn't buy a toilet or anything. They didn't want to import anything that was so expensive. We had everything made here. They had the water closets made out of copper by coppersmiths, beautifully done, wall hung.

The last letter just before he died, he asked me, "What can you do about removing those dreadful inscriptions like 'Premier' and 'Imperial Hotel,' which I've seen in photographs?" Well, of course, I didn't dare to tell him that that was the least objectionable part of what they did to the hotel.

He was a real American in his emotional originality. He was the opposite of Mies van der Rohe or Gropius or any of these cerebral Germans, just the very opposite.

Le Corbusier

"PEOPLE SAID I LACKED COURTESY. BUT I WAS ONLY POINTING OUT THINGS THAT ARE FUNDAMENTAL."

Le Corbusier's usual somber attire—a double-breasted dark suit, blue shirt, and thick, black, round, horn-rimmed glasses—befitted the nickname "Corbu," a corruption of the French word for crow. He was born Charles-Édouard Jeanneret, but adapted and adopted his maternal grandmother's name, Lecorbesier. His animated face seemed surprisingly intense even in repose. Just as poor handwriting is sometimes explained by a quick mind that runs ahead of the hand, so with Le Corbusier I had the feeling that his mind was running ahead of his words, leaping from thought to thought.

He had an abiding frustration born of his complex nature and uncompromising vision. A remarkable number of his plans, generally drawn up on his own initiative, went unexecuted, and he viewed the unappreciative world as an implacable enemy. He was a highly gifted thinker and artist. It has been observed that he designed an entire city before he executed his first significant building. His books and other writings nearly outnumber his buildings; in addition, he devoted a significant portion of his time to painting. Though

he insisted on speaking French on all occasions, I have repeatedly heard him correct the English of the translator.

Corbusier had many admirers, but few close friends. I met but did not really know the man. However, I take some comfort in the observation of his friend the Swiss historian Sigfried Giedion: "He is as mistrustful as a mountain peasant. Nobody knows who he really is." Though frequently sarcastic and even arrogant, he could also be charming and witty with students. He said, "I am St. Thomas without the saintliness. I have been led by my doubts." But he expressed little uncertainty about where these doubts had led him.

Due to a tape-recording malfunction during our meeting, I have supplemented this section on Le Corbusier with some excerpts from recorded interviews on Radio Française. Following Le Corbusier's own observations are two views of the master by the architect Alfred Roth and the engineer and architect Paul Weidlinger, both of whom worked with him.

LE COUVENT SAINTE-MARIE-DE-LA-TOURETTE. Le Corbusier. *Eveux-sur-l'Arbresle, France. 1959. Located on a sequestered, gently wooded slope, the raw concrete building is a modern monastery with medieval power.*

1961

QUESTION: *You have taken France as your adopted country.*

LE CORBUSIER: Not my adopted country. I am of French origin, here for centuries. I am from the south of France, from Languedoc. I'm from the terrible persecutions of the thirteenth century, and they dare not say so because I've already built some pretty fair churches. The interesting thing about this is that those who were not massacred were able to escape. They climbed, and they established themselves there at all the high points. There they built Languedoc houses—farmhouses from the year thirteen hundred to the year fifteen hundred. This is why, as far as I am concerned, I have always had a great affinity for the southern regions, for the Mediterranean, and I have looked for an art which is Mediterranean amid the world corruption.

1958

My direct family, father and mother, influenced me by creating a harmonious environment, a simple milieu, dignified, not at all bourgeois. My mother played music. My father worked in the watch industry. He made white enamel dial plates, one of the most difficult artisan professions. I never had any desire to follow this career. My father never proposed for me to do so. My brother was destined for music. He gave his first concert at the age of eleven. The entire activity of the family concentrated on him. In the meantime I was left on my own. I was with my friends in the street. I followed my little path on my own.

I stopped school at age thirteen. Then, as I had a thing for drawing, I was stuck in a school called an art school. But the first day I came home and said to my parents, "Do you believe they want to make me a watch engraver!" My father said that it was a profession like any other. I was not at all pleased to engrave the bottoms of watches that were to be exported to South America. I came to the attention of a teacher, L'Eplattenier, who said, "Don't worry, we'll see what we can do with you." Then one day he said to me, "You will be an architect." I thought, "No way, I hate that." I based my opinion on what was being done around me, which I didn't like at all.

In my school a member of the commission wanted to build a house. I said to him, "I will design your house." He answered, "But you aren't an architect." I figured a house has to be done like anything else. I made some plans, which he liked. I was eighteen years old. I had my first skirmish with public opinion. It continued from then on. This experience allowed me to hold bricks in my hands, to weigh how heavy they are. I figured, "If I put one thousand one over the other, that's very heavy." It made me aware of the question of materials, the specific value of materials. It made me think of ways to overcome their resistance. I became an architect in the sense that is lawful with the Lord, though maybe not with the schools.

The money I made with this house, fifteen hundred francs, allowed me to go to Italy. Why Italy? To see things that are different. Why that rather than a school, as my father recommended? Because I didn't know what a school was going to teach me. I first wanted to have a look around. I bought a little Kodak camera. But then I saw that by confiding my emotions to the lens, I forgot to look myself. So then I said no. I dropped the idea of a camera. I took a notebook and a pencil since I have always

LE CORBUSIER *in his Paris studio, 1961*

TRAVEL SKETCHES. *Le Corbusier. 1911. Sketching was part of Le Corbusier's self-education in seeing, not just looking. His sketch pad became the source book of many of his later ideas.*

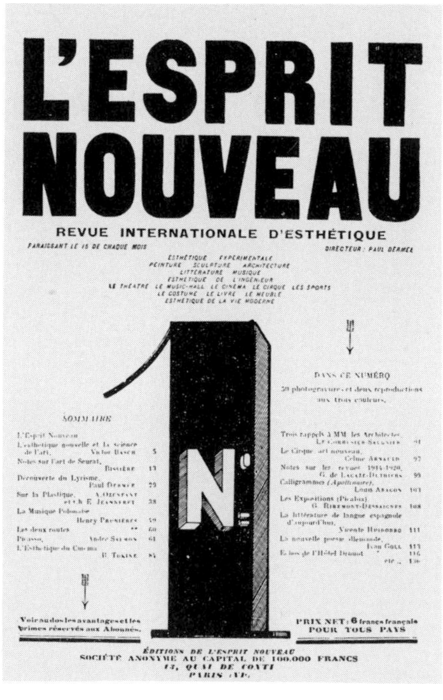

L'ESPRIT NOUVEAU. *No. 1, 1920. In this review Le Corbusier introduced his avant-garde architectural ideas with Amédée Ozenfant and Paul Dermée.*

drawn, everywhere, in the metro, everywhere. If it goes from my head to my hand then it's memorized, but if I only press a button then I don't participate. Then I went with my backpack on through Bohemia and the Balkans, as well as Greece, with the pretext of seeing the Greek works. I had the luck of never having been in school and to have at ages twenty, twenty-one, and twenty-two been to the Balkans, to Greece, to Turkey, to Asia Minor with my backpack. I traveled for seven months in all sorts of vehicles and saw architecture wherever I went. There were temples, and then for entire days there were farms, houses, buildings at all times around me. The most modest constructions of stones which made me say that folk buildings which took centuries to evolve are carriers of architecture.

In 1908 I arrived in Paris, where I knew absolutely no one. I had no contacts, no money, I didn't know where to go. One day by accident I found the artists' directory. I found the name of Eugène Grasset, who had reformed decorative art and who had impressed us in my school. I went to see him. He said that he didn't have the time to see me, but I insisted. I blocked the door with my foot—"I want to see you." I showed him my portfolio with my drawings from Italy. He looked at them and asked me to sit down. He looked at them with great interest. He started explaining a lot of things. He said, "I'm going to give you a compliment. You know how to listen and that's very important." He told me about the Perret brothers, who put concrete in boxes with steel and it holds. I went to see Perret with my drawings of Italy. He hired me immediately. He would say in a loud voice: "I make reinforced concrete." It was a proclamation that brought on him the hatred of people in the profession who accused him of not being an architect, of not having the right to claim that title.

I traveled some more. I saw Peter Behrens in Germany.

In 1918 I was one of the founders and directors of the review *L'Esprit Nouveau*, with Ozenfant and Dermée. At the last minute, when the proofs were done, Ozenfant said, "We should really do something on architecture." So I wrote something. I remember it was a Saturday evening. I wrote "Three Reminders to Architects." I decided to put the article under another name. I decided to sign it Le

Corbusier. My real name is Jeanneret. That doggone Le Corbusier was born that day. That article and the next made a lot of noise. The name Le Corbusier became known worldwide on the first day. The three reminders were: plane, volume, and surface. The article caused me a few problems with the profession. People said I lacked courtesy. But I was only pointing out things that are fundamental. This article exploded. We had letters from all over the world. People came to see Le Corbusier and I had difficulty believing I was the person in question.

In 1923 a businessman from the Bordeaux region wanted to build houses for eighteen thousand francs. I told him we would need a machine for seventy-five thousand francs. He was a little shocked. Then later he said to me, "I bought the machine. I bought the land. We can start with fifty houses." The guy tried hard, but he sowed hatred under his feet, jealousy, ferocity, and the most implacable opposition. I got splashed with it, too. We created the Cité de Pessac. It was a little paradise. But the water company refused to connect the water. The director of the company considered the houses to be inhuman and took it upon himself to refuse to supply the water. Thus the village remained unoccupied for eight years. In the meantime, the municipal council of Paris was studying what my German colleague, Gropius, a great architect, was doing in Dessau, where he was building houses inspired by Pessac. In its wisdom the municipal council decided to send a commission to study what was being done in Germany, while in France Pessac was slowly dying.

VERS UNE ARCHITECTURE. *Le Corbusier. Édition G. Crès, Paris. 1923. In one of the most influential books of modern architecture, Le Corbusier advocated a revolutionary architectural aesthetic based on the efficient modern machine. The English edition,* Towards a New Architecture, *was published in 1927.*

1954

Q.: *In 1925 you did the Pavillon de l'Esprit Nouveau for the* Exposition des Arts Décoratifs.

L.C.: They kicked me out. They refused to give me any land. In the end there was one piece that was left. A young guy from the administration called me and said, "Come, take it immediately." I told my draftsmen to occupy the land with their drawings for several days, which they did. So no one was able to steal it from me. I built the Pavillon de l'Esprit Nouveau, which is a fantastic avant-garde work for the period. The entire modular order of housing was created in it, with surprising pomp yet without any sumptuosity.

PESSAC HOUSING ESTATES. *Le Corbusier. Pessac, France. 1926. Despite political delays, Le Corbusier's first executed community plan, with one hundred thirty reinforced-concrete houses, had immediate international influence.*

LE PAVILLON DE L'ESPRIT NOUVEAU. *Le Corbusier with Pierre Jeanneret. Paris. 1925. Sited in a far corner of the* Exposition des Arts Décoratifs, *this two-story apartment showcased Le Corbusier's daring ideas for modern living.*

Voisin was the name of an automobile constructor and not the term "neighbor," as many people thought. They thought it was an illusion of optimism to call it that. The plan was done in 1925, no, 1922, and it is still waiting. However, events have passed and people's eyes are opening. The pavilion was ready in 1922, but the outside was shocking and naturally everybody screamed at the outside without bothering to see what was inside.

Currently the world is covered with pustules that are called big cities. They have become monsters, like New York and London and even Paris now. That is, of five,

VOISIN PLAN. *Le Corbusier. Paris. 1925. There was little chance Le Corbusier's many unsolicited Paris plans, such as this one with its cruciform skyscrapers, would be adopted, but they did promote his influential concepts of city planning.*

seven, eight million inhabitants—pure folly. These people finding only noise and bad smells in the city react with an attitude of everyone for himself. People fleeing the cities figure since they can't move around in their own city they might as well get out. They can cover forty kilometers out of the city faster than five kilometers in it. Cities are one hundred kilometers in diameter. The sun turns unrelentingly and people spend their time running after the sun and the sun after them. The meeting never takes place and the day lacks balance.

The point is, therefore, to try to get rid of the waste in the way the public travels, a terrible burden for people which costs a country fantastic sums and which finally deprives a society which has submitted to it despite itself.

HOUSE, WEISSENHOF EXHIBITION. *Le Corbusier. Stuttgart, Germany. 1927. This most ambitious and influential housing exhibition featured buildings by sixteen international architects. The house on pillars is one of three designed by Le Corbusier.*

Q.: *What do you propose?*
L.C.: To reinstall, in our machine society, the conditions of nature which have been disrupted. That is, sun, space, and greenery, which are the cosmic factors of life and without which we would die.

The new techniques bring about freedoms. You can now go where you couldn't in the past—the conquest of the horizons. Instead of having views onto other houses, building houses that are tall allows a liberation of grounds that can be counted in acres. Multiply the experience and you get a city that is green through your windows. They aren't even windows any longer. They're bays, loggias. You obtain wonderful views.

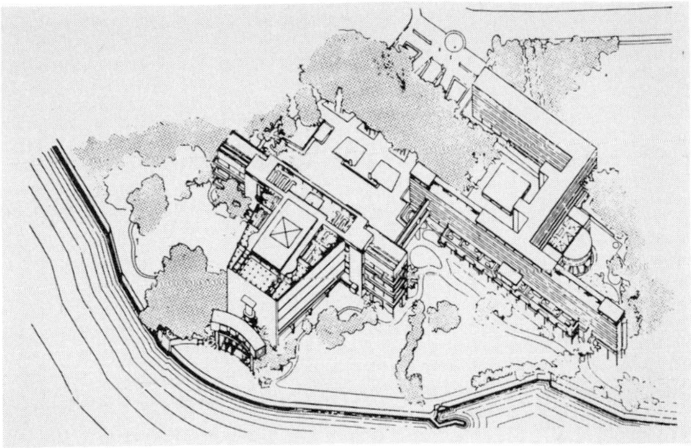

I won the first prize for the international competition for the construction of the building for the League of Nations. But one of the delegates, I won't mention names, had me pushed aside. They said my project was unacceptable because it was drawn with printing ink instead of India ink. That was enough for people to bow to the pressure. There was a worldwide protest.

LEAGUE OF NATIONS PROJECT. *Le Corbusier with Pierre Jeanneret. Geneva. 1927. Le Corbusier's imaginative entry to this worldwide competition presented a wedge-shaped assembly hall raised on pillars over a landscaped garden. The project was rejected on the technicality that the drawing was not done in India ink.*

1961

Q.: *You worked with the people who are building Brasília, with Costa who, some say, was your student.*

L.C.: No, Costa wasn't my student. He was my first adversary. When I arrived there in 1929, for three or four days' time, I made two reports on architecture. From that moment on, there was a faithful friendship.

In 1936, when he had the commission for the Headquarters of the Ministry of National Education and Public Health, that of the University City, he said, "I will not put up my building unless Corbusier has reviewed the plans. Then I will not make the plans for the University City unless Corbusier has done the initial one."

1962

In 1930 I tried to establish a doctrine of urbanism. My associate asked me: "What does V.R. stand for?" I answered, "Ville Radieuse." He asked me, "Why don't you call it something more solid, like 'Locomotive,' something that works." The critics who accuse us of building army barracks, Prussian towns, should be obliged to read my work before destroying it. Once they have read it, they will realize that the city is radiant and I don't give a damn about locomotives.

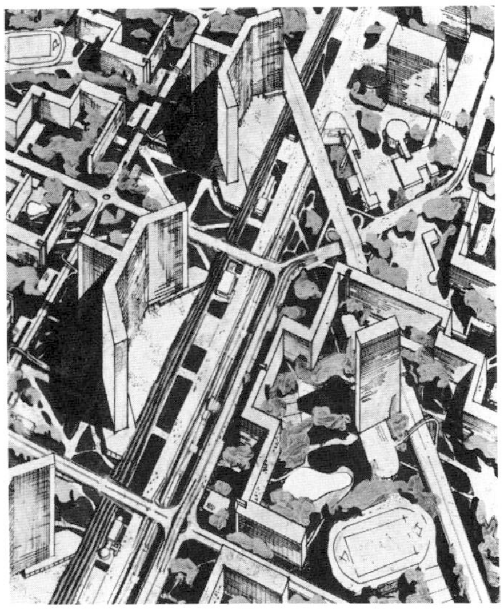

LA VILLE RADIEUSE, PLAN. *Le Corbusier with Pierre Jeanneret. 1930. Le Corbusier's visionary plan shows an entire parallel city of megastructures lifted on pillars above one great continuous park.*

I have thought a house alone in a city does not create the city, it destroys it. It is the immense illusion of people who want to have their house on the ground among the noise, the dust, and the dog droppings. Whereas by studying the problem in all of its aspects, I realized that I had to consider not the individual home that satisfies one family, but urban planning. That is, the other part, the collective, which is either a great constraint or a great liberation. That is the problem. There is the role of the artist to be a prophet, creator, inventor, and organizer of all the resources present in time to lighten man's load.

When a society wishes to build new homes, a new state of consciousness is born, the conscience of the machinist civilization. The fundamental premise of this architectural as well as social revolution is encompassed by the three fundamental elements that have since the beginning of time conditioned the life of man and which are sun, space, and trees. These three factors become the very condition of the immense reform that will take place in the uses of architecture. It is here that the failure is total. Cities have become inhuman, hostile to man, dangerous for his physical and moral health.

1961

Dautry was the first to show courage. One day after the Liberation, he called me in and said to me, "Corbusier, what town are you rebuilding these days?" I said, "None. What a question!" So then he said, "Nothing at all?" I said, "Nothing at all." He said, "Well, do you want to . . . Marseilles is planning a big thing." I said, "Certainly, Mr. Minister, but on one condition, that I be free from any and all regulations." He said to me, "Fine, fine, agreed, agreed!" For he's the only guy in the world to be able to build without regulations. It took five years and it was an incredible experience.

At the beginning, after the work had been under way for some time already, there was a newspaper headline that read, "All the architects of the Morbihan except one request that the government stop construction work immediately." So then, for four pages, disgusting, nasty rubbish. So I said to my secretary, "Listen, starting today I don't want to read one line on Marseilles till we finish." And I kept my word. I didn't read one line of a newspaper for five years. And some got on my case. They said, "Do you know what they're doing to you?" But I told them, "At least I have the satisfaction of being able to say that I haven't read them." So Marseilles is a big thing. It's considerable for the future.

I had said, "We will make the man of 1983." Well, the engineer who was in charge of the works was quite stirred up and said to me, "We cannot, we don't have the time. We are pouring in three days." I said, "You are not going to get me! Put that seat by the blackboard over there, and I'll design the frame myself." And while he was yelling, I was drawing. In half an hour I had drawn the two figures, chalked them in. It was life-sized, you know. I told the designer to put Decaze on it. I phoned Lagar, who had a workshop, and said to him, "Come tomorrow morning to get this. You bring it back tomorrow evening, we'll carve it the day after," because I had it carved in wood, five centimeters thick, and the trick was done! With all that, that moron then took four months to put it in a mold.

Marseilles is something for the future, instead of serving as a guideline of conduct to be adopted. I said, "People of Marseilles, do you want to raise your family in quiet? Do you want to raise them in conditions of nature? Do you want a totally private life, to meet no one, in complete intimacy? Good, well then, let two thousand of you get together, enter by a single door, take a bank of elevators consisting of four elevators. You go fifty meters up and that way you will have elevators available at all times, right? You will never meet anyone in the corridors that I call indoor streets. When you are in your apartment, through a fifteen-square-meter window, you will be overlooking the sea or the mountains." Two extraordinary sights which do not exist for any of the eighty thousand residents of Marseilles. They all live behind closed shutters. Marseilles is the city of closed shutters, not only the red-light district, but everywhere.

Whereas the Marseilles building which I made has three sides one hundred percent glass, but provided with sun protection. Sun protection with a veranda, which is the most traditional and most antique thing in the world. Old Socrates used to say, when you build your house put a portico in front of it. In the summer it will keep you in the shade, but in the winter, when the sun is low on the horizon, it will enter in all the way. Well, I was told that after I finished Marseilles, because I don't read Socrates every day. Actually, not at all, though he may be superb, I don't have the time.

In any case we now see that everywhere, under the influence of largely American lack of constraint and thoughtlessness, the curtain wall has been invented. They did this in the United Nations building, which they stole from me. They did not want to put a sun shield on it, because that would have looked like Corbu, right? So they invented the curtain wall, which simplifies things so much that they say, "This is fantastic. This is very modern." There is no protection from the sun and in temperate countries the sun is as hostile as in tropical countries in certain seasons, isn't that so?

Air-conditioning costs a ridiculously high price. It doesn't keep the sun from coming in. There is the example of UNESCO—the same thing, and the Family Allowance Building. There is a revolt on the part of the personnel. People don't want to work there anymore, right?

A few months ago, six months, last winter, the faculties of the university asked me to speak at the Sorbonne. There were forty-five hundred people there and fifteen hundred in the street who had to go home. I spoke fairly well, like a colleague.

You see, in this genteel country of Descartes—where Descartes emerges only after his death, because then posthumous studies can be published, right?—here, inventors are relentlessly pursued. This makes up the quality of France because this country is somewhat hard, difficult. It gives its value to Paris, for Paris is a city, the first city in the world all in depth, all in profound amazement, right? Except in the thirsty soil you cannot plant roots. You choke on it. It's a place of lusts, of fierceness, a terrible place.

1959

Q.: *How did you receive the commission for Ronchamp?*

L.C.: It's guys from the Monuments Historiques who gave me the contract. Jardot, the inspector at the Monuments Historiques. Young guys, who are reviving the administration of the Monuments Historiques. It's a rather peculiar site. It's a hill above the valley of the Saône and has always been a location for places of worship, occupied long ago by pagan temples, and then with the advent of Christianity by churches. They were always destroyed, throughout the centuries, without stop, in 1871, in 1914, 1939, and at the Liberation.

The bishop's council met to discuss the chapel project, which was not going any further. They were giving up when someone said, "Go ahead, say the name!" and he said, "Well, what about Le Corbusier?" They said, "Well, maybe." Then the archbishop said to the priest, "Go see him and see what he's like." So the guy came to my

NOTRE-DAME-DU-HAUT, INTERIOR. *Le Corbusier. Ronchamp, France. 1955. Light entering through the wedge-shaped stained glass windows in the side walls gives the chapel a remarkably spiritual atmosphere.*

house. I said, "I don't care about your church, I didn't ask you to do it. And, if I do it, I'll do it my way. It interests me because it's a plastic work. It's difficult. Twenty years ago I was asked to do one, but I refused. Now I think I would like to do it." He was so enthusiastic he gave a very good report to his bishop.

So I went there and looked at the land. I won the local people over, the priest, the sister of the priest. I said so many silly things to make them laugh. They must have thought that I'm not a very serious guy. Then I went on the site and seriously worked like a slave for several hours the way I know how to. I made it a work of art.

Q.: *Do people like it?*
L.C.: Ah, that I don't know. There are twelve thousand pilgrims twice a year; a mass is given inside for the initiated and a mass outside for the crowds.

Q.: *What is the capacity inside?*
L.C.: Only two hundred. There is a place above the sacristy for music. They will be able to make incredible music, an unbelievable sound when they have twelve thousand people outside, with amplifiers. I said to the priest, "You should get rid of the kind of music played by an old maid on an old harmonium—that's out of tune—and instead have music composed for the church, something new, not sad music, a loud noise, an unholy din."

I had the burned stones left from the church before the war. They couldn't carry anything, but I still didn't want to get rid of them. I made curved walls so that they would hold. This curve is useful for acoustics. It is an acoustic of space that receives the four horizons, all different from each other. In it there is a gesture, not a sign, not an artificial tool created by centuries of decadence. For instance, I put the cross in a very significant place. At first it was in the wrong place. It was in the axis, it looked solemn. No, it looked silly. Then I put it to the side like a witness, and when you think that they crucified someone on it, that is dramatic.

Q.: *Later, in 1921, there was the Monastery of La Tourette.*
L.C.: I had been very interested because Father Couturier had explained to me the Dominican ritual which is eight hundred years old and very human. Naturally they had no money. People always come to me and say, "I have no money, but do something nice." The church that is part of the whole that is a box. There is a sense of proportion in it, a radiant spirit, a feeling of harmony. It is built with the most fantastically simple materials that can be. Never did anyone build in a more direct fashion. I was a little curious to see how it would turn out.

When I went to the inauguration ceremony with the solemn mass and the wonderful Gregorian chants that were sung in it, I was delighted. The goal was met. I think it made a great impression on everybody there. Even the archbishop of Lyons, who made a little speech, said that he was converted to Le Corbusier, because until this day he had always thought of Le Corbusier as a devil. He realized that I can create an art which is perhaps not religious, but an art of places of prayer and meditation, which is the phenomenon and the manifestation of the sacred in the human heart.

Q.: *Are you still in agreement with what you wrote on the Modulor, for instance?*
L.C.: It's part of the definition I gave of taking care of man. There's a famous man, Luca Pacioli, who around 1400 wrote *De Divina Proportione*, On Divine Proportion, that came from the past, from the Egyptians, the Pythagoreans, etc. Well I brought something new to this golden number because of the metric system that came from the French Revolution. Before that they had the foot-thumb measures. It was based on the human scale, whereas now with the metric system we've lost all that. So the metric system of measurement is depersonalized. We have dehumanized our system of measurement. The meter, the tenth of a meter are not proportions that are linked to the human scale. Well, I linked the Modulor to the human scale. I took the proportions from the solar plexus of man to his head and raised arm, I found the Golden

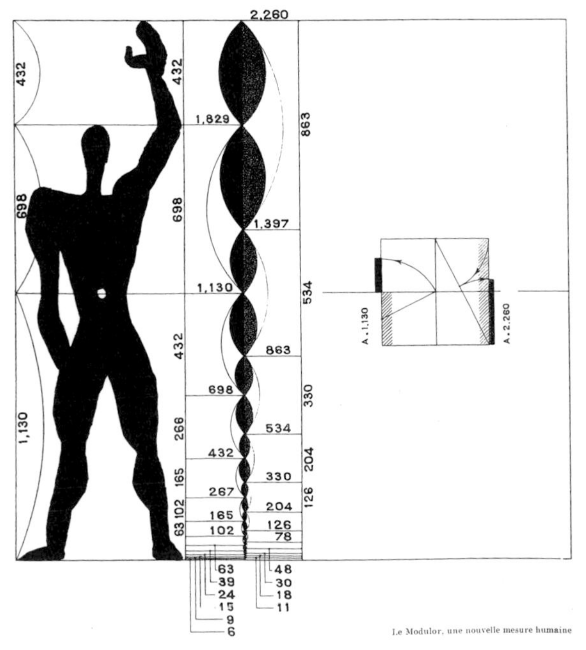

LE MODULOR FIGURE, SECOND VERSION. *Le Corbusier. 1955. This version of Le Corbusier's proportional system based on the human body is convertible from meters to feet and inches.*

Section in that and created a dimensional system that answers all of the needs of man, seated, standing up, lying down, etc.

I happened to find that system by chance. I am without pretensions naturally, but it is very important and opens to industry unlimited possibilities, a tool of modern times. An inexhaustible source of amazement to see that a piano made to human measures is an incredible innovation.

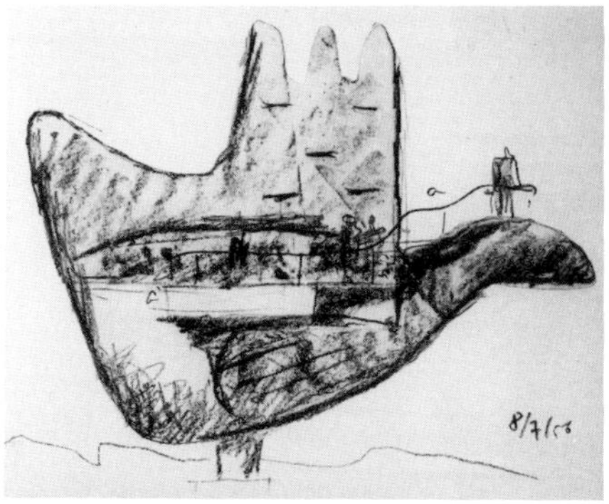

THE OPEN HAND, SKETCH. *Le Corbusier. Chandigarh, India. 1956. Le Corbusier's monument for Chandigarh's Trench of Consideration is a symbol of democratic dialogue.*

Q.: *What is the meaning of the upraised hand like that of the Modulor figure to be erected in Chandigarh?*

L.C.: It is the expression of a philosophy, in all modesty, the fruit of a life of studying, of fighting, of defeats, and possibly of victories as well. The open hand was present between Nehru and myself from our very first meeting in Delhi on. Over the years the open hand became the crowning element in the Trench of Consideration, which is a tool for the discussion of public matters separate from what the established authorities designated. This basin was dug at the top of the city and was dominated twenty-eight meters above by the hand, which explodes in the sun with the Himalayas as a backdrop.

This Trench of Consideration—consideration because things are considered, thought about—contains two seating tiers, for the two sides of a discussion, the duality of opinions. There are seats for those who are to speak on a given evening. The podium for the speaker has a sound shell to project and spread the speaker's voice. Over all of this, the hand mounted on ball bearings, so that it turns with the wind, not as a weathervane, but to express what is life itself, the constant changes that are part of daily life, that are valid and which must be taken into account. I have made only one political gesture in my life: that is the open hand. People said it was anticommunist. I say, no, it is the hand that gives, that receives, that distributes, a sign of optimism in the face of a world that is in a state of catastrophe.

Q.: *Could you have conceived of your architecture without the existence of concrete?*

L.C.: Concrete developed, from 1920 to 1960, in forty years in a prodigious way, allowing us to make curves, etc., which we couldn't do before. The concrete of Auguste Perret at rue Franklin, a wooden framework, was the starting point. Whereas now we make forms with concrete. So I take advantage of these resources. Why not?

I wrote in *When the Cathedrals Were White* that with stone and no cement people in the Middle Ages built formidable arches and vaults. We, with our extraordinary materials—steels, cements, etc.—were frightened of architecture. Engineers sometimes showed us some courageous constructions. Our vocation lacked the intimate contact with the modern techniques brought to us by the nineteenth century, and on which the twentieth century now focuses, which can solve architectural problems ranging from happiness in the home to great constructions intended for crowds.

Pierre Jeanneret and I did some extremely revolutionary things. They amazed people. Friends instinctively rallied whereas others shouted, "What?"

CARPENTER CENTER FOR THE VISUAL ARTS, HARVARD UNIVERSITY. *Le Corbusier with José Luis Sert, Huson Jackson, and Ronald Gourley. Cambridge, Massachusetts. 1961. Le Corbusier's only building in the United States is a statement of his late architectural ideas. With winding ramps and articulated spaces he made the most of the restricted site.*

Q.: *How do you feel about ornament in architecture?*
L.C.: I have been at war with decoration for a long time. My youth was spent doing decoration and since then I have become hostile to the whole idea. It is excessively superficial, pasted on. It takes on obsessive and immutable space. In public buildings its purpose is to consecrate public figures and that is understood. We don't need to look at them all day long. But in a dwelling an element of decoration is there at all times. It becomes obsessive. I often noticed that people who live in a house with decoration don't even see it anymore. That is sad, and I dream of people who are stimulated.

Q.: *Then should painting and sculpture be banned?*
L.C.: Ah, this is a journalist for you. You always distort what we say. Not at all. Look at art history in general, decoration in temples, in palaces—that is a frightful distortion. It is a serious fault. We have around us natural emotions which are very beautiful. That is why I require intense art and won't tolerate mediocrity. There is art and not Art Deco. Art is the way of doing things well. Decorative art is doing things quickly, making noise, approximations.

I prefer a pebble on the beach made by the Lord or a butterfly or an old bone if it's cleaned by the ocean, than an object representing doves embracing or an ashtray representing saints of the church. I am an architect. I work in planes, profiles, and sections. Well, a bone gives you all of that. A bone is an admirable object which is made to resist all shocks and to support dynamic efforts. A bone is a very subtle object. The section of a bone can teach a lot. I still have a lot to learn. I have had a weakness for seashells ever since I was a boy. There is nothing as beautiful as a seashell. It is based on the law of harmony, and the idea behind it is very simple. It develops in a spiral or it rays out, both in the interior and exterior. You can find these objects everywhere. The point is to see them, to observe them. They contain the laws of nature and that is the best instruction.

UNITÉ D'HABITATION.
Le Corbusier. Marseilles, France. 1947.
The brise-soleil facade of Le Corbusier's famous ferro-concrete apartment house protects the occupants from the strong southern sun.

1961

Q.: *In summary . . .*

L.C.: In this morning's paper, *L'Humanité,* on the first page, a headline saying that Le Corbusier is passé, that young people are turning away from Le Corbusier, that he is history. You are not going to write my eulogy, are you?

I would have to reply this way, that for thirty years I have not built a single housing unit in Paris. Yet I am the man who has addressed the housing problem everywhere in the world successfully, because, in short, while these ideas are appreciated everywhere, here I am treated strangely.

If I have the right to a little public recognition it is not because I have built palaces, even though I did build a few, but because as soon as I approached the problem of architecture, I had the feeling that the home was the temple of the family and that there was something noble in working in that direction. There is in that a great part of human happiness. I don't know why I feel obliged to concern myself with human happiness, but I would just as soon approach the solution of such a problem to bring to it this vital factor of life which is joie de vivre.

ALFRED ROTH ON LE CORBUSIER

1961

It happened on Christmas. Mr. Moser came to my drafting board and said, "My dear friend Roth, I have no more work for you. Why do you not go to work with Le Corbusier in Paris?" Corbusier was just then working on his famous project for the international competition for the League of Nations building in Geneva and he asked Professor Moser for students or young architects to help him to finish his drawings.

Well, I went to Paris and entered Le Corbusier's office. There I found a completely new world of architecture. An architect who works in a close relationship with painting since he is himself a painter. It was a new world and that was the decisive moment for me to say, yes, now I'm going on the way of an architect. I discovered myself there as an architect. I was completely, what would you say, taken, passionately taken, by the idea of architecture of that type by Le Corbusier. Paris was an intensive center, not only Corbusier, there were other architects and Picasso. I met all these people. Then I met Piet Mondrian as a very young man, you know. But there, in Paris, I made the decision to stop painting and to go on with architecture. I was convinced from that moment that it was the right way.

At that time, '26, Corbusier was nearly an unknown. His two first books were published—*Vers une Architecture* and *L'Urbanisme*. They were just published, '25, '24—no translations, so they were rather unknown. We knew about Le Corbusier. [Karl] Moser told us a little about Le Corbusier, but he was not the famous man at that period that he had become later on.

During that period for us, the younger generation, the Bauhaus was rather a stronger attraction. Germany, Holland, were stronger attractions than Paris and, in fact, I had already written a letter to the Bauhaus and wanted to go there. They accepted me to go not on the basis of my architectural work, since I had done nothing at that period, but I sent them some photographs of my paintings. They accepted me, but I did not go. I went on to Paris and I was indeed very fortunate with Le Corbusier. After the work of about only two months he sent me to Stuttgart.

In '27 the very famous first international exhibition of modern architecture and art in Europe and in the world was held in Stuttgart. He had to design two houses there. Since I spoke German, I was of very great service to him to prepare his plans for Germany. He sent me to Stuttgart to supervise the building of these two houses. I was obviously very young. I had very little practice, just a new, fresh diploma in architecture from Zürich. I stayed through the whole summer to build his two houses and that was again, for me, a wonderful experience because in Stuttgart the international elite of modern architecture and art met at this exhibition. So I came in during the very early years, at the very center of the modern movement in Europe. Mies van der Rohe was the chief architect. Gropius designed two houses. Stam from Holland, Oud from Holland, Le Corbusier from France, Frank from Vienna, and some two other Germans. It was a wonderful period.

I was twenty-four. World War I was over. It was a wonderful period of optimism. Everybody was convinced there would be no more war and ideas and everything was spreading out. It was a creative atmosphere in Europe which produced the work of the twenties, which is really one of the great periods of the modern movement in Europe and in the world.

Also in Stuttgart I published my first booklet, a small publication on the two houses of Le Corbusier, which I wrote in Stuttgart. It was printed just for that exhibition. It was then sold in the exhibition. It was the beginning of my publishing work.

But the fact was that Corbusier never came to Stuttgart. He left me completely alone in Stuttgart to handle these two jobs in a very short time. He never came to the exhibition. The drawings were somewhat detailed in Paris and then designed by myself when I was still in his office. The rest I did in Stuttgart in an improvised little office. I sent them back to him, he made some corrections and sent them back to me. Then he wrote me a letter with such things as you do not have to bother about the furniture, I shall send you our most recent designs of chairs and tables and beds. Nothing arrived. I had to design them myself. He sent me a letter, I shall send you paintings by myself, by Fernand Léger, maybe by Picasso to decorate my rooms there in Stuttgart. Nothing came.

For the color schemes I sent him perspectives of the rooms and the outside. He sent the drawings back with very small samples of colors. He cut them out of wallpaper collections and stuck them on the plans. They were one centimeter by one centimeter. Out of that I had to do the whole room. He never came to the exhibition. He went to Stuttgart weeks after the exhibition was already closed.

That's typical Le Corbusier. He was quite pleased with the work I did. He found that maybe somewhere a color was a little bit too strong, but that was natural. He was quite pleased, but that was typical of Le Corbusier. He has wonderful ideas, but he does not care too much about carrying out these things. When he sent me to Stuttgart, for him, everything was over. It was done.

PAUL WEIDLINGER ON LE CORBUSIER

1989

Moholy-Nagy said something very important. It influenced me a great deal. He said, "Why don't you go and work for Le Corbusier?" At that time that was an impossible thing. People used to pay a fee to work there. He said, "I'll write to him and I'll arrange that you don't have to pay. You can work for free." I said to him, "Well, you know, Le Corbusier, it's like working for God, I will never see him and what do I get out of being there?" He said, "You are absolutely wrong, go there even if you never talk to him, just breathe in the air, look at the drawings on the wall, listen to what other people say, it will be very important." He was right in a way. It sounded convincing. I think in my youth it's probably the only advice I ever followed from a grown-up.

Maybe when I think about it, it's the reason why I say I don't know about individual buildings, I know only about the work. Because I learned it there. It was a large office. I was amazed by what was going on there. I saw things which I never heard about. People were designing cities! They were designing countries! It was incredible. It was wonderful to be there.

I mean this is all very personal. Le Corbusier is very typical, you know. He, all of a sudden, changed his whole direction, perhaps a lot of uproar and upset about him. I understood that. I mean, here's a guy who's trying to do something and all of sudden, he said, maybe I was doing it wrong and I'm trying to do it this way. That's what excited me about that work, not a particular building. I couldn't pick out and say this is a great building. I don't know how to do that, I'm not good enough. But I can look at his work and I can look at his process and that I understand. I didn't work that closely to him.

1956

The best advice I think I learned from Le Corbusier. I received that advice from him many years later in connection with the Pan American competition, which I had won at the time as an architect. I was supposed to execute the buildings, build them as an architect and an engineer. When I was just about ready to go, the committee who sponsored this huge university city came to me and suggested that I modify my design completely and put all the buildings on top of each other, make it a skyscraper and what have you. I refused very indignantly to change my ideas and the committee proposed that I write to Corbusier as an arbiter and ask him what he would think about such a proposal. I wrote to him and he wrote a wonderful letter. He said, "All my life I've been dying to get a project like you have and my advice to you is just to do anything they tell you as long as they let you build." This was the day when I stopped being an architect and became an engineer. I am still very grateful to him for it.

1989

When he was in New York he pretended he didn't know English. I used to hang around with him and act as an interpreter. We had conversations and some odd ones, because ninety percent of the time I totally disagreed with everything he said. But almost one hundred percent I agreed with what he did. When this whole United Nations thing started and he just published his Modulor book. When we met he said, "Ah, you are a mathematician. What do you think about this great work?" Like an idiot I told him, "Master, this was published, I think, in the eleventh century by Leonardo Pisano called *Tillio Bonanci*. Everybody knows that. It's a great thing, but this is old hat. I don't know what it does." He got incredibly angry at me. He said, "You don't always know enough. I have to meet a new scientist." He, in fact, said, "I'm going to make an appointment with Einstein. I'm going to show him that." This was ages ago. I was very upset because Einstein was working on the general theory that he had only a few years to live. I said, "Please don't go and bother him." But, of course, he didn't listen. He disappeared for a few days and I didn't see him.

All of a sudden he appeared in my office. He called me in, unrolled a big roll, and pasted it on the wall. At that time it was not so easy to make an enlargement. He went to see Einstein to show him the Modulor, explained it to him, and Einstein, you know, he was a very nice person, said, "This is wonderful." Le Corbusier said, "Write it down." So, he wrote something to the effect that, "The Modulor is wonderful. It makes the beautiful easy, the ugly difficult." Corbusier had it photostated and he pasted it on my wall and he said, "Look at it, this is what Einstein says."

Ludwig Mies van der Rohe

"I CANNOT TELL YOU AT THE MOMENT WHERE I READ IT, . . . THAT ARCHITECTURE BELONGS TO THE EPOCH AND NOT EVEN TO THE TIME, TO A REAL EPOCH."

Ludwig Mies van der Rohe was an imposing man with a hewn-granite face. His attire—usually a Saville Row suit—as well as his surroundings had the same sense of quality and elegant style as his architecture. We recorded Mies at his suite in the Waldorf Towers in New York in 1955 and at his Chicago apartment in 1964. This undistinguished building was located not far from his celebrated Lake Shore Drive apartments. When I asked him why he did not live in one of the Lake Shore apartments, he replied with a hearty laugh that he did not think it was a good idea for an architect to be traveling in the same elevators as the occupants of one of his apartment buildings. His spacious five-room apartment was sparsely furnished with large, comfortable leather chairs, and a wonderful collection of art by Paul Klee, Georges Braque, and Kurt Schwitters hung on the bare white walls.

Mies was not given to conversation. With his somewhat monastic life-style, it was almost as if he had taken the vow of silence. There is more blank tape on his reels than on those of any other architect in the Oral History. My questions were sometimes followed with a noncommittal "Ya," or with such a long pause that I felt compelled to ask another question.

ILLINOIS INSTITUTE OF TECHNOLOGY. *Ludwig Mies van der Rohe. Chicago. 1939–56. The site plan for this one-hundred-ten-acre urban campus and eighteen of its beautifully proportioned buildings, employing a common module and materials, were designed by Mies when he was director of the Architecture Department at IIT.*

However, in several sessions, amid clouds of Havana cigar smoke and innumerable double Gibsons, I gathered enough comments and reflections to surprise some of his closest associates, to whom his statement, "Less is more," applied also to their infrequent discussions.

In our conversations Mies left no doubt about his beliefs. He articulated them with unmistakable conviction. With patience and persistence, he followed his own architectural vision. Though the many adjectives—solid, unswerving, honest, unyielding, rational—used to describe Mies are true, I was repeatedly struck by something else—the emotion and enthusiasm with which he expressed his ideas. It is only in person or in listening to the recordings that one can appreciate this side of him.

For the most part Mies let his buildings speak for themselves. However, on occasion he quoted philosophers discovered in his lifelong search for meaning in architecture. In one session he repeated St. Augustine, "Beauty is the radiance of truth," and added, "I think that is a wonderful motto for architecture. It has to be truthful, otherwise I don't believe it is really beautiful."

Following Mies's own words is a view of the man by Philip Johnson, one of his closest architectural associates.

1964

JOHN PETER: *What first interested you in architecture?*

LUDWIG MIES VAN DER ROHE: I learned from my father. You know, he was a stonemason. He liked to do good work. I remember in my hometown in Aachen was the cathedral. This octagon was built by Charlemagne. In different centuries they did something different with it. Sometime in the Baroque they plastered the whole thing and made ornaments in it. When I was young they took the plaster out. Then they hadn't the money to go further so you saw the real stones. When I looked at the old building that had nothing on it, just fine brickwork or stonework, a building that was really clear and with really good craftsmanship, I would have given all the other things for one of these buildings. Later they covered it with marble again, but I must say it was much more impressive without the marble.

J.P.: *Tell me, were you influenced in your thinking by things other than architecture—music, or painting?*

L.M.V.D.R.: Yes, it may have been later. But not when I was young, you know. I didn't have any relation to other arts particularly.

J.P.: *Did reading have anything to do with your thinking?*

L.M.V.D.R.: Yes, quite a lot. You know, I left school when I was fourteen years old. So I had no education. I worked for an architect. When I came to his office, he said, "Here is your table." I cleaned it up and looked in the drawer. . . . What I found there were two things, a magazine called *The Future*. It was a weekly magazine. It was a very interesting magazine. It was partly a political magazine, but in the way as Lippmann would talk about politics, not a party affair. It was a cultural magazine, let us say that. It talked about music. It talked about poetry. It talked about architecture, but very seldom. That was one thing.

Then I found another pamphlet about the Laplace theory. That was these two things, you know. From there on I started to read this magazine, *The Future*. I bought that every Sunday morning and read it. Then I started to read.

A few years later, when I came to Berlin, I had to build a house for a philosopher. It was at the university in Berlin. There I met quite a number of people and I started to read more and more. When this philosopher came to my office the first time—I had an office in my apartment, my books were lying on a huge drafting board, about a foot high. He looked around and he saw all these books—he said, "For Heaven's sake, who advised you on your library?" I said, "Nobody. I started to buy books and read them." He was very surprised, you know. He saw no discipline in it or anything like that.

At that time, we were working for Behrens. There were other architects in Berlin. Messel, he was a very fine architect, but a Palladio man or something like that.

I was interested in what is architecture. I asked somebody, "What is architecture?" But he didn't answer me. He said, "Just forget it. Just work. You will find that out by yourself later." I said, "That's a fine answer to my question." But I wanted to know more. I wanted to find out. That was the reason I read, you know. For nothing else, I

LUDWIG MIES VAN DER ROHE
in New York City, 1955

wanted to find out things, I wanted to be clear. What is going on. What is our time and what is it all about. Otherwise, I didn't think we would be able to do something reasonable. In this way, I read a lot. I bought all these books and paid for them. I read them in all the fields.

J.P.: *Do you still read?*

L.M.V.D.R.: Yes, I do. And I read very often the old books. The New York Chapter of Architecture once had some affair going on. I said, "When I left Germany I had about three thousand books. I made a list and they shipped me three hundred." I said, "I could send back two hundred seventy. Thirty is all I wanted to have."

I was interested in the philosophy of values and problems of the spirit. I was also very much interested in astronomy and natural sciences. . . . I asked myself the question, "What is the truth? What is the truth?" until I stopped at Thomas Aquinas, you know. I found the answer for that.

So, for other things, what is order? Everybody talks about it, you know, but nobody could tell you what it is. Until I read Augustine about sociology. There was a mess as great as in architecture then. You could read a lot of sociological books and you were not wiser than before.

J.P.: *Do you feel that the thinking of people who sought truth in other periods is applicable today?*

L.M.V.D.R.: Oh, certainly, I am sure. There are certain truths. They don't wear out. I am quite sure of that. I cannot talk for other people. I just followed what I needed. I want this clarity. I could have read other books, you know, a lot of poetry or others. But I didn't. I read these books where I could find the truth about certain things.

J.P.: *Did your father or mother influence you in thinking this way?*

L.M.V.D.R.: Not at all. No. My father said, "Don't read these dumb books. Work." He was a craftsman, you know.

1955

J.P.: *Were there great works or great masters who influenced your own thinking about architecture?*

L.M.V.D.R.: Yes, there is no question. I think if somebody takes his work seriously and even if he is relatively young, he will be influenced by other people. You just cannot help that, you know. It is a fact.

First of all, I was influenced by old buildings. I looked at them, people built them. I don't know the names, and I don't know what it was . . . mostly very simple buildings, you know. When I was really young, you know, not even twenty years old, I was impressed by the strength of these old buildings because they didn't even belong to any epoch. But they were there for one thousand years and still there, you know, and still impressive, and nothing could change it. And all the styles, the great styles, passed, but they were still there. They didn't lose anything. They were ignored through certain architectural epochs, but they were still there and still good as they were in the first day they were built.

Then I worked with Peter Behrens. He had a great sense of the great form. That was his main interest; and that I certainly understood and learned from him.

"A GREAT STYLE MAY BE EXPECTED IN COMING TIMES. A STYLE WHICH SHALL NOT SIMPLY BE BEAUTIFUL BUT WILL ONCE MORE BE ABLE TO ATTAIN SUBLIMITY."

Hendrik Petrus Berlage

J.P.: *By great form what do you mean?*
L.M.V.D.R.: Oh, let us say like the Palazzo Pitti. It is something, the monumental form. Let me put it this way, I was lucky enough, you know, when I came to the Netherlands and I was confronted with Berlage's work. There, was the construction. What made the strongest impression on me was the use of brick and so on, the honesty of materials and so on. I never forget this lesson I got there just by looking at his buildings. I had only a few talks with Berlage, but not about that. We never talked about architecture together.

J.P.: *Do you think he knew that you sensed what he was doing?*
L.M.V.D.R.: No, I don't think so. I cannot see any reason why he should have because we didn't talk about it. I was really a young boy then. But I really learned this idea from him. I must have been open for this particular view because of the old buildings I had seen.

And I learned a lot from Frank Lloyd Wright. I would say that. I think more as a liberation, you know. I felt much freer by seeing what he did. You know, the way he puts a building in the landscape and the free way he uses space and so on.

J.P.: *Then those were the influences in your approach to architecture?*
L.M.V.D.R.: But my architectural philosophy came out of reading philosophical books. I cannot tell you at the moment where I read it, but I know I read it somewhere, that architecture belongs to the epoch and not even to the time, to a real epoch.

Since I understood that, I would not be for fashion in architecture. I would look for more profound principles. And since I know by reading and studying books that we are under the influence of science and technology, I would ask myself, "What can that be? What result comes from this fact? Can we change it, or can we not change

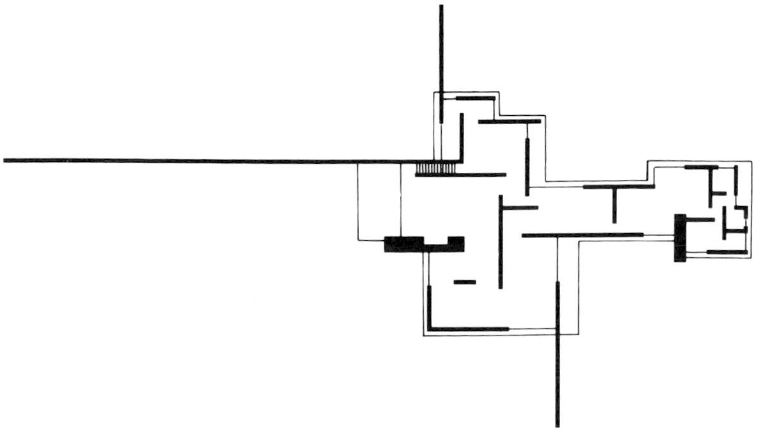

BRICK COUNTRY HOUSE PROJECT. *Ludwig Mies van der Rohe. 1923. The floor plan of the house shows a De Stijl influence and extends Frank Lloyd Wright's ideas for free-flowing interiors with walls running into the landscape.*

it?" And the answer to this question, you know, gave me the direction which I followed, not what I liked. I throw often things out I like very much. They are dear to my heart, but when I have a better conviction, a better idea, a clearer idea, then I follow the clearer idea. And after a while, you know, I find the Washington Bridge most beautiful, the best building in New York. Maybe at the beginning I wouldn't. That grew. But first I had to conquer the idea and later I appreciated it as beauty.

J.P.: *So you sought what was characteristic of the epoch.*

L.M.V.D.R.: What is the essence of the epoch. And that is the only thing we really can express, and what is worth to express.

There is another thing that just comes to my mind. Thomas Aquinas, he says, "Reason is the first principle of all human work." Now when you have grasped that once, you know, then you act accordingly. So I would throw everything out what is not reasonable.

I don't want to be interesting. I want to be good.

You know, you often find in books, they have nothing to do with architecture, the very important things. Erwin Schrödinger, you know, the physicist, he talks here about general principles, and he said the creative vigor of a general principle depends precisely on its generality. That is exactly what I think about when I talk about structure in architecture. It is not a special solution. It is the general idea.

Sometimes people say, "How do you feel if somebody copies you?" I say that is not a problem to me. I think that is the reason we are working, that we find something everybody can use. We hope only that he uses it right.

J.P.: *In other words, copies are an affirmation that you have found a general solution.*

L.M.V.D.R.: Yes, that is what I call the common language, too. That is what I'm working on. I am not working on architecture, I am working on architecture as a language, and I think you have to have a grammar in order to have a language. It has to be a living language, but still you come in the end to the grammar. It is a discipline. And then you can use it, you know, for normal purposes and you speak in prose. And if you are good at that, you speak a wonderful prose, and if you are really good, you can be a poet. But it is the same language, that is the characteristic. A poet doesn't produce a different language for each poem. That's not necessary; he uses the same language, he uses even the same words. In music it is always the same and the same instruments, most of the time. I think that is the same in architecture.

You know, if you have to construct something you can make a garage out of it or you can make a cathedral out of it. The same means, the same structural methods we use for all these things. It has nothing to do with the level you are working on. What I am driving at is to develop a common language, not particularly individual ideas. I think that is the biggest point in our whole time. We have no real common language. To build that, if possible, if we can do that, then we can build what we like and everything is all right. I see no reason why that should not be the case. I am quite convinced that will be the task for the future.

I think there will be certain influences, climatic influences, but that will only color what is done. I think a much greater influence is the influence of science and technology that is worldwide that will take all these old cultures away and everybody will do the same. Just this light coloration.

J.P.: *In other words, you feel we are in a period where there can be an architectural vocabulary?*
L.M.V.D.R.: Oh, certainly, there's no question about that. I think that this is a human desire to do something reasonable. I see no difference if there is something reasonable in California, in the Mediterranean, or in Norway. They should do it with reason. If they would work with reason and would not have fancy ideas, particularly architectural ideas, everything would be much better.

J.P.: *You would say that the people recognize a reasonable and honest approach.*
L.M.V.D.R.: Certainly. Let us take an example, the mechanic in a garage today. He is very much interested in all the technological means we have. He takes that all for granted. You have no personal ideas about these things. You know, when he sticks to that, then he is on the common plane.

J.P.: *Do you mind working with engineers?*
L.M.V.D.R.: No, just the opposite, I love it if I get a good one. There are things that cannot be done without engineers. You cannot know everything. I think architects should understand more about engineering and the engineers should know a little more about architecture.

J.P.: *Will new materials greatly change the style of our times?*
L.M.V.D.R.: No, I don't think so because what I tried to do in architecture is to develop a clear structure. We just are confronted with the material. How to use it in the right way is what you have to find out. It has nothing to do with the shape. What I do, what you call my kind of architecture, we should just call it a structural approach. We don't think about the form when we start. We think about the right way to use the materials. Then we accept the result.

Grand ideas, you know, we keep high in the air when we are working. We don't want them to come down. Often we are ourselves surprised what comes out of it. I

NEW NATIONAL GALLERY. *Ludwig Mies van der Rohe. Berlin. 1966. This masterpiece, located in the city of his youth, was one of Mies's final works. The great steel roof is supported on eight massive steel columns erected on a lower gallery pedestal. Glass walls enclose the resulting undivided, universal space.*

collect the facts. All the facts as much as I can get. I study these facts and then I act accordingly.

J.P.: *Maybe one of the problems of Wright's style is that it is not a vocabulary in that sense.*
L.M.V.D.R.: It is not that. It is much too individualistic in order to be that. We know he's a genius. There is no question about that. But I think he cannot have real followers. In order to do things as he does it, you need a lot of fantasy and, if you have fantasy, you will do it differently. I am quite sure it is an individualistic approach and I don't go this way. I go a different way. I am trying to go an objective way.

J.P.: *Have there been architects of the past who have developed a style that lasted as a vocabulary?*
L.M.V.D.R.: Palladio, certainly. You know, it lasted. It is still among us in certain cases. Even though his forms have changed, his spirit is still there in many cases.

J.P.: *Do you think there is a desire on the part of people for natural materials that are in a sense rich? For instance, I've always felt disappointed that the Resor House was never built.*
L.M.V.D.R.: Yes, I was sorry, too. I think it is a very good building.

J.P.: *Do you think these rich materials tend to give a humanity to it?*
L.M.V.D.R.: It is not necessary, but it can be rich. But it is not necessary. It could very well be simple. It would not change that.

J.P.: *You mean the Resor House wouldn't have had to be built with teak?*
L.M.V.D.R.: No, it was not necessary at all. That could have been in any other kind of wood and still be a good building. It would be not as fine as teak.

In fact, I think that the Barcelona Pavilion, if I would have built it in brick, it would be as good a building. I am quite sure it would have been not as successful as marble, but that has nothing to do with the idea.

J.P.: *What do you think of the use of color in architecture?*
L.M.V.D.R.: In our IIT campus I painted the steel black. At the Farnsworth House I painted it white because it was in the green. It was in the open. I could use any color, you know.

J.P.: *And you've even been known to chrome it as you did in the Barcelona Pavilion.*
L.M.V.D.R.: Oh, certainly, yes. I would do that. I love natural materials or metallic things, you know. I very seldom have used colored walls, for instance. I would really like to give it to Picasso or to Klee. In fact, I ordered from Klee a large picture, two pictures, one side white and the other black. I said, "I don't care what you paint on it."

J.P.: *So if it were a problem of color you would give it to a master.*
L.M.V.D.R.: Oh, certainly, yes. I would do that.

1964

If I were subjective I would be a painter, you know, not an architect. There I can express anything I like, but in buildings I have to do what has to be done. Not that I like it particularly. Just what's best to be done. I often throw out ideas I was in love with, but when I thought it through I just had to throw them out. That is the difference. It is not so much the function. You cannot be really subjective. It looks funny in buildings. You have to be good, a stonemason or a timber man. There is nothing funny about that. In painting you can express the slightest emotion, but with a beam of wood or a piece of stone you cannot do much about it. If you try to do much about it, then you lose the character of your material. I think architecture is an objective art.

J.P.: *What was the Bauhaus? Why did you associate your own name and talents with it?*
L.M.V.D.R.: I think Gropius could answer this question best because he was the founder and to me that is the Bauhaus. He left the Bauhaus and gave it into the hands of Hannes Meyer. At this time it became more a political instrument or was used not so much by Hannes Meyer but by younger people. Hannes Meyer, in my opinion, was not a strong man. He was taken in by these young people. I can understand that, too. But there was a certain difference. You could say that was the second phase of the Bauhaus, quite different from Gropius's phase. The Bauhaus from '19 to '32 was no way one affair. It was quite different.

I came to the Bauhaus when the Bauhaus had trouble for political reasons. The city, which was Democratic or Social Democratic, had to pay for it. They said we will not do that anymore. Gropius and the mayor of Dessau came to me. They explained that to me and asked me to take it over. They thought if I would not do it, it would be closed. I went there and made it clear to the students, as clear as I could, "You have to work here and I can assure you who doesn't work I will throw out. I have nothing against any political idea that is here." I spent my time to teach them something and they had to work on it. But I was not so involved as Gropius was. That was his idea. We were working in the same direction.

At Gropius's seventieth birthday I talked about the Bauhaus. I said that I didn't believe that it was the propaganda which made it known all over the world, but that it was a new idea. Propaganda would never be so strong as to do this work. But I think Gropius can tell you more about it than I can.

J.P.: *Would there have been a Bauhaus if there had been no Gropius?*
L.M.V.D.R.: No, I think there would not have been a Bauhaus. There would have been another school. The school was there when it was in Weimar. If I'm not mistaken, I think that Gropius was proposed by van de Velde, who was the head of the school in Weimar. When he left Weimar he proposed Gropius as his successor.

Getting the different people was Gropius's doing. There is no doubt about that. He brought these people. He must have seen that these people were driving in a different direction, too. But that they were good people, that was Gropius's doing.

J.P.: *How important to the Bauhaus was the climate of the Werkbund?*
L.M.V.D.R.: That may have had an influence. Gropius was one of the leading people in the Werkbund, particularly so, say, after 1910. There was this Werkbund exhibition in Cologne where he built one of the important buildings. I think his building and van de Velde's theater were the real buildings there. He certainly was very active in the Werkbund. There were other people, not often architects, but craftsmen. They tried to use good materials. They had a sense of quality. . . . I had nothing to do to the Werkbund then. I came much later. It was in '26 when I came to the Werkbund when they gave me this job to do, the Weissenhof exhibition.

J.P.: *Has working in America changed what you think or what you do?*
L.M.V.D.R.: I think you are always influenced by your environment. There's no doubt. I think that teaching helped me a lot. I was forced to be clear to the students. You know, students are funny people. They perforate you with questions. You look like a sieve. You have to make it really clear and you cannot fool them. They want to know and you have to be clear. That forces me to think these things clear through so that I could answer them. I think teaching had this influence. It was in the direction I was going anyway.

J.P.: *So that was not a waste of time as far as you were concerned?*
L.M.V.D.R.: Oh, no, no, on the opposite, I think it was really good. I don't think you have to build a thousand houses or a thousand buildings. That's all nonsense. I can make a statement about architecture with a few buildings. If I would do nothing else that would make absolutely clear what I mean.

I remember the greatest impression I had the first time in New York, that an elevator could take you up in no time, fifty stories high and really hit it on the head. I was very much impressed by that.

J.P.: *You once mentioned the Pennsylvania barn.*
L.M.V.D.R.: Yes, the good Pennsylvania barn, I really like better than most buildings. It's a real building and the best building, for that reason, I know in America.

The Washington Bridge, I think, is a fine sample of modern building. It's direct to the point, you know. Maybe they had ideas about these towers, but I'm talking about a principle and not about that. But to go in this simple straight line from one bank of the Hudson to the other, this direct solution, that is what I am driving at.

There's something else. We use in German the word *Baukunst*, that are two words, the "building" and the "art." The art is the refinement of the building. That is what we express with Baukunst. When I was young, we hated the word architecture. We talked about Baukunst, because architecture is that you form something from the outside.

S.R. CROWN HALL, ILLINOIS INSTITUTE OF TECHNOLOGY. *Ludwig Mies van der Rohe. Chicago. 1955. This exquisitely detailed steel structure is one vast undivided room raised a half a level above grade and enclosed by transparent and translucent glass. In Crown Hall Mies realized his concept of a universal space.*

J.P.: *Would you say that a characteristic of Baukunst has always been a certain reasonableness?*

L.M.V.D.R.: Yes, at least that is what I like in Baukunst. Even though we had to make a lot of Baroque things when I was young, I was never much interested in Baroque architecture. I was interested in structural architecture, I was interested in Romanesque, I was interested in Gothic architecture. They are often misunderstood. You know, the profiles of a pillar in a cathedral, that is still a very clear structure. The refinements were to make it clearer, not to decorate it, but to make it clearer. People think when they see one of these buildings, they say it is too cold. But they forget what they are asking for because, they think, that is too strong an order. They have it on Michigan Avenue, on the lakefront, everywhere. That is what they really ask for. They are not clear about it. They ask for chaos. But there can be a richness. It has not to be a chaos. I think you can use clear elements and make it rich. Any medieval city used the same plan all over. What was the difference was the doorknob or bay window and that depended on the money they had. But the plan was about all the same. They had the stable culture.

1964

J.P.: *What about technical developments?*

L.M.V.D.R.: People are surprised that I used construction in different materials, but that to me is absolutely normal. In the one case the roof plate is a real plate and has to be supported. It doesn't matter if you build it in steel or in concrete. Nearly all the cathedrals have the same structural principle. What is wrong in that? You can change. You need not copy it really, but you can use it as a structural principle.

That was, in fact, our idea when we started to work. We wanted to develop new structural solutions which could be used by anybody. We were not after individual solutions. We were after good structural solutions. We are not hurt if somebody uses that. We are hurt if the somebody doesn't use them well. There are certainly many

GLASS SKYSCRAPER, MODEL. *Ludwig Mies van der Rohe. 1921. In this and other experimental designs, Mies sought with all glass walls to reveal the structure of the building and to explore the play of reflections on curving glass.*

more unknown students of mine than direct students. But certainly I am not hurt at all. On the opposite, that is what we tried to achieve, and we did it. There is no doubt about that.

J.P.: *And your sketches for the glass skyscraper?*
L.M.V.D.R.: That was another problem. There I was interested in glass and what can be done with glass buildings. I tried to avoid certain glare or dead front. So first I bent these large pieces so that they had the character of a crystal. Under no circumstances was it a dead solution. Then later I thought that maybe it could be much richer if I would make it fully curved, but they were just studies in glass. I was thinking about a building all right, but that was a particular study in glass.

J.P.: *As far as the buildings you now build, are they more characteristic of steel or of glass?*
L.M.V.D.R.: Some people say the Seagram's Building is a bronze building. They don't talk about a glass building because there is so much metal there. I think that there are glass buildings, but that is when one works the problem through.

J.P.: *When you use concrete you waive the plasticity of concrete?*
L.M.V.D.R.: The plasticity of concrete, that is very funny. The plasticity of concrete is not necessarily the best way to use concrete. I think I use concrete, if I use it, in a structural manner. What I call a structure. I know you can use it in another way, but I don't like the other way. I still like it for building a clear structure. I don't care about the plastic solutions. I just don't.

J.P.: *Even in your chairs?*
L.M.V.D.R.: See, that is the same. The chair is an arc chair with this half circle in front of it. That is a skeleton structure, you know. Even the Barcelona chair is still a

skeleton structure. I made some designs in plastic chairs. I didn't follow them up. There I used the mass, you know. If you want to use a plastic material, then you have to use the mass. But because you can form the concrete, it is not necessary to form it in a plastic manner. It's just because that is a possibility you can do it.

You see, when we used aluminum, there you can use extruded materials. When we used it for the first time we tried for our mullions. Then we hung it on the roof of 860 to see how it reads. I tell you that the simple I-beam worked much better. That is why we used, even in aluminum, the I-beam structure. It reads better. It is much clearer.

J.P.: *You say clear. Do you think there's a relationship between clarity and goodness?*
L.M.V.D.R.: Yes, to me, certainly. Yes, I'm quite sure about that.

J.P.: *If you had lived in another period might you have used . . .*
L.M.V.D.R.: Oh, certainly, if we didn't have other materials, but we have steel. I think that this is a fine material. By fine, I mean it is very strong. It is very elegant. You can do a lot with it. The whole character of the building is very light. That is why I like it when I have to build a building in a steel construction. What I like best is when I can use stone on the ground and then come up a little.

J.P.: *Do you like steel because of the factor of economy?*
L.M.V.D.R.: It is an economy factor, but it is not an architectural factor. It is a factor here in our country. When you have to build something, you take a sheet of paper

SEAGRAM BUILDING. *Ludwig Mies van der Rohe with Philip Johnson. New York City. 1958. Mies's first major office building was a thirty-eight-story tower richly sheathed in bronze and boldly set back from Park Avenue on a broad granite plaza. It is a master statement of a modern building type, the skyscraper.*

and write down what the site costs, the architect's fee, the engineering fee, and God knows what we get back. If that is not twelve percent or fifteen percent, it will never be built. That is the economical question you were talking about. Not the greatest idea will be built if it is not economical in this sense. . . . I am not talking about this economy. I am talking about a spiritual economy, the economy of means. The clearest sentence is, to me, economy. That is the economy that has an influence on architecture.

You can build in concrete. There are the Maillart bridges in Switzerland that are wonderful bridges, very clear. I have nothing against that. But if you build in steel it gives you a lot of freedom inside. People say, "Ah, that is cold." That's nonsense, you know. Inside you can really do what you like. You are free to do something. But you are not free outside.

You have to remember in an enclosed building you have a few floor-plan possibilities. When you really work in one of our buildings you will come to the conclusion there are only a few good solutions. They are limited even though you could do anything you like.

J.P.: *However, if the use of the building changed, say the museum building became for some reason a century from now . . .*

L.M.V.D.R.: Yes, it could be something else. I would not hesitate to make a cathedral in the inside of my convention hall. I see no reason why not. You can do that. So a type, like the convention hall or like the museum, can be used for other purposes just as well. . . . This is not anymore that the form follows function or should follow function. I am, anyway, a little dubious about these statements, you know. There was a reason when somebody said it. But you cannot make a law out of them. . . . You very well could make an apartment building from an office building. They are similar in the fact that you have twenty or thirty floors one on the top of the other. That is the character of the building, not to talk about what is inside. In an apartment building you may use, for economical reasons, smaller spans or something, reduce the size, but you could very well live in an office building with the large span and have a fine apartment in that.

The sociologists tell us we have to think about the human beings who are living in that building. That is a sociological problem, not an architectural one. That always comes up, you know. But that is a sociological question. I think the sociologists should fight that out. That is not an architectural question.

J.P.: *And can't be solved architecturally?*

L.M.V.D.R.: No. It could be solved if they would give us a program. But first they have to prove that their idea is a sound one in the sociological field. They would like to make us responsible for that, you know! No, not with me!

J.P.: *When I look at these projects I have been struck by the fact that there is a sense of continuity in your work. Is there a relationship?*

L.M.V.D.R.: It is always the same problem. It is only that in one case you have just, say, walls to work with and, in this group of buildings, you have to have buildings to work with. But it is the same problem. You find a good relation among them, you know. It's always the same. It is a very simple problem. We had in our school a space problem which every student had to go through and work on, and that is the same for a small apartment as it is for a hotel or a bank lobby. There is no difference in these. It is the same problem.

J.P.: *Is it the same for a city plan, almost?*
L.M.V.D.R.: I would say yes. You know, in city planning you have the traffic problems, but in itself it is the same problem. It is a very simple problem of the good relation of one to another. In some we had first a free plan and then we were bound by streets, so it became a geometric plan, not a free plan. But you can make a free composition or a geometrical composition just as well. In principle there is no difference in it.

J.P.: *But the fact that streets are a gridiron, does this tend to suggest a . . .*
L.M.V.D.R.: Certainly, to me it suggested a geometrical solution. Not that I am for it out of principle, but that is what I have to work with. That is a material to me, you know. I can make a building or a group of buildings. I can make it symmetrical or I can make it asymmetrical, that is just what the problem is about. Some people think it has to be asymmetrical: that is not the case, you know. Maybe they are tired of a lot of things, and they just try something else.

I remember when I made the symmetrical solution, somewhere, and I was told, now we have to learn again that there can be symmetry. But the symmetry was the reasonable solution, not that I particularly liked it or not liked it. That was the reasonable solution for this purpose. I would not hesitate to do that, you know. I think that is more an aesthetic speculation. I don't care much about these things.

J.P.: *In regard to your buildings—the Krupp office building for instance?*
L.M.V.D.R.: The Krupp is an enormous skeleton building. If you use a skeleton you would come to a similar solution. You can do something that is not similar but of form is the same. The skeleton is just a skeleton.

MELLON HALL SCIENCE CENTER, DUQUESNE UNIVERSITY. *Ludwig Mies van der Rohe. Pittsburgh, Pennsylvania. 1962. In this science building, in pure Miesian style, he introduced space beneath the floors to accommodate the mechanicals supporting the laboratory equipment.*

FEDERAL CENTER. *Ludwig Mies van der Rohe. Chicago. 1964. The three black steel-framed buildings of varying heights and bulk, masterfully grouped around a large central plaza with a flaring red stabile by Alexander Calder, are one of Mies's finest works.*

The Duquesne is a laboratory. Since we did not know what would be inside, we thought we would give a possibility to let the pipes go wherever they like to go. We made the first lab building in Chicago, the Metals Building, that was kind of a laboratory, but it was not a chemical laboratory. There we used glass on the outside.

J.P.: *Do the plans for Montreal, Toronto, and the Chicago Federal buildings have something in common?*
L.M.V.D.R.: We put the buildings so that each one gets the best situation and that the space between them is about the best we can achieve. They all have that in common. Even if I would build a group of single houses, I would use the same principle there. Only that the space between them maybe would be smaller.

1955

J.P.: *You once told me how the Barcelona Pavilion evolved around a slab of marble that you found.*
L.M.V.D.R.: Since I had the idea about the building and I had to look around. We had very little time. It was deep in the winter. You cannot move marble from the quarry in the winter because it is still wet inside and it would freeze to pieces. You had to find a piece of material which is dry. We had to go and look around in huge depots. There I found an onyx block. This marble block had a certain size so I had only the possibility of taking twice the height of the block. Then making the pavilion twice the height of the onyx block. That was the module.

J.P.: *Would you be interested in doing another exhibition type of building?*
L.M.V.D.R.: You know, I went through a lot of different possible types of building.

There are only a few left. I would like to do this convention hall. This is an enormous building, seven hundred twenty feet by seven hundred twenty feet. I would like to see it myself. I know the drawings. I know the idea behind it. But, in fact, there is a certain size that is a reality. Take the pyramids in Egypt and make them only fifteen feet high. It is nothing. There is just this enormous size that makes all the difference.

J.P.: *Do you feel in the Seagram Building on Park Avenue that the size of the sheer wall going up will have a lot to do with its impact?*
L.M.V.D.R.: Yes, I am quite sure. Because of its simplicity, again, it will be much stronger. Some other buildings are much higher and richer in the grouping and so on. I think, at least that is what I hope, that the Seagram's Building will be a good building.

I must say that when I came first to this country, I lived at the University Club. I saw the main tower of the Rockefeller Center every morning from my breakfast table and it made a great impression on me. That slab, yes. It has nothing to do with style. There you see that it is a mass. That is not an individual thing, thousands of windows, you know. Good or bad, that doesn't mean anything. That is like an army of soldiers or like a meadow. You don't see the details anymore when you see the mass. I think that is the quality of this tower.

1964

J.P.: *You set the Seagram Building back at a time when nobody else set buildings back.*
L.M.V.D.R.: I set it back so that you could see it. That was the reason. You know, if you go to New York you really have to look at these canopies to find where you are. You cannot even see the building. You see only the building in the distance. So I set it back for this reason.

J.P.: *Why was the material bronze?*
L.M.V.D.R.: We used bronze because of the client. Just in the talk we had, he said, "I like bronze and marble." I said, "That's good enough for me!"

J.P.: *In designing your building the way you do, somehow the Seagram respects other buildings like the McKim, Mead, and White building across the street.*
L.M.V.D.R.: Oh, certainly, yes. The Lever House was there when we started. When we moved the building back we didn't know what would happen on each side of it. After the Seagram's Building was finished, there you had the Lever House and the Seagram's Building, so it was quite easy to set back the next building that is right between them. But they didn't! That was so funny. That was a great help for any architect, but that is just what happens, you know.

J.P.: *Unlike the Seagram Building, the two Bacardi buildings were different problems.*
L.M.V.D.R.: Yes, it was certainly a different site. The first building in Cuba, the client wanted to have a large room. That is what he liked. He said, "I like to have a desk in a large room. I like to work with my people. I don't need a closed office

BACARDI ADMINISTRATION BUILDING. *Ludwig Mies van der Rohe. Mexico City. 1957. With walls of gray glass, exposed steel columns painted black, and a setback entrance hall, the office block of this refined building is raised above the nearby highway.*

because I work more than anybody else, so it doesn't hurt me that they see me." We tried to solve that.

But in Mexico there were two factors which changed the character of the building. The one was that the highway is higher than the site. So if we would have built a one-story building there, you would see only the roof. That was the reason that we made a two-story building there. It was a more normal office building because the leading people insisted on separate offices.

J.P.: *How important do you regard historical influences?*

L.M.V.D.R.: I am not interested in the history of civilization. I am interested in our civilization. We are living it. Because I really believe after a long time of working and thinking and studying that architecture has, in fact, only to do with this civilization we are in. You know, that is really what architecture is about. It can only express this civilization we are in and nothing else. There are certain forces that are in contrast to each other. But if you really look at it, you'll find leading forces, sustaining forces, and you'll find superficial forces. That is why it is so difficult to give a definition of civilization and to give a definition of our time. In older civilizations the superficial forces are gone. Only the deciding forces become historical forces, the exceptional forces.

Often you cannot make a definition of something. But then you see something that strikes you in the bones. You know that is it. You cannot express it, but that is it. It's like if you meet somebody who is healthy. What could you say, but you know when somebody is healthy or not. That is what I find so important, particularly in the time we are in now when this Baroque movement is going on. You call it Baroque or whatever. But I think it is a form of Baroque movement against the reasonable, the direct. In particular, in the time where there is confusion, what could be leading if not reason? That is why we were trying so hard since the '20s, the early '20s, to find what is a reasonable way to do things. There were people who had a lot of fantasy and sculptural interest in the Jugendstil and the Art Nouveau period. They all were, more or less, fantastic. But very few were reasonable then. I decided when I was quite young to accept this reasonableness.

1955

J.P.: *Do you think that new ways of living will change things?*
L.M.V.D.R.: No, I think in principle it will be the same. It can be richer as it develops. You know, that is very difficult just to make something clear. Then express it in a beautiful way. They are two different things. But first it has to be clear. I cannot help it if somebody wants to have forty-story apartments and the apartments have to be all the same. I can only try to express it in a way that it really comes out and that in the end it is beautiful.

J.P.: *Are you optimistic about the future of architecture?*
L.M.V.D.R.: Certainly, I am. I am absolutely optimistic. I think you should not plan too much and not construct too much these things.

J.P.: *So do you envision a time later when a person working from your architectural style may evolve a richer . . .*
L.M.V.D.R.: I would not even use this word style for that. I would say if he would use the same principle, the same approach. Then he, certainly, if he is talented he can make it richer. That depends, but it would be in principle not different.

There is obviously visible now a reaction to my approach in architecture. There is no question, but I think it is just a reaction. I don't believe it is a new approach. It is a reaction against something that is there. The reaction is a kind of fashion.

COLONNADE PARK APARTMENTS. *Ludwig Mies van der Rohe. Newark, New Jersey. 1960. In the first building built under Newark's redevelopment program, Mies placed five hundred sixty units along a single central corridor, providing half of the tenants with a view of the Manhattan skyline and the other half with a view of the adjacent public park.*

1955

I'm working with Mies van der Rohe. I've known him for some thirty-five years and I was his biographer.

The elegance of simplicity always attracted me to Mies. His Barcelona Pavilion, the simplicity of which I found only one other place in the history of architecture, and that is in the Temple of the Sphinx and the entrance to the pyramids in Egypt. It's done entirely differently, but it's what you can do with the least possible means for the maximum effect. His slogan "Less is more" means that you'll get the greatest effects by the simplest means, and that is the highest form of art to him. . . . That appealed to my Puritan spirit. Somehow I thought we could gain richness through simplicity. I don't think you can take Mies's words for really what he means. Maybe he has more emotional content with glass than he admits, but there's no doubt that time, light, cold and heat, and those things don't appeal to him. His emotion is taken care of with the shape of the space involved.

There's no reason why the ground floor of Seagram's is twenty-four feet high instead of twelve feet high. In fact, it's unreasonable from a financial point of view. But he never even told anybody how high it was. It was just that high. Nobody ever asked. Of course, if it was put up by a developer like the Uris brothers they would have asked. But it's just that was that.

1963

He once told me, as sort of being off the record, that he had the H in mind first for the mullions, because it was a rolled section, you see, in the steel buildings. . . . When he came to the bronze building or aluminum, there was no point to keeping the H-section at all for the mullions. Then he tried other shapes. He used to make them out of wood and hang them on his window and look at them. He said, "Philip, we came back to the H-section." Although it's an extruded thing, you can extrude any shape you want. . . . I can analyze it after the fact that, without his consciousness, what he was doing was creating another plane, another skin now eight inches out from the other side. But he didn't know that, I don't think. I don't think he's that articulate and conscious of his own motives. You see, to me, he is a very emotional man who does these processional things with his passion, and then afterwards says, "All I did was build as simple as possible the thing you could have asked with durable materials. You must admit, Philip, that bronze is more durable than iron that you have to paint." He comes back to those simple reasons. Whereas his real impulse is just as passionate as any other architect's, of course.

He's very much like Mondrian because they're exactly the same age and were good friends. I mean it's perfectly natural that this would be exactly what he wanted. Yes, he wanted to restrict his palette. "Less is more," all very Mondrian, very much his time.

Mies has much more of an idea for processional space than he admits because ver-

bally he always talks about good building, "*gutes bauen*." . . . However, in the Seagram Building, for instance, you walk at an angle always across the plaza. He made that plaza very wide, wider than I would have proposed it. So that you walk up or down the avenue. You can't walk across it, because it's a street with a barrier in the middle, you see. So, you cross at an angle in Seagram's. . . . But once in, you go like a bee to your own elevator. There's no doubting. There's no twisting. There's no turning. There's no looking up at signs. It's the only building in New York where the elevators are turned the way they are. I remember when he said that, he said to me, "Philip, we will not turn the elevator bank, no matter what that does to the practicality of the rooms above. You must walk from the street to your elevator." It's that kind of sense of clarity which I inherited from him.

SEAGRAM BUILDING. *Ludwig Mies van der Rohe with Philip Johnson. New York City. 1958. The meticulous and masterful detailing of this celebrated Manhattan skyscraper reveals why the word Miesian was introduced into the vocabulary.*

1986

There's no question about the historical roots of this modern movement, but the fact that it was carried furthest by a couple of very great geniuses is interesting. Corbusier and Mies. There were very good people on the side. There was J. J. P. Oud, who was my best friend because he talked language you could understand. He was an intellectual. Mies wasn't and Corbusier wasn't. But they were geniuses. But, you see, people didn't believe that. People believed that Mies, and Mies himself believed, that Mies was something you could learn. It was too bad that you can't learn Mies. I never could, so why should anybody be able to? I'm as good a pupil as you can get.

Walter Gropius

"THE BAUHAUS WAS MUCH MORE THAN A SCHOOL OF ART OR ARCHITECTURE. WE REALLY HAD AN APPROACH TO A NEW WAY OF LIFE."

Walter Gropius looked and spoke like a professor. His conservative tweed jacket and bow tie bespoke the campus, and his considered, measured words had an educator's tone. Characteristically, to assure the accuracy and precision of some of these recorded remarks, he read a portion that he had prepared ahead of time.

Gropius fits the professorial image so perfectly, and so much has been made of his educational contribution to modern architecture in establishing the Bauhaus and heading the Department of Architecture at Harvard, that his talent as a creative architect is frequently underestimated. Gropius's pioneering works, the Fagus Factory in Alfeld-an-der-Leine and the Bauhaus at Dessau, were remarkable buildings that had significant impact on the shape of architecture. The Chamberlain House in Weyland, Massachusetts, which he designed with Marcel Breuer, became the prototype of small modern cottages in New England.

I first met Gropius through his daughter Ati, who once worked with me. He smiled when I told him that as a youngster in Seattle I discovered one of

GROPIUS HOUSE. *Walter Gropius and Marcel Breuer. Lincoln, Massachusetts. 1937. In his first building in the United States, Gropius imaginatively combined Bauhaus design with the vocabulary of traditional New England residential architecture—brick chimney, screened porch, fieldstone foundation, and wood clapboard, painted white but applied vertically.*

the Bauhaus books and hid it behind the other books in the museum library so others would not find these incredible ideas. I later learned that the Bauhaus, the atom bomb of modern design, was a poorly kept secret.

We recorded Gropius in his Lincoln, Massachusetts, home and in the Brattle Street, Cambridge, offices of TAC, The Architects' Collaborative. Both the modest house and the name of the firm reflected his quiet but solid convictions about modern architecture.

1964

JOHN PETER: *You studied where?*

WALTER GROPIUS: I studied for a while at the so-called Technische Hochschule. But I didn't go to the end because I got fed up with it. The students queued up with their work, then either the professor or the assistants sat down, drafted a little bit in that design, connecting his own stuff onto the student's design. Then, we took it under our arm and went away, until the next time, we came again. So it was not our work, and it was just absolutely childishly done. One day I turned around to say, "I don't do that anymore," and went into practice. That was the architectural school in Berlin. The classic order was the first course, which didn't mean anything. There was a big revolution due.

1955

My teacher from whom I learned most was Peter Behrens. He was the architect of the AEG, the big electrical concern in Germany. He built some of the factory buildings and some office buildings which really showed the new trend in daring construction and different use of materials. At least, it was the beginning of this line.

1964

Behrens was a personality. He was very clever in many fields, you know. He also went into industrial production. He did many things for the AEG. He did all the products for them. I took part in it myself and it turned out very well. So this was a very good school for me. It was definitely fundamental for what I did later.

J.P.: *Would you say that Behrens, to an extent, is one of the sources of the Bauhaus idea?*
W.G.: Well, perhaps that goes a little bit too far. I mean, the direction, the working together with industry was very much in Behrens. He came from painting. He was not an educated architect. He was a painter and made layouts and so on. Then, all of a sudden, he started to build a house for himself in the colony in Darmstadt. Then he became interested in architecture, and as a layman he marched into it. He was a talented man, he made something out of it.

I was in his office for quite a while as his right-hand man and we did all these things together. He was my master.

1955

I learned from the practical man in the field. As the foreman of these men I learned something of building. I cannot separate building from designing. I think the architect should be well trained in all the technicalities and know them. Of course, the field is so large today that one man cannot know all these things, but the main things he can absorb, then use specific materials and specific constructions where they fit best.

J.P.: *Did anybody give you any architectural advice?*
W.G.: There are so many things, you know. I mentioned Peter Behrens, who was my master, though I, perhaps, have gone beyond what basic things I learned from him which were most valuable to me. Then, of course, reading and seeing other things, as well as a personality like Le Corbusier, who really has a great hand in the development of modern architecture and a consistency in the development, has also made an impression on me.

Also, in my early times, I saw a lot of things of Frank Lloyd Wright, who interested me very much. Of course, in the philosophy of architecture I am on another limb than he is. He is very strongly an individualist whereas I am very much in favor of teamwork. I think that the field we have to see today is so large that it is impossible to have everything in one head. I dare say that even a genius, if he understands how to develop teams around himself and lead these teams, that the spark that he can give can come more to the fore. It can be used better when he has many team helpers

WALTER GROPIUS *at his office in Cambridge, Massachusetts, 1955* than when he is all alone in an ivory tower by himself.

J.P.: *Do you recommend this notion of teamwork to your students?*

W.G.: When I started these things with my students, they were very much in agreement. When I checked the next day, everyone was in another corner and their connection was not forthcoming. We have to train ourselves to do these things, but I think it is a definite necessity and it is now building.

I believe that not only in our field but everywhere the alignment of many groups will come more and more. For instance, I just came across a very interesting case recently. New Jersey did a very good thing as to traffic and roads. But it has put some neighboring states in the greatest traffic difficulties. You have to relate to the neighbors and to the whole country. With our exchange of traffic, we are bound to line up with our neighbors and, in the end, with the whole world.

Architecture is coming more and more into the field of planning. Seeing the whole community build up organically is more and more necessary because the community is really the projection of the whole life of a certain region. We have to line up with everyone in that region to know what to do. That doesn't mean that the architect, who is by nature a coordinator, because he works with so many people in building and in planning, has to bring the architect into the most important spot on the team.

Twenty-five years ago the best European architects on the modern line joined hands and built up the so-called CIAM, the Congrès Internationaux d'Architecture Moderne. There we developed from the bottom up the whole approach to rebuilding our communities. First, by making very broad and very deep analysis in thirty-five different countries. Then, in the end, building up what arts were necessary for it. . . . Now, after twenty-five years, we want to put the CIAM into the hands of the younger generation. Next Sunday I have a meeting here with Canadians and with people of this country preparing for the next congress, which will take place in September in Algiers.

So it is already on the way, that responsible architects think very much in terms of the whole community. I have always told my students, "I am not interested when you

FAGUS FACTORY. *Walter Gropius and Adolph Meyer. Alfeld, Germany. 1911. With an early steel frame and free-standing glass curtain walls, this shoe-last factory was a pioneering development in the International Style.*

build a beautiful design in a gap of a street if you have treated it only as a unit in itself, not considering the neighborhood which is already there. You have to blend in with the larger circumstance. This larger circumstance is the main thing and all limited objectives have to be subordinated to the whole."

PACKAGED HOME SYSTEM, PLAN. *Walter Gropius with Konrad Wachsmann. 1942. This innovative house of bearing wood panels and metal wedge connectors, designed for the General Panel Corporation, suffered the disheartening fate of all prefabricated home ventures launched at that time.*

J.P.: *Have you seen in your time a development that makes you optimistic about this?*
W.G.: I definitely have. But I should say that when I was a young man and started out with these things, I thought we would do it for three years, everybody would accept it. But I see now that such a process goes much, much slower because I think the inertia of the human heart is too great. Man sticks, particularly in our time where everything has changed, to some visual things he has inherited from his grandpa and he doesn't let it go.

1964

J.P.: *What was the Bauhaus and how did it begin?*
W.G.: Early in my life I discovered that there was so much discrepancy in art and architecture that I felt that if a man really wanted to make a dent he couldn't do it alone, but that it would be necessary to build up a whole school which would take as their task to investigate into all the conditions of the present time and find a new approach to all the problems. Out of that came the Bauhaus, which I didn't do alone but with a group of a lot of well-known people today, like the painters Klee, Kandinsky, Moholy-Nagy, Lyonel Feininger, and others, and out of that we built a method of approach how we should prepare our students for life. It was much more than a school of art or architecture. We really had an approach to a new way of life. The students took part just as much as the faculty of the institute. I must emphasize that even seen from today this was not an attempt to create a style or dogma or so. On the contrary, we fought heavily against doing that. We wanted to find a proper research process, an open process which remains open and is still open today. Because it was not for this or that personality, but we tried to find an objective means of informing the younger man how he should approach all these problems.

"THE BAUHAUS WAS NOT AN INSTITUTION WITH A CLEAR PROGRAM. IT WAS AN IDEA AND GROPIUS FORMULATED THIS IDEA WITH GREAT PRECISION. THE FACT THAT IT WAS AN IDEA, I THINK, IS THE CAUSE OF THIS ENORMOUS INFLUENCE THE BAUHAUS HAD ON EVERY PROGRESSIVE SCHOOL AROUND THE GLOBE. YOU CANNOT DO THAT WITH AN ORGANIZATION. YOU CANNOT DO THAT WITH PROPAGANDA. ONLY AN IDEA SPREADS SO FAR."

Ludwig Mies van der Rohe

BAUHAUS. *Walter Gropius. Dessau, Germany. 1926. This landmark building with its pinwheel plan and early glass curtain walls introduced into architecture many of the new concepts generated by the celebrated design school.*

I may illustrate that with an example. You know Frank Lloyd Wright, who was a great personality. About a year ago I went to see his school. His widow very brilliantly has taken over this school. There are still about sixty students. I went around from place to place and found that everyone is making second-rate Frank Lloyd Wright designs. This definitely cannot be the aim of a school. I repeat—for every young man it must be a great experience to come across a personality like Frank Lloyd Wright, but from the educational point of view, this is the education of assistants, but not of independent men.

At the Bauhaus, we tried to find an objective approach, to find all the things that are derived from the psychology and biology of human life which are objective, which are proper for everyone who ever takes it. We wanted to inform the student with all these definite details from these fields and in that way bring him into the position to find his own way. We definitely tried to destroy any imitation.

It is quite natural that every student will, to a certain degree, imitate his teacher. That doesn't do harm as long as the teacher tells him, "That is not you. You have imitated me." Then he will slowly come to his own. I might mention in this regard Josef Albers, who was a prominent teacher in the Bauhaus and who, in my opinion, is the ablest teacher in these fields. He, so to speak, throws every student in the pond when he cannot yet swim. When the student starts drowning, he is then open for advice. This is the objective way to come to it. Albers has brought that beyond what we did in the Bauhaus. He found an approach to treat every student in a different way, individually, but always giving him only the objective information. He never puts his own approach on him. This we did all together in the Bauhaus, and such independent men like the names I mentioned joined hands with me to really carry this way through.

J.P.: *Tell me, how did the name Bauhaus come about?*

W.G.: I have coined this word. You know, *bauen* has a much wider meaning in the

German language than it does in the English one. The *Bauer* is the peasant. Bauen is very broad, you know, and so we want . . . I wanted to have an expression of an institute which treats bauen with a very wide variety in any direction, even building up the human being, you know. So this is a much wider margin than, say, "architecture" or "building" in the English language. That was the reason for this word. The house for bauen, the house for building.

J.P.: *Was there something in the Deutsche Werkbund that established the climate in which the Bauhaus was created?*
W.G.: You must remember that the German people had lost this big war, the First World War. In everyone's mind was now we have to start fresh again. We have to investigate everything which we have done and try to get into a fresh approach. This was really very definite in everyone's mind when I made this first pamphlet to call people to the Bauhaus, and students came who had just returned from the war, were in a rather shaky position, without any money and so on. But I managed somehow with the wording of this pamphlet to stimulate them. They came and were open to find, to start a new approach to all these problems. And you know, so far the academies were rather sterile. They were separate from the life and we wanted to bring these things together again. We wanted to investigate what were the instruments of our life and how can we work for them and not have this separating wall between art on one side and the flowing life on the other side. So we had to investigate step by step the means of production today.

We started out with a craft because, in my opinion, the machine is only a refined hand-tool, and without knowing the basic things of hand tools, the basic crafts, we don't understand the industry. So we asked everyone to go for a few years in one of our workshops and learn the craft properly. And you know, the craft in Germany was still a very strong thing. The craftsmen were still organized—that's something one doesn't know here, for instance, that the craftsmen had to fulfill certain requirements. We wanted somebody to take his exam as a craftsman before three craftsmen in the community.

In addition to that, in the Bauhaus, were also all these technical staffing problems involved. For instance, when I tried to find teachers for the Bauhaus, I knew that there was no man in the world anymore who simultaneously was able to design a new chair and to make that chair. There were excellent craftsmen who could do anything—a Rococo chair, or a modern chair, or whatever—when the design was given him. On the other side, there were good designers, but they were not integrated. In the beginning I put as the heads of the workshop one artist and one craftsman, and in the second *Hof,* in Dessau, it was not necessary anymore to have this separation because now there was a new crew where in one man we had the knowledge of the craft as well as the artistic approach.

J.P.: *Did other people feel that the artist and the architect should be joined with industry?*
W.G.: Some people have felt the same thing, but as it always is with new ideas,

there were a lot of fights against it. We had to fight our way through every day. Every day it was very hard to come through. I look backwards today, after what I know now, I wonder if I would dare to start something like that again. I would say, "How could I?" But at that time, you know, when you are a young man and full of beans, then you have the impression that you will never die, and you go on, on, on. But it was a very, very heavy uphill fight and only very slowly was it recognized.

Particularly the problem to bring art and production of the day close to each other were looked very askance from many people, particularly the artists. They didn't like that at all. They wanted to be entirely separate in their ivory tower and we wanted to have that ivory tower destroyed. We wanted to pull the artist into the life of the people again, you know. We all agreed it was the right way of doing it. This, of course, took a long while before it was recognized in a broader way because we were not only fought by the population, but also in the end by the government, where we were pushed out of Weimar. That's how the mayor of Dessau gave us the opportunity to build everything up again. Then came the Nazi regime and destroyed the Bauhaus altogether. I had been in the Bauhaus only nine years and my successors had been there altogether for five years. That was the whole Bauhaus. But in spite of that, in spite this uphill fight, I can state today that the idea of the Bauhaus has really spread, has penetrated through, not only in this country, but very much so in England, in Italy, in Japan, and even other countries. From Russia all of a sudden quite a lot of examples that they recognize also the possibilities of the Bauhaus. Because it was not a style approach, but it was an idea approach, and an idea is not personal but impersonal. Every day it can be in a new way. It's a method of approach.

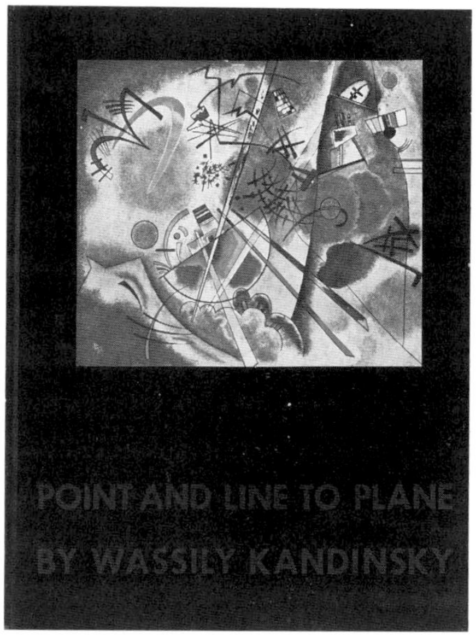

POINT AND LINE TO PLANE. Vasily Kandinsky. Solomon R. Guggenheim Foundation, New York. 1947. Originally published in German as Punkt und Linie zu Fläche, *Bauhausbucher, Munich. 1926. This is one of the fourteen books published by the Bauhaus to present the school and its teachings to the public.*

J.P.: *The Bauhaus lasted only fourteen years, from 1919 to 1933. What were the standards by which you were able to choose the people who taught, or how did they happen to come?*

W.G.: You know, I obviously had a lucky hand to get my people because all these names like Kandinsky, Klee, and Feininger were utterly unknown at the time. I knew they were strong in themselves, but it was a jump into the dark to get them in.

This is an answer for those who think this was a very rigid, rationalized approach. It was not. How else would I have taken these artists into the institute? I wanted to have infiltration from both sides, the technical and the organizational part on the one side and the richness of the artist on the other. Out of that came what I called, when we made the first exhibition, *Art and Technique in New Unity*. That was the title of the exhibition. We were pressed to make an exhibition by the government of Weimar. So we went out and did it in 1923. This exhibition made quite a bit of clash. Many people also came from other countries. We see, already, the beginning of this method or approach, as I call it.

Klee was teaching. Klee was perhaps the personality that was never put in question by any one of the faculty or the students. He was always somewhat aloof, but he was strongly in the whole thing. His teaching was very basic, completely fresh and new. We still have quite a lot of his type of teaching. He was very strong. Kandinsky also had a strong line of himself, which he developed. My point was that if I nominated somebody for the staff in the Bauhaus, he was on his own. One can only say to a personality completely "yes" or completely "no." Then you have to let go. But there were some basic things we agreed upon in our meetings, particularly in the first years. We had an enormous amount of meetings between the faculty and the students to come to terms, to a certain understanding, particularly to find these objective things.

When I came to this country, I heard at Harvard this expression, "the arts and sciences." So I tried to investigate this. In science, I found everything was very clear. Art? Art was always art appreciation, or reading poetry or looking at paintings to appreciate them and so on, but not making paintings, making poetry, making architecture. This is still so, you know. It is a little bit better now in Harvard. Now they have a visual art institute which tries to go in there, but it isn't believed in yet properly. Art is still on the margin. It is not really absorbed or integrated into the whole. This goes away only by a deep educational system starting from the nursery on through the whole system.

J.P.: *There is no such thing as science appreciation, is there?*
W.G.: No. I think a true democracy must be balanced on all sides. Today we have an overemphasis on the science side because we think too much of all the practical outcome of the sciences. From the cultural point of view I think art must balance that out. There, we are in abeyance because the artist is still the forgotten man. He is not really recognized as an essential member of society, which he is.

J.P.: *Is this partly the artist's fault?*
W.G.: Sure. It's always from various sides. But with less and less understanding for art because it is pressed aside by this enormous science development. I by no means talk against science. It's something wonderful that has to be developed. Only the

GRADUATE CENTER, HARVARD UNIVERSITY. *Walter Gropius with The Architects' Collaborative. Cambridge, Massachusetts. 1950. Designed in the new International Style, these seven residential blocks with interlocking courtyards linked by covered walkways around a commons building represented a bold departure from the traditional Neo-Georgian red brick style of Harvard.*

effort was too much on one side and the other side was forgotten. The artist felt he was forgotten by the people, he went into his ivory tower and worked there for himself. For me, the explanation for abstract art is that the artist couldn't give the content any more of what was happening in the time. He was apart. He was on the margin. Now we try to pull him in again, and for that the Bauhaus was instrumental.

Imagine in the Middle Ages, the craftsman was the artist. He made the thing and he was the businessman. He did everything together. Then came the subdivision of all these things and the craftsman was left only with some handwork, doing something which others told him to do. They were no longer the rounded, independent personalities that the craftsmen of the Middle Ages were. In this country where are the craftsmen? The best craftsmen have gone into industry, making models and dies because that's the best paid. It needs a very neat hand, you know. But the craftsman of old hardly exists.

J.P.: *You still feel the importance of working in collaboration with other people in your own profession.*

W.G.: Very strongly so. The time has become so complicated. There are so many phases that one individual is unable to cover it all. In my field, in architecture, it's so obvious. How can you bridge that? In my opinion you can bridge it only by creating a well-oiled team. What is that? It's not so easy. It's easily said, but the team cannot be made by a boss who says you and you and you work together. This doesn't work. Teamwork must be done on a voluntary basis. If I like a person and we want to do something together with this third one and the fourth one, that's a group. They want to do it. But then they have to learn among themselves, first to take criticism from one another and not feel offended. We have to learn that. It's a long process.

Now it's true, of course, that the spark comes always from the individual. When you have a team and they are really vibrating, they are interested in carrying through certain ideas. In discussion you make a remark which stimulates something in me and in the end I don't know anymore who was the initiator of that idea. It's a chain process from one to the other. Out of that develops something further and something better. Particularly my ideas are controlled by others and I control the ideas of others. We enrich each other if it is done in the right way. But the spark comes always from the individual.

We've worked here in this office seventeen years together. It so happens that a job has one of us as the leader. We come together several times a week to discuss all our design work and the leader has to present what he has done so far and then we criticize, very much so. He still may take or leave our criticism. The decision is left to him. Of course, he has learned to listen to get the good suggestions and work them in. There's still a lot of things which can be improved, but teamwork is not such an obvious thing. It has really to be developed. I think in the future we will come more and more to it. For me it is the basis of democracy, because I have to work together with another person. The basis of democracy is the collaboration from man to man, and then we can build up something which works also in larger units.

I forgot to say something which just came to mind. How can something like an idea like the Bauhaus spread? When we say that we have to improve education, that education should incorporate these things, then I say we can do it only by creating small concentrated nuclei from which the idea spreads. This nuclei should be built up in a very strong way, taking in only the very best and dropping everything else. It is not a problem of magnitude. Bauhaus was very small. We had eighty to one hundred and twenty students, you know, and we had such a short time. But still it spread because it was intense in itself. This intensity is necessary. When there's a new idea and something new has to be tried out in, say, a children's school, you should select a few of the best teachers one can find as well as the students. It will make itself felt, if they put themselves in it and do a good searching. I always say that we need search more than research.

J.P.: *How many teachers were there?*

W.G.: Well, all in all, perhaps twenty. Over the first years there were not more than eighty students, and later it came to, as I remember, one hundred and fifty students. That was the maximum, never more.

The orientation course was the basic thing of the Bauhaus. It was started first by Johannes Itten and then was taken over by László Moholy-Nagy and Josef Albers. Everyone contributed to it including myself. We developed a course to bring the young man, quite unprejudiced, into doing things with his hands with different materials and learning by going into these things. I did not project my own approach into the student's mind but tried to help the student on his own line. This is what's necessary.

Even within the Bauhaus, you know, there were very strong viewpoints. We were able to handle it on an objective basis. A certain unification of ideas came out of all of us together. The young students took part in this strongly. There was a very strong personality in Oskar Schlemmer, who is not yet known enough in the world. I'm absolutely sure that he's the coming master because he had such a strong personal approach, particularly from the painter's point of view—a very individual approach to space. I have seen an exhibition of his life work now in the academy in Berlin half a year ago. It was wonderful, really wonderful.

We had a Bauhaus orchestra and they did quite a lot. They even made some compositions. They were in all our festivities. When there was some cramp in the school, or some fight in the school, I right away made a fête and gave them two days to arrange that fête. The most wonderful things came out of what the Bauhaus made for these festivities. Then the air was right again. It was a safety valve all the time. They were really creative in these things. There was Schlemmer, who was excellent as a stage man. He very often did the themes. For instance, the white fête or striped fête. Then everyone developed his costume on that theme. It was wonderful.

J.P.: *Some people have associated the use of an all lower-case alphabet with the Bauhaus. Others have said that this was partly because there was a strong feeling against the excessive capitalization of the German language.*

W.G.: Yes, this was part of it. Of course, it goes faster on the typewriter if you have only small letters. We did it for a long time. We tried all these things. There was always some practical meaning as well as some aesthetic intentions. But definitely this was done for several years. I also wrote my letters that way. I gave it up later on, particularly in the English language where it doesn't mean that much.

J.P.: *You had worked in architecture before. Was architecture the base or the catalyst in which all could participate?*
W.G.: The basic idea was to develop architecture. But as it was the last thing, after everyone had gone through the workshops, I never had sufficient money to build it up in the ways I wanted to build it up. It was always a small cell. That small cell, of course, had a strong influence on the institute, but I wanted to have a real institute built up out of it and I couldn't do it because I didn't have the money. Then my successor, Hannes Meyer, did a little bit more of that. He somewhat widened out architecture. Mies van der Rohe, the last director, did a little bit more for the architecture department. But none of us could really build it up in the way that we wanted to have it because the time ran out.

The most lively time, of course, was when we came to Dessau. I designed the new Bauhaus building and had all the workshops collaborate on the whole thing. All the lamps, furniture, textiles, lettering, and everything was done in our workshops. This was a very lively time, of course, because this was for real. We have a lot of examples of what became of certain Bauhaus models. We find them everywhere, the lighting fixtures, chairs and things, which everybody knows the source of today. We made contracts with firms to give them fully executed models, not just on paper. We sent people out into the factories to study their methods of designing and producing. They came back and we developed the full model for them. Then we got royalties from the business of these various manufacturers.

J.P.: *Do you feel that designers should do a wide range of activities?*
W.G.: I'm very much against artificial boundaries because the principles are all the same for everything in our surroundings. It's left to the individual to decide what he's most interested in. I have gone in many directions myself and tried this and that because I was interested in it. I have built quite a few vehicles, not only automobiles, but some sleeping cars for the German railway.

J.P.: *Was this possible because of the times?*
W.G.: You hear now the expression, "the Golden Twenties," you know. In Germany that was really from the cultural point of view, because everyone was terribly poor. There was this terrific inflation. When I, as the director of the Bauhaus, got my salary, I rushed into a grocery and bought because after an hour it was worth half that much. Money was just absurd at that time. It was incredible.

When we opened the exhibition in 1923, which is still talked about today, the money we got from the government ran out completely. We didn't have anything left because inflation had just swept it away. We didn't even have the money to have people who could wash the floors. Our wives did it. We did everything to the very last

BAUHAUS MASTER HOUSES. *Walter Gropius. Dessau, Germany. 1925. The cluster of three semidetached duplexes and a separate house for the director related in style to the nearby main building, also designed by Gropius.*

ourselves. We used to laugh about how little money there had been for the Bauhaus. There were so many factors that came together. There was that push after the war, when some people really got fed up with what happened, you know, the kaiser and all that. Of course, there were terrible political dangers because the young people went too far left. I had to be very tough and say, "In the Bauhaus there are no politics. What you do outside, I don't care, but as soon as we become host to the left, we are immediately destroyed." I was very strong to hold the line. Otherwise we would have been lost.

The beginning of the Nazis was in Weimar. They became stronger and stronger. They pushed us out and didn't give us any more of our money, which we needed for the institute. We declared the Bauhaus closed in order to end it quicker than they. We got offers from four different cities in Germany. Dessau was the best offer and we went there.

J.P.: *I didn't realize that the first closing was also affected by the Nazis.*
W.G.: Yes. They made it a bargaining apple for the party, you know, which is always wrong to do with cultural things. Cultural things must be left out, otherwise it's very dangerous because the artist has no way of defending himself on a political level. He can't do that. So they squeezed us out because the Nazis smelled what we were doing was certainly not on their line. So they were automatically enemies from the beginning.

J.P.: *Were you able to carry on the Bauhaus approach at Harvard?*
W.G.: No. At the very end of my time in Harvard I had fought for it. President Conant gave a little sum to build up such a preliminary course for the student. But we didn't have any workshops, you know. Because I believed that designing and building were too much apart, I asked the school to take care of the student on the building site. Then I made a contract with the contractors' organization of Massachusetts

IMPINGTON COLLEGE, CLASSROOM WING. *Walter Gropius and Maxwell Fry. Cambridgeshire, England. 1936. The classrooms of this early modern, single-story school enjoyed natural light from both sides and opened onto the surrounding lawn.*

to place my students in the field during the summer. I do not mean laying bricks—this is also very good—but I mean that an older student should learn the process of building, because you cannot learn how to flash a roof well from the drafting board. You have to see it in the flesh. You don't even know the sequence of all the processes. How a building is put together. You have to see that in the field. But our people don't learn that way.

J.P.: *Architecture does not have an internship, like medicine.*
W.G.: Internship is an office, but this is something else. I think he has to be in the field.

You will not find that many of my students at Harvard are Gropius imitators. I destroyed that. I wanted to have a man who is as strong as possible in himself, perhaps completely different from myself. Then he could build up something on his own. Some brilliant architects today who have been my students are completely different

UNITED STATES EMBASSY. *Walter Gropius with The Architects' Collaborative. Athens, Greece. 1961. The two-story marble-clad building features a formal square plan with an open central court. It is a handsome realization of Gropius's desire to respect Greece's classical spirit in thoroughly modern terms.*

from myself—like Paul Rudolph and I.M. Pei and quite a lot of others. This is what I wanted to happen.

In Germany I was the successor of van de Velde, who was a very great artist and a wonderful personality, but who also educated only small van de Veldes. I ended up with that. I thought that was not the right thing. This was the real change in the Bauhaus, a completely different approach.

J.P.: *How do you feel specifically about the future of the Bauhaus idea?*
W.G.: I think as long as I look back it increases all the time. It still increases, you know. It's so enormous. Everything is alive and has to be changed. The conditions are different every day. We have to be flexible. We should take this on with our individual gifts. This is only a direction. Everyone with their individual gifts will do something with it. I'm very much against these fixed ideas, you know. The moment they are fixed, they have to move. As long as it's an open process, it's alive. When it's closed, it's dead. The Bauhaus is a ferment which is still there and growing.

Eero Saarinen

"A BUILDING IS A FORM PLACED BETWEEN THE GROUND AND THE SKY. THEN YOU ASK YOURSELF, 'WHAT IS THE BEST DAMNED FORM TO PLACE BETWEEN THESE TWO?'"

We recorded Eero Saarinen in his office and in his comfortably modern, remodeled nine-room Victorian house in Bloomfield Hills, Michigan, not far from Cranbrook Academy, where his father, Eliel, had been director. Like his father, Eero believed, "Architecture has always to be considered an art." "Until his death," Eero explained, "I worked in the form of my father." In the next dozen years of Eero's abbreviated career, he created both forms and a fame of his own.

With his staff or a stranger, it was his nature to turn a talk into a discussion, asking questions as well as offering answers. He combined casualness with intensity to a greater degree than anyone I ever met. His shirt collar open and sleeves rolled up, between slow puffs on a briar pipe, he explored ideas with a probing mind, often clarifying them with diagrams and quick sketches. Whether he was talking, as we walked through the General Motors Technical Center, or at work on the model of the St. Louis arch in his studio, I was struck by Eero's characteristically methodical exploration of options. His solutions were varied but never cautious. Eero's Scandinavian

heritage came through not only in his accent but also in his concerns. He said, "I look for the day when our spiritual qualities catch up with our physical advances. Then our architecture will take an important place in history with the Gothic and the Renaissance."

TWA TERMINAL, KENNEDY INTERNATIONAL AIRPORT. *Eero Saarinen. New York City. 1962. With its great interlocking concrete vaults and sculptured forms throughout, this passenger air terminal anticipates the excitement of flight.*

1956

JOHN PETER: *When you were young, did anybody give you some particularly good advice regarding architecture?*
EERO SAARINEN: The great majority of advice I have received comes from my father. You see, I practically grew up under his drafting table and then when I was old enough to get on top, I was drawing on the other end of it. Of course, there is much advice, like when he would erase things he would say, "It's never too late to change," and so on.

J.P.: *Do you feel that way yourself?*
E.S.: I feel that way up to a certain point. He also corrected me when I took that one too seriously, but I think that the greatest advice I've had is, maybe, an advice in attitude. I am talking about the profession of architecture now. We've only been architects of single buildings, with very little regard for what goes on left or right or in front of that building. Partly because we've been in such a tremendous growth that whatever was to the left or right of our building would be changed in a few years

GENERAL MOTORS TECHNICAL CENTER. *Eero Saarinen. Warren, Michigan. 1956. This structure is typical of the gleaming complex: twenty-five buildings with brightly colored side-walls surround a formal man-made lake with programmed fountains and a stainless steel water tower.*

later. This has meant that we've concentrated on the single, lone building only, but we have accomplished very little in total look of our cities.

I think that it is now time that we take that Cinerama view of our work instead of the narrow-angle view of our work. I've been fortunate in projects that I've been working on, which are mostly university problems, and the same thing holds true in this respect for the General Motors Technical Center. They've all been projects where the total environment is the important thing. In the university plans where you have several existing buildings like the rocks around a Frank Lloyd Wright house, they influence, they tone down, or they do certain things to whatever you build. For instance, the domed auditorium at MIT and the chapel next to it, a great deal of effort and time was spent trying to relate those to the surrounding buildings. In architecture, just as in color, you either contrast or you complement. That is the situation, but it is not as easy as that.

In other problems, such as university campuses, I am very concerned with just how we build within the modern idiom to go with older buildings that are its permanent neighbors. Frankly, I see very few of my colleagues really taking on that responsibility. Sometimes they are forced into it by the client and the result usually is the same kind of material or the same kind of color or something.

In Europe they have older permanent cities. I think the tradition of the Scandinavians is different from the Germans, where the whole city planning is influenced. Thanks to my father, probably, I am very interested in this. I think the Latins have done very little in that. They would like to fight the old and impose a completely new. That's quite a strong contrast between those parts.

Specifically at MIT, I was not so much concerned with the dome having a relationship with the other domes. I was more concerned with what is the best possible building to place in among several, approximately five- or six-story, buildings. An auditorium done as a squarish box, which can be done, would have been lower than those buildings and it just did not seem to fit there. It would have blocked the space, would have just looked like a lesser cousin of the other buildings. Maybe without windows, because an auditorium has less need for windows or windows of a different scale. Therefore, its shape that started from the ground, went up and then returned to the ground seemed to be in better contrast with the surrounding buildings.

Just one more moment on relating buildings to buildings of another period. The example which I always use, and which I guess everybody uses and which is the best one, is Piazza San Marco. Piazza San Marco is the most beautiful place in the world. It has four different kinds of architecture, built during a period of one thousand years, four or five different materials. But in its space, in the mass of the surrounding buildings, in the ultimate use to which each style is put to emphasize the total, it's probably the best. I think it is the best that man has achieved or probably ever will achieve.

1958

J.P.: *You have often talked about the relationship of architecture to its surroundings.*
E.S.: I am really very enthusiastic about that phase of architecture, how that phase of architecture was really sort of a completely forgotten one, how we in America had made sort of terrible blunders in that—that thought really took me back to the care that was put into the unity of the public square or the unity of the city, really, in my father's time in Finland and also in present-day Scandinavian environment.

Now because I'm enthusiastic about that, I think that when you have an environment like a university or a campus where most of the surrounding buildings are of a permanent setting, boy, you have no right to ruin that setting by your individual fancy or by just producing something straight out of the *Architectural Forum* or the other magazines. I think you have this obligation to look at the problem very, very carefully. But these kind of problems become really terribly complex. If you get all enthusiastic about just conforming with the surrounding buildings, what do you really do? Are you then apt to weaken the architecture by adding some little frills and little things?

Well, as an example, three or four days ago, I looked at a campus where a very good modern architect did a building which went well with the eclectic surrounding buildings. In fact, he did an extremely good job of tying the old and the new together in his building, and his building is a very interesting building. There were several interesting things produced in that building because of that need of tying the two together, but then one also asks oneself, "Is his building a significant building?" And that's where it might fall down. Not only do you have to be in scale, in material, in mass, and in plan, not only do you have to do that, but do it in relation to the surrounding. Boy, you also have to be a proud builder of your own time. Don't show weakness. These are all specialized problems. These are really mostly campus problems.

J.P.: *In your Women's Dormitory at the University of Pennsylvania was this a part of the problem?*
E.S.: Well, there were many other problems such as a right-of-way running diagonally through the site, which made it almost impossible to make any kind of site plan except the one that we did make.

In the case of Pennsylvania, I felt that brick, which is so dominantly their material, just had to be also the material for this building in spite of the fact that I was more interested in building in some other materials, which I'll come to later. But in this case brick seemed to be the answer.

Now then, the other problem that we faced and, I think, solved. The surrounding buildings are fairly old buildings and, therefore, their floor height was fifteen, sixteen feet. Dormitories that you build today, for economic and other reasons, have floor heights of eight foot six inches. In other words almost half this scale. So you have the problem of relating a building with floor heights almost half the scale to these tremendously scaled buildings around, more or less, in the Renaissance and Gothic style, whichever they were, but always of brick.

What we did was actually knit the wall together into a pattern of vertical and horizontal windows. Now this sounds terrible, but we really have three kinds of windows, vertical, horizontal, and square. Then placing them in a pattern over the elevation, we really created, with the vertical windows, sort of an impression of double scale, double of the single room, double of the room in width, and double of the floor in height. In that way we sort of pulled it back into the same scale as the surrounding buildings. Otherwise it's a very simple building.

Now, I want to get on to the second point. I believe very much that you test the thing by the extremes. How could you not honor that? Think of some of the things that are going on where architects are putting onto campuses, in the abstract, perfectly good modern buildings that in their own surroundings, or in no surroundings at all, would be a perfectly good piece of architecture, but in the total relationship with other buildings are just horrible.

J.P.: *Eero, you mentioned this thought in relation to buildings like the MIT buildings.*
E.S.: Good question. That's why I hesitate. I was there about three or four days ago just at MIT itself. I was looking at the buildings in relation to the surrounding buildings and possible future buildings and so on. I must say, the brick of the chapel blends in extremely well with the total picture. The chapel was really too small a building to separate itself out completely. Now it separates itself out in mass. I can ask you, would you rather have seen a square chapel? Do you think it would have gone better with the other buildings? Or should we have put fake windows to make it go with the other buildings? You see, here was a building of an entirely different kind, different use. All the buildings that it has to go with are brick walls punctured with little windows. The chapel was a building that did not need that kind of window, so you can't relate them by knitting the surfaces together. Besides, the buildings immediately around that are no damned good and may come down. I hope so. But by doing it round, by getting the round surface in relation to the square surfaces, sort of separated out, by the

KRESGE AUDITORIUM, MASSACHUSETTS INSTITUTE OF TECHNOLOGY. *Eero Saarinen. Cambridge. 1955. This thin-shell concrete dome resting on three points on a grassy plaza provides the auditorium with a great, unobstructed interior.*

EERO SAARINEN *at home in Bloomfield Hills, Michigan, 1956*

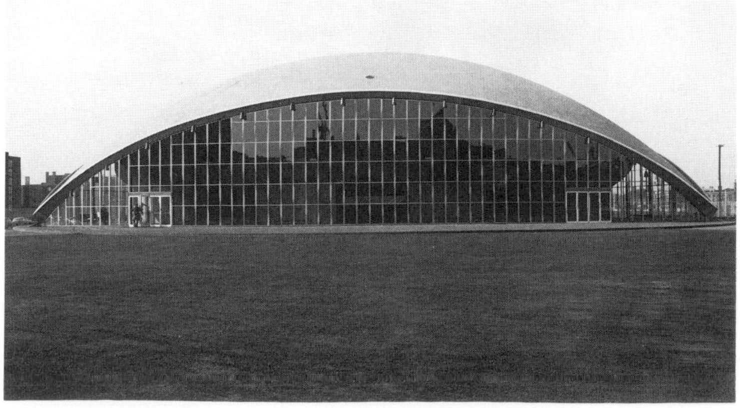

material being the same, but only more forceful in the chapel, by being round and by being the stronger texture of brick, I think it goes very well there.

Now, the auditorium, again, I say the same thing. The problem was we were surrounded by a ring of roughly six-story buildings on all sides and the auditorium was to be in the middle. Now, what better can you do then place a form there which grows from the ground up and then returns to the ground again, sculpturally, I think, it has the right relationship.

J.P.: *It's a relationship in the sense of contrast.*

E.S.: Yes. Now London—I think the U.S. Embassy in London is a different kind of a problem. You see, there we are not building a chapel or an auditorium, we are really building a building that has to have windows roughly spaced equally as all the other windows around.

On Grosvenor Square, you know, the buildings around are pseudo-Georgian buildings. Georgian is basically a three-story architecture with a beginning, a middle, and an end. The end being a roof with the dormers in it. On Grosvenor Square the buildings have a definite plan for continuing that so that it becomes a solid mass of this type of neo-Georgian. It's like if you take a face and you have the chin and the mouth which is the base but instead of a nose you put in about four noses in height, and then, instead of a forehead, you add a couple of foreheads on. It's sort of overgrown Georgian with these eight-story buildings all the way around. Now, they are not great buildings, we recognize that, but they are permanent. They are the permanent surroundings of that square. Whatever we place on that square really has to live with them.

We worked quite hard to determine what was the right thing in mass. Really the problems are mass, material, scale, and how do you answer those? Do you carry any lines around? Do you put a Georgian roof on it? Do you make it out of brick? Do you have the same kind of a base, this low chin again? What do you?

I felt very strongly that this was a case where the total of the restful square, which this has an opportunity of being, should not be violated. Just suppose again an extreme, just suppose we decided to do a Georgian building exactly like the others

UNITED STATES EMBASSY. *Eero Saarinen. London. 1960. This chancellery was designed to dominate Grosvenor Square, although its Portland stone is harmonious with the Georgian-style buildings along the other three sides of the square.*

there. Well, this is an embassy. The others are apartment houses. It would not only be wrong against our time, but it would also be wrong against the meaning of the building. This embassy really has to, in a sense, capture the square. The other three sides are really the setting for this most important building on the square.

In the buildings on the other three sides, brick is the dominant material, but stone, the Portland stone, is the trim material. By using the Portland stone, by making the entire building out of that material, making the three other sides of the square just the beginning for the fine side, the embassy, the proudest side of the square. And by, in mass, creating a base so that the building stands a little bit higher than the other buildings, it doesn't come straight down to the ground. It has this sloping base and then the fence around it. Then the building cantilevers up above the piano nobile. I think we've created enough of a special thing out of this building and still in total not violated the square at all.

Boy, I really had a terribly interesting time in London. I was talking at the AA, Architectural Association, and gave this speech. Afterwards the English students and the young architects were there with the most gracious thanks which they put in the most beautiful English language. They speak marvelously. They don't do terribly good architecture, but, boy, they can speak about architecture. They told me how well I presented the case and so forth.

Then with a knife they got in after it. In general, they were saying isn't this rather a reactionary thing to put on Grosvenor Square, to bow to the material, to bow to the surroundings to that extent. Well, for the particular place, for the particular problem, and for the total problem of government architecture, I sincerely don't think of bowing to the place as much as they think it is.

You see, everybody is fighting their own battle and are looking for support for that battle. That's the way we read history. That's the way we look at other people's architecture. These English are terribly enthusiastic about curtain-wall construction. They would just have loved it if I had built a building with glass and aluminum. If I had put General Motors there. That's what they were looking for because that would support their own fight.

Now, I think we were the first ones ever to do curtain-wall construction and I think we really know more about it than anybody else and so on. But this just did not seem to be the place for it and that I'm sure of. Now, we talked long enough about how to relate buildings to older buildings, which sometimes is quite a burden.

J.P.: *What about the relation of an architect to a civic problem, such as your own Jefferson Memorial?*

E.S.: I'm terribly interested in Jefferson. That one I would like to build more than anything else. As you know, we have now come to an agreement with the railroad, so that if Congress says yes to the whole thing we may go ahead. I would very much like to build this stainless-steel arch and the whole park. The design now is really a much simpler thing than the original design that we did in '48. Now, the lines of the park, the approaches and everything, are really the same kind of linear forms as the arch itself.

JEFFERSON NATIONAL EXPANSION MEMORIAL. *Eero Saarinen. St. Louis, Missouri. 1962. This audacious stainless-steel arch, sited in Jefferson National Memorial Park along the Missouri River, dramatically commemorates the city's role as the gateway to the beckoning West.*

J.P.: *Do you feel that you've lost something?*

E.S.: No, gained in everything. You know, architecture is really impact. The value of architecture is the impact it has on human beings. Now, if you dissipate your impact by saying different things, either contradictory or confusing things, then it loses its strength. Also, I think, you have to overstate. In going back to some of the work that we've done and completed, looking at it with the cold eyes of daylight, some of the work was just terribly good ideas but they were not stated strongly enough or they were dissipated with lots of other ideas. Now, how do you correct that?

First of all, I'm beginning to feel more and more that your idea has to be strong enough. It has to be good enough. Then you have to put all your eggs in one basket—that idea. Everything in the building has to really support that idea because, going back to impact, people really don't look. Most people are blind. If you get too subtle about architecture, if you go from one proportioned room to another proportioned room to a third proportioned room and you plan well and beautiful how these proportions relate just one to another, well, people come in and walk through it and never notice the difference. We're cultivated people, more or less, in other things, but

MILWAUKEE WAR MEMORIAL. *Eero Saarinen. Milwaukee, Wisconsin. 1957. Designed both as a monument on a high bluff and a gateway to the park extending down to Lake Michigan, this dramatic concrete building houses an art museum, meeting halls, and a memorial court with a pool.*

as far as appreciating architecture, we are a nation of barbarians. I think you need the strong impact to be appreciated. But that isn't all, you also need the strong impact to really get the idea across.

J.P.: *In the case of Jefferson Memorial in St. Louis, you would say that the changes have ended up by making it better.*

E.S.: Yes. Let's say we made two kinds of changes in the plans. One, to solve the practical problem of the approach, putting the railroad tunnels underneath without too much grades and without too much cost. In doing so, we have actually relocated the monument. The arch in the earlier plans was right on the levee. From the city you went down to it. It was almost at the bottom of the bowl. Now, because of practical things, we had to raise it up. It's not only the practical things that made me want to raise it up. I also started thinking what vertical monuments are there that you approach going downhill and the only one I could think of was the sunken ship at the bottom of the Spanish Steps in Rome. You cannot place a vertical monument at the bottom of some steps.

Now the arch is in a sense a vertical monument on one axis and a wide monument in another. I think now we have the approaches worked out just right so that in a thousand years this will still be the right relationship between the monument, the river, the park, and the city. You become much more conscious of the relationship of the monument to the city because there are some fairly high buildings there. It's also good to bring the base of the arch up. Actually, we may want to make that arch a little bit higher.

The second thing was in the reworking of the lines of the park, the roads, the approaches to the thing to introduce the same kind of lines inherent in the arch itself, the parabolic line.

You see, all these things relate. You know, you work on a chair, you work on getting the same kind of lines on the top of the chair, on the bottom of the chair, and so on. That then relates and through that you get a certain dexterity with curved lines. That dexterity is then built up more in a problem like TWA, which was all curved lines and curved planes. In fact, with all the fellows in the project, not only myself and Kevin Roche, but also Cesar Pelli and the others, who worked for months and months on these curved lines, really for about half a year, didn't work on a single straight line. They become terribly good and terribly sensitive to the curved line, the curved plane, and so on.

Now, in the middle of the changes I saw for the first time that really in relation to the arch, the park, the roads, the approaches to the park should all be done within that same curved-form world, which it wasn't before. You see, before it was put together with many different, well related things, but of many different form worlds. Now it's going to be all one.

J.P.: *You, in a sense, are replanning a section of St. Louis, which is perhaps the most exciting part of that city.*

E.S.: Yes. In the problems of urban renewal, I really can't say very much because

I've not had enough experience in that. We've not done an urban renewal project. The St. Louis one is, of course, peculiar. We are doing the design. We have a client which consists of many city officials, the National Parks Service, the interested citizens, and the mayor of St. Louis, Mayor Tucker, who is a marvelous man. These are all people we enjoy working with greatly.

There were, of course, the days when your client was just one big man with a big mustache or something and those days are gone. You just work with the corporate client or the sort of the urban client.

J.P.: *You haven't found this much different than when you were working with a corporate body?*

E.S.: Well, in the sense the corporate body is lots of people and so is the city. Sometimes the corporation has a way of making up its mind a little bit faster than a city, but I have no criticism in relation to the arch.

1956

We were talking about concepts and how a building is conceived. I think maybe one of the things which has been lacking in our day is how is a building perceived. The seldom-perceived thing in architecture is perception. You come to a building in a certain way. You enter a door. You grasp a door handle. You see the frame of the door. You come into a space. You don't know what is going to happen beyond it. You come into a dark space and then it opens up into a light space. The series of perceptions that happen to you when you come in, we're not master of that in our modern architecture.

For instance, I always remember one traditional, awful French house north of Chicago where this was marvelously done. The series of things that happened to you, the surprises, the development from one space to another space. Modern architecture is something that you come in, you can practically see the inside from the outside, and there's no surprise. Then you have to evaluate: How important is it really toward the total? How much has it been forgotten? How much should you do it and in what kind of a problem can you use it? Can you add that to architecture? Is that something we've lost? Is that one of the babies we threw out with the functional bath?

Take another thing for instance. Basically one might say after one is through talking about all architecture, functional and so forth, one might say that a building is a form placed between the ground and the sky. Then you ask yourself, "What is the best damned form to place between these two?" Then you look at the French château and maybe that is a better thing than some of the supermarkets that we're building today. Maybe that line, the top line of the building should not be a straight line, maybe a better relation with the sky is reached with a roof—daring thoughts. There are so many of these things that we should sort of reexamine and then, as I told you earlier, the whole problem of relating buildings to old buildings.

Some of these elements are interrelated, then in certain problems they become dominant and in others they don't. We have to think much more about architecture than we've done. The things that we take for granted we should reexamine.

J.P.: *This is the art of the building and not techniques. We've made great advances in techniques.*

E.S.: We've made marvelous things. We could make anything look like anything else. There used to be just stone, plaster, and tiles. Now we have fifty different plastics and a hundred other different materials but basically it comes down to our ability to use them, and sometimes it is harder to use the greater number.

Just take the example of a little town in Indiana or some other state built during the period with a bearing brick wall. The high vertical window with the arch over it was the only way you could build that gave you unity, because the only way you could build gave a discipline throughout the town. What has happened to that town? Bond Clothes and a few others that are rich and successful put these glass fronts on these things and those are published in a magazine as great improvements, and prizes are given by the local chamber of commerce for "beautifying" the town. But they're terrible. They hurt the basic rhythm of that town, the total environment of that town was better when everything had the same rhythm, which came from a basic material.

The total environment is always more important than the individual building and that's why, when we built this medium-sized bank in the little town of Columbus, Indiana, our big concern was how to put up a building so as not to hurt but to help the town, to respect the integrity of the town and also to build an uncompromisingly modern building. I think we solved that problem, actually, and I'll show you the drawings.

J.P.: *How do your projects evolve?*

E.S.: We go through the most terrible labor pains sometimes. There's so many ways and there's so many solutions to any problem. If you don't believe it just look at the results of any competition. There's so many reasonable ways of getting into entirely different solutions. Now, in this whole problem of architecture one has to know what one is doing. In other words one not only has to know what one wants to do, but one also should know what other possibilities there are in order to come to that solution.

One has a feeling that in so many cases architects don't know what they're doing. They're just riding with the punches of the latest magazines. Theoretically, one should sort of survey the entire field of what can be done in this instance, and then choose one's direction. I think it was Sullivan that said, "Each problem has within it its own solution." Where we might be criticized is for almost trying to find a different solution for every single problem, trying to just bend over backwards to do that.

Let's take the problem of a chair. There are many ways of doing a chair. In the problem of a chair, in this last line and also the earlier lines that I did for the Organic Design Competition of The Museum of Modern Art, what interested me was to find a prototype of the chair for mass production, for use in the normal situations within homes or within offices. On chairs I've deliberately not gone off in seven different directions to see how clever we are. Because I feel that's not the problem. I just wanted to design what, in my mind, was the final and right solution for the chair.

INGALLS HOCKEY RINK, YALE UNIVERSITY. *Eero Saarinen. New Haven, Connecticut. 1956. The soaring curve of the reinforced-concrete spine, hung with steel cables and supporting a wood-decked roof, encloses a regulation-size hockey rink.*

Within architecture, I believe there are many, many different problems that cannot be answered by one prototype. Skidmore, Owings, and Merrill, I would say, tried to answer it with one Miesian prototype. I don't agree with that. They got as far as the chapel at the Air Academy and then they had to switch because there they realized that it wasn't proper.

J.P.: *In the case of Mies it was interesting that he didn't depart even for the IIT chapel.*
E.S.: I was just going to bring up Mies. I'm an enthusiastic admirer of Mies, but I can only go with him as far as the chapel at Illinois Tech. There I separate from him. I think these are not all problems under the same prototype. In fact, for myself, I would put architecture under more prototypes. What I am interested in doing is trying to create the prototypes. Not in certain cases where the problem is so special that it cannot become a prototype. All right, then it has the right for a separate solution. I mean it's obvious that a hockey rink is different from an office building. It's obvious that in that kind of case the structure is such a strong, dominant thing that you recognize it in the form. You don't just build a box. Also certain locations and certain relations to other buildings are so dominant and so strong that you have to give it the special solution. But, perhaps, also I've been terribly worried that architecture was just going to get itself into a box and there was a very strong need for spreading out, for finding the new solutions. That's why the value of the work of Paul Rudolph, the work of Matthew Nowicki, and the work of Minoru Yamasaki is very valuable. And the work of Wright, yes. We're a civilization that in architecture really has these marvelous two poles right in our backyard, Mies and Wright. Boy, that's why there is so much interest in architecture in America today, because there's always the challenge of these two poles. Of course, there's Corbu as the third pole, but we have these two in our backyard and should be very proud of it.

Along these lines, I would very much like to produce a real steel building. I would very much like to produce a real concrete building and think that Milwaukee came out very well, really better than I expected. I shouldn't really say that. It's a concrete

JOHN DEERE AND COMPANY ADMINISTRATIVE CENTER. *Eero Saarinen. Moline, Illinois. 1963. In this eight-story headquarters building, Saarinen used Cor-Ten weathering, self-protecting steel to celebrate the toughness of the company's farm machinery.*

building that has guts. I have great hope for the John Deere building, which is a real steel building, a real iron building. It is in the right kind of a setting and for the right kind of a client for an iron building. It, too, has a lot of strength.

J.P.: *As opposed to the elegant use, the refined use of steel or chromed steel.*
E.S.: Yes, and I think TWA will, as a concrete building, also have the sort of the total unity of the flowing, cast material of concrete. I have great hopes for that. Now I see the problem much more clearly. Let's design the best building in concrete that we can for its purpose, but a building that in every part smells concrete. Let's also design a building in steel that in every part and every joint smells steel. Very strongly I feel now that a building has to be all one thing—a sense of unity, a sense of unity in philosophy, a sense of unity in form, a sense of unity with its purpose. A building should just be one thing. A building can't have many ideas in it. It can only have one idea. You look at Wright's Guggenheim, which really looks as if it's going to be a great building. That's an all-concrete building. Sure, it has windows, but you don't see them. Now, maybe we shouldn't carry it that far. But there is an example where actually it's a concrete building and there's nothing else than concrete.

Now, we are also doing a building of all glass, the Bell Telephone Laboratories. It's a concrete building inside, but it's all covered with glass. That idea of the glass and how it's covered is all related to the plan. It's all related to the function of the building and to the total thing.

J.P.: *Do we take function for granted now?*
E.S.: Well, I've gotten terribly interested in it just lately. Somehow, you are quite right, one has a feeling that everybody has forgotten about it. That it's not the fashion anymore. But that's what we're working on. As I showed you, in the new international airport for Washington, in Chantilly, Virginia. We're working together, as a team, with Ammann & Whitney and Burns & McDonnell. It's a team of really several firms, but we're working on the terminal and the function of the terminal. Just how should an airport terminal function? What is the best method? What really hap-

DULLES INTERNATIONAL AIRPORT. *Eero Saarinen. Washington, D.C. 1958. Steel cables, suspended from beams supported by concrete piers, hold the concrete roof, hammock style, in this compact terminal. Saarinen addressed the problems of extended and crowded airports with specially designed mobile lounges.*

pens in a terminal? What do people really do? How do they move around in a terminal and what takes time in a terminal? All these problems are fascinating and we're right in the middle of a real analysis of the problem.

We've taken an existing building such as St. Louis Airport, Washington National, and the airfield in Dallas and made studies. We've made counts finding out exactly how these function and what is wrong with them, what is wrong with the circulation. Really sort of documented every part that can have any relation to our project of a much larger terminal where the distances become larger, where the times become longer. How can one fight that problem?

J.P.: *All these problems are going to be exaggerated and extended as time goes on.*
E.S.: That's right and, boy, we're all experts on airport terminals. That's where we spend most of our time nowadays. We don't expect that our research will create the architecture of the building, but we are terribly interested in making a really well working terminal. The ideal that we have is really Grand Central Railroad Terminal. I mean this is a marvelous building that was built, whenever it was, I think just before World War I, and is still functioning. It is still working substantially the way it was planned at that time and is maintaining well. People go through it without any major gripes and that's terribly important.

J.P.: *Is there a Grand Central in the field of air terminals today?*
E.S.: No, there is not and I would say definitely no.

J.P.: *Eero, have you ever designed a house? In your own house here you certainly designed parts. Does the problem of a house seem to challenge you?*
E.S.: The house isn't really architecture. I think it's been much too overblown and much too important. Let's sort of relate this to other things. Now we know that the family is not as strong as it used to be. It's not as strong as an educational element. The education that children got through the family was much greater in earlier days than it is today. Yet the house as a piece of architecture has become terribly impor-

tant. It really wasn't until the Victorian times, you know. They built the palaces and so on. This has become a terribly important part of architecture. But lots of civilizations have lived with the house being an unimportant part, an anonymous part of architecture.

Look at a place like Orvieto in Italy. When you drive up you see all the houses around. They are really almost like prefabs, made out of masonry, but they all have windows which are essentially the same. They all have tile roofs the same way and so on. Then the whole grandeur of the civilization that built that town was placed in the cathedral. I think there has been an overemphasis on the house.

Now I made this statement that the house is not architecture. What I really mean is that the house has been too emphasized as architecture. All this to-do about your personality in your house and how each house has to be done right for that personality. All that is going on when, at a time, everybody is getting more and more alike. I'm not sure that we should live in houses. I mean houses really create suburbia and here we sit and talk about houses and take it for granted that we should live in houses. But should we? I mean do we really want the city the way it is today?

1956

We can compare the European city, whether it's Paris or any other one, as a thick rug. If we think of the little threads in the rug as the paths that each individual took from their place of living to their place of work and to their place of eating, all by foot. In a flosser rug the threads don't go very far. They stay near. But many make this one city. Now, today we have this pattern of the city where people streak out from one side to the other, from living to place of work may be the same, but the distances are about one hundred times greater.

The automobile, you know, also takes an enormous amount of space. We figure about three hundred square feet for parking a car but that is at the house, add at the factory, at the shop, at the beauty parlor, at the movie. So that you get into many thousands of square feet of space in addition to all the enormous road systems. All this has changed the city.

J.P.: *Do you think that an architect can affect the city only to a certain point?*
E.S.: I think that is the right thing. I don't think any one individual has all the sensitivities to assemble the total of the orchestra which should be architecture, or which is architecture. But there always has to be an orchestra leader. I think the architect is the one that it should be, obviously. Just imagine an orchestra leader not wanting to delegate some of the responsibility and running from one instrument to the other. You can't operate that way.

You once asked me about group practice. That implies many things. Let's think about this. It is a subject that interests me. First of all, one category is the individual designer that does a building, has complete control over every detail and carries it through from beginning to end. That's one category. Second category is the group of people that work together enthusiastically all on one thing, several of them doing design. Third is the group practice, which is the very large office which has several designers in it. We have all of these three at this time.

These different phenomena really produce different kinds of architecture. There are certain pitfalls in this whole thing that we should be aware of. But to examine what's good and bad, let's look at the product. Let's think about architecture and not get too enthusiastic about the system because the end result is what counts. The play is the thing, somebody said.

Now when the one individual, as in the first case, deals with all the problems, where he designs the thing through and through from the beginning to end, I think of this as an example like my father's art center in Des Moines. There the total is one piece of architecture because it is the work of one man doing the whole thing. That is a terribly satisfying thing. You don't change philosophy in midstream during the process of designing a building. It just hurts and weakens the building.

When you get to the second case, a group of people, more or less of equal status, working on the same thing, when nobody is the dominant force in that group, you get a result which you can see is several people trying to contribute something. I can, for instance, think of one concert hall which shall remain unnamed, which looks as if twenty designers were put in one room full of architectural magazines for twenty years. Then they were let out to design this building. They all enthusiastically added everything they knew and had seen to the building, but these things destroy each other. A building has to be all one thing. A building has to have an overall concept which is, in a sense, a design philosophy, a design religion, we might call it, which filters down to every little detail.

It is the same thing as when you look at an Egyptian or a Greek piece of sculpture. The same philosophy is applied to the nose as to the small toe. But each is entirely different. Therefore, I think a building cannot be done with many different philosophies. Basically somebody has to be the captain, but others can work within that concept. Only so can great architecture be done.

Now let's go to the third kind of thing, the group practice, where a very large office has a great practice. Perhaps the danger with that kind of practice is that every problem has to be designed really in the same way or else such an office doesn't work. You might say it is a gradually developing formula for doing good architecture. It has its merits, but it also has its dangers that everything is seen too much in a similar way. I believe that.

Thinking of Corbu gives me strength in this, that every significant piece of architecture is a different thing and has to be considered as such. From the problem, from its location, from the client's problem, and so forth, comes more or less an approach. It becomes the principle. Then every part of that piece has to be part of that principle. I think, for instance, that when the General Motors people first came to my father for the General Motors Technical Center, they probably thought and imagined in their mind that they would get something like Cranbrook. But the problem was a different one. The whole spirit of what they stand for is a different one. The time was a different one. The General Motors Technical Center is very, very different from Cranbrook.

J.P.: *On the other hand, Eero, I can't escape this thing that I did see out there at GM today. The fact was that there is a certain continuity from Cranbrook.*

E.S.: I hope it's true. I think that all past experience, all past influences should be playing on every one of these problems. I don't mean that one starts as newborn everytime. There is also the use of water, of which my father was a master. There is also the problem of the overall relation of buildings, to which I owe my father much and which I have inherited from him. Maybe not so much the great axis but the many minor axes, which was more a characteristic of his than others, the use of color, and maybe also the sense—and this may be presumptuous to say, I think, from having been brought up by my father—I have gotten from his work and his generation the sense that architecture is a broader thing than some think of it today.

You met John Dinkeloo, who has been the project manager for this and who has really thought through it, but then there are the designers like Kevin Roche, for one, and Warren Plattner. I owe much to that group. In a way we all decided that this is

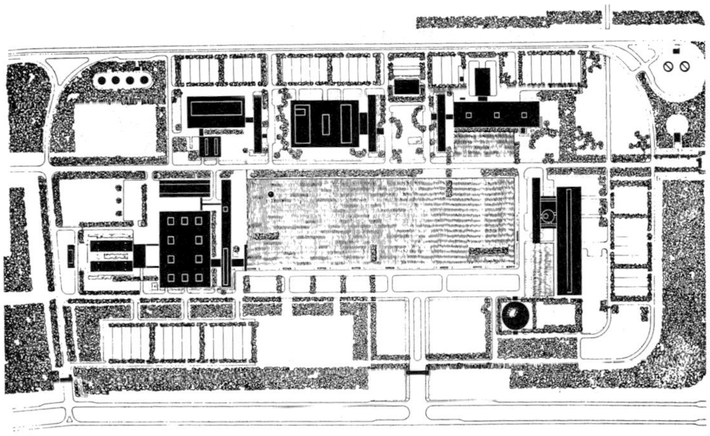

GENERAL MOTORS TECHNICAL CENTER, PLAN. *Eero Saarinen. Warren, Michigan. 1956. Three-story buildings set around a twenty-two-acre lake in masterful interrelationship earned the Technical Center the sobriquet "The Industrial Versailles."*

one concept, that we better stick to it. Then we all tried hard so as not to wander away from that. One danger is to be too much the same. The other is to wander away from it too much. I think we have done that fairly well. But we also have this code between us. When we tackle another problem, such as the MIT auditorium or any other problem, then we realize that this is another concept, we think freshly on everything, including the door butts, for this particular thing.

It is less convenient than doing everything the same, I can assure you. But this is much more fun. And I think it is a very needed thing in architecture because I sort of see architecture today as something closing in and being taken for granted as a package. Some work is done well. We all like it, but then the mediocre and the bad stuff is all the same kind of stuff.

Two years ago, when the Missouri Synod of the Lutheran Church came to me and wanted a senior college for Fort Wayne, Indiana, they probably imagined they would get something like the General Motors Technical Center. But they didn't. I think they might have accepted such a thing, but in talking with them, trying to find the core of their problem and the feeling for the land, out of it grew an entirely different thing.

We're doing this factory for IBM in Rochester, Minnesota, which incidentally has one of the thinnest curtain walls in the world. It's only three-eighths of an inch thick. It's a porcelain-enameled wall. There was a chance to experiment with ornament and to use two tones on the panels. We did hundreds of experiments and finally ended up with the simplest possible thing. It was just a slight reinforcement of the vertical lines, which in a sense is ornament.

IBM PLANT. *Eero Saarinen. Rochester, Minnesota. 1956. Saarinen, a recognized pioneer in curtain-wall construction, enclosed the nine two-story building blocks of this IBM facility with remarkably advanced thin walls.*

I think we have to be terribly careful about ornament, that we don't put ornament on for ornament's sake. Ornament has to be a natural development out of the structure and the fabrication of the building. Now that doesn't mean that in the year of functionalism that we should sit around and wait for ornament to come. It won't come. It's a thing that one should experiment with, it's a thing that one should flirt with. I mean you have to constantly sort of exercise your ability to see further in architecture.

You know, I was saying that a building should be all one thing. If you take that to its ultimate conclusion, it's really the architect who should do the mural or do the sculpture and the landscaping and everything else. I don't mean an office, I don't mean many people. I mean just one individual, Michelangelo or a Frank Lloyd Wright. Have you ever sat on his chairs?

That could be one ultimate conclusion, but I don't mean that. I mean because architecture should not be the sort of the egocentric glorification of an ego. Architecture today is something where many, many people are involved and particularly in larger products. I mean a house can be done all by one person from the very beginning to the very end. But in larger projects there are many involved. For instance, in our office the technical developments that John Dinkeloo is working on relate very strongly to the design things that myself and Kevin Roche are working on, and so on. We also get the help of Dan Kiley on landscaping. Really what I'm sort of thinking of is that the building is the thing. Many personalities have to be subjugated in the process, but the personality of the building has to be saved or has to be made. That's the important thing.

Now, in that total picture, the artist, the Roszak, the Stuart Davis, or the Calder, brings to the building the special sensitivity that he has. It is a terribly, terribly important thing provided, it's an enhancement of the theme of the building. If it is something that diverts from that, then it shouldn't be there. But if it's something that enhances it, it should be there, by all means. It shouldn't be there as an afterthought, because how can it really be part of the whole thing if it's a total afterthought? At the same time, let's be practical also about it. It depends on how integrally it relates to the architecture.

Let's take the problem of the London embassy. The eagle that Ted Roszak is doing for that. We talked very much about just the character of the whole building. How it should relate to that. He did many sketches. From the very beginning we had the intention of the spot which really marks the central axis of the building, also marks the entrance down below.

Now we did not bring Roszak in the day we had the intention of that spot. He came much, much later. It's not practical to bring artists in at the very moment you have an idea that there should be art. If they gripe about that, that's all right. You've heard gripes by artists before, haven't you? It's a natural gripe. It's really how does it end up? Does it end up as an integral part of the building with a piece of art enhancing and enthusiastically really carrying the building further, or is it something which is in a fight with the building?

1956

I think we have to design within our time, uncompromisingly, but we have to broaden the alphabet of modern architecture to face problems that it hasn't faced before. . . . God knows I am very, very enthusiastic about Mies van der Rohe and the almost common vernacular style he has created and that we all accept as a very fine thing. However, I cannot help but think that it's only the ABC of the alphabet, that architecture, if we're to bloom into a full, really great style of architecture, which I think we will, we have to learn many more letters.

Louis Kahn

"THE SEMINAL IDEA OF MY WORK IS THE CONSTANT DISTINCTION BETWEEN THE AREAS THAT ARE SERVED AND THE AREAS THAT SERVE."

Louis Kahn was a small man with some of the biggest ideas in modern architecture. He expressed them in the language of a poet and sketched them with the hand of an artist. His earnestness was compelling and his enthusiasm contagious. To Lou, architecture was a living "persona" that "wants to be."

The true value of a challenging client with a clear functional program to a talented architect was brought home to me in the intense conversations I observed between Kahn and Dr. Jonas Salk at the stunning oceanside site of the Salk Institute. Lou later said he was the ideal client, "who knows not what he wants but what he aspires to."

On one occasion we recorded him in his office, surrounded by associates as eager to be with him as we were. One does not have to listen to him for very long on these recordings to appreciate why he was one of the most inspiring teachers. His commitment to education, which he pursued as a professor of architecture at Yale and the University of Pennsylvania, was such that his important architectural works were packed into the last eighteen

SALK INSTITUTE. *Louis Kahn. La Jolla, California. 1965. This research institute, built among rolling hills with a breathtaking view of the Pacific, is composed of eight concrete study towers backed by two laboratory blocks. The structures flank a broad, paved plaza.*

years of his life. With his tousled white hair and bow tie in disarray, he gave the impression of a man on charrette hurrying to accomplish a life's worth of work in the little time left.

However, there was nothing hurried about his buildings. They represented, as he said, "the thoughtful making of spaces," executed with a root respect for the great architectural periods of the past, a love of building materials, and a firm grasp of modern technology. He viewed architecture as a fine art, and it is no accident that three of his most renowned designs are art museums.

1961

JOHN PETER: *How did you become interested in architecture?*
LOU KAHN: I have been very reluctant about anything personal because I felt what I really wanted to have a person do is to write something like Viollet-le-Duc, you see. Not a personal history, which is really different from the work story.

One question was, "Who inspired you . . . to do the work you do?" And I said the inspiration is somewhat classical. It is really Greek, Roman, Gothic, Romanesque, Renaissance architecture. It stands there constantly as a marvelous challenge, you see, for what I do now. And then from that kind of general thing sits another man

who is most significant to me. That's Le Corbusier, you see. Most significant to me. Now the significance, of course, lies in the images that he created. But I always sensed that the image belongs to him, that I'd never copy him, you see. But what activated a sense of architecture in me was really he, you see, and not the old stuff. The old stuff was ready there to be plucked, you might say. They were so very general in their way that no personality really entered the thing at all. And he, in his case, there was a personality who said certain things differently from anyone else. But he was answerable to what would later become the common stuff called architecture. So I always wanted to work for him. But I always felt, well . . . if I were a youngster I'd work readily for him. Because I must find my own way, so it made me reluctant to work for him, you see.

Now when I did the bath house, the Trenton Bath House, I discovered a very simple thing. I discovered that certain spaces are very unimportant and some spaces are the real raison d'être for doing what you're doing. But the small spaces were contributing to the strength of the larger spaces. They were serving them. And when I realized there were servant areas and there were areas served, that difference, I realized I didn't have to work for Corbusier anymore. At that moment I realized I don't have to work for him at all.

JEWISH COMMUNITY CENTER BATH HOUSE. *Louis Kahn. Trenton, New Jersey. 1957. In this brick bath-house with pyramidal roofs, Kahn first gave form to his concept of served and servant spaces.*

J.P.: *That wasn't very long ago.*

L.K.: That was just a few years ago, you might say. All the other times, I had my own way of expressing things aesthetically. And I modified, you might say, almost, the images which were created by other men. I had always a feeling that I was not in the depths of architecture really. I was in the depths of design, I was in the depths of knowing about things and could see that the variation on the theme of the works of other architects was very akin to me. But I did not find something of a truth which belonged to me, which belonged to architecture, from which I drew because I had discovered it, you see. It drew in greater richness than others because I knew the aura of its essence. I knew very well.

LOUIS KAHN *in his Philadelphia office, 1961*

RICHARDS MEDICAL RESEARCH BUILDING, UNIVERSITY OF PENNSYLVANIA. *Louis Kahn. Philadelphia. 1961. Kahn found the form of this research building in its need for uncontaminated air. He linked four separate laboratory areas and surrounded them with tall ventilating stacks that rise two stories above the roof.*

At that moment, I realized that what I had discovered in the way of the hierarchy of spaces, of the servant areas and the areas served, that I had discovered something that belongs to everybody else, but from which I would base my own designs very clearly and strongly as a way of life. I began to see architecture as a way of life at that point, where previously they were the artful manipulation of spaces appropriate to use. But as a way of life, something which everyone could use quite freely, like the invention of an ax. At that moment it doesn't belong to you. It belongs to the woodsman. It belongs to making houses. It belongs to a lot of things. So this thing is of the same nature.

You might say we are a scientifically resourceful society. There's so many laws we now have by the tail and we're not making good rules to work with them. The law is a completely unchangeable thing, but rules must always be considered as being changeable. The rules should never be given to anybody cold without telling the law that is back of it.

J.P.: *In the field of technology, we have invented a whole new set of rules.*
L.K.: No, we've found new laws. We have found new harmony of laws, but we have not found good rules to live by.

J.P.: *Your "served and servant areas" concept is almost the opposite of Mies's universal space, in which the structure permits flexible and different uses over time.*
L.K.: I am at complete variance with it, but understand now what Mies is. I would say he is really sensitive and is as sensitive as any man I know. His personal way of expressing things is different from my way—I most humbly present as my way, which may be a way of life. Whatever can be taken from Mies is fine, but I don't want to say one is better or less.

J.P.: *Tell us, Lou, how your thoughts about the servant order apply to some specific buildings.*
L.K.: I can show you that very easily. You see, in the laboratories of the University of Pennsylvania, I realized that the air you breathe should not come in contact with

the air you throw away in a laboratory, because the air you throw away in a laboratory is germ infected. It is noxious. It is not good to breathe. If you used it, the law would say you're not in good shape. It's not only waste air, but it's dangerous air. It has germs in it. If you were to get anywhere near the breathing apparatus for this air, you would be a dead duck.

I make a good rule and say that the air you breathe should never come in contact with the air you throw away. It's a rule I made. So, therefore, I put all the exhaust towers high, and I put all the air intakes low, on the other side. It never comes in contact with it. Now this shaped the building, don't you see?

J.P.: *Take another laboratory like your Salk Institute.*

L.K.: Here I made the distinction between the wonder and knowledge careers. In the wonder—here's the Salk site—there's the Pacific Ocean and the canyons, the garden entrances in the arcades below. The studies open to the laboratory areas.

In a biological laboratory, as distinguished from other laboratories, the air must be as free of spores as possible because it's not only injurious to the man, but it's injurious to the experiment, which many consider more important than the man. So the architecture must be a completely cleanable architecture. It must be the architecture of stainless steel. It must be the architecture of clean air.

But the study, the place where I hang my hat and just brood over things, and even go to sleep, is a room where you get away from the laboratory. It is really the architecture of the oak table and the rug. It is completely different. Therefore, I divided the studies from the laboratory itself. I put the studies over arcades which enter from gardens. The laboratories overlook the gardens. A library of immediate use to the laboratories overlooks the canyon.

A quarter of a mile away is the meetinghouse, which is where all minds come together. Dr. Salk is particularly concerned not to isolate research into a clannish, self-centered, limited mental experience, but to be constantly in the presence of wonder in the work, so that men come to visit in this château like Bertrand Russell, like C.P. Snow, who are in constant touch with men concerned with biology. Yes, they are always reminded, you see, that man is not just this.

Here, again, is the assembly hall where, of course, assembly is a deliberate thing. This is a complex of a kind of great house where men get together, without thinking of biology so much as a problem as it is of all nature and all things.

Therefore, an architect, when he gets a program from a client, should begin . . . right from the start to say, "What is the nature of this institution?" His first duty is this. He must take all the areas which are given to him by the client and translate them into spaces. The client knows only about areas. Then he must take all the corridors that the client has in his mind and change them into galleries because corridors only lead you to places for lockers and return air ducts. That's all it gives you. But a gallery, which probably has natural light, may even reach higher and above all other functioning areas because natural light is the only way you can distinguish space from an area. An artificial lamp will never do this because it's only one incidence in light, where natural lighting has all the seasons and all the nuances of the time of day in it. So how can you compare one with the other? The architecture of space must be that which is bathed in natural light.

I was asked to do a monastery in the high desert near Los Angeles. I lived with the monks for a day. I sensed out of the very position, that is to say, the location, that one of the most important things I must remember about this place is that water is scarce.

Who will deny the importance of water? But if you imagine as a city planner that water is always in pipes, then you're not thinking fundamentally enough about city planning. You must think of water as being water and not necessarily in pipes. If it is conveniently in pipes, that's okay, too, but you must think fundamentally.

Now they didn't have any pipes. Their water came from wells. They, of course, are using pipe water now in the lower part of the development, but where I'm going to build this monastery, there is no water. There are also very strict laws about using water, pumping water, which will take away some of the pressure which now exists. They said to me, "We know where water is." I said, "If you do and have trust in this, we'll start the plan with the source of the water. Then, at the source of water, you must build something, a monument to the source of the water. . . . This has nothing to do with your religion, which I know nothing about." I was very frank, but I said, "I know enough about the sense of man existing on earth to know that you must give respect for the fact that you have found water."

Then I said, "From this water source, you must then build the contour so that you make as much use of law as possible, gravity being very important for water. Water wants to go downhill. Or you can find another law that says you can have water go uphill. We couldn't build a tall building unless we did have it go up, right? And so you combine the gravity, which costs you nothing, with the pump that costs you something. You make a good rule in establishing this and you develop an order out of water.

"An order of water, just that, which, in a way, is a kind of aqueduct architecture. This aqueduct architecture gives you the systems to house water which can be made beautifully in architecture expressing these systems. Aqueducts carry the water off to places where you can do your irrigation, where you can even build your buildings. This will establish the position for your church, for the chapel, for the monastery cells, and for the little workshops, because that water is of prime importance in the establishment of life in this area." Water at work. Good rules at work.

Now I say, "All right, you're living in a high desert, it gets cold here. Also, it gets very warm here. I propose that you consider walls, which are of a certain nature. The nature of a wall is that on the outside you expect certain things to happen to the wall, and on the inside you expect certain things to happen to the wall. If it's cold outside, for instance, you want it warm inside. This wall must be made so that warmth can be retained on the inside if it's cold outside and vice versa. You don't want dampness to come in. So this wall must have good rules in its making to be able to respect the laws which are playing on this thing, and have to do with your desire as man to control these laws. . . . Instead of having, let us say, a single wall, why don't you have two walls? One an outside wall and one an inside wall, which do not come together at all. And you have a passage between them in which you can walk causing

ST. ANDREW'S PRIORY PROJECT. *Louis Kahn. Valyermo, California. 1966. Kahn keyed this building, sited high on a barren hill, to the need for water. He placed the reservoir atop the entrance tower and arrayed the monastery cells, with their irrigated terraces and gardens, at the edge of the slope overlooking the desert.*

a venturi of air, which will cool the interior airs in the summertime, which will form an insulation for the interior in the wintertime by placing doors in this avenue that you can walk into, in other words, this little street. You will close the doors on either side. And you will have a beginning, let's say, of a kind of cloister, but not in the old terms. It's a new law which makes a cloister."

Then I said, "Now you have a possibility of using your adobe. After all, you're not rich. You make everything you live by. Therefore, I say we should bring the most marvelous experts in the building of concrete frames, which will span your roofs and span your floors, but the walls will be enclosed on this framework or lattice of concrete, which is the proper way of using concrete, by the way." Now I did not make any drawings on paper. Realizing nature's way, I made rules which would apply to beginning a way of life of a monastery in this locality.

So from the beginning, you see, greatness can emerge in architecture. Beginnings are very necessary today, new beginnings of expressing spatially our institutions. Our institutions are miserably expressed under paneled curtain walls, sort of homogenized, anonymous looking buildings.

We are simply clothing, you might say, old things. We are not contributing to the making of our institutions greater and greater and greater. So that the spaces themselves can evoke a creative attitude toward the institution because men who work in it will be greatly elevated into the seriousness, or you might say into the glory, of contributing to this institution. Architecture, at least, can do its part in the making the spaces in it great.

The seminal idea of my work is the constant distinction between the areas that are served and the areas that serve. And that distinguishes, in my opinion, modern architecture from old architecture. Because the spaces, the servant spaces are different in every age. You still have round rooms. You still have great halls. You still have light from above or below. You see, you can't get away from the fact that space enclosed is of a nature quite like other spaces of old. The Pantheon is a beautiful example of a terrific space which you can't surpass no matter what age. It really spells enclosure. It spells a world of its own, you see. And that's what a building is. A building is a world of its own.

There must be a kind of new belief if you want a new city. It just cannot be because the other city's overcrowded that you begin a new city. No, a new city begins

YALE ART GALLERY, YALE UNIVERSITY. *Louis Kahn with Douglas Or. New Haven, Connecticut. 1953. The severe brick and glass exterior of Kahn's extension to the Yale Art Gallery offers no hint of the interior with its remarkable honeycombed ceiling, which freed the inside of columns for completely flexible planning.*

with belief of some kind. All cities have belief. New York has a belief, though it may not be clear. It must be made more clear. Almost the first purpose should be to clarify the belief of the city.

Around this realization of areas that serve and are served, which I call a realization, immediately many things went into orbit. City planning became absolutely clear to me at that point because I realized that a plan of a city had to distinguish between that which serves the spaces of the city or, I say, the institutions within which the spaces live. . . . Let's put it the other way. The institutions live in the spaces. Everything we build we build for an institution. It's the institution of home. It's the institution of learning, institution of government, institution of recreation, institution of health. They're all institutions. Every single thing that we established as part of a way of life is an instituted thing. It's a supported thing.

J.P.: *Is our architecture different from the earlier civilizations because our institutions are different?*
L.K.: There are now more institutions. There are institutions going into being. The architect must make the institution great by the way he puts the spaces within which they will do their creative work. It depends on how great he makes those spaces.

J.P.: *So this hierarchy of spaces applies not only to architecture as a building or a complex, but to the total environment in which we live.*
L.K.: Exactly. From this I derived the idea that there is a difference between the viaduct architecture and the architecture of the institutions of man. The institutions of man sit as in the complexity of movement, which is part of the viaduct architecture, in contrast with the toughness of the viaduct architecture and the gossamer delicacy of the buildings of the institutions of man.

To me, it is a beautiful distinction because buildings know how they should be built and roads know how they should be. And as the roads enter the city they change their character because they're entering precious areas. Viaduct architecture is the architecture of movement, which involves coming from distant spaces and are of major concern to the city. When they are entering the city, they must be more respectable. Their construction must be finer, and because they occupy very strategic spaces, as expressways do, they must contain more than just the road itself. They are the places for the storage areas of the city.

Mostly we talk about the center part of the city because it is the image that one associates with city more than any other part. And almost every other part is more or less answerable to it, is inspired by it, and relates itself to it. The center of the city must become great again. That's what I want to say, really.

Time usually brings about a realization of how backward the city is. I think it's happened through the ages, that suddenly you realized that you were not the city you were before, or in relation to other places, you're not as great as you were before. New things have happened in which you must take care. So now the city has been dismembered or deformed, you might say—deformed is a good word—because the way

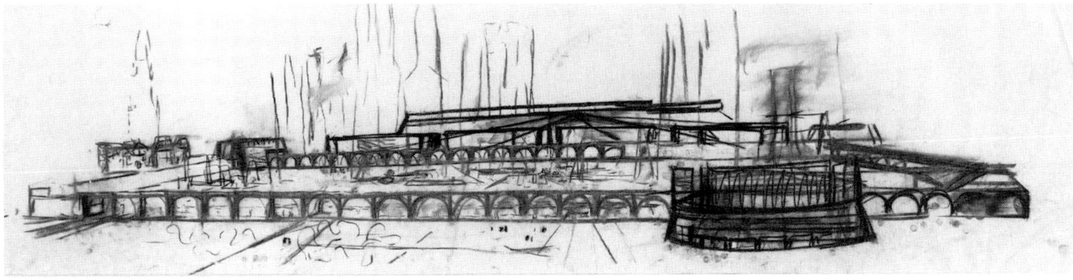

CENTER CITY PROJECT. *Louis Kahn. Philadelphia. 1956. In this sketch Kahn applied his servant and served concept to urban planning with a multilevel viaduct accommodating various forms of transport traffic.*

of life is different. The car has made life very different. The viaduct architecture is the architecture of movement involving a car and it has a tendency now to actually deform the city.

What I'm trying to get at is this. If you think of the viaduct, the viaduct architecture is the architecture really of the street, which has become more than just a road. It requires a flowing architecture. And a flowing architecture is really the architecture of movement. No other architecture requires flow, because a man can dodge very easily around corners and around circular areas, or go straight, or jump over something. He can do anything. But a car, really, is a flowing thing when it is moving. Its objective is to stop. No matter what its movements are, its objective is finally to stop, and in the center of the city especially. So the center of the city is really the stopping place for the car. It's a resting place for the car. The city is something to come to and not go through.

Already the city planners and road builders realize this by making circumferential roads and getting from the circumferential roads into the center of the city. But they do not consider the road as architecture. They consider the road still as the Appian Way, you know, with things either under it or not. But no, that road pattern is also the pattern of service to the city. Therefore, that road must be considered as a building on which you're riding the roof of, below which are pipes and maybe storage spaces, for both the car and wares and goods, let's say, for the service of the city.

J.P.: *In other words, the way it developed, the roads were considered engineering problems at best? They were never considered architecture.*

L.K.: Well, let me say this. There are major roads coming from outlying places to the city. When they enter the city, they must become different roads than they were outside because they're entering strategic, valuable, and viable land. Their position is in a service relationship to the city. They are not just any roads, but they are a particular road which I like to call the viaduct. A "via-duct," a way of going. This could just as well be related to other services which a city needs, storage houses, related to central air-conditioning centers, the centers of all piping.

J.P.: *Huge mechanical cores . . .*

L.K.: Yes, so that these viaducts should be so carefully planned as part of the architecture of the city that the center becomes intensely served by their presence. This would make it possible to economically place them closer to the center because they are doing more work than just being a road. They must be buildings because you never want to tear them up in order to get at the pipes, in order to get at the ducts, in order to get more electrical service, which is constantly happening in the city. The road must be made so that it is never torn up for any purpose.

Therefore, you must walk into the road with its elevators, you might say, and with its stairways, into the places where piping exists, in their own rooms and their own fixing areas, in the storage houses for the cars or storage houses for goods, but they are really a very important architecture of their own which filters through the city in a highly organized way, constructed not as a road one day, as a garage another day, or by one man or another, or storage houses built by another group and air-conditioning centers by another interest, but that this joint interest of service be attached to the service of entrance to the city. This is called the beginning of viaduct architecture, as

PROPOSAL FOR CENTER CITY. *Louis Kahn. Philadelphia. 1950. As a member of Associated City Planners, Kahn translated the committee's report into sketches and a gigantic model of the imaginative but ill-fated Philadelphia redevelopment plan.*

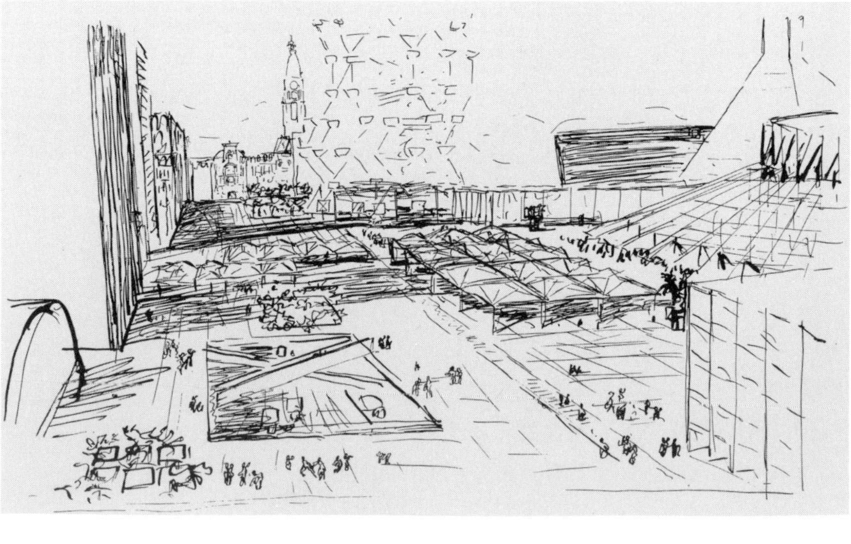

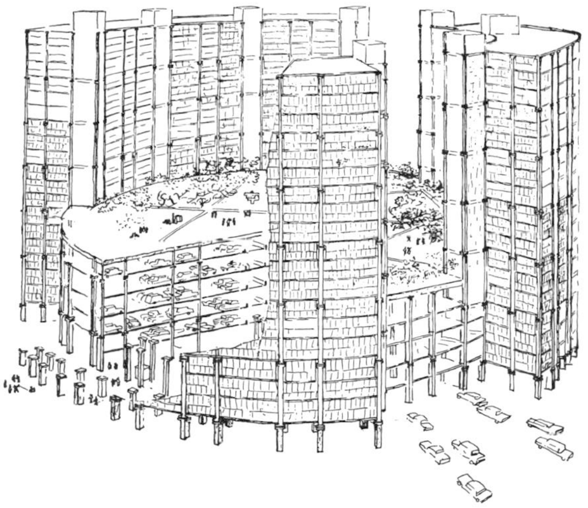

PARKING TOWER PROJECT. *Louis Kahn. Philadelphia. 1956. Envisioned for Philadelphia's Civic Center, the parking tower, shown here in a cutaway perspective drawing, was conceived as a cylindrical building with the parking area surrounded by tall towers.*

contrasted with the architecture of the institutions of man, which are free from all these problems.

J.P.: *In earlier periods when the street was a pedestrian street, or a piazza, it was really part of architecture, wasn't it?*

L.K.: Oh, yes, it was a room. The street was an outside room. The piazza was an outside room. In fact, many times a piazza was as long as a cathedral was high. Because one measured the details of the cathedral by the clearance in front of the cathedral. Many times things were laid out on this piazza before it was erected.

So they were very alive, these places, and they were all part of the way of life. Now I'm making a distinction between a way of life and the way of living. A way of living is a personal thing. You live your own way, but a way of life has to do with the rules of living. We've found new laws. We have found new harmony of laws. Remember, these rules are only great if they follow the laws of nature. If you're going to the moon you should feel the kind of sameness of purpose, it should be something that we all really want to satisfy our sense of wonder.

Philip Johnson

"ONE THING THAT I REALLY THINK RUNS AS A THREAD IS MY PASSIONATE INTEREST IN PROCESSIONAL SPACE, SPACE AS APPREHENDED BY WALKING THROUGH IT."

Philip Johnson is known as an articulate observer and practitioner of modern architecture. Through his work as a historian and author with Henry-Russell Hitchcock of The International Style *and as the first curator of the pioneering architecture department of The Museum of Modern Art, New York, he made a major contribution to the early recognition of the modern movement.*

Johnson's political excursions, acerbic wit, and controversial works have kept him in the center of the architectural storm. His trim, urbane appearance and sophisticated life-style reinforce the image of an aesthete. Yet I am reminded of his determined return to Harvard University, at the age of thirty-three, to obtain an architectural degree every time I pass his tiny Ash Street house in Cambridge. In his generation, not many people went back to school to start a new career at that age. Not many students build their class project and live in it while earning their degree.

I recorded Johnson in his Connecticut Glass House and twice in his architectural offices in New York. His architecture is an accurate mirror of the man and the times. An early apostle of modern architectural orthodoxy, he

now feels, "There are no rules anymore!" Though he is quite justly known for his buildings, it is in the tranquil setting of his New Canaan house, the sculpture garden of The Museum of Modern Art, or the cascading fountain at Fort Wayne that he exhibits a talent for landscaping uncommon among modern architects.

GLASS HOUSE. *Philip Johnson. New Canaan, Connecticut. 1949. With sweeping views and privacy provided by surrounding landscaped areas, Johnson's famous transparent pavilion of steel and glass is a single room, punctuated by a circular brick fireplace and bathroom and divided by teak storage units.*

1955

JOHN PETER: *How did you first become interested in architecture?*
PHILIP JOHNSON: When I was eighteen years old I read an article in the old *Arts Magazine* on architecture. I was a major in college in Greek. I picked up this magazine article by Russell Hitchcock on the work of J. J. P. Oud, one of the Dutch pioneers. That afternoon as I finished the article—it was practically illegible, but the pictures were there—I decided that I was going to change my career and I'd be an architect. It happened in exactly three hours. I had never thought of being an architect before that time.

1963

J. P.: *Phil, what do you think you will be remembered for?*
P. J.: Mendelsohn once wrote that architects are remembered by their one-room buildings. How true. The only buildings that I got prizes for were this house, the reac-

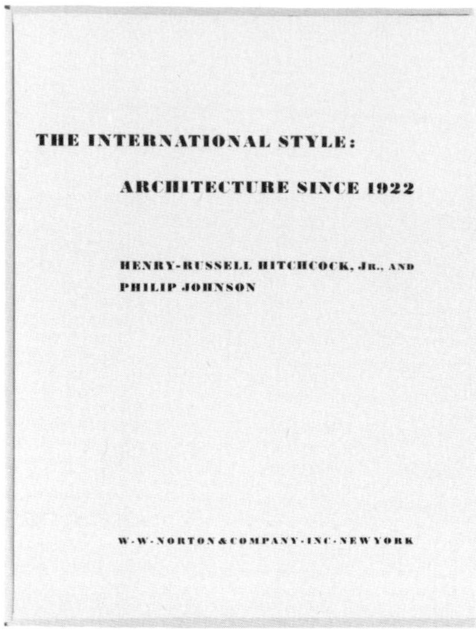
THE INTERNATIONAL STYLE:

ARCHITECTURE SINCE 1922

HENRY-RUSSELL HITCHCOCK, JR., AND PHILIP JOHNSON

W·W·NORTON & COMPANY·INC·NEW YORK

THE INTERNATIONAL STYLE: ARCHITECTURE SINCE 1922. Henry-Russell Hitchcock and Philip Johnson. W.W. Norton, New York. 1932. This influential book was published in conjunction with the first architectural exhibition at The Museum of Modern Art, New York City. It announced and documented the emergence of the new modern style.

tor in Israel, and the church in New Harmony, not by my dormitories or office buildings. No, you're remembered by your one-room buildings or your one-court buildings, like Eero's dormitories. It's a single conception. I mean it's the one-shot deal that you're remembered by. Of course, Mendelsohn put it in architectural terms, but maybe it's also your great chance, you see.

J.P.: *A one-room building, for instance, like a theater.*

P.J.: A theater is a place where a community meets to be elevated. If there's one time that architecture's going to be frozen music, it better be a theater. To me, workshop theaters, like the Loeb Theater in Cambridge, don't interest one. The ceiling's too low, there's no lift, everything's mechanics. The money went into moving the chairs around. It's a typical American aberration. If you move it enough then you get out of being an architect. It's a crutch. It wasn't one of my "Seven Crutches of Modern Architecture," but it should've been. If you leave it all to the consultants you don't have to do the work yourself. Well, the electricians want that and the lighting people want this. What's a poor architect to do? An abdication of the will and the right of an architect to his seats.

You've got to whip your consultants and somehow overcome them to make a monumental space out of a theater. Because if you feel good, you feel well dressed and you're going to enjoy the play more. So the theater, if there's anything to it from an architectural point of view, it's the glamour. Not whether the seats turn around with the press of a button, you see. I feel that the basic experience of going to the theater is the proscenium. I don't want somebody coming out on a platform that I see, and talk to me. I want that sense of the curtains going up. To me, it's of the essence. Now I admit that this is a personal reaction, but it's one that I just don't mind continuing if I have a chance to continue it.

J.P.: *What about Lincoln Center?*

P.J.: My first sketch was not unlike what turned out to be the present Philharmonic. I said, "Look boys, since nobody's going to do any good architecture

NEW YORK STATE THEATER, LINCOLN CENTER FOR THE PERFORMING ARTS. *Philip Johnson and Richard Foster. New York City. 1964. The handsome State Theater was designed to relate to the other buildings surrounding the plaza and fountain. It seats twenty-eight hundred people and is used primarily for ballet and opera performances.*

here, let's get a module. Let's come to what we can all stick to. Let's take a twenty-foot bay and just repeat it around." Well, Abramovitz ran with it. My committee who was over me said no. They're opera people. They're not interested in art or architecture. I showed them my semicircular one that, in my book, was the proper thing to do. They just didn't do it. So we lost the exterior, but I've got some wonderful rooms in there.

Of course, there's that other question of the theater as a processional thing, which I spent more time on than any other architect might. As usual, it's my interest. In my theater you get to your seat in a most wonderful way. You get to the great room in an easy and logical way. Even Paris, as grand as it was, is a little bit complicated. If you're handling three thousand people, you want to give them a good time. You have a lot of things they have to do, like buying a ticket, giving it up, getting a drink, going to their seats, getting out of their seats, finding a taxi. All these things they have to do. It does seem to me incumbent on the architect to make these things as easy as possible, as gracious as possible.

For instance, one thing the owners tried to force me to use was an escalator because, you see, you're handling these great crowds and we have all these wonderful new methods of changing levels. I tried to say it was too expensive because it cost $100,000 and they said, "Well, we'll raise that $100,000." All of a sudden they had money. There wasn't any money for other things, but they wanted the gadget.

The other thing I refused, even though they requested it, was the revolving doors. It's not gracious living to go through a revolving door. If you have to go into an office building you do, but you don't enjoy it. You're in a different atmosphere. You're on business. You're pushed through revolving doors. That's an awful thing that revolving door. The whole sense of the thing is "Where am I?" department.

J.P.: *Does the fountain prepare you for the Lincoln Center buildings?*
P.J.: Actually, that square is going to be very pleasant. People make fun of it. They're all surprised at how small it is. Which, of course, pleases me very much. Because it's exactly the same size as the Capitoline Hill plaza of Michelangelo. Not that that's good or bad, but it's that small, you see. But who wants a larger one?

J.P.: *I think they were comparing it to the Piazza San Marco in Venice. Given the size of the Lincoln Center plaza, one of the many suggestions you made was to enclose the front.*
P.J.: Oh boy, that would have been a thing. Because then you would've entered through a screen as you used to enter into St. Peter's Square before they ruined it by opening the front. We used to filter through the columns. The disclosure of a square through those columns is a semi-enclosed feeling that's delicious.

Right now we're going to have a bad opening onto the city on one of the four sides of the square. It'll be all right as you approach, but when you're walking out, you'll be in the city. It's just a bay out of the city instead of a square of its own. Even in San Marco, you come through colonnades, except for that one place the Piazzetti. If you saw New York, as you would've, through my colonnade, it would have been wonderful. But that's what I mean by committee architecture. Architecture aside, who's going to bell the cat? For instance, who's going to be allowed to design that colonnade? Since it was my suggestion, everybody thought that I would design it and, therefore, of course, they threw it out. Jealousy being human, you can't blame them. But the fountain, of course, will be stupendous.

J.P.: *You've done a lot of both museums and exhibitions.*
P.J.: Yes. My main group of work is in museums. I think it's the most important job of the day for the simple reason that there is no more possibility of having churches as the monumental building of a community. The thing that people vicariously enjoy.

I noticed that in Utica there's great nineteenth-century buildings, but there's no twentieth-century building. When we built the museum, the pride of the town is in that museum. You arrive in the town and they say, "Have you seen our museum?" The period of saying that about a church is, for reasons we can't go into, gone. I'd say, well, what about a city hall? That's gone, too. Or even the idea of saying that about a university, there are towns that don't have universities. In other words, there's no vicarious pleasure in a palace, let's say, that you might find in a provincial, central European town. A factory has never been something that you can say, "Oh, come and see our factory."

The one building that's viable in America as a symbol of the importance of their town has become the museum. The civic symbol, instead of being either a civic building or a library or a school or a palace or a town hall or a church is now a museum. This is for many reasons true. I think one of the strange ones that makes it true is that Americans are education mad. We have no limits to the amount we spend on automobiles and education. A museum just barely gets under the category of education. So it's not waste. You see, Americans cannot waste anything. It's not antibusiness, because education is still allowable as a value, you see. For one reason or another, the museum has become the essence of the town pride.

My main interest in life is to build buildings that people are going to have a pride in. It becomes a building with overtones of art, magnificence, monumentality, emotion. Therefore the museum is, to me, the most interesting job for an architect today. The theater might be, but the theater, since the 1920s, has not been built in this country. Maybe Lincoln Center will change that and all the theaters that are now going up. Lincoln Center is, of course, a pleasure to work on for exactly the same reason. That it is the thing that New Yorkers are going to be proud of. Whatever they think of it now. It gets into that museum world, the type of building that one likes to build.

Since I was a museum man before, it was perfectly natural that I would try to get museum jobs. It was first started, of course, in Utica. That was a job I got first many years ago. The pleasure of a museum is that it is a manifold problem of a functional and emotional nature. Of course, my interest, as Frank Lloyd Wright's was in the Guggenheim, is the monumental nature of it. As a former museum man, I couldn't do a Frank Lloyd Wright type building—a Guggenheim. I had to do a building that would work. The Guggenheim is fine, but you can't hang pictures in it. The Museum

PHILIP JOHNSON *at his office in New York City, 1955*

MUNSON-WILLIAMS-PROCTOR INSTITUTE. *Philip Johnson. Utica, New York. 1957. With the lower floor enclosed in glass, the bulk of this museum appears as a granite-faced cube suspended from a monumental bronze-covered concrete frame.*

of Modern Art, you can hang pictures in, but it's not fine. My job, I felt, was to make a building that was fine but you could still have pictures in.

Now my first one, the Utica building, has a great central hall, which has been criticized by the Museum of Modern Art staff. René d'Harnoncourt, for instance, at the opening, leaned over my shoulder and said, "It's magnificent, Johnson, but is it a museum?" The Museum of Modern Art staff puts it in the same category as Wright, which shocked me, rather, because I thought I had hung pictures. But if you look at the total cubage given to *grandezza* versus the total cubage given to hanging pictures, maybe he has a point.

I agree perfectly with them about The Museum of Modern Art in New York. You could hang pictures literally in a garage. Then it would be perfectly acceptable because we've arrived, as it were. We no longer need that museum as a community pride symbol. New York doesn't need it. They need Lincoln Center. They need the Metropolitan. They need Central Park. They need the tallest building in the world. But they don't need another museum to express it. But the other towns do. I feel, and it's proven, that way.

For instance, the big court at Utica is used for speeches, concerts, meetings, festivals, changing shows, anything that plays. They use the stairs there to act Shakespeare on, you see. It becomes a community center which is certainly, to me, part of the duty of public-spirited citizens that are giving museums. There's no way that Utica could have a great collection of The Museum of Modern Art's caliber and I feel that you need to sell, in that horrible American sense of the word sell, art by means of architecture. Therefore, to me, museums are community centers and community centers are museums.

We went on from Utica to Fort Worth, that was my second. Fort Worth, of course, had a slightly different point in that it was a memorial building to a great public-spirited citizen. It was built in a public park. The city gave the land and the family gave the museum. I was told when I got the job that this job was to be a memorial to Amon Carter. This is an interesting reversal, you see, of the usual thing. They said, "We want a monument to Amon Carter." So I built a monument in a park. Then, because of the brilliance of the family and the ownership, they found out what a community service the museum really was. In other words, this is the cart before the horse. We built the shell, then they found people liked the shell so much, they had to build a museum. We are now engaged in more than doubling the cubage of that building. We're making a museum out of it, as well as a monument to Amon Carter. The wing that is going on behind it is more than the size of the part that I built. But, you see, so important is the civic symbol there that the museum part almost got lost.

Then, when you take another example, Lincoln, Nebraska, was the third museum that I built and that was the university museum. Now there we had the central part of our country, the heartland of America. Nebraska is absolutely the center of population, the center of geography of the United States, but they feel quite neglected. There's no oil. There's no industry. There's no new discovery. It's farmland. It's the old American stock. The twentieth century has passed Nebraska by. By creating a monument there, we reestablished Nebraska as one of the pioneer states which they used to be with the great capitol they built by Goodhue. Once again, Nebraska can pat itself on the back with pride that they are in the forefront of design. They cannot ever have a great collection. Again, it was the importance of showing to the undergraduate body, some fifteen thousand American heartland children, that there were other values besides the sciences and the books that they're working in. To get them into the museum, we created a monument.

It was also, as it happened, the wish of the donor to spend all the money on the building. The will specifically states that they cannot take one cent from the will money to use for anything but the building. So convinced were they, the donors, that it was important to create a symbol building. Of course, it worked out exactly that way. There were editorials in every paper that this great building, which cost four or five times as much per square foot as any other building, should be regarded as a gift for the future of Nebraska and not compared with what the recreation buildings across the street cost. Of course, the fact that that could be a controversy is a very interesting point, isn't it? Actually, one legislator went as far as to say that the university had no right to accept money to be spent on a wasteful building.

AMON CARTER MUSEUM. *Philip Johnson. Fort Worth, Texas. 1961. Set behind a formal facade of five carved arches, this memorial museum has teak-walled galleries arrayed around a double-height central hall. It is faced with Texas shellstone and occupies a stepped and landscaped site.*

SHELDON MEMORIAL ART GALLERY, UNIVERSITY OF NEBRASKA. *Philip Johnson. Lincoln. 1963. The museum has a classicism befitting its location at the heart of a university campus. Ten travertine-encased piers and solid windowless walls enclose the galleries and auditorium.*

This is a great battle in this country, between the cost-per-square-foot people and the people that want to do something grand. In this case the donors made it perfectly clear the university would have to assume the maintenance of this building. So the legislature, who has to accept it, finally, for the university, because it's a state university, has the right to refuse the money on the grounds that the cost of maintenance would be too high. But, finally, the university, through its enlightened chancellor, agreed to it.

A miserable building would have had exactly the same maintenance. I sound like a very wasteful architect. But I consider myself a very strong functionalist. When the museum director wanted the skylighting, I made the daylight lighting on the pictures. I made a study of the air-conditioning costs and found out that for another $40,000 a year in air-conditioning cost they could have a skylight. Well, that ruled it out, of course, because that wasn't in the will to maintain any such costs. My point was to make a maintenance-light building, although, very, very expensive. I didn't spare any costs on the glory of the carving of the marble, for instance, or anything like that. The marble was carved in Italy and sent over in numbered pieces and fitted together here. A man from our office went over. When he found a piece that didn't fit, he took a sledgehammer and broke it, to the tears, of course, of the men who had done all the carving. At least, then they didn't do it wrong the next time.

It's absolutely amazing, Peter, to see it in this age. It seems like from another era because nowadays we don't carve marble buildings. I mean this doesn't look like you just built it. You have to blink. I think in a few years you'll never know the age of it when it gets a patina on the travertine, because it's so unlikely to find a building with carving.

I first started the carved arch idea in the pavilion, down there by this house, by trying to invent a new column. I've always been annoyed by what I call the Brunelleschi problem. That is something Brunelleschi could never do in an interior court. He didn't know what to do when he got to the corner. You can't take a column that's at a corner. It disappears. So all you see in Brunelleschi's court is a little bit, about an inch size, of Ionic column left over from each piece of the final column. It wasn't until the Baroque times when Laurano first, in Urbino, created the column that would be in the corner. He pulled it out and made two columns of it. In other words, what you can't do with the columns is to go around all the corners. My main aim was to make the universal column with an arch that would go around outside corners, inside corners, and flat, and could also be made into a pilaster without changing the form of the column. That occupied me for a couple of years. One application of it, of course, is my pavilion in New Canaan, and one is the new house in Dallas that's just being finished now with four hundred of these columns.

The third, and by far the best, is the museum in Lincoln, Nebraska. Where we didn't use concrete, but where we carved every single piece and fit it together. There I found out something. Like all amusing inventions something has to be added by accident, like the waving of the bead curtains at the Four Seasons restaurant, which I didn't know was going to happen. What happened, with these columns, is it appears that when you carve marble concave, it makes very interesting shadows that you don't get by carving it convex. A concave carving proves in the first place that it's hand carved because you can't get in there with a machine. In the second place, the shadows change as the sun and the lights move around it. It gives it a third-dimensional feeling that you never can get from flat surfaces built up or from concave surfaces. Even if you're outside the building, it's a sense of semi-enclosure bubbling up around you, and it has to be done in good stone. The concrete doesn't do the same thing.

Then I did another thing in the central space, which I always use in my museums, to give you a sense of awe as you enter a building. It does seem, to me, the most important thing in a museum, if you're trying to sell anything, the building itself or pictures or whatever you want to sell, is to give the feeling of awe. I mean it is the main principle in any architectural design, whether it's a boudoir or not, to get the sense of awe as soon as you can. In that court, which is a room, with the use of these arches, with the sense of being enclosed, the floor is travertine, the walls are travertine, the ceiling is travertine, with gold leaf medallions on it, the curved corners curving toward you, the curving in of the ceiling corner, the curving in of the floor corner and the fact that it's all the same travertine. I hate to use words like womb, but you do feel involved in it. Much as you do, I think, in a different sense, you do feel involved in the TWA of Eero's. You feel the roof coming down to the floor. The floor engaged with the walls and the walls engaged to the ceiling. Of course, I do it architecturally and not physically. In other words, I don't actually bend the ceiling down. However, it does get you a sense of being wrapped in travertine.

It's a form I'm used to. It's a form I used in my own pavilion, which I'm used to, in precast concrete. It wasn't only the scale that impressed me as I came to the finished building, it was the fact of those fantastic materials.

J.P.: *Mies likes fine materials, whether it's marble or raw silk.*
P.J.: Of course, I get that from him.

J.P.: *Isn't doing an exhibit building, such as the one at the New York World's Fair, a completely different thing than a museum?*

NEW YORK STATE PAVILION, WORLD'S FAIR. *Philip Johnson and Richard Foster. New York City. 1964. The tallest building in the fair, Johnson's pavilion featured three cylindrical observation towers rising over a translucent circular suspension roof supported on sixteen concrete columns.*

P.J.: Of course, because that's not a permanent building, it's a tent. In this case it's a purely external thing. I'm interested there, again, in space. I got the design space by doing a roof without walls there. A great many people never built a space that big. I mean it's big, so a football field sits comfortably in the center of it. It's the size of a football stadium with a roof on it. It's the roof that gives it the sense, I hope, of absolute staggering space. I don't know this, of course, since I've only seen it here in my mind. The model, of course, shows nothing. Nobody's even bothered to publish the pictures of the model. They won't even look at it, but it's going to be twenty times that impressive once it's got a roof on it without any other supports. In this case, I didn't worry about processionals because I'm filtering in from all directions.

I'm counting on one hundred thousand people sort of wandering from the Vatican show to the General Motors show because everyone will want to see those two. Nobody could care less about New York State, but we have a very good restaurant. A place to eat, in my tent, which should be rather a fantastic place, just physically, to be in.

Now the crazy way the program is written, Nelson Rockefeller walked in one day and said, "Philip, I want the highest building at the fair." I said, "Well, Nelson, there is my project." He said, "Well can't you take one of those sixteen towers and carry it up?" I looked at him and said, "Nelson. . . ." He said, "Yes, I see. It would be aesthetically bad." I mean there's one of our few people who knows what you're talking about when you use words like aesthetics. He said, "I suppose you can't. Figure it out. I want the highest building at the fair." I said, "Well, there's a law at the fair." He said, "Law? At the fair? But," he said, "well, we're the whole state, I guess we can do what we want." And we did.

We do have the highest building at the fair. Now my three towers, of course, are not spatial. The towers are sculptured, not space. The architect has sometime to be a sculptor like the Washington Monument or anything that you only look at. The tower has no interior space in it. After all, the definition of architecture, as Nowicki said, is the decoration of interior space. Even if you're in front of Notre-Dame, you're enclosed by that persona. So all architecture is interior space, although you're looking at it from the outside.

But this tower all by itself, like a needle, is truly a sculpture. Now it may not be a very good sculpture, we'll find out. But these things are rather fantastic in the model. Again, rather childish, even though it's awfully low. It's two hundred and fifty feet. But two hundred and fifty feet is more than twice as high as anything else at the fair. Somebody should say, "That's a very amusing cluster of towers." Then another person should say, coming in from the other should say, "Jeez, that's quite a space there with that big two-hundred-and-fifty-foot roof."

J. P.: *Philip, what about the free-flowing space in the Glass House?*

P. J.: About six years ago it was a conscious shift of wanting to do something on my own. I mean as different as this house is from the Farnsworth, it couldn't have happened without it and nobody's saying it could. It's different enough. More different than I thought. Well, of course, at the time I thought it was identical. Now I see how very different the space of these things are. At the time, I was completely devoted to making it identical, showing you're never conscious of your own motives.

One thing that I really think runs as a thread is my passionate interest in processional space, space as apprehended by walking through it. It isn't just a space. It is the procession of the appreciation of space. This I get a little bit from Mies. Then I got interested in more complex processionals.

You see, in this house, the processional into where we're sitting now, in the living room, is much more complicated than the Farnsworth. The Farnsworth is a single-unit space. Here, there's a very important vestibule outlined by the chimney and the kitchen before you debouch into the living room. I think I'm more elaborate perhaps. You get out of your car, which is the entrance to the building, and you make many turns. Of course, it comes from a definition of the Parthenon that you always approach a building at an angle. That kind of development very consciously influences me. There's always that sense of processional space that may make a line in my work, I hope.

Now I'm working in quite a different direction. I have no idea what it is. You can tell me or somebody can tell me. But now I see one thing, that I'm as inconsistent as all us modern contemporary architects.

Oscar Niemeyer

"ARCHITECTURE SHOULD BE DIRECTED TOWARD BEAUTY, TOWARD A DIFFERENT SOLUTION, A NOVEL AND CREATIVE APPROACH."

Oscar Niemeyer, tanned, slim, and serious, is a born Carioca. One of Rio's broad boulevards is named Avenida Niemeyer, after a distinguished uncle.

We made the first recording of Niemeyer in a canvas-covered field office on the dusty construction site of Brasília. He graciously drove my wife and me in his Mercedes around the new city, describing Lucio Costa's master plan and his own buildings. We were grateful that the broad avenues in this capital designed for the automobile age were completely empty, as he regularly turned around while driving to talk to us in the backseat. The second interview was made thirty-four years later, in his top-floor office on the Copacabana with a sweeping view of the world-renowned Rio harbor.

When interviewed he sometimes gave one the feeling that he had other, more important things to do. Indeed, he did. The first time he was designing an entire city and the second, in his eighties, he had buildings under way in both South America and Europe. He has strong opinions concerning critics and he may have included me as one of them.

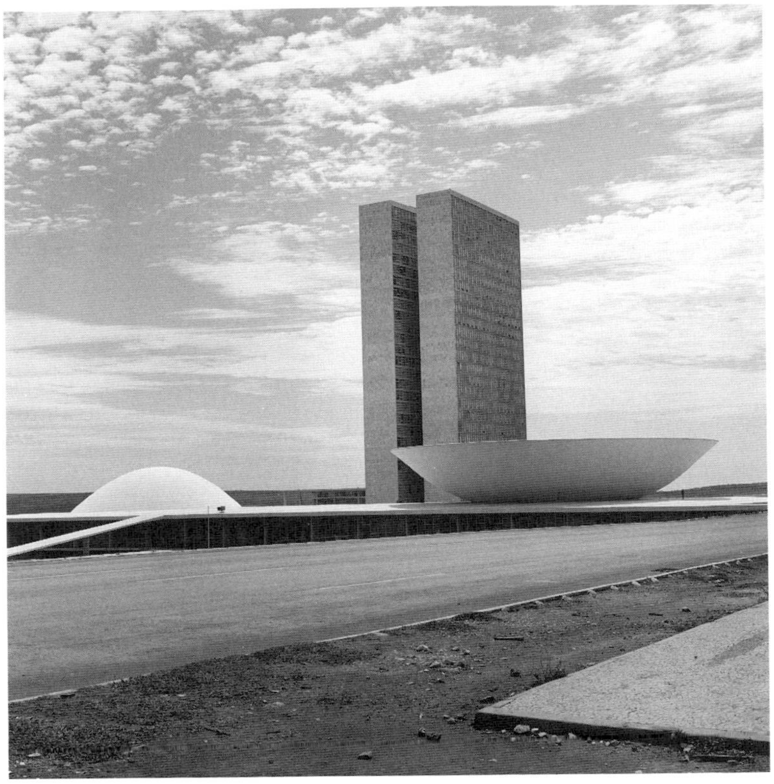

PLAZA OF THE THREE POWERS. Oscar Niemeyer. Brasília, Brazil. 1960. *The focal point of the new capital city, Brasília, is a Senate dome and an Assembly bowl resting on a broad horizontal base, which Niemeyer contrasts with a monumental tower containing the legislators' offices.*

Niemeyer also has strong social views, but he practices architecture as an art. When I asked him for his definition of an architect, he said, "An architect should have an understanding of and interest in things of the world, in social issues, and also possess the qualities that should lead him to the profession. I think an architect should be born an architect just as a painter is born a painter."

1955

JOHN PETER: *Tell me a little of your background.*
OSCAR NIEMEYER: I was born in Rio de Janeiro, which today is in the state of Guanabara. I am the son of Oscar Niemeyer Soares and Delfina Almeida de Niemeyer Soares. Since I was a child I've enjoyed drawing and I think it was this affinity for drawing that brought me to the school of architecture. During my days as a student in architecture school, I worked in the office of Lucio Costa and with him I learned about the profession.

J.P.: *What were the most important influences on your work?*
O.N.: The professional influence of Lucio Costa and the work of Le Corbusier, for which I feel the most enthusiasm.

PRIVATE HOUSE, DRAWING. *Oscar Niemeyer. Rio de Janeiro, Brazil. 1949. This compact three-bedroom residence shows the purer International Style of Niemeyer's earlier work.*

PRESIDENT'S PALACE OF THE DAWN. *Oscar Niemeyer. Brasília, Brazil. 1958. Approached by a ramp, Niemeyer's huge two-story building has a broad roof resting on a stunning series of sculptured, reinforced-concrete supports.*

J.P.: *What is your philosophy of architecture?*

O.N.: I can't understand criticism of art, though fair and honest often enough, but it is my opinion that the architect should pursue his work in accordance with his art and its possibilities. Countless are the examples that justify this point of view and the works that were not originally understood, which later gained absolute respect and admiration. They were the subject of speculation upon problems in form and architecture. They are the testament of an architect whose ideas are often theoretical. But they were based mainly on his work and his professional experience.

I am in favor of an almost unremitted plastic freedom. A freedom that is not slavishly subordinated to the principle of functionalism, but one which makes an appeal to the imagination, to things that are new and beautiful and capable of arousing surprise and emotion by their very human creativeness. A freedom that provides scope. Of course, this freedom cannot be used freely. In European localities, for instance, I am all for restricting the architecture. I am for preserving the unity and harmony of the overall plan by avoiding solutions that do not really fit into it.

In Brasília, in this view to which I am alluding, restrictions are there to cover volumes, facing materials, etc., in order to prevent the city from proliferating, like other

BRAZILIAN PAVILION, WORLD'S FAIR. *Oscar Niemeyer, Lucio Costa, and Paul Lester Wiener. New York City. 1939. The free-flowing plan of this exhibition building and its tropical gardens designed by Roberto Burle Marx brought worldwide attention to modern Brazilian architecture.*

modern cities, in a regime of disharmony and confusion. In isolated buildings surrounded by free space, total freedom is possible. Naturally, we respect the rules of proportion that have always been required of architecture. However, this plastic freedom is bitterly opposed in certain sectors of modern and contemporary architecture. It is a position that comes from the timid, from those who feel that they are better off and more comfortable conforming to rules and restrictions. It is a system that permits no fantasy, no compromise, no contradiction of the functionalist principles they adopt which lead them unprotestingly to solutions so often repeated as to at times become vulgar. These are tenets that are unsound when it is a question of special jobs where the problems of function are secondary. Thus public building, schools, theaters, museums, residences, and so on all come to have an identical appearance despite their widely varying programs. Programs that should lead to solutions of the utmost interest in which full use is made of the possibilities of modern architecture.

It is my opinion that the architect should not get stuck on the impositions of criticism. Criticism is made many years later. Each should follow his inclinations. He will only be successful if he does what he likes without being worried about what they're going to think of his work. His work should be interesting to himself above all. In making these comments I do not mean to be adversarial to what is current, but simply to show the weakness of these arguments and the critics who support them.

I endeavor to shape my projects never based only on compositional functionalism, but always on a sense of new and varied solutions, logical if possible, within the structural system. I feel no contradiction of form with technique and function in the certitude that they alone command the solutions that are beautiful, aesthetic, and harmonious. To that extent, I accept any advice, any compromise, convinced that architecture is not just a matter of engineering, but a totalization of mind, imagination, and poetry.

In the Congressional Palace, for instance, the composition was worked out according to this principle, taking into account the demands of architecture—volumes, free space, visual depths of perspective, and especially the intention of endowing it with the character of great monumentality by means of the simplification of its elements and the adoption of a few simple forms.

The whole project was based on topography, on creating a monumental esplanade on a level with the avenues flanking it. Had the Palace been designed in the academic spirit instead of on the esplanade, we would have had a tall structure blocking the view that now stretches out beyond the building over the esplanade between the Palace of the Three Powers, as well as the other architectural elements that compose it and give the overall perspective more inviting variety. Now in the Palace of the Three Powers—which encompasses the legislative, judicial, and executive branches—I did not want to adopt the identical standard sections, which would have been simple and cheaper, but sought other forms that might run counter to perceived functionalist precepts and would give the building character. Designing the Presidential Palace, I was also concerned with the atmosphere they would give to the Plaza of the Palace of the Three Powers.

It was important for me to forge a link with the architecture of old colonial Brazil and the elements common to those days by expressing the same plastic intentions, the same love of curves, rich and refined form, that are so characteristic of the colonial style.

J.P.: *In what you just told us, you talked about the relationship between the colonial style and the buildings that you created here in Brasília. Could you explain this relationship a bit further?*

O.N.: What exists is the following. There is the relationship between the attitude of the architect of the colonial period and the attitude of today's architect. I mean, in Brazil we like to retain the concern for the shape, the curve, in other words, for a more aesthetic architecture. We know that there cannot be only one relationship because what suggests the style is precisely the progress of technology. Since today we work with different materials, our work has to be done in a different way also. But we keep the same attitude.

1989

J.P.: *In what way does Brazilian architecture, most particularly your architecture, reflect the social and economic climate of Brazil?*

O.N.: Any architecture, wherever it is made, always reflects the technical and social progress of the country in which it is made. For that very reason, Brazilian architecture presents certain deficiencies. It is an architecture that discriminates. It is only at the service of the rich and of governments—that is known. But that does not prevent it from having creativity, does not prevent it from being, I believe, good architecture.

The Brazilian problem is very clear. Our heritage, our cultural heritage, is poor. We have little left of the Indians. If you compare what the Indians of Brazil did with what was done by the Indians of Peru or of Mexico, it's practically nothing. On the other hand, the older Brazilian architecture is the descendant of Portuguese architecture. In truth, it is not even Brazilian. It is Portuguese architecture which was brought to Brazil with modifications. In view of all this, we are bothered by not having a rich past like other countries, even countries of Latin America. On the other hand, the lack of the burden of the past gives Brazilians greater freedom. We are free to try out all we wish. We are free to do what we judge appropriate. We have concrete in our hands. We have the carefully developed techniques of our engineers, and with that, within our possibilities, we try to create our own architecture.

However, I didn't want to do architecture based only on techniques, on the need for steel-reinforced concrete, or on the conveniences of calculations. I wanted to produce architecture that I feel is different because I think architecture is beyond these things. Architecture should be directed toward beauty, toward a different solution, a novel and creative approach.

J.P.: *What material do you like to use most?*

O.N.: In Brazil we work with steel-reinforced concrete, which we like. It is a material that can be molded. It is gentle and does everything we want. With steel-reinforced concrete, for example, if a span is too long, the logical solution is the curve. In other words, we don't fall into the rigid architecture that metal structures justify.

The structure of the buildings is what suggests the architecture. When the structure changes, the buildings change also. In this way the styles appear as a function of new materials and new technology.

I think the works of Le Corbusier are the greatest works of modern architecture as much for the buildings constructed as for those which didn't get built. He is like Picasso, a man full of imagination who isn't stuck in any doctrine. He does exactly as he pleases.

J.P.: *Do you have specific examples?*

O.N.: The Marseilles building, the Ronchamp church. That church has a freer inclination, which is the inclination I prefer, making things with the greatest freedom of form, without concern for whether the form is based on professional reasoning. He did it only because he thought it was beautiful.

J.P.: *What do you think is the future of architecture?*

O.N.: The future of architecture is to serve everyone, not to remain, as it has until now, as a privilege of the more powerful classes. It should be directed to all the people. The architects should work for the people, not just for those who, at the moment, possess the money and can pay for the architect's work.

CHURCH OF ST. FRANCIS OF ASSISI. *Oscar Niemeyer. Pampulha, Brazil. 1943. The undulating form of this uniquely modern church, with its color tile mural by Candido Portinari on the rear wall, is a striking blend of modern art and architecture.*

PAMPULHA YACHT CLUB.
Oscar Niemeyer. Pampulha, Brazil. 1942. Niemeyer designed this small building with economy and precision to provide Pampulha with a boathouse, swimming pool, tennis, basketball, and volleyball courts, as well as a restaurant and lounges. The inverted gable roof offers maximum height where needed and enhances the roofline of the low, long building.

J.P.: *Has your work changed?*

O.N.: I divide my life as an architect into distinct phases. First, was Pampulha. Pampulha was against the right angle. I found then that it was madness to speak of right angles when concrete is continuously suggesting the curve. For that very reason I made the church full of curves, with a variety of curves. I also made the Marquessa do Bali of curves. Le Corbusier liked our work. One day he said that I had the hills of Rio inside my architecture.

In the second phase, from Pampulha to Brasília, I was concerned with the intent of architecture. I found that architecture had to be something different. If you go to Brasília, you may like or not like the sections already built, but you cannot say that you have ever seen anything similar. That for us is what is essential. At that time, I sought new solutions, solutions that should create surprise. I once read in a book by Baudelaire that someone asked, "What is surprise?" Variety, inventiveness are characteristic of beauty. That is what we base ourselves on.

Consequently, I was horrified when more reactionary individuals, those of architectural rationalism, complained loudly against the freer forms I made. They found

HOTEL DIAMANTINA.
Oscar Niemeyer. Belo Horizonte, Brazil. 1951. With characteristic imagination, Niemeyer endowed this small hotel with sloping supports, which carry not only the second floor, but also the dramatic, overhanging roof that shields the front rooms from the sun.

OSCAR NIEMEYER
on the construction site of Brasília, 1955

them to be gratuitous. I thought that one day they would grow tired of copying each other so much, that they would advance to a different architecture. That is happening now: extremely functionalist, a neat architecture drawn with triangle and ruler, as if it were just the building of a metallic structure. Today, they are part of the modern corps, which represents an adventure without too much interest. They are dying out.

In Brasília my reaction was different. My reaction was in favor of form that goes beyond its own beauty. I found that to seek form after the technical, structural solution has been found was not enough. It could allow for some imagination if it was beautiful. So I attempted a freer architecture in Brasília. I had the option, for example, in the Plaza of the Palace of the Three Powers to build the structures with thinner columns, as if they were resting on the ground. It was one of many options. In Brasília, at least those who go there are surprised by a different architecture.

BRASÍLIA CATHEDRAL. *Oscar Niemeyer. Brasília, Brazil. 1959. Arrayed in a circular plan, twenty-one converging curved buttresses open at the top in a halolike ring to admit a strikingly spiritual cone of light.*

1955

I wanted the Plaza of the Three Powers in Brasília to not have the cold feeling that is sometimes characteristic of modern architecture. I wanted it to have more of a surrealistic aspect, more dreamlike, as is seen in the paintings of Grasuto, which I think are marvelous. For example, sometimes architects show up at the Congressional Palace who want to know why the curves were made with that shape. There was a functional reason. The shape of the curves allows for a view. But I don't care for that answer. I think what's essential is beauty. When we are in front of a very important work from the past, such as the Cathedral of Chartres, those which have remained as monuments of art, we become emotional without knowing if the works were based on functional needs because they are very old. It is only a sensation we feel toward beauty.

1989

Then I left Brasília. Brasília was finished for me. The military came and I did not get along well with them. I was on the left. They were on the right. So I went abroad. There I tried an architecture closer to the earth with larger beams. I also wanted to highlight the importance of our engineering.

J.P.: *What is the relationship between the exterior and the interior of your buildings?*
O.N.: I find that those two things are linked. The interior, the workings, and the external side of architecture are done at the same time. I find that architecture must, above all, express technique. The Brazilian architecture we are engaged in expresses the present technique in all of its fullness. We do not build small staircases in concrete. We aim to conquer great spaces.

I do not believe in an architecture constrained by dogmas and preconceived notions and rules. I find that architecture is a thing of fantasy. It is the quest for beauty. I find that when a form is pleasing, it possesses the beauty of its own significance. So that the freedom we require of our own world must also be present in the way we act, in our attitudes, in our works. Based on the technical, to see beauty: that is our objective.

J.P.: *You're one who accomplished the modern architect's great dream of building a complete modern city. How do you feel about Brasília today?*

O.N.: In Brasília I was just an architect. I only worked on the architecture of Brasília, but I admire Brasília as an interesting option. I find it to be the modern city that expresses a modern option better than any other city of Brazil. Brasília is the accomplishment of Lucio Costa. He built it with great talent. He chose to give the city a different character. He wanted to create a city connected to the automobile. He created the great avenues. He divided a standard plan into sectors and he gave it its monumental side, the monumental character that it should have. He made the living sections inviting, lined with trees, with parks, with schools, with clubs. I find Brasília to be a good example of a modern city . . . a city which works well. It is a city without pollution. Access to it is easy. Distances are short by automobile. It is a city of the greatest importance. If you go to Brasília and talk to the people who live there, you'll find no one wants to leave. I am not referring to my work, I am referring to the work of Lucio Costa.

NIEMEYER HOUSE. *Oscar Niemeyer. Rio de Janeiro, Brazil. 1953. Niemeyer sheltered this pavilion under a serpentine roof. The open living areas and kitchen offer sweeping views of the ocean and surrounding hills.*

1955

I had no intention of making Brasília cold and technical with the purity of straight lines. On the contrary, I wanted it to abound in forms. I think of dreams and poetry.

José Luis Sert

"I'VE ALWAYS BEEN INTERESTED IN ARCHITECTURE AS AN EXTENSION OF HUMAN PROBLEMS, NOT ONLY TECHNICAL, BUT HUMAN PROBLEMS."

José Luis Sert was an international architect with work on three continents, but he never strayed far in spirit from his Spanish roots. Animated in conversation, short in stature, swarthy in complexion, with his dark suit and narrow black bow tie, he would look admirably at home sipping coffee in a Catalan sidewalk café.

I recorded him in his gem of a small house in Cambridge, not far from Harvard's Graduate School of Architecture, where he was dean. Designed in the Mediterranean spirit, the house turned inward, with blank walls to the street and rooms open to a grassy patio. Sert explained, "A new pattern of living has to be devised so that people can live closer together, can enjoy the sun, the trees, and the sky without looking on the disorder of a neighbor's backyard or the pace of traffic on a busy street." The interior rooms displayed art that ranged from an impressive fifteenth-century Spanish altarpiece to works by his friends Picasso, Miró, Calder, Léger, and Nivola.

Indeed, art and artists were his abiding interest. He designed the Spanish Pavilion for the 1937 World's Fair in Paris, for which Picasso painted

MIRÓ STUDIO. *José Luis Sert. Palma de Mallorca, Spain. 1955. With this glass and white-walled concrete building topped by a curving roof, Sert created a wonderful light-filled studio for his friend, the artist Joan Miró.*

Guernica; the Fondation Maeght museum in St.-Paul-de-Vence, France; as well as Miró's studio in Mallorca and his museum in Barcelona.

Though art was his love, the city was his concern. Sert was an ardent and articulate advocate of city planning. He told me, "It became a joke among our friends that every time I went to South America there was some revolution with some city burned so that we could come in and replan it. I had to assure them several times that I had nothing to do with this series of coincidences." However, Sert never permitted the disappointment of his numerous stillborn urban schemes to destroy his optimistic, ebullient disposition.

1959

JOHN PETER: *Could you tell me a little of your background?*

JOSÉ LUIS SERT: I was born in Barcelona, in Catalonia, the part of Spain that is close to the French border, across the Pyrenees with a very direct link to France. My mother came from the north of Spain and my father from Catalonia. The name is a Catalan name. My father's family was in the textile business, which my family still has. My mother's family has a Spanish steamship company, the Transatlantic Company.

I was very interested in art from my very early years. I was much more interested in painting and sculpture in the beginning than I was in architecture. In my family I had a painter, the muralist José Maria Sert. I had seen, of course, his work. From a very early age I started getting art books and seeing pictures.

Barcelona was quite a center of the arts at that time. There was a great influence of the French Impressionists, although in my early years Picasso was already painting. He had practically finished his Blue Period and was doing his best Cubist pictures, which had been seen in Barcelona. He was known much more for what he had done before he left Barcelona.

Through my uncle and members of the family, I got to know quite a few painters. I became acquainted with people who were interested in the arts and were patrons of the arts in my native city. At the same time important museums like the Museum of Primitive Romanesque and Gothic Art were formed in Barcelona. I had the opportunity of seeing that. When I was very young I remember seeing the Diaghilev ballets and the show of modern French painting with the best Impressionist painters and some of the Post-Impressionists that came to Barcelona during the First World War. Barcelona became a very important center of culture and the arts because of the war situation in Paris at that time.

The first time I went to Paris I was about twelve years old. That was just at the start of the First World War. After the war I went to Paris several times until I went to live there for a longer period starting in 1928.

It was around my late teens that I started my interest in architecture. It came through friends I knew. In the beginning I never thought I was going to become an architect. I was still much more interested in painting than I was in architecture. I took up the study of architecture in my early twenties. One of the things that influenced me most was the discovery of Le Corbusier's books in Paris when I went there in 1924 or 1925, when those books had just been published—*L'Urbanisme* and *Towards a New Architecture*, his very first books.

After I got these books in Paris and before I had finished my studies in Barcelona, we got a group of young people together and formed the first group of modern architects in Spain. That was around 1927. We had a first show at the galleries where Miró and Dalí showed in those and later years.

There was a community, on the Catalan coast, that we planned in the modern idiom, or what we knew of it at that time. To insist in designing buildings in the modern way caused me several failures in architectural school. My first modern design at the school in Barcelona was a building with a vaulted roof because in Catalonia these very thin vaults were not new, they were very old. These very thin brick vaults had been very well developed in Barcelona by the local craftsmen.

J.P.: *Was this perhaps the Moorish influence?*

J.L.S.: It may have been. It certainly is an Oriental influence. How much came directly from the East and how much came across the Pyrenees from the Gothic master builders is difficult to tell. But it did certainly originally come from the East. This particular way of working the brick, I presume, is mainly imported from the Eastern

JOSÉ LUIS SERT *in his Cambridge, Massachusetts, office, 1959* countries, where they do these things with practically no scaffolding. It's really a feat in architecture even today.

After that, this group prospered and had great success among the younger people. When we finished our studies, we set up a sort of center for the modern arts in Barcelona. At first we only exhibited architecture and then painting and sculpture. We had them both working together. The group was really a little club of its own, starting just about the days that the Spanish Republic was proclaimed. That was April 1931, I remember that very clearly.

We then started a little magazine that we sent all around the world. It was little more than a student magazine. We got people from industry interested in advertising in the magazine. We started publishing articles not only about architecture, but modern painting and the relationship of architecture to city planning.

Some members of the group saw a Madrid paper announcing that Corbusier was coming to deliver a lecture. We were very thrilled to hear that. We made a very ambitious plan to try to get him to come to Barcelona. That was 1927 or 1928. As students, of course, we didn't have much money to pay a man who was already celebrated and was very well paid for his lectures, although he hadn't built many buildings at that time. But we got him there. He was interested because we were a group of young students. He came, he lectured, and we had long talks with him.

He then asked me, "When you finish your studies, why don't you come to work in my studio in Paris?" I immediately accepted. Even before I quite finished my studies in Barcelona I went to work, for a few months, with him, and then came again in 1928 and 1929 and again in 1931.

J.P.: *What sort of work was Le Corbusier doing at that time?*

J.L.S.: When I arrived at his studio, he was doing the second project for the League of Nations. The first one had been rejected and he was doing a variant of that project, Projet d'un Immeuble, in Switzerland and also a very large project, the Villa Savoye and the Palace of the Trade Unions. The Palace of the Soviets was designed, but never built. That was, of course, a very interesting moment in my career because Corbusier's place was composed of amateur draftsmen. I think there was only one paid man on the staff. We were a lot of people from different parts of the world. There were people from Czechoslovakia, Germany, Holland, and the Scandinavian countries. There was one Russian, one Greek, and a Turk. I represented the Iberian Peninsula. I don't think there were any Frenchmen. There was an American, I believe, but no Frenchman. It took a long time before the French even half accepted Corbusier. They were the last ones to accept him.

We had a wonderful time, I remember. I met people that I've known for years after that, like Oscar Stonorov, Albert Frey, and Pierre Jeanneret, who was his associate then. There were also a few Japanese. They were very good, the Japanese. They've done a lot of buildings since they left Corbusier's office. So we are now dispersed all around the world, but we were a group working enthusiastically and very closely together at that time.

Then I got to know Fernand Léger and had gotten to know Picasso through my uncle and Edouard Vuillard. That got me very much in this Paris group. I came back to Barcelona, and back and forth, and then started working in Barcelona. Our group prospered from 1931, when it really started this magazine, until the civil war came to interrupt it.

J.P.: *What was the magazine's name?*
J.L.S.: The magazine was called AC, which means Arquitectura Contemporánea or Contemporary Architecture. It was an illustrated magazine and was also critical. We got into trouble more than once by criticizing buildings, brand new buildings that had just been built in our city. It prospered during the period and was very interesting for us because at that time there was a great change in Spain because of the coming of the Spanish Republican government, and the government—the independent government of Catalonia—and the Basque provinces. There were a whole lot of things happening at that time in the country. It became very much alive and architecture and city planning came into the picture. We then got interested in the problems of the city of Barcelona and worked together with the local government.

We did some public housing. Then I got involved in a general plan for Barcelona. We worked together with Corbusier, who said he'd like to work with us in this plan. We had a show in Barcelona and brought the international congresses, the CIAM, Congrès Internationaux d'Architecture Moderne, into Barcelona. That was in the year 1932.

J.P.: *At what point did you join the CIAM?*
J.L.S.: I joined the CIAM after its founding because it was founded and started in 1928 in Switzerland. I joined them at their second congress in 1929 in Stuttgart. After that I went to the Brussels congress and I became the second Spanish delegate. Finally, I became the first Spanish delegate in the congress. I then continued to work with them through the congress in Athens in 1933 and in 1937. There was a congress meeting at that time in Paris and I was appointed vice president of the congress. I also worked with Le Corbusier in that big tent they had in 1937, where we had a CIAM section of the city in different phases.

At the same time, I was working for the Spanish Loyalist government in Paris. We were organizing displays and shows in the little room we had in the Boulevard Madeleine. The treasures of the Catalonian Museum had been brought in to Paris for safeguarding. So I also worked on the show of Catalan arts. I was on a committee then with Pablo Casals and Picasso and so on. We worked on the display of the show in the Jeu de Paume Museum in the Tuileries.

After that I was asked to design the Spanish Pavilion for the Paris World's Fair in 1937 for the Loyalist government. That was very interesting work. It wasn't a large pavilion. It was relatively small, but it became very alive with all the events in Spain and, especially, we got very interesting collaboration of the painters and sculptors. We got two people interested because of the conditions in Spain and the issues that

SPANISH REPUBLICAN PAVILION, WORLD'S FAIR. *José Luis Sert. Paris. 1937. The two-story exhibition building was constructed of prefabricated elements. It was included in the fair to represent the wartime struggle of the Spanish Republic.*

were being fought there. Picasso was very interested in this matter and Miró, also, became very interested. They both offered to paint something for the pavilion.

J.P.: *They both offered spontaneously?*
J.L.S.: Yes, spontaneously, to make this gesture for the Spanish government to try to help the people of Spain by attracting people to the pavilion, where they would become more aware of what was happening in Spain. It was, perhaps, the first political pavilion, especially of a small country, because, of course, there were both the pavilion of the Soviet Union and the German pavilion a little farther down from our place, which were tremendously big things, very imposing in their own way but completely different in spirit.

We had a small pavilion with very beautiful trees and a courtyard. We were very lucky because beside getting Spanish artists like Picasso and Miró and González, the sculptor, who did a very extraordinary piece, we also got people who were not Spaniards.

J.P.: *Tell me, did Picasso know where his painting was to be placed?*
J.L.S.: He came to the pavilion, we discussed this thing together. He asked me about the colors and the materials. I showed him how this was going to be done, the size of the wall and the position of the thing, which he studied rather carefully. This was very specially designed for that space, taking the space, light, and other conditions very carefully into consideration. Of course, one of Picasso's qualities is he's unpredictable. So you never know, he may do it one day and not do it the next. He did do it that time because we were very much together. I used to see Picasso and a group of friends in the café every evening. He came several times to the pavilion. Each time we talked about these things. It worked extraordinarily well. *Guernica* was a great success and one of the great paintings of all time possibly, and perhaps the greatest mural he has ever painted. It was something that had great repercussions. It was kept in the pavilion until the last days.

Somebody suggested that it should be replaced by a more realistic painting. I don't want to mention names, but he was quite a well-known writer at the time. He may have changed his mind by now. We did not want to change it because we were aware it was one of the greatest factors that we had in this pavilion.

There was a group of people who recognized the greatness of this thing immediately and responded to it. There was tremendous world publicity around it. Many people, perhaps, were not convinced in the beginning, but after they saw the publicity, they were convinced by that, surprised and convinced.

At the planning stage I was asked to install a mercury fountain in the middle of this open space in front of *Guernica.* When I saw the fountain I was horrified. It was a most uninventive little design with an odd sort of fake stone. It was very ugly and you couldn't even see the mercury. I knew Alexander Calder very well and I thought he would be the best man to do that kind of work. It took a little bit to convince the people that it should be Sandy and that there was no Spaniard who could do it. He did a brilliant piece of work. It had a great success and was going to be repeated later in the other Spanish Pavilion in New York that never got built. That was in 1939. So that was a very thrilling moment and it was an experiment for me and for a group of people working there in how the arts could get together.

SPANISH REPUBLICAN PAVILION, WORLD'S FAIR, INTERIOR. *José Luis Sert. Paris. 1937. The memorable works of art—Picasso's* Guernica *mural, Miró's painting* El Segador Catalan, *and Alexander Calder's mobile* Mercury Fountain*—made Sert's Spanish Republican Pavilion famous.*

J.P.: *Tell me, then what happened to you after the pavilion?*

J.L.S.: Well, after that I continued working in Paris doing several things, but the premonition of World War II was already there. I made a couple of trips to Spain at that time. Spain, of course, was in very serious condition, cities were being bombed constantly. When the Spanish war was over in the beginning of March 1939, I decided to come to America. I had always wanted to come to America. I thought that was the right time to do it because I had been uprooted from Barcelona. I didn't want to go back to Spain and there was nothing much one could do in France with this menace of war constantly over our heads.

J.P.: *You felt this in Paris?*

J.L.S.: Oh yes, at that time in Paris we felt it very definitely. I remember being with

CAN OUR CITIES SURVIVE?
José Luis Sert. Harvard University Press, Cambridge, Massachusetts. 1942. In this influential work, Sert articulated the concern of modern architects with urban planning. He examines the modern city's four elementary functions—dwelling, recreation, work, and transportation—from a realistic and human point of view.

Picasso when he was drafting his will. That was the eve of the Munich pact. We all felt something, some great world events were in the making and that we could not continue working in the same kind of way as we had been doing. In the very early spring of 1939 I left Paris.

I came to this country. Then I was invited by Harvard University to lecture. I had an old friendship with Walter Gropius, whom I had met in 1929 in Frankfurt, Germany, at the CIAM conference. At that time I spoke no German. I still don't. He spoke no English, which he does now. I saw him after that in Barcelona. He came to our CIAM conference in 1932. We had a very nice time together.

I came to this country with a visitor's permit for six months, but before the six months was over—that was September 1939—the war had started. I had been working in the library of the Harvard Graduate School of Design preparing a book, *Can Our Cities Survive?* It tied all the urban design factors together. I think in that respect it was one of the first, together with some of Corbusier's books, which did that. It was not only the city planning factors that are understood generally, but also tied to the architectural and urban design factors which I have always been interested in from the very beginning. That was my first job in this country. The book appeared shortly afterwards, I think, in the end of 1941. Harvard University Press printed it. After that, I started working in an office in New York, doing work on prefabrication of structures for the War Production Board during the war years, 1941, 1942, 1943.

At that time, due to my friendship with Gropius and Breuer and I knew Moholy-Nagy well also, I met Albers over here and Serge Chermayeff and some of the people of the Bauhaus group. What was interesting was that the Paris group also started arriving in New York. Everybody was arriving there. A few weeks or months after I had arrived, Chagall, whom I knew from Paris slightly, came to New York. I got to know him much better in New York. Jacques Lipschitz, who was a friend from Paris, came to New York. Georges Duthuit, Yves Tanguy, and Fernand Léger, who was a very old friend, came to New York. L'Ozenfant was also here in this country by that time. We had a wonderful time together here.

Mondrian, who was a close friend, actually lived on the top floor of our house on Fifty-ninth Street and I used to see him from time to time. We used to walk together on Madison Avenue. So that really the remnants of the Paris group were together again in New York.

We had a wonderful time in a little cottage we rented on Long Island. We had these weekends with just gallons of California wine which were very fine. Some very interesting discussions came to pass there. It was a continuation, strange as it may seem, of things that had happened before. But at the same time, of course, we were becoming more acquainted with the American picture and with friends over here. We did have American friends, like Sandy Calder from Paris, that we knew over there. We saw him very frequently here and we spent some time with him in his house in Connecticut. I came to spend some time with Gropius in his own house. So for us it was a very interesting period of our lives and a very exciting one. That lasted through the war period.

As I told you before, I was working for the War Production Board then devising structures that could be easily built and knocked down. Some had to be exported and taken overseas. I became associated with Paul Lester Wiener, who had an office in New York, and we formed this group called Town Planning Associates. We then came into the field of urban design and city planning and shortly after that, there was the war years where we worked on prefabrication and after that we went to South America.

J.P.: *You did a good deal of architecture and planning in South America.*

J.L.S.: Before the end of the war, we started on this work for South America. First for Brazil and then for Peru in '46. Just after the war, March '46, we went down to Brazil and worked there for a while and got familiar with that country. And after that, in the end of '47, we came back and went down through Yucatan and Central America to Peru, and worked there for about six months.

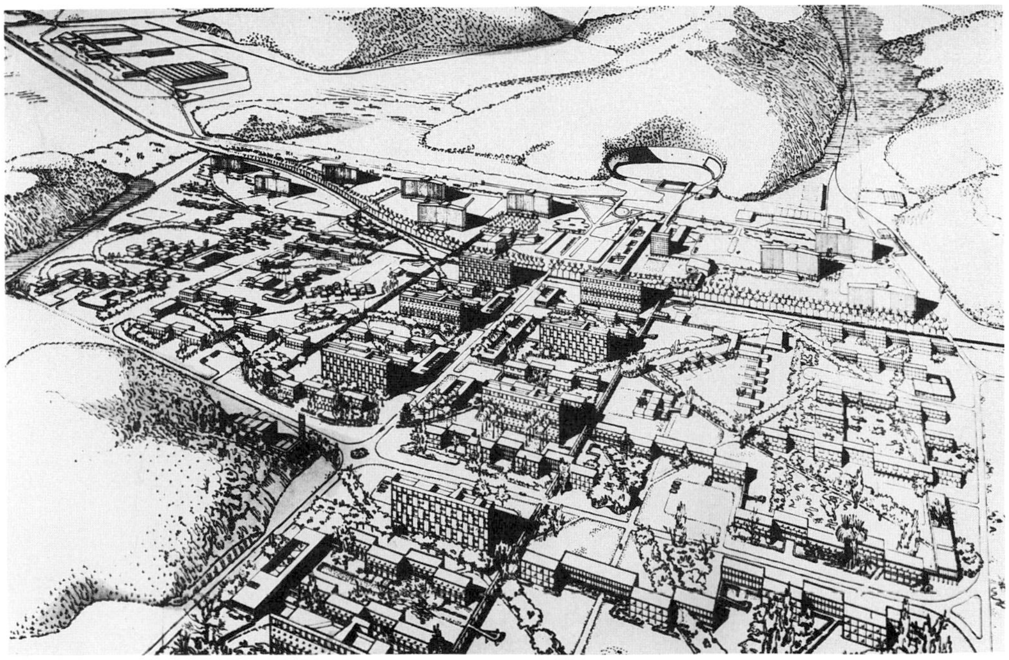

CIDADE DOS MOTORES, PLAN. *José Luis Sert with Paul Lester Wiener. 1947. This plan for a Brazilian city of 25,000, showing a civic center, factory tract, and residential housing, is typical of a number of Sert's unrealized plans for Central and South America.*

I had been in Brazil in '46. That was my first trip, but then went to Peru later on in the end of '47 and the beginning of '48. After that we worked in Colombia for many years. I worked on the plans for Medellín first of all and for Cali.

Corbusier was supposed to work in Bogotá and we worked together on the plan of Bogotá. So that was, again, an opportunity to work together with Corbusier, which I hadn't done for many, many years. It was a very agreeable experience. We worked together in Bogotá and traveled up and down to South America from New York. He stayed with us in Long Island for some time. We met in the south of France in his house and worked partly there, partly in New York, and partly in Bogotá. That lasted for quite a few years, and then after Bogotá the Venezuelan government and the United States Steel Company asked us to design some of their new communities down there with a Venezuelan group. After Venezuela we started working for Cuba and that was just finished last July.

I've always been interested in architecture as an extension of human problems, not only technical, but human problems. I'm very interested in this side, of how this is an expression of a way of living and of certain approaches to life. Perhaps I was interested in a less-abstract expression of architecture than were some of my colleagues. It had to be, of course, to be satisfactory in a way, a work of art. I always defended that point of view and its connection with painting and with the other fine arts, the world of vision, but I saw it on this broader picture, and also was very interested in how architecture was going to change, not only because new materials were coming into the market, but because new needs asked for the new materials. That meant that there was a new approach to life and a new way of living, and that cities were being transformed. I was working with a group of young people in CIAM. We were all aware of the problems of architecture, let's say, from the individual buildings to the problems of mass production and the industrialization of buildings. But then, we saw that that is also linked to the cities and the development of communities. One thing led into the other. There are no real borderlines, no limits, so we got increasingly interested in problems that were human problems, social problems, economic prob-

HOLYOKE CENTER, HARVARD UNIVERSITY. *José Luis Sert, Huson Jackson, and Ronald Gourley. Cambridge, Massachusetts. 1960. Serving as a link between two busy streets, this H-shaped, multifunctional building is thoughtfully set back from both thoroughfares.*

PEABODY TERRACE MARRIED STUDENTS HOUSING, HARVARD UNIVERSITY. *José Luis Sert, Huson Jackson, and Ronald Gourley. Cambridge, Massachusetts. 1962. With three twenty-two-story towers set among many low, terraced units, this landscaped cluster by the Charles River is one of the most successful modern housing developments of its kind.*

lems, technical problems, and problems of aesthetics. They all came together to make architecture more interesting for us.

Of course, having lived through the changes in Spain and having seen the war in Europe, what came before the war and in all these postwar years, what happened with the development in the South American countries. . . . I got more and more involved in this kind of world that is between the architecture of individual buildings and the architecture of the city—the structure of the bigger problems. And that's what has been my work for the last years. Although I have continued designing individual buildings and building them whenever I could, I have given a lot of time to the problems of what we call today urban design. What is interesting for me and very thrilling is that at the time I began to talk about these matters in this country, a majority of people were absolutely unconcerned. The architects thought it was none of their business. The planners were just not interested in that kind of physical world. Now today the architects have extended their viewpoint to encompass not only buildings but neighborhoods and parts of cities, at least, especially with the urban renewal problems. The planners feel that they do need some planners to be trained in design.

I must say that the situation has changed totally from the first lecture I gave in Harvard, where I sort of tried to summarize the contents of my book, *Can Our Cities Survive?*, in a couple of lectures, with the pictures which I used in the book, to the situation today. I think there is an awareness today that was nonexistent then. Nobody was aware of that. They were much more concerned with detail problems and with other matters that were not exactly the broader picture. Today, I think, they feel that you have to take care of both things. You can't neglect details. They're as important as anything else. Buildings have to become a reality, but I think there's an awareness of the allover picture that did not exist at that time.

I think on the part of the public, the press, and the popular magazines, awareness has increased tremendously. I was aware of that, at that time, in this country as it had much more of an echo than in Europe. I remember one of the illustrations in *Can*

UNITED STATES EMBASSY. *José Luis Sert. Baghdad, Iraq. 1955. Sert designed this three-story reinforced-concrete office building and residence around palm tree gardens, pools, and canals.*

Our Cities Survive? is a pasteup that I made of American papers with headlines dealing with problems of the cities. I also remember going to London one day and trying to get information on this subject in one of their big libraries. They didn't know where to place my questions because they were tied to architecture and to buildings, but at the same time not very much concerned with the structure of cities themselves.

J.P.: *How did you get into education?*
J.L.S.: At the beginning, I didn't want to go into the field of education at all because I had my own independent profession and I had been working freely all my life like that, but finally Gropius convinced me that it was important. I told President Conant of Harvard when he came to see me that I would like to orient the school and give it a certain approach to the problems of architecture and planning, but at the same time I would like to keep myself rather free to do my own work. I took the job on a part-time basis.

PRESIDENTIAL PALACE, MODEL. *José Luis Sert. Havana, Cuba. 1955. This unrealized palace is a group of related buildings under a concrete parasol shell. With its colored glass, glazed tiles, sun baffles, and surrounding patios, terraces, and pools, the complex employs many elements of traditional Cuban architecture.*

I came here to Cambridge in 1953. At the same time I designed a studio for Miró in Mallorca. I built a big scheme for the Baghdad Embassy. I've done the design on the Havana plan, which we are publishing now. It will be out in a few weeks, as well as the studies for the Presidential Palace in Havana. And now the museum, the Fondation Maeght in the south of France.

I was interested in taking the fourth year that Gropius had been working with, the masters class, as it is commonly called, because you get people not only from every school in this country, but also practically every school in the world. It is a small group of people who come here in search of certain solutions and a certain philosophical approach to architectural planning. That is what we try to do and it's very stimulating to work with this group of young people. It's something that keeps one up-to-date on the problems of the world. Otherwise, in one's own office, one is sort of inclined to become old-fashioned and forget some things that are happening around us. You have to keep up-to-date if you have a group of students to work with.

FONDATION MAEGHT. *José Luis Sert. St.-Paul-de-Vence, France. 1964. Making the most of the dramatic Côte d'Azur site, Sert designed a brilliant white concrete, clear glass, and stone building with an upswept, light-reflecting roof. It is a remarkable modern museum design.*

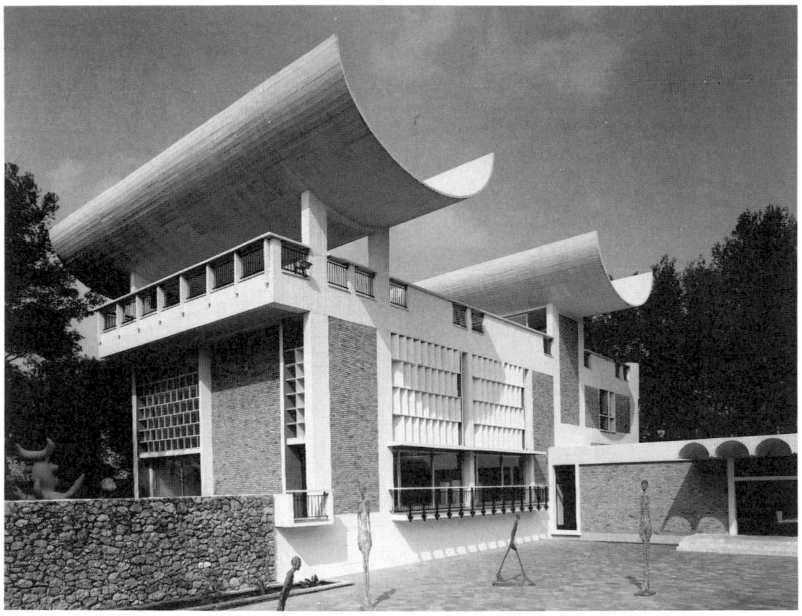

I. M. Pei

"I THINK TO DESIGN WITH STYLE IS ONE THING, BUT TO DESIGN WITH STYLE IN MIND IS SOMETHING ELSE ALTOGETHER DIFFERENT."

Ieoh Ming Pei was working for that improbable real estate impresario Bill Zeckendorf when I first knew him. We shared adjacent top-floor workrooms in the old Margery Residence Hotel on Park Avenue. Later, at the time of these interviews, with his tailored, double-breasted dark suits, round-rimmed glasses, and engaging enthusiasm, he had not so much changed as he had grown. It would be only an unperceiving few who would mistake his easy smile or frequent laughter for lack of serious intensity or tenacity of purpose.

A French critic once said to Pei, "You're an American so you don't respect tradition." Pei replied, "But I'm also Chinese and we respect tradition." In a way this also represents his position in modern architecture. He has created his own distinctive body of modern work without rejecting the basic tenets of the architectural revolution. An example of this approach is his respect for early modern architecture's emphasis on social concerns. It led to his early involvement in public housing—Kips Bay in New York City and Society Hill in Philadelphia—and his city planning work at Boston Government Center and in the Bedford Stuyvesant section of Brooklyn, New York, where, at the time, he told me, "The community is our client."

UNIVERSITY PLAZA, NEW YORK UNIVERSITY. *I.M. Pei. New York City. 1966. This admired complex for urban living groups two New York University apartment buildings and a matching tower for government middle-income housing. They are adroitly juxtaposed on a landscaped site that is enhanced by a sandblasted concrete sculpture by Pablo Picasso.*

Over the years I. M. has consciously explored, in turn, each of the major building types. He said, "There's a tremendous variety of work that this firm has undertaken, partly by choice and partly by chance." Pei recognizes the realities of chance and timing in the affairs of people and architecture. I. M. knows that architecture, like politics, is the art of the possible, but he pushes the possible past what many would consider limits. Like that of several important second-generation modern architects, his work is not marked by an instantly identifiable style but is recognized for its consistent quality and imagination.

1956

JOHN PETER: *Let's start after you graduated from Harvard School of Architecture and you began teaching.*

I.M. PEI: I stumbled into teaching, John, by the way. I definitely stumbled into it. That was not planned. It was at the end of the Second World War. I was all set to go back to China and I wanted to spend a few more months here. I didn't want to go into a very definite job, you see, which would commit me to a certain period of time, and teaching happened to offer that flexibility. I took it. I had no experience in teaching. I never thought I would make a good teacher. I must say that I have gained more from those three years teaching than all the years of education preceding it. I know I learned more by teaching than I did when I was a student.

1987

It was the right time for me to take stock, so to speak. What I learned. Where do I go. I think the most important single reason for saying that teaching was important is because I was able to then avoid the tremendous urge to go home at that time. I wanted to go home. I wanted to do something there. Yet I knew it would not be right to go back at that time. Teaching was the only thing I could do because I couldn't go in and say to someone, "I'm going to work for you, but I may leave six months from now." In teaching you can.

I intended to go back, you see. I hadn't given up, even when I came to work for Zeckendorf. I still wanted to go back because it's only natural. My family's there and my mother, and at that time my future had to be there. It wasn't until the early 1950s, I think I will say 1954, 1955, that I decided that there's no chance.

J.P.: *You couldn't do the kind of work that you wanted to do there?*
I.M.P.: That's right. Even if I worked when I went home. So it was a struggle with myself when to return and then it eventually became should I return. Teaching bought that time for me. It enabled me to stay here, think about it and wait until political situations settled down.

1956

J.P.: *Was there anything you read that you could say had a considerable influence on your design thinking?*
I.M.P.: Yes. I read Lao-tse a very great deal, especially since I graduated from school. When I was in college, I really did not have the wisdom to read Lao-tse, although I did read it when I was a child. I forgot it as quickly as I read it. But I have read Lao-tse a great deal since then and I think that his writing has probably more effect on my architectural thinking than anything else. I think perhaps that many modern architects would tell you the same. I would certainly recommend it. It's a very difficult book to read. I can only take about one page at a time. You are sort of exhausted when you get through that page. It's not the kind of book that you would really want to read in your light moments. Yes, I would strongly recommend his writing.

J.P.: *What technical or social development promises to make the greatest change in architecture?*
I.M.P.: Well, I would like to modify this question a little bit, if I may. If you isolate architecture from planning, architecture meaning single buildings or a group of buildings, then you have one answer. But when you take planning into consideration, then that is something else again. I, for one, don't believe that the threat of the atomic bomb will ever have any effect on the design of our cities. But I do think that the continued expansion or the centralization of the city itself, if that should be allowed to continue, will have a great deal of effect on planning.

Traffic, for instance, is a very serious problem. We face that everywhere when we build on Manhattan Island. I would say that transportation is a very serious problem

I. M. PEI *in his office in New York City, 1955*

and, as such, will have a tremendous influence on planning, which, in turn, affects groups of buildings. As such, I think that its influence may be even more widespread.

J.P.: *Does architecture have a future?*
I.M.P.: The answer can only be yes. I should like to express it this way: I think those of us who expect to see a tremendous revolution to come will be disappointed. I don't think so. Architecture has already gone through this revolutionary period, and I think the future, the buildings—let's not call it the future of architecture—may not be unlike the buildings that are being built today. There will certainly be improvements in techniques. The power plant may be in one drawer, instead of occupying a very large basement space. Things like that may take place, but the building itself, the exterior expression and the form of the building, may very well be similar to the type of buildings we are building today. I don't expect that there will be too great a change in quite a few decades to come. I think that we have a lot to digest and a lot to refine.

Now I expect there will be greater richness. By that I don't mean lots of colors and lots of forms and so on, but there will be richness. I expect that will come, especially with the public acceptance of modern architecture. As soon as they accept it and understand it, they'll be prepared to invest more money in it, demand more of it, and better quality. And I think you will find a greater change in that aspect of architecture rather than more novel types of building or new construction methods that will completely change the shape and form of buildings. I don't look forward to that, at least in the near future.

J.P.: *What about air-conditioning or other developments? Has that changed architecture?*
I.M.P.: Air-conditioning, of course, is a tremendous influence on building expression and building design. All we have to do is to look at Lever House on the one hand and look at the Marseilles apartments on the other hand. One undoubtedly does not have the benefit of air-conditioning, so they have to take care of the natural elements such as the sun. They have to resist against it. Whereas in the other building you can afford to ignore the sun and, as such, you get into a totally different building construction and building design.

HELIX APARTMENT, MODEL. *I.M. Pei. 1949. The unrealized helix tower lined with wedge-shaped apartments was Pei's solution to changing family requirements.*

1987

Talking about air-conditioning reminds me of something. Le Corbusier was here during the United Nations building. It was around the early fifties, I think. I was designing the helix, you remember that, with Zeckendorf. Zeckendorf, of course, was very proud of the helix. He planned to show it to Le Corbusier and asked him to come to meet me. He showed the design to him. Corbusier looked and looked and looked. Well, the fact that he looked impressed me. He didn't just come out and dismiss it. He looked very hard and, finally, he said, "You know, where is the sun?"

"Where is the sun?," because the helix is completely nondirectional. Why? Because of air-conditioning. It's not like Brazil. It is no longer an important consideration to those of us who design in America. If you have an apartment, the important thing is view, actually, more so than sun. If you have sun, so much the better. Why defend against it? Bring it in. So there's a difference there. But the fact that he asked that question jolted me. I never thought of it. I sort of accepted it. But that jolted me and that is very important. Sometimes, even though you may not in the end agree with a position, the fact that it made you think is what makes one grow because then you change. Then you react. That was just one case.

J.P.: *In the future, will there be less concern with the individual building and more with multiple units?*
I.M.P.: Definitely. Let me give you an example. Just my very limited experience alone has convinced me of this. A few years ago, five or six years ago, we were planning small buildings and a building at a time. Today, and it is only five years hence, eighty percent of the projects on our drafting boards are projects that involve a city block, or many, many city blocks. You see that this type of planning, of course, will not bear fruit for another five or ten years. I'm sure that on many drafting boards throughout the country you have a similar experience such as mine. Ten years from now, if we are allowed to, or are fortunate enough to see our plans realized, you can imagine what that would do to the city. The city will, for the first time, I think, have a certain planned look, which is completely lacking today.

Rockefeller Center is probably a very good illustration in a very limited sort of a way. Already any one of us walking through this group of buildings may have quibbles with its architectural style and so on, but still there is a certain feeling of satisfaction when you walk into this complex of buildings because there is a relatedness. The buildings are related to other buildings and each building is related to the open spaces. I think that is going to be the important thing, as I see it.

The pioneers did not really have that opportunity. I think that opportunity is the right word. They did not have it. I think we are about to inherit it and, as such, we should do the best we can.

At this point in time, I think the emphasis on architecture as a social art is less. Not for me, it's not less. I continue to consider some of the work I've done in the urban renewal area in the 1950s and 1960s very important work, because it dealt with urban housing. But as an art form, they are limited. They are really limited.

KIPS BAY PLAZA. *I.M. Pei. New York City. 1956. The innovative poured-in-place honeycombed concrete walls of these two apartment slabs were an architectural breakthrough within the confining requirements of Federal Housing Authority rules.*

Architecturally there's nothing much to talk about. I mean it's very simple, straightforward. Kips Bay will have to be looked at within the context of time. It was conceived in the early 1950s. It was finished in the early 1960s. It was one of the first projects I worked on with Zeckendorf. People do not pay much for apartments with rent control and everything else tends to force the cost of construction way down. If you remember, the forerunners of Kips Bay were Peter Cooper Village and Stuyvesant Town, built by Metropolitan Life Insurance Company. They were brick buildings in a checkerboard pattern with punch windows. That's the approach and that's what the FHA wanted. We came on the scene at that time. We needed FHA financing. Yet we tried to do something different from the accepted formula. I think in that sense we broke new ground and it's important for that reason. The fact that we built it with very little money was not in itself a triumph. It's just that we built it in a different way and still achieved it with very little means. In other words, we found an alternative to building brick buildings with punch windows with steel sections. We found an alternative and that alternative was not to be denied at that time.

Social housing was very satisfying for me. We built it in Philadelphia. We built it at University Plaza in downtown New York on the same principle. We haven't done much in the way of apartment design since then because we moved on to other areas. Kips Bay is the best I could do based on means and the components I had to work with, including the FHA. But it does not give me the same kind of satisfaction. It gives me the satisfaction I was able to provide decent housing, but your objective, your accomplishment also has to be limited. Architecture as an art form, I don't think you'll find it in social housing because it's very limiting, extremely limiting. But that doesn't make it unimportant. That makes it all the more important simply because providing low-cost housing for people is very important. Also, to create an environment, a physical environment for urban life is very important, very important.

The exploration of form, the exploration of space is something you have to find in other types of architecture, like museums. I went into public buildings for that reason. They're social of another dimension, you see, another dimension. They are less limiting. They enable the architect to go more deeply into the artistic aspect of

SOCIETY HILL APARTMENTS AND TOWN HOUSES. *I.M. Pei. Philadelphia. 1962. The sensitive relationship between Pei's thirty-one-story concrete apartment towers and the existing three-story Flemish brick town houses in downtown Philadelphia helped make this a successful and widely hailed urban renewal effort.*

expression. It's different, but it doesn't make one more important than the other.

J.P.: *You have also been involved in town planning, like Boston.*
I.M.P.: We did the plan for the Government Center for Ed Logue. That's executed. We didn't do any buildings, but we did the master plan. I would like to say that we got a lot of satisfaction out of that if for no other reason than to save the scale of Faneuil Hall. In the competition program for city hall, we ruled out a tall building and specified that it must be a horizontal building. We recommended that to Ed Logue and Ed Logue accepted that. It was written into the program for the first time in a competition in America. It said this building cannot be a tower because of enclosure. We needed enclosure to give Faneuil Hall an environment, a scape, that's in scale suitable to it.

I was severely criticized by many of my architect friends who entered the competition, saying, "How could you do that? How could you write that kind of restraint into the program?" Well, I'm glad we did. Because as the consequence of that we created two different spaces out of an enormous area, the city hall plaza in the front, and Faneuil Hall. Each suited for the other in two different scales. That is the greatest contribution we made in planning, not in architecture.

We were asked to design a building in Paris at La Défense and it ended up as just a plan. We replanned La Défense in order to find a place for the building. The place was then at the head of La Défense. At that time they wanted that place empty, because they wanted it to go on, like a boulevard all the way to Saint-Germain-en-Laye. I said no. I said, if you don't terminate it, you will never have a space, you don't have a focus for life. They bought that, but they couldn't buy the fact, at that time, for an American to come in and do the most important building in La Défense, which is the axial building. Frankly, that's what Pompidou said: "It's a great axial of France, it must be done by a French architect." I think it's on record.

I think planning is very important and architects should do more of it, but it is a lot of effort and in some ways you don't get the satisfaction that you deserve. Let's put it this way, unfortunately, because it should be important. It should be important.

J.P.: *We know that in earlier periods, art had been much more integrated into architecture, the element of ornament, the element of decoration, that kind of enrichment. Of course, in the revolution they stripped it clean. The public has felt it's not as human or as rich. Is there any validity to that point?*
I.M.P.: Oh, sure, because people always yearn for richness. Color always attracted people. I think that modern architecture did sweep much of that away. I think for good reason. Because we don't have stonemasons anymore to carve stone like they did in cathedrals. This started way back in the Greek times and before, actually. We don't have that anymore. If we tried to do it, we'd be doing it less well, wouldn't we? So, therefore, you obviously don't want to do something less well than a thousand years ago, or even fifty years ago. You have to move on. We have to move on with the times. As you strip ornament away you don't have to do all of it. I think the modern movement did try to strip all of it away. However, it has one good thing, it really does

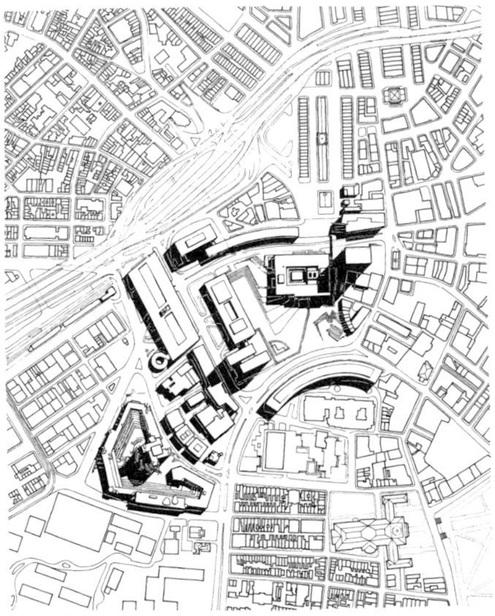

GOVERNMENT CENTER MASTER PLAN. I.M. Pei. Boston. *1960. Pei and his associates established the redevelopment program for the City Hall Competition and the Government Center on the sixty-six-acre site in historic but neglected downtown Boston.*

LA DÉFENSE, MODEL. I.M. Pei. Paris. *1966. Pei's unrealized plan for this satellite development was conceived around the twin office towers that preserved the view down the Louvre-Concorde-Étoile axis.*

something to call attention to architects and training my generation, to look at other things than ornament—space. Space needs no ornament. Space is really a surface. It's how you position walls. That, I think, can be a very abstract thing. In fact, even if you have no color. It can be all one color, all white, all blue. You have space to deal with. You have form, with or without ornament, there are beautiful forms. Look at modern art, for instance. It's all form. Architecture should deal with the essence, and not with something which we like, but is no longer appropriate to our times because we cannot do it as well. That doesn't mean we should not do it. I think the revival is now taking place. There are possibilities of ornament without stripping it to the bone. But I think the fact that we had to strip away ornament in the beginning of the modern movement, called attention to the possibility of form and space without ornament.

1956

J.P.: *There are people who feel that modern architecture is colorless or too pristine or restricted in its palette.*

I.M.P.: Well, of course, form is far more important than color. Any use of color, if it's going to be used in such a way that would clarify or express the form of the architecture, well then it should be used. Only when it starts to compromise form will I take a different stand. When you think in terms of the monochrome of the building—about which the public, in particular, worries very much, especially when you see a modern building like Lake Shore Drive—don't forget that there is color in the sky. The blue sky gives blue to the glass on a building, that is also color. So one must not forget the background. Oftentimes, a rather simple and even a severe building, with a proper setting, can be most attractive.

1987

J.P.: *Every time I drive past the site in Cambridge where the Kennedy library was going to be, I always feel bad that it isn't there.*

I.M.P.: Here I think it's circumstances. I think it's time. I started the project in 1965. I was selected as the architect in 1964 and there were a number of sites offered to us by Harvard on both sides of the river. Finally, we, meaning the then Mrs. Kennedy and her advisors and myself, all felt very strongly that the car barn site was the right site. It's in the center of life. It's near transportation, which is important. It just was right. But, unfortunately, by the time we got around to planning, designing the building—1968—just the beginning, the Vietnam War really had taken its toll and the people's power, in terms of community, in terms of students, became very, very obvious at that time. They all wanted a say, and, of course, they were very anti-establishment. The Kennedy aura by then faded, to a certain extent, because of his supposed involvement in Vietnam. We had to fight all these political and social forces at that time and that was not to be won.

On top of that, you had to add to it certain other sentiments in the university, in Boston, in Cambridge itself. You have a lot of forces all working against us, all working, and, of course, the traffic problem. People thinking that this would draw millions of millions of people. Therefore, it would absolutely ruin Harvard Square. Of course, it was not going to be. That was a great disappointment to me.

J.P.: *Was it the design of the building?*
I.M.P.: We hadn't reached that point. We just never reached that point in considering a design. We had lots of designs but I don't think the community in the Cambridge area or the public in general was that much interested in the design. They're more interested in the idea of the presidential library coming there and the number of cars that would have come to the area. That's why I say you have to get lucky at the right time.

J.P.: *There was an element of luck with office buildings. How do you feel today about Hancock?*
I.M.P.: I still think it's a good building. I tell you why, because first of all I think Henry Cobb had more to do with it than anybody else in this firm. So I can praise him. It's a minimal approach, but then, it shows that richness can come without carving, without pediments, without different kinds of granite. It doesn't have to have all that. And it's still a rich building, minimal, but still rich. Because he played with form. He played with light, he played with illusion or the reflectivity of glass. Those are elements you can play with in modern buildings.

Now you couldn't do that building in Raymond Hood's day. You couldn't. Today we're doing shadows of buildings, like Ray Hood. Ray Hood could do better buildings than we could. Why? Because the craftsmanship was there. It's no longer here today. We think those buildings are great and we're trying to imitate that. But how can we succeed? There's no way to succeed.

Rockefeller Center, on the other hand, is a triumph. It has nothing to do with a style of architecture, it is an urban complex of great quality. I would say that is the single most important work. If you ask me to include urban design into my evaluation of modern architecture, I would put Rockefeller Center up there. It's very important and also the time. It was built at a time, built during the Depression, as a matter of

JOHN HANCOCK TOWER.
I. M. Pei and Henry Cobb. Boston. 1966. The bulk of this sixty-story tower is minimized by its elegant, slim shape and the reflective glass walls, which mirror the surrounding cityscape.

fact, when construction costs were relatively low. So the Rockefellers could afford to do many things that most developers could not afford to do today.

J.P.: *Is modern architecture a style?*

I.M.P.: I think it's very dangerous for architects to consciously keep style in mind in design. I mean it's a very dangerous thing because that is not the beginning. I think to design with style is one thing, but to design with style in mind is something else altogether different and I would not approve of the latter. I think an architect, like a poet, like a writer, has a style and that style comes from his own way of doing things. But should he consciously want to design a building with style, I think he would fail. On the other hand, if he is a good architect, his work has to have style.

Even in a certain movement styles are very different one from the other, one individual from the other, like painting. They are very different. But still, you take Braque and Picasso. They're both involved in the early Cubist work but I can tell them apart. Is it Cubism that's the common element of time? Or is it the style that makes them different, Picasso from Braque? I think it's the personal style.

J.P.: *What would you say have been the accomplishments of modern architecture?*

I.M.P.: I think it's a major shift in the ways of designing—of ways of looking at architecture. The Beaux-Arts tradition is one that dated quite far back in France, if not the eighteenth century, certainly early nineteenth century. Quite old and it's sort of no longer relevant to our times. Therefore, this revolution in architecture had to take place. Had to take place because it had been going too long. You built buildings and you somehow feel that the buildings have no relationship to our life.

So that happened after the First World War, although it started before that because history's continuous. It's very hard to say this is the moment, but I would say after the First World War in Germany, that is the beginning of the change into modern architecture. The Bauhaus happened to be there at that time. But that was certainly not the only place where they were thinking about it. But that one was a very important change. So much so that I call it a revolution.

Now when you want to change a way of thinking, you have to oversimplify, like adopting slogans. Communism did that, fascism did that, and modern architecture. I'm not equating the two, political and architectural, but "Form follows function" is an oversimplified term, but, nevertheless, very effective as a slogan. "Machine for living." Did Le Corbusier finally regret that he ever said that? I don't think so. At that particular moment it shook up people and they had to begin to think about a house as not a comfortable rocking chair. It became something else. They had to simplify. They had to make it powerful as a statement. Many of them probably didn't really believe in all of it. But, nevertheless, it served their purpose.

J.P.: *You might do that yourself in making a presentation.*

I.M.P.: Sure. I think that there lie the shortcomings, but I wouldn't say it's the shortcomings of the movement. It's the shortcomings of that particular need to get people's attention.

J.P.: *Is the revolution over?*

I.M.P.: I see continuity. We're only at the beginning. I think that the premise, or rather modern architecture as we now come to define it, is fundamentally sound. It has a great deal of limitations in the context of time. I think tremendous limitations, but the limitations do not make it invalid. It came out at a time when the whole . . . the architectural scene was dominated by the Beaux-Arts tradition and, all of a sudden, it's a new way of looking at architecture. That's why it's called a revolution. Even though we continue to pick at it and say, oh, gosh, it's monotonous, you know. It's so dogmatic and how can you continue to justify "Form follows function" as a slogan? You can't do that anymore, but never mind. The premise is sound. The times had changed and architecture had not changed with the times, and something had to be done. So now it's a question of continually developing and refining and enriching. This process is going on, but I don't think the basis for that change is in question, is invalid. It continues, it's still there. But it will continue to evolve and develop.

As for those men at the forefront of change—Wright, Le Corbusier, Gropius, Mies—these are all men who made this change come about. They will continue to be up there. Their names are going to be shining brighter and brighter with the times. Absolutely, it will be brighter and brighter.

Brunelleschi, Michelangelo, but then the difference between them. Why Michelangelo is important, I think, that was a change from Renaissance to Baroque. But it's still that same Renaissance tradition of design. Michelangelo changed it. With him and Bernini and a few others it went into Baroque. Therefore, you have another group of masters coming out, Borromini, Bernini, and so on, and then the Mannerists to follow. So you have this kind of change, but they're still of one tradition. But the ones who started the change will always be remembered much more sharply than those who eventually evolve, enrich, you know, the tradition. They were there, they were there first. They're the ones that made the break. I think the fact that they were there first, at that moment in time, their names will always shine bright.

There are lots of very uninteresting buildings that have cropped up under the name of Modern Architecture. But that's not their fault. I think this movement will continue to go on, as Renaissance adds things to the fourteenth century. It came to a high point in the fifteenth century, went into Baroque in the sixteenth and seventeenth century, but it's the same continuity. It just goes on and moves on.

SOUTHWEST WASHINGTON, D.C., PROJECT, PLAN. *I.M. Pei. Washington, D.C. 1953. Pei's remarkable urban renewal plan for a neglected section of downtown Washington, D.C., centered on a three-hundred-foot-wide mall. The project was rejected, but major portions were subsequently built.*

ASSESSMENTS

Modern architecture is the architecture of today. It is safe to say that the revolution is over. Architecture is evolutionary as well as revolutionary. The revolutionary phase recorded in this book, in which the modern movement was initiated and established, had ended by the mid-1960s and was replaced by an evolutionary phase. This was indicated by the widespread acceptance of the phrase "Post-Modern" to describe contemporary architecture. Its arrival was confirmed in 1966 by the American architect Robert

Venturi, in his book Complexity and Contradiction in Architecture, *published by The Museum of Modern Art, New York. In 1972 he followed this book up with* Learning from Las Vegas, *a Yale School of Architecture study written with Denise Scott Brown and Steven Izenour. The two publications articulated an influential reaction to modern architecture, advocating greater freedom, increased variety, recognition of the vernacular, and employment of historical imagery.*

NEW NATIONAL GALLERY.
Ludwig Mies van der Rohe. Berlin. 1966

In Complexity and Contradiction *Venturi stated:*
Architects can no longer afford to be intimidated by the puritanically moral language of orthodox Modern architecture. I like elements which are hybrid rather than "pure," compromising rather than "clean," distorted rather than "straightforward," ambiguous rather than "articulated," perverse as well as impersonal, boring as well as "interesting," conventional rather than "designed," accommodating rather than excluding, redundant rather than simple, vestigial as well as innovating, inconsistent and equivocal rather than direct and clear. I am for messy vitality over obvious unity.

It is generally admitted that the description Post-Modern is imprecise, and while others disagree with Venturi's thesis, clearly the obvious deficiencies of early modern architecture have generated both questioning and change. However, those who posed these challenges were not the first to recognize the shortcomings of modern architecture. The Oral History *is replete with criticism by some of its most ardent advocates and practitioners. As with any revolution, there were early supporters who questioned some of the tenets of modern architecture, and there were those who later became troubled by its consequences. Others recognized its failures, assigned the causes, and saw a still bright future ahead. One of the latter, Philip Johnson, shared his views with us.*

PHILIP JOHNSON: 1955

Architecture is a terribly foolish profession to go into. I think most students know that. At least I always tell them. But I think we should talk about the future of the art of architecture.

Of course, I am very optimistic. I feel that we are in one of the great golden ages of architecture. And I can't say that from my meager knowledge, anyhow, of painting, or of the theater, or even of writing—since I know less about it, I don't want to say that. But I do know that in architecture we have reached, or are beginning to reach, and that's why you can talk in terms of the future, beginning to reach a wonderful style background on which to build. Imagine if I had had to practice seventy-five years ago, I'd have had to invent a new style for every building I built, like Richardson or poor Sullivan, for them every building was a challenge. They had to start from nothing. Now I can use all of Mies's work, all of Corbusier's work. I can't use Wright, there's the significant part. Wright is of today, lives today, but is not of it. His work, I think, gives us a thrill much as the Parthenon might, but has just about the same amount of message content. It's just about as relevant to our work as the Parthenon is. But all of Mies's work, all of the International Style, to use the phrase, is grist to our mill. We start with that, as with the lenses of our eyes. More and more as you read the magazines and go to the schools, that is the architecture that is practiced, taught, and publicized. The half-modern works, the compromises with the Beaux-Arts, nobody takes seriously anymore.

The future of architecture is completely and absolutely sure because no matter how it is battered at by the Goffs at one end, the classicists at the other, the mainstream seems now to have caught on after these thirty years. We've come to a period which is, I believe, the first time since the Baroque synthesis of the eighteenth century, when we have a stylistic background that is part of our bloodstream on which we can start designing.

Now I'm not telling you that you have to go and do International Style work. Let them break away if they can. Let them even try to bend the style, by so much as the crook of a finger, as Saarinen is trying to do, which I am trying to do. Any architect worth his salt is trying to break loose. It's that tension between the disciplines that you know you've got and you've inherited from Mies. In the case of Saarinen, or Pei, or myself, we're trying to develop from there, trying to stand on the shoulders of those people. It's amazing that our best work is the most restrained. It's the most typically in the straight line of style, I think it will be a few years to find out whether Saarinen's Lutheran College will be better than General Motors or not.

History, of course, will be the final arbiter. But how wonderful, I feel, as a semi-historian to live in a period where you have that calmness of acceptance of a style of architecture. The first time since the eighteenth century, when everybody knew when a window was well spaced or not. In Wren's time they knew the difference between a thick muntin and a thin muntin. Now we know the difference between well-spaced columns and oversized, lumpy columns, or whether you are introducing brick in a place where there should be tension.

What style would be in this sense would be a corpus—I use that strange word just because it helps me—a corpus of commonly understood concepts and principles of design. It's just a group of clues like, for instance, the fact that every one of us, in building a tall building such as Seagram's and 860 Lake Shore Drive and Lever House and Marseilles, put our building up from the ground. That is a basic feeling of our style.

Now whether it's expressed as Russell Hitchcock did twenty-five years ago in his book, that it is a feeling of volume, not of mass, or whatever the cause, it is instinctual in every one of us. We don't feel that we're copying anybody simply because we show the underside soffit of our second stories. That is an absolute characteristic of our style. The same thing is true of the method of the treatment of symmetry and of ordering the facade. We use what Hitchcock called the principle of regularity. That is a sort of ground base, a boom-boom-boom, of spaced columns. For instance, many of us notice in looking at the boom-boom-boom underlying Lever House that one of the columns is misplaced, which is disturbing to those who are in tune with regularity as a basic theme in development of architecture.

Then there's another characteristic that we don't talk about, but we all practice: none of us use ornamentation. It's no accident that Wright and Goff use more ornament than Welton Becket and myself because in that case Welton Becket and I are identical. Both believe in the same style. Naturally, he has a slightly different interpretation, which is fine. I think the more the better.

In fact, I think the striving that Saarinen is going through, which is a real struggle in his soul, his Finnish, Nordic temperament is really hard at work trying to break this effect that he thinks is one influenced by Mies van der Rohe. I feel more happy about it myself if I think that if I go off the deep end, as I did in my house or the synagogue, history will bring me back, or I'll find my way back, if back is to be back. But if anybody can change this style, or change this style phase, to use a minor subdivision of a style, let them try.

Certainly, the Gothic changed during its period. In England especially, in three different manners, although it remained Gothic, although the period didn't look like Early English. Modern architecture today doesn't look like a stucco box with windows thrown around it as it did in the 1920s.

Take Catalano's new house, a hyperbolic paraboloid out of laminated wood with a clear plastic roof, so that as you approach the house, you see the laminations held up at the ends, enormous spans, by this structure. The glass walls are put at the neutral axis of the hyperbolic paraboloid, which is perfectly level, horizontal. You see none of the solecisms that you usually see in concrete with glass following it up. All right, that fascinates me. I don't want to do it. It might not be my dish of tea, but my eyes are in that direction. Catalano is in the mainstream of pushing the boundaries, the edges of our style. I welcome the hyperbolic paraboloids and the thin-shelled dome boys. They don't invalidate any of the basic theses. They don't start using ornament. They don't say let's not use regular column-spacings and cover our columns up. No, the regular columns are still there—all the basic characteristics. What is changing is it's becoming richer, as all styles have.

Look at the difference as Romanesque developed. The Greek, of course, is an exception. They didn't develop. They became more like Mies. Mies is the Greek of the modern style. He refines, refines, refines, until his final building will be his most perfect building, which is very Greek in a restrained sense. Where Saarinen is more outgoing and Corbusier, especially, the most Baroque spirit, is ending up at Ronchamp in the chapel. It should have been built in Gunite and glass, a light, weightless cage of miraculous shape-abilities. But the technicians are rather a dull lot these days. They can't keep up with Corbusier's genius-type ideas. Ronchamp is built, but since Gunite can't do it, it is built in rubble, masonry, and any old things they could put together, then stuccoed over. In other words, the idea has gone a little bit ahead of the techniques, which is only right. Those are the extremes, the Seagram Building and the Ronchamp Chapel. They still both admire each other, which is no accident.

It's amusing to look back at the birthday of the style, 1923, which is now thirty-two years ago. I don't think there is anybody, even among architects younger than I am, that wouldn't look back to, let's say, Mies's brick house that wandered off in all directions, or to Le Corbusier's Ozenfant House, to pick two different examples, without a feeling of perfect familiarity and admiration.

A better example of this, though, that no one can deny, is the wonderful one of the chair. The greatest chair of our time designed in 1928, the Barcelona Pavilion chair by Mies van der Rohe. That chair I now specify, as do all my fellow young architects, whenever we need a large monumental chair. All right, that's a twenty-seven-year-old chair. You stand at the year 1928, when that was designed, and look back twenty-seven years at the chairs. The Art Nouveau, the curvilinear whiplash chairs may be objects of beauty as some of van de Velde's work, or you could look at the Arts and Crafts Mission style with square stick backs, or Frank Lloyd Wright's, which was Mission of the period, with their pegs, their squares, and their flat arms, you just feel a sense that, "Well, there's history, boys. What are we going to do?" But who feels that of the Barcelona chair? Who feels, "That piece of old-fashioned nonsense?" Nobody can say that. We have a style. Now I don't mean to say that that was the last good chair or the first. It wasn't. Eames has refined on the ideas that have come up, technically and aesthetically, by using the thin wires, as Bertoia and others have. It's perfectly legitimate, but those don't deny the validity of the Barcelona chairs. The Barcelona, the Stuttgart, and the Breuer chair completely deny the validity of the approach of the Mission and the Art Nouveau chair.

You stand in 1923 and start looking back. You can't look two years back, much less ten years back. There is no building in 1913 that would be even recognizable, either to us or to the men of 1923.

There are, of course, exceptions to all rules. And what exceptions! There are two in history that come to mind quickly: one of them is Michelangelo and the other is Frank Lloyd Wright. Frank Lloyd Wright founds styles as anyone else founds manners. He just starts a new one every time he turns around. He did another one when he went to California in 1923. He did another one after this war with his circles and cylinders, and, no doubt, he will do another one yet if given time. But his period when he was relevant to this period was 1900 to 1908. You date from the Riverside Club when, practically single-handed, he founded the style of 1923, to give it a quick name, and then went off to invent many other architectures after that. But that is the one that caught. That is the one that for some reason became the touchstone, the touch-off of what we know now as modern architecture.

Of course, there are many differences. There are many handcraft approaches. There is a great sheltering roof, it's very massive and meant to be, you see. The jump had to be made by the boys over there, Gropius, Mies, Oud, and Corbusier. That jump was not made here.

But if you were to analyze what caused it to come together in the year 1923, you have to start with Frank Lloyd Wright. You can't name any other architect. Almost, just Frank Lloyd Wright, and then you have to go into modern painting, into modern technology, into the Crystal Palace and other extraneous matters to explain what happened in 1923. The defeat in the World War of central Europe. Modern painting being by far the most important.

But much the same, you see, in Mannerist Italy in Michelangelo's time. Michelangelo was very impatient with Bramante's classical Renaissance and he was darned if he was going to follow the rules. He really exploded the whole thing. If it hadn't been for Michelangelo, both Mannerism and Baroque would have been different, although he was not a Baroque architect. Yet almost single-handed, in the rear of St. Peter's, he started the colossal order in the use of strange contrasts, of small windows and enormous columns that later became the Baroque style. So Frank Lloyd Wright did found modern architecture and yet he has nothing to do with it today. On the contrary, he has as much to do with it as the Parthenon has, or the Crystal Palace.

Not that you can't misunderstand Mies just as you can misunderstand Wright. But you can't misunderstand him to such an extent. It's moot because the answer's in the style.

The patronage we have today for great buildings, which is just beginning with General Motors and the Seagram's company, would not be possible without a style. They see it coming. Some people in the companies see this common denominator of the basic style that is not expensive and not nonsensical. It's a way to monumentality without arrogance, without stupidity. It is making patronage possible and probable. It's now got to that point, which is a very good point to get to, because the patronage today will be by business, just as it was with the Medici in Florence.

Each one of us says, I know I'm changing quite a lot. It gives us pause. But we do it, I notice. We're restless. We're striving for—I don't know what. Maybe this whole generation will be written off. I think we'll just have to wait for the history books.

From the beginning modern architecture had certain inherent inconsistencies. For example, in line with egalitarian social goals, group practice was urged as the appropriate architectural organization. Though Rockefeller Center, the United Nations Headquarters, and countless other projects were produced by architectural group effort, in most architectural offices egalitarian group practice as advocated by Gropius did not prevail. The makers of modern architecture were decidedly individualistic.

MAX BILL: 1961

This Gropius group practice is a special case. This philosophy of teamwork seems to me a bit artificial. But maybe such combinations are very useful. We have here in Zürich a combination between Haefeli, Moser, and Steiger. They work together. They have worked with others together and the architectural expression is perhaps not so expressionistic. But it's, in a certain way, clear, reasonable, and, for this, perhaps really right. I personally like to cooperate with others when a team is strong enough. When the team is not good enough, it's better that one is doing it himself.

WILLEM DUDOK: 1961

I should say a good city planner is in principle the architect. Once Berlioz or Wagner said, when they asked him, "What is the finest instrument?" he answered, "The finest instrument is the orchestra." In the same way, I say the finest building is the city. Understand what I mean? Then the city is an architectural problem. Of course, there must be a teamwork with engineers and different businessmen and financiers and all the things. But the conductor, that is the architect, because it is an architectural problem.

CARL KOCH: 1956

We pay a lot of lip service to the group, but training is still very much that of the individual and the artist. We are not yet good as team members. The first thing is to find out what sort of team it is. Then if the architect can get to be captain, why, fine. But if he sets himself up as captain, without understanding the game, he is going to find it hard to get any players.

I think architects, when they talk of teams, are too prone to think of teams of architects. Instead of thinking of the team as one on which the architect plays a part, and the manufacturer, the businessman, the politician, the statesman, and so on are the other members of the team. Very often we think in architectural terms of a team being a group of guys who get together and, therefore, are stronger to fight the other members of the team, which we are still prone to call the opposition. As far as architects are concerned, they will play a part in it if they broaden their horizons considerably. We still look at an individual building as the end product of an architect.

We talk about city planning and regional planning and so on. But even there we only look at the technical aspects of it. We have got to learn the rest of what makes it necessary to build buildings well enough, and how to speak the language of the other members of the team. How to understand their problems well enough so that we can help. That's the first step that most of us don't take. A politician is a politician, and our idea is you can't talk his language. A result is that he doesn't care about or feel it important to understand ours. A few people have got to be able to talk to each other to bring in planning that has to do with any municipality. Though buildings are built by a team of people with many capabilities—owners, investors, engineers, contractors, constructors—the new doctrine automatically designates the architect the head of the team.

A principal charge frequently leveled against modern architecture was that the practice did not match the theory. This is not an unusual charge, but in the case of modern architecture it is significant because of the moral fervor with which the new era was proclaimed. Form did not inevitably follow function. The idea was a cleansing one, but the function of a given building can be fulfilled with many different forms. The final form selected may have a great deal to do with art, style, economics, legalities, technology, and many other factors, including simple preference.

LE CORBUSIER: 1950

"Functional architecture" is a journalists' phrase. It is redundant because architecture is functional by definition. Otherwise, what is it? Garbage. I have defined architecture. It is the scientific, correct, and magnificent play of forms in the light. This is the first sentence I wrote about architecture. That means you have to be plastician, poet, and, at the same time, informed technician. It opened the whole front and allowed creation.

KUNIO MAYEKAWA: 1962

When I studied at Corbusier's office in 1928–30, I recall that European modern architecture had laid hopes on what is called mechanization. People were quite optimistic in the hope that mechanization would save human beings as well as human life. However, that hope seemed to be betrayed twenty to thirty years after that. The environment where people lived had become dehumanized. Unfortunately, this mechanization is not only impacting on the technological side of human life, but it is also involving wider areas of human society itself in its big, dehumanized network of mechanism. Such bureaucratization has been spreading in our society. Therefore, all human beings are experiencing great difficulties, not only in architecture, but also in our society, in the entire environment where we now live. How to overcome this is our most important problem. Modern architecture should address this difficult problem.

I am most interested in economic problems. No matter how much technology develops, if society in general is barren, or it does not have enough wealth to utilize it, that new technology will not bear fruit. In this connection, as far as both technology and design are concerned, I am very much interested in whether society can afford it or not.

RUDOLF STEIGER: 1961

I think that architecture, in all periods, was a very complicated subject, and I remember a letter of Alberti in the time of the Renaissance. Alberti wrote to a friend, "It is amazing that we have no artists and architects in our time." That was in the Renaissance. Today we have the impression that it was the most important time for the architect. That is always the impression people have when they are in the present.

It is important that the range, the vision of the architect be as broad as possible. I said this afternoon that it makes a big difference whether my camera has a telephoto lens. This corresponds to the specialist who, in the great distance, sees a small field, or a medium lens, which corresponds to the average architect, but we must aim for a wide-angle lens to master as wide a field as possible. Here it is the development that is unsatisfactory, that is the excessive specialization of the architect.

J.J.P. OUD: 1961

If I have to find an architectural philosophy in a few words, then I would like the description I gave in the initial stage of my career. Seek in clear forms for clearly expressed needs. Silently included in this formula is the necessity of giving the work a lucid aesthetic shape.

Later on, startled by this dead end of one-sided abstraction, I extended this formula to the following four sentences: The drive to abstraction demands completion by striving for melody. Pure abstraction is like religion without humanity. Humanity is life in the flowing continuation of daily existence. The course and rhythm of daily existence demands architectural melody.

At present, we have not yet realized this in architecture in a satisfactory way. The architecture today lacks, first of all, the distinguishing mark of high quality, whereas this is essential for modern architecture. There is, of course, a kind of modern style nowadays. But it is still too much a matter of mode. It lacks deepness and devotion. Nearly everyone can design, at present, a good building. But we want more, we want buildings which can move us.

Another frequent fundamental criticism of modern architecture has been that it lacks humanity. Perhaps some negative response was inevitable, given the increased size of buildings, but architects of past ages have managed to endow even huge buildings with human warmth and appeal.

FÉLIX CANDELA: 1961

The matter of monumental architecture is very interesting because that is one of the most difficult things to do at this moment. I mean, specifically, because we don't have this ornamental idiom with which to express ourselves, you see. I mean all these decorative elements which acquire a symbolic significance, we have not given time for them to become symbols.

According to many critics of modern architecture, the best it has been able to do regarding enrichment is to employ the wide variety of textures and patterns in natural materials—marble and other types of stone, wood, and so on.

MINORU YAMASAKI: 1960

One of the things that has caused the reaction of modern architecture, early-twentieth-century architecture, was narrowing our horizons in every field. Simplicity, lack of color, everything reducing the materials which were popular. For instance, you couldn't use stone or marble, for a while anyway. All of this, I think, is tending to erase itself and now we're starting to broaden our horizons and include our whole palette. Heaven knows our palette isn't large enough really to use tastefully because I think that man needs variety.

Modern architecture disowned the ornament of the past and never developed its own. The other fine arts, sculpture and painting, which had enriched architecture throughout history, had also become abstract. With few exceptions, abstract painting and sculpture added little warmth or humanity to the abstract forms of modern buildings.

WILLEM DUDOK: 1961

In my opinion, what is wrong with architecture equally applies to all other arts—music, painting, sculpture, poetry. This need not surprise us, for in every art society is reflected. This society develops at a formidable and alarming pace, but ours is not a culture in which the focus is human interest. Man does not spend much time on his cultural development. It appears that he accepts literally everything that is served as art. He knows that great artists have always been in advance of their time and he is afraid of staying behind, not to be modern if he does not keep pace with his time. It's a kind of social snobbism, which in Andersen's famous fairy tale, "The Beautiful Clothes of the Emperor" ["The Emperor's New Clothes"], was ridiculed in an immortal way.

I must go into this more deeply. Art is a communication. This, at any rate, is an important aspect of art. It is a wonderful communication, full of sense, from man to man, that is, from the artist to the layman. Every art has a language of its own. No philosophy explains how it is that a melody can be so moving, that a building can be so touching. But this fact speaks for the existence of eternal values, to which all people appear to be susceptible. Values to which the artist is able to give expression. It is certainly true that artists in all times have shifted the boundaries to express themselves in their own way. All this on the basis of values which have made art comprehensible for all times, values which have their natural limitations. The unlimited is chaos, degeneration.

Of course, pictorial or sculptural art need not be descriptive, let alone photographic. Abstract art which can move is certainly conceivable. But pictures like scribbling paper on which one has wiped off one's paintbrushes, sculpture like rubbish, music as if a cat has come down on the piano—all that is for me degeneration. I speak out freely because I prefer to be considered as a kind of obsolete modernist by contemporaries to being considered a fool by posterity.

Ironically, this lack of human appeal is most grievous in the area where early modern architecture showed its most ardent dedication and made its initial efforts—housing.

EDWARD DURELL STONE: 1963

Well, first of all, actually very, very few private dwellings that are built in the United States are ever done by architects. They're done by speculative builders. It's a matter of simple arithmetic that neither the owner nor the architect can afford to have houses that are designed by architects. So as a result, this country, especially in the last twenty to thirty years, has seen all private dwellings done by speculative builders, with the result that all of the suburbs of our cities are being used up by these little boxes, which are probably the most impractical way in the world to build. It means, first of all, that our land is being consumed. They are the largest contributors to what is popularly known as "urban sprawl." We're beginning to witness the spectacle of cities that run on for a hundred miles, like Los Angeles. It is threatened that we will have such a city reaching from Boston to the Potomac. We almost have it.

Now if this country had originally been settled by the French or by the Spanish, we would have fallen heir to a completely different tradition, or the Italians—completely different tradition in building. If you'll notice, the French countryside is made up of compact villages. The houses are built wall to wall with courtyards for privacy, walled off. You can practically shake hands with your next-door neighbor here out your window. You've lost all privacy. There they have privacy. They have convenience. They have the economy of building compactly. But more than that, they have open country between the little villages.

It's a Latin tradition. Italy, France, and Spain all build this way. Well, it's a Mediterranean tradition. You could see this if you visited Pompeii. Now the Pompeians built their houses wall to wall. They were completely anonymous. You had a door that led you into your place. You were confronted with solid walls. When you got in and you first came into a beautiful atrium, a top-lighted room, and then you went into a second room—open courtyard—where the rooms were all grouped around this courtyard. You had complete privacy. Even the most affluent people lived this way.

So it wasn't a, you know, you visit a suburb—an expensive suburb like you'd find out of Houston and so on, and you get into a lot of status symbols. Somebody has a great Colonial house, with four columns. Somebody else has an English Tudor house—all very artificial, anachronistic.

Well, in light of this I thought, and have for a long while, that we should build, instead of kidding ourselves, recognize that land is precious, that we would be better to build in, to cloister our houses for that precious commodity, privacy. You'd in effect wall in. You can use a smaller plot, wall that in and live within this where you're cut off from the world and you can have some peace and tranquility. This means that a community would look quite different. You'd come into a house like this, it's located in the suburbs. It would be located on little dead-end streets. We probably wouldn't line these up on streets with traffic.

STEIGER: 1961

All sorts of minor considerations of all kinds gnawed away at architecture. At the moment this creates a somewhat pessimistic period in our architecture because we see that more and more the purely material aspects are decisive, such as the price of the land, utilization of real estate, the highest possible investment return, all of these factors, which are a burden to architecture. This situation is, especially for young architects, very difficult and many wonder nowadays whether it is still possible to make headway with architectural forms, means, and ideas.

JUAN O'GORMAN: 1955

The box in modern architecture is probably an expression of a greater importance of commodities than of human beings. In our time, the human being is measured like a commodity and, therefore, he's housed like a commodity. When you have to stack up a lot of apples or pencils or some commodity like that, you put it into a box. Today, a great deal of the thinking is around the idea that everything that is important in our lives is a commodity, including the human being, which, of course, is very, very wrong.

However, housing was only one of the concerns the architects voiced on the future of modern architecture.

MARC SAUGEY: 1961

We are at an intermediary stage right now. Over the past decades we have witnessed strong disagreement between the supporters of a certain classicism or conventionality in architecture and the advocates of a radical change to go hand in hand with the change in our life-style. Between these two extremes, we have seen, little by little, like a growing tree, other possible paths emerge. There are even paths of compromise. I think we've reached a stage where there is a synthesis of all contemporary generative ideas and that, from this stage, we will take off on different paths. I think architecture ought to be less schematic, less hard, less, how should I say, less a weapon. In a new stage, it should be much more a function of man, a function of ease of living, much more adapted to the problem of life.

L.L. RADO: 1956

Mr. Wright said that modern architecture is in the gutter. Well, I wouldn't say we are in the gutter exactly. There is something happening to today's society that we seem to overemphasize material values. Our advances are mainly in the field of science and technology. I think we are somewhat off balance and architecture reflects that. But I think that there are some indications that the pendulum is swinging back. Now whether that will take five years, ten or one thousand years to really swing back, I don't know. But we do have to strive for that balance.

MARCELO ROBERTO: 1955

What is somewhat wrong in today's architecture is excessive inventiveness. Invention, in the Greek sense of the word, meant the constant improvement of a process or a technique, but in the architecture of our times, invention is just that, invention. The architect feels constantly pressured to create something new, something different, and that uninterrupted series of changes detracts from the quality and the importance of the work. I think the fault lies not with the architects, but with the agitation of the modern world that is always asking for something different, demanding change. The architect simply satisfies that exaggerated insistence. It isn't up to the architect to change things. As long as the world is in such a state of unrest and needs constant invention, the architect has to oblige.

MARTÍN VEGAS: 1955

In architecture there is maybe a certain confusion because of a continuous and excited search for what is new, without thinking of the consequences. I believe there is a certain chaos taking place in the urban environment. The cities have lost unity. Here, every architect is attempting, in every work, for what you would call, a masterpiece, without taking into account the surroundings of his work. As a consequence, I have a feeling that the urban environment is losing a lot of quality.

JOSÉ MIGUEL GALIA: 1955

I agree with my partner, Martín Vegas. I believe that I could say the same. I think there is in architecture a process of decantation, not of invention. You can't invent every day. I believe it's better to let things settle, that is, to work along a line. If, after some time, one year, five years, you change mentally, you have other thoughts, seek something, but not for the sake of seeking, not because three months ago I did something this way, now I have to do it differently.

EDGARDO CONTINI: 1956

The pace of architecture through the ages was always disciplined by economic factors as well as by the slow pace of development. Our whole contemporary picture is, in more than one field, affected unfavorably by the speed with which new developments are presented to us and the inability of man to cope with such rapidity. His ability to absorb and become aware of changing conditions is more or less constant to the time.

Architecture has always existed in time. Modern architecture has been the expression of such time. But we have reason to be concerned, I think, about what modern architecture has been in the last quarter of a century and what it's going to be in the next quarter of a century, in the broad terms of the expression of a society. The expression of a society, of which it is a part, because of the tremendous rapidity with which designers, architects, and engineers are faced with new materials, new techniques, new methods. Our inability to absorb these new techniques to such a degree that they become a tool in our hands for the production of real architecture, rather than something to play with, to experiment with. Too much of our architecture has had, in one form or another, in one direction or another, this eclectic quality of experimentation, indeed, of a period that is probably very significant to mankind otherwise.

I am, therefore, deeply concerned about the future of architecture. This, probably, because we all are deeply concerned about our own future in broader terms and the indecisions and nervousness of architectural expression reflects such broader indecisions in our rather human problems.

DUDOK: 1961

The fact that the technique of construction allows us unlimited freedom has, more than once, given rise to forms which seem rather to be applied, because they have never occurred before, than to give a suggestive expression to the building.

Architecture is the beautiful and serious game of space. There are many modern buildings to which this statement cannot be applied. We see churches looking like exhibition buildings, schools like factories, government buildings like offices, without the least suggestion of dignity. Even famous colleagues sometimes disappoint me when I see in their work new stunts to strike us dumb. To build only to amaze the world is not the way to a beautiful development. In every one of us there lives the hope of originality. This will always remain so. He is original who comes, in the most natural way, to amazingly simple solutions, which lead to unlooked-for new forms. In this way, building can become a reflection of the inexorably practical.

CANDELA: 1961

One of the worst things with architecture today may be that we are too concerned about originality. I mean everybody wants to be original and in some cases this is almost pathetic to see. In order to have architecture, I believe that we must have a language in common, something which people can understand. If you change this language, this idiom of vocabulary, people cannot understand what is happening. Then you cannot have a style, a permanent vocabulary, which I think is necessary to have in architecture. Then what's happening, really, not only in architecture but probably in most of the arts, is we are doing painting for painters, architecture for architects, and music for musicians.

JUNZO YOSHIMURA: 1962

I think the current architecture is too conceptual. In order to solve this problem, we must find the real meaning and purpose for architecture. Then it will become what human beings really need. It will no longer be an odd and unrealistic thing. In other words, if we design individual architecture on the basis of necessity, architecture will not be alienated from human life any longer. I think current architecture the world over is designed for its own existence. We have to design architecture for the use of human beings. I think only such architecture will remain.

PAUL RUDOLPH: 1960

What we really need is a sense of hierarchy of building types. Traditionally, the place of worship, the palace, the governmental building, the gateway to the city were given real emphasis. They were made very plastic. They had the most adornment. There was the greatest play of light and shadow. They were sited so that you could see them from the greatest distance. The buildings for finance and for housing and so forth were background buildings, so to speak. They were relatively quiet. This set up the whole hierarchy of building types, which was made into a meaningful whole, which was called the city.

Today this has been turned upside down. Industry quite often has the most money to spend, so these become the dominant buildings. The church quite often is lost in the shuffle. At the University of Mexico there is a building which tends to dominate that whole campus, which merely holds a machine. Our whole sense of symbolism is upside down. We need today, perhaps more than any other single thing, a hierarchy of building types, and this has to do with where the most advanced structures should be used. The most advanced structures, which tend to call the most attention to themselves, should be relegated to truly important buildings. Not every hot dog stand should be a hyperbolic paraboloid, or whatever. Every age that has produced architecture worth talking about has had a hierarchy of building types all its own. But we, today, do not have this. I would say that this has to do with the whole environmental aspect of architecture.

YAMASAKI: 1960

It would be deadly if we narrowed our sights to the point where we only had one kind of architecture, one solution, one kind of material, for our total environment. This would be really a kind of sickening environment, monotonous and boring.

In a sense, to focus our thinking, and it is very necessary, simplicity is the early part of any period in architecture. In Romanesque, in Gothic, it was the same thing and then it flowered into a richer kind of architecture as it matured. In the same way, I think that our architecture had to sort of focus our sights by returning to the simple, basic thing.

But then, because we are such a complex civilization, because we do have this incredible amount of material on hand, because of our technology and methods, we have really an immense horizon. I think it's wrong to say to society that you should limit yourself with one kind of thinking, with one kind of architecture. The richness of our society is going to be evidenced by what we can produce with the materials on hand and the gauge is how tastefully and how thoughtfully we can do this.

RALPH RAPSON: 1959

Acknowledged scientific and technical progress has placed in our hands the means to create a truly superior environment. We have the ability to control architectural form almost at will. The dilemma is that we live in a cultural vacuum. We just don't seem to be able to absorb the ever expanding and increasing scientific and technological innovations and to assimilate all of this into our daily lives. As we add more and more gadgets to our way of life, we often do this under the delusion that this is culture. We flatter ourselves that this is real progress when so often it is simply escape. Rather, it is, as Frank Lloyd Wright says, a cheap substitute for culture, hired and paid for by the hour. Technical means have always been the means to achieve and enrich the environment, but our great advantage will be of little value unless inspired by truly cultural values.

I think if our era is to produce significant architecture, significant environment, in keeping with the highly developed technology of our times as well as our own striving for a better world, then we have to have a new scale of values that are based on sound, orderly research. Knowledge that is applied creatively to the technology of today. Values based on creative thinking, beauty, order. Let me remind you that order is inseparable from fitness of use, honest application of technology, and genuine aesthetic values. All of these values should be based on a genuine desire for harmonious and beautiful environment, stemming from great understanding and appreciation for the dignity of man.

GORDON BUNSHAFT: 1956

I hope that we tend toward doing good buildings where each one is not an individualistic, unusual attempt at being different, but attempts more and more to fit in with the buildings around it in unity, scale, and a few other things like that. I hope that as we get more mature in our modern movement we will feel that we do not have to have each product be entirely a new concept. In other words, I'm a believer of evolution rather than revolution. I'd rather see a street of neat, simple structures than a street full of nine eccentric geniuses, mixing up the pattern of that area.

WILLIAM WURSTER: 1955

I feel that architecture has broadened its face. In the years past, when I was in school, the emphasis was on the solo performance. I think the emphasis has become on the total environment, and as such it is much more important than it used to be. The only reason to split off architecture and planning is purely of the weight of the work to be done. It's like psychology split off from philosophy. It's like statistics split off from mathematics. The weight of the knowledge becomes so great that you can no longer treat it in one compartment, that's the only reason. It's a total picture that you're after.

AFFONSO EDUARDO REIDY: 1955

The future of architecture is not in an isolated building. The future of architecture is entwined in urbanism because the big problem of architecture is urbanism. Urbanism has been forgotten and greatly transformed into only a scientific object. It is necessary to humanize urbanism.

Urbanism must have more of the architect's help. It should not only maintain the theoretical aspect of planning, which is necessary and indispensable, but should feel the creative influence of the architect as the humanizer of the city. In solving housing problems, the architect has to create functional spaces, volumes, good conditions, but also make it beautiful and pleasant so that people feel comfortable.

One prominent characteristic that the modern architectural revolution had in common with all revolutions was a strong sense of optimism concerning the future. This vital and durable conviction, along with accompanying concerns, was evident in the comments of the early founders and the current practitioners alike.

OUD: 1961

If I was not optimistic, I would not be an architect.

FRANK LLOYD WRIGHT: 1957

It's not the future I'm worried about. It's the present. When you get pessimistic concerning the future, the thing that you love, why, then you are done.

LUDWIG MIES VAN DER ROHE: 1964

I'm absolutely optimistic because I think the forces, the economic forces are so strong. I think you are always influenced by your environment, you know.

LE CORBUSIER: 1950

I will say something that will surprise you. I have never claimed to be smarter than the others. Only I have made personal judgments that I maintained against all odds, judgments that I tried to make explicit to myself in my practical life. I have a head that is rather well organized. Though I am self-taught, I have an insatiable curiosity and am a student more enthusiastically today than ever.

WALTER GROPIUS: 1955

I'm definitely optimistic about the future. Let me read this. It's something I've prepared:

We can see that through the enormous speed of development we have come through, I daresay that happened in my lifetime in the practical problems of life, as well as the philosophy behind it, there have been greater changes than in the whole time going back to Jesus Christ. So I think if we look back to see what has been achieved during the last thirty or forty years, we find that the artistic gentleman architect, who turned out charming Tudor mansions and Renaissance skyscrapers with all modern conveniences, has almost vanished. This type of applied archaeology, as I call it, is disappearing fast. It is melting in the fire of the conviction that the architect can conceive buildings not as monuments, but as receptacles for the flow of life which they have to serve, and that his conception must be flexible enough to create a background fit to absorb the dynamic features of our modern life.

Modern architecture is not a few branches of an old tree. It is new growth right from the roots. This does not mean, however, that we are witness to the sudden advent of a new style. What we see and experience is a movement in flux, which has created a fundamentally different outlook on our architecture. Its underlying philosophy knits well with the trends in today's science and art, steadying it against those forces which try to block its advance and to retard the growing power of its ideas.

The irrepressible urge of critics to classify contemporary movements which are still in flux and to put each neatly in a coffin with a style label on it has increased the widespread confusion in understanding the dynamic forces of the new movement in architecture and planning. What we looked for was a new approach, not a new style. The attempt to classify and thereby to freeze living architecture and art while it is still in its formative stage into a style or ism is more likely to stifle than to stimulate creative activity.

Steel or concrete skeletons, ribbon windows, slabs cantilevered, or wings hovering on stilts are but impersonal contemporary means, the raw stuff, so to speak, with which regionally different architectural manifestations can be created. The constructive achievements of the Gothic period, its walls, arches, buttresses, and pinnacles, similarly became a common international experience. Yet what a great regional variety of architectural expression has resulted from it in the different countries.

But what is far more important than structural economy and its functional emphasis is the intellectual achievement which has made possible a new spatial vision. Whereas the practical side of building is a matter of construction and materials, the very nature of architecture makes it dependent on the mastery of space. Architecture is becoming again an integral part of our life, a thing dynamic, not static. It lives, it changes, it expresses the intangible through the tangible. It brings inert materials to life by relating them to the human being.

GIO PONTI: 1961

There is nothing today that is wrong with architecture because there are marvelous things. What is wrong in architecture is bad architects, and this was also the case in the past. There's not a crisis or something that demands change because we have a richness of architecture that has never before existed in the world.

Wherever town planning is possible, there are enormous possibilities that didn't exist in the past. With the presence of men the likes of Le Corbusier, Mies van der Rohe, Gropius, Aalto, Neutra, Kenzo Tange, and then people who have died such as that Dutchman, what was his name, van de Velde, and Frank Lloyd Wright. There has never before been such a wealth of such extraordinary men, and I've overlooked many. Then the works of Nervi, works as large as we can build them and that we do build, marvelous reinforced concrete and steel and plastics. Large and special problems which create a type of architecture in itself. For example, all the nuclear stations had created an architecture before the architect thought of it. It is a marvelous period.

My advice is to treasure the future and never look back. The glory of the past was made by others. We have the future, the great unknown, that mystery in front of us. Our architecture must look to the past only to be worthy of the burdens of the past.

BRUCE GOFF: 1956

Our civilization is a different one than we've ever had and naturally our architecture has to be different to go along with it. We hear talk if we try to do something that we're going too far, but if we look back a little ways, no one ever went too far. No architect, composer, anyone, ever went too far. It seems to me that anything we can do now, and that we need to do now, and can actually realize now is not too far. It's part of what we are capable of in our own civilization. No matter how different it may seem to the so-called cultural lag.

EDUARDO CATALANO: 1956

Modern architecture is based upon a dynamic concept and develops without preconceptions. Although we have development of ideas and social structures, it will never reach a climax because climax means decadence and death afterwards. I think that modern architecture will be always modern and will change. Change is the only permanent thing that we have in the universe.

It's based upon a dynamic concept. We will have modern architecture for a long, long time. I don't mean the present modern architecture, but the modern architecture of its time, expressing its ideas, its social structure, its technology, and so on. Regarding the expression of architecture, I hope that we will never have an international pattern. It will have many patterns and always different.

EERO SAARINEN: 1958

Let's review a little bit what has happened. Let's go back to almost around 1900. In 1900 there were several pioneers breaking out of the rut of the old by their own strength. There was Peter Behrens. There was my father. There was Mackintosh. There was Berlage and many others. Those were all great and strong individuals that through their own strength were breaking away.

Now then in the twenties—the socially conscious twenties—and thirties, and forties, socially conscious architecture came with functionalism, with all the hoopla about the International Style. Everything really channeled down to one sort of style.

It wasn't proper to step outside of that style at all. In fact, it was most improper. The exhibit at The Museum of Modern Art, you know, where you were judged whether you deviated from that style one bit or not. If you didn't, you got in.

Then one man, Mies, really came along and codified all these attempts into one beautiful line and it became the gospel. It became one straight line and it was a beautifully clear thing. It was open for everybody to copy if they wished and, by God, that's what they've done, too, and sometimes it was done very well. But that was about the state of things in 1950.

Since then, a curious thing has happened. A new set of pioneers have come up who have strained to get out of that one single rut, because as much as I admire—I'm a great, great admirer of Mies—but if a thing just becomes used in an undigested way by others, it becomes a rut.

We now have a whole spread line of attack on the problem of architecture. There is all the folded-roof experiments on the one side. The experiments in relating things to surrounding buildings. There are all the grille experiments. There are all the structural experiments. There's a whole new growth of enthusiasm for concrete in many different ways and for decoration.

Everybody is really working hard to spread out from the sterile little line, but then we have to ask, "Is that really what we want architecture to be?" I think if we regard what everybody's doing as an experiment spreading out, then it's all right. But if we think of it as, "Ah, this is what architecture is now," then it's not all right. What should grow out of this? That's, of course, the question. That's the thing that I'm terribly interested in now.

As in earlier periods, sweeping changes in the late nineteenth century generated a new architecture. This architecture responded to new attitudes in people's minds. It recognized an industrialized economic system; it responded to and shaped the different circumstances in which twentieth-century people worked and lived. In a society that was becoming ever more global, it became an international style.

The revolutionary founders of modern architecture proclaimed a total break with the past. They embraced technology by using new materials—steel, glass, plastic, reinforced concrete—and electrical and mechanical innovations. Influenced by modern art, they created an architectural aesthetic based on abstract form, space, and light, and frequently employing bold primary colors. With determination these pioneers sought improved social goals, dedicating the machine age to democratic values. In the perspective of history, their accomplishments will loom even larger than they do today.

Modern architects displayed their zeal and audacity not only in buildings, but also in the modern cities they designed to replace the accumulated architecture of past generations. The dream of creating new cities was partly realized in places like Chandigarh, where Le Corbusier designed a modern acropolis in a traditional city. But it was fully realized in only one place—Brasília, planned by Lucio Costa with buildings by Oscar Niemeyer. Brasília has prompted many of the criticisms discussed in this chapter—excessive inventiveness, lack of enrichment and human scale—but there is no doubt that it is distinctly different from all preceding styles.

At the turn of the century, when the Oral History *begins, there was no modern architecture. Sixty-six years later, when it closes, nothing was built throughout the civilized world but modern architecture. Within these years a style of architecture was created that ranks in unsurpassed quality and remarkable beauty with the great styles of the past.*

Biographies

ALVAR AALTO (1898–1976). Born in Kuortane, Finland, Aalto attended Helsinki Technical School. In his Turku office he executed his first independent work, a complex of exhibition buildings at the Industrial Exhibition at Tampere, the year following graduation. He was an early and active member of CIAM (Congrès Internationaux d'Architecture Moderne). His Town Hall in Säynätsalo and his Paimio Sanatorium gained the admiration of the architectural world. He also earned renown as a furniture designer, introducing the use of molded plywood. Through his sensitive and sympathetic use of natural materials, Aalto brought humanizing elements to the pure International Style and gained worldwide recognition as an important innovator and leader in the modern movement. Other outstanding works include Library, Viipuri, Finland; Villa Mairea, Noormarkku, Finland; Finnish Pavilion, 1939 World's Fair, New York; Baker House, Massachusetts Institute of Technology, Cambridge, Massachusetts; Civic Center, Säynätsalo, Finland; Sunila Pulp Mill and Workers Housing, Kotka, Finland; Culture Center, Wolfsburg, Germany; National Pensions Institute, Helsinki.

PIETRO BELLUSCHI (1899–1994). Born in Ancona, Italy, Belluschi graduated from the University of Rome and received a degree in civil engineering at Cornell University. After working as a chief designer in the office of A.E. Doyle in Portland, Oregon, he became an associate, and the office later reorganized under his name. His Equitable Savings and Loan Association Building was a pioneering structure, but the churches and houses in his Northwest style, influenced by the Japanese residential wooden vernacular, made him internationally renowned. As dean of the Department of Architecture at the Massachusetts Institute of Technology and an active consultant, Belluschi has been an important influence in education and the architectural profession. Other outstanding works include Portland Art Museum, Oregon; First Presbyterian Church, Cottage Grove, Oregon; Central Lutheran Church, Portland; Portsmouth Priory, Rhode Island; and as consultant, Bennington College Library, Vermont; Goucher College Center, Towson, Maryland; Northern States Power Company Building, Minneapolis, Minnesota.

MAX BILL (b. 1908). Born in Winterthur, Switzerland, Bill studied at the Bauhaus under Walter Gropius and Hannes Meyer. His buildings such as the School of Design in Ulm, Germany, attest to his special architectural talent. With the exception of his years teaching in Ulm, he was based in Zürich. His work as a sculptor, painter, designer, and important educator demonstrate his wide-ranging abilities in and influence on all the modern arts. Other outstanding works include Bill Studio House, Zürich; Swiss Pavilion, 1936 Triennale, Milan; Radio Zürich Studio and Administration Building, Zürich.

OSWALDO ARTHUR BRATKE (b. 1907). Born in São Paulo, Brazil, Bratke studied civil engineering there at Mackenzie University. After erecting over four hundred houses as a builder, he became a professional architect. He devoted his career to developing the human element in architecture, stressing simple design and easily maintained materials. From his own admired residence in São Paulo to entire new towns in the Amazon, such as Vilas Industriais Amazonas, Amapa State, Brazil, Bratke is internationally honored for his sympathetic architectural environments. Outstanding works include Grande Hotel, Campos do Jordão, Brazil; Morumbi Children's Hospital, São Paulo; Legislative Assembly, São Paulo.

MARCEL BREUER (1902–1981). Born in Pécs, Hungary, Breuer studied at the Weimar Bauhaus and became a master at the Dessau Bauhaus. There he created his highly influential tubular steel furniture. After opening an office in Berlin, he spent four years traveling. Breuer worked in England and then moved to the United States, where he joined Walter Gropius on the faculty of the Harvard University School of Architecture. First with Gropius in Cambridge, Massachusetts, and later in his own New York City practice, he designed a series of notable houses, combining modern and traditional American influences. In major international commissions, with unusual clarity of expression and attention to detail, he employed concrete in massive and sculptural forms. With his teaching and architecture, Breuer became the most celebrated of first-generation Bauhaus students. Outstanding works include Chamberlain House, with Walter Gropius, Weyland, Massachusetts; Breuer House, New Canaan, Connecticut; Robinson House, Williamstown, Massachusetts; IBM Research Center, with R.F. Gatje, Grasse, France; UNESCO Headquarters, with Pier Luigi Nervi and Bernard Zehrfuss, Paris; Whitney Museum of American Art, with H. Smith, New York City.

GORDON BUNSHAFT (1909–1990). Born in Buffalo, New York, Bunshaft graduated with a degree in architecture from the Massachusetts Institute of Technology, Cambridge, and continued his education in Europe and Africa on a Rotch Traveling Fellowship. After serving with the U.S. Army Corps of Engineers, he joined the New York City firm later known as Skidmore, Owings, and Merrill. As partner in charge of design at SOM, he received worldwide recognition for consistently innovative and quality work, ranging from a single building such as Lever House, New York City, to large projects like the U.S. Air Force Academy in Colorado Springs. A master of his craft, Bunshaft was one of the most significant second-generation modern architects. Other outstanding works include H.J. Heinz Company, Pittsburgh, Pennsylvania; Manufacturers Hanover Trust Building, New York City; Reynolds Headquarters Building, Richmond, Virginia; Connecticut General Life Insurance Office Building, Bloomfield, Connecticut; Beinecke Rare Book and Manuscript Library, Yale University, New Haven, Connecticut.

FÉLIX CANDELA (b. 1910). Born in Madrid, Candela graduated from that city's University of Architecture, where he concentrated on mathematics and structural theory. He enlisted in the Spanish Republican forces, was taken prisoner, and later went to Mexico City. He adopted Mexican nationality and, with his brothers, established an architectural and construction company. He designed over nine hundred shell-dome structures, exploiting the tensile strength of reinforced concrete. From low-cost family housing to a major cathedral, the Church of the Miraculous Virgin, Mexico City, Candela transformed the science of engineering into the art of architecture. Other outstanding works include Cosmic Ray Pavilion, University City, Mexico City; Market Hall, Mexico City; Chapel at Lomas de Cuernavaca, Temixco, Morelos, Mexico.

EDUARDO CATALANO (b. 1917). Born in Buenos Aires, Argentina, Catalano graduated with architectural degrees from the University of Pennsylvania, Philadelphia, and from Harvard University, Cambridge, Massachusetts. After running an independent architectural practice in Buenos Aires, he moved to the United States. Catalano taught at the University of North Carolina, Raleigh, and later at the Massachusetts Institute of Technology, Cambridge, Massachusetts. His buildings display his unique technical talents and concern for the broad social responsibilities of the architect. Outstanding works include Raleigh House, Raleigh, North Carolina; Julius Adams Stratton Student Center, Massachusetts Institute of Technology.

MARIO CIAMPI (b. 1907). Born in San Francisco, Ciampi studied at Harvard University, Cambridge, Massachusetts, and the École des Beaux-Arts, Paris. In addition to his architectural work, such as the Corpus Christi Roman Catholic Church in San Francisco and numerous important school buildings, including Westmoor High School, Daly City, California, and Oceana High School, San Francisco, he designed master plans for universities, school districts, and private developments. He also served as urban consultant for the general redevelopment of the city of San Francisco. Ciampi's notable career emphasized and advanced the role of the modern architect as an urban planner. Other outstanding works include Saint Peter's Roman Catholic Church, Pacifica, California.

EDGARDO CONTINI (1914–1990). Born in Ferrara, Italy, Contini was educated in Rome and served as an engineer in the Italian air force. He moved to the United States and joined the office of Albert Kahn in Detroit, Michigan. With responsibilities for the design of concrete and steel structures for naval bases and power, defense, and industrial plants, Contini created the first thin barrel-vaulted project in the United States. He was awarded the Legion of Merit for his wartime service with the U.S. Army Corps of Engineers. He became partner in charge of engineering with Gruen Associates, supervising design for the public and private sectors throughout the world. As a lecturer in urban design at the University of California at Los Angeles, he combined his architectural talent with sensitive dedication to the environment. Outstanding works include Midtown Plaza, Rochester, New York; Mid-Wilshire Medical Building, Los Angeles.

WILLEM DUDOK (1884–1974). Born in Amsterdam, Dudok graduated as an engineer from the Royal Military Academy of Breda. After ten years of military work, he was appointed city architect for Hilversum, the Netherlands, where for decades he shaped the city and designed many of its principal buildings. He served as town planner for The Hague, Velsen, Wassevaar, and Zwalle, and designed many buildings in his private practice. Dudok's unadorned massive brick buildings in simple geometric forms established his early reputation as an International Style architect. Outstanding works include Town Hall, Hilversum; De Bijenkorf Store, Rotterdam; Vondel School, Hilversum; Netherlands Students House, Cité Universitaire, Paris; Crematory, Westenwelt, the Netherlands; Erasmus Huis, Rotterdam.

R. BUCKMINSTER FULLER (1895–1983). Born in Milton, Massachusetts, Fuller studied briefly at Harvard University, Cambridge. As a member of the U.S. Navy during the First World War, Fuller, with assignments in applied engineering and global strategies, initiated his "comprehensive anticipatory design science." Fuller was an American original. He was not an architect, but he is considered one of the architectural innovators of this era. He lectured in major universities and architecture schools throughout the world. He developed a new type of fibrous building block for lightweight structures and invented the circular Dymaxion House and the Dymaxion Car. His most significant contribution was the geodesic dome, based on the concept of the space frame and made in a variety of materials, including plywood, aluminum, and prestressed concrete. Some of the best known large-scale examples are the United States Pavilion, Sokolniki Park, Moscow; Ford Rotunda, Dearborn, Michigan; DEW Line Radar Stations, the Arctic and Antarctica; Union Tank Car Dome, Baton Rouge, Louisiana.

JOSÉ MIGUEL GALIA (b. 1924). Born in Gualegua ychú, Argentina, Galia studied at the University of Montevideo with Julio Vilamajó. As a partner with Martín Vegas in Caracas, Venezuela, he designed a series of important modern buildings that encouraged the adoption of the International Style in Venezuela. Outstanding works include Polar Building, Caracas; Commerce and Agriculture Bank, Caracas; Eastern Professional Center of Sabara Grande, Caracas; Twin Morochos Apartments, Caracas.

BRUCE GOFF (1904–1982). Born in Alton, Kansas, Goff received no academic architectural education but was apprenticed at the age of twelve to the firm of Rush, Endacott, and Rush in Tulsa, Oklahoma, where he later became a partner. During the Second World War, in the Construction Battalion of the U.S. Navy, he was recognized for his ability to design using improvised materials. Later he was appointed chairman of the Department of Architecture at the University of Oklahoma in Norman, which attracted widespread attention for its unique, creative design curriculum. In numerous unconventional, single-family houses, Goff explored an unprecedented variety of building materials and inventive construction techniques. He designed a number of major buildings in his idiosyncratic style. Outstanding works include Boston Avenue United Methodist Church, Tulsa, Oklahoma; Rudd House, San Francisco; Ledbetter House, Norman; Ford House, Aurora, Illinois; Bavinger House, Norman.

CHARLES GOODMAN (1906–1992). Born in New York City, Goodman studied at the Illinois Institute of Technology, Chicago. He founded Charles Goodman Associates in Washington, D.C., and built a nationwide reputation in the residential field. Goodman's numerous housing developments and his pioneering work in prefabricated homes was marked by award-winning planning and design. Outstanding works include Hollin Hills, Alexandria, Virginia; River Park, Washington, D.C.; National Homes, Lafayette, Indiana.

WALTER GROPIUS (1883–1969). Born in Berlin, Gropius studied architecture at the Technical College in Berlin-Charlottenburg. Like Ludwig Mies van der Rohe and Le Corbusier, he worked as an assistant in the Berlin office of Peter Behrens before beginning his own practice. With Adolph Meyer, he designed the famous Fagus Factory, Alfeld, Germany, in which he utilized curtain-wall construction well in advance of its time. An active propagandist for new social, artistic, and architectural goals, Gropius was appointed head of two art schools in Weimar, which he combined as the Bauhaus. He remained director when it moved to Dessau; there he designed its famed glass and steel building. As Hitler came to power, Gropius left Germany and, after an interval in England, moved to America, where he was appointed chairman of the Department of Architecture at Harvard University, Cambridge, Massachusetts. He also returned to private practice, with Marcel Breuer, and subsequently formed TAC, The Architects' Collaborative, in keeping with his convictions concerning group design. Throughout his long and active career, Gropius was one of the most influential international educators and architects of the twentieth century. Other outstanding works include City Employment Building, Dessau; Impington Village, Cambridgeshire, England; Graduate Center, Harvard University; United States Embassy, Athens; Pan American (Met Life) Building, New York City.

VICTOR GRUEN (1903–1980). Born in Vienna, Gruen attended the Architectural School and Academy of Arts there and went into private practice. In 1938 he moved to New York City and later to Los Angeles. He pioneered a new architectural complex, the shopping mall; a series of prototypical examples featured colorful, multistoried interiors with gardens, sculpture, and cafés, and addressed the urban problems of traffic and parking. He applied his ideas to city plans such as Fort Worth, Texas, which were unrealized yet widely influential. In his work, Gruen strove to create an environment of comfort and convenience rather than stylish buildings. Outstanding works include Lederer Shop, New York City; Northland Shopping Center, Detroit, Michigan; Southdale Shopping Center, Minneapolis, Minnesota; Museum of Arts and Sciences, Evansville, Indiana; Midtown Plaza, Rochester, New York.

HELMUT HENTRICH (b. 1905). Born in Krefeld, Germany, Hentrich was educated at the University of Freiburg and the Technical University of Vienna. He received an architectural degree from the Technical University of Berlin. After working in the offices of Ernö Goldfinger in Paris and Norman Bel Geddes in New York City, he opened an office in Düsseldorf and worked with a series of partners. HPP, Hentrich-Petschnigg and Partner KG, has been honored for its careful restoration of historic buildings, but Hentrich is most widely recognized for the numerous outstanding office and administration buildings that introduced American corporate-style architecture to a rebuilding postwar Germany. Outstanding works include BASF Tower, Ludwigshafen,

Germany; Thyssen Building, Düsseldorf; Horten Department Store, Neuss, Germany; Europa Center, Berlin.

ARNE JACOBSEN (1902–1971). Born in Copenhagen, Jacobsen attended the Copenhagen Technical College and graduated from the Royal Academy. His early residences and apartments followed the International Style. He was influenced by Erik Gunnar Asplund during his wartime work in Sweden. Back in Copenhagen after the war, he created designs indebted to Ludwig Mies van der Rohe. He developed his own distinctive style characterized by a sensitive aesthetic and meticulous detailing. Jacobsen's widely admired Town Hall in Rødovre, Denmark, initiated a series of notable international projects. Celebrated for his light and delicate interiors, Jacobsen worked with the idea of total design, creating furniture and furnishings that helped make Danish design world famous. Other outstanding buildings include Aarhus Town Hall, Denmark; Row houses, Søholm, Denmark; Royal SAS Hotel and Air Terminal, Copenhagen; Munkegaard School, Copenhagen; Saint Catherine's College, Oxford, England.

PHILIP JOHNSON (b. 1906). Born in Cleveland, Ohio, Johnson graduated from Harvard University, Cambridge, Massachusetts, with a degree in classical studies. He was appointed the first director of the innovative Architecture Department at The Museum of Modern Art, New York. There, with architectural historian Henry-Russell Hitchcock, he curated the landmark modern architecture exhibition *The International Style*. The show and accompanying catalogue, cowritten by Hitchcock and Johnson, introduced the vanguard European architecture of the twenties to America. Johnson returned to Harvard to obtain an architecture degree and then resumed his position at MOMA. In private practice, with a series of partners, he designed a number of residences, including his own famous Glass House in New Canaan, Connecticut, as well as major cultural and office buildings, in the evolving modern style. A historian, advocate, critic, and talented practitioner, Johnson is one of the most widely recognized figures in modern architecture. Other outstanding works include Hodgson House, New Canaan; Munson-Williams-Proctor Institute, Utica, New York; New York State Theater, Lincoln Center, New York City.

LOUIS KAHN (1901–1974). Born in Saarama, Estonia, Kahn emigrated with his parents to the United States. He attended the University of Pennsylvania, Philadelphia, under the Beaux-Arts curriculum of dean Paul Philippe Cret. Remarkably talented in drawing, he worked first as a draftsman, then as a principal designer for a series of Philadelphia firms. He became design critic and professor of architecture at Yale University, New Haven, Connecticut, and subsequently accepted a similar appointment at his alma mater. In a stunning series of buildings ranging from museums to laboratories, he pursued an intuitive search for the fundamental principles of design employing brick and poured-in-place concrete. His unfulfilled city plans reveal not only his abiding social concerns but also his inspired creativity. With his teaching and his buildings of extraordinary strength and beauty, Kahn influenced the development of modern architecture and earned recognition as a twentieth-century master. Outstanding works include Yale Art Gallery, Yale University, New Haven; Mill Creek Redevelopment, Philadelphia; Richards Medical Research Building, University of Pennsylvania; First Unitarian Church and School, Rochester, New York; Salk Institute, La Jolla, California; National Assembly, Dacca, Bangladesh; Kimbell Art Museum, Fort Worth, Texas; Library and Dining Hall, Phillips Exeter Academy, Exeter, New Hampshire.

CARL KOCH (b. 1912). Born in Milwaukee, Wisconsin, Koch graduated from Harvard University, Cambridge, Massachusetts, and began his practice in Boston as a designer of luxury homes. He soon addressed the larger social problem of low-cost housing, convinced that an answer lay in industrialized housing. He pioneered in the field of prefabricated homes with the innovative foldout Acorn Prefabricated House, Weston, Massachusetts, which was opposed by unions and local building codes. Later he designed a series of modern Techbuilt houses, with factory-manufactured modular parts. Continuing his lifelong concerns, Koch worked to bring human values to high-density housing. Other outstanding buildings include Eastgate Apartments, Cambridge, Massachusetts; Public Library, Fitchburg, Massachusetts; Lewis Wharf, Boston.

LE CORBUSIER (1887–1965). Born Charles-Édouard Jeanneret in La Chaux-de-Fonds, Switzerland, he is known by his adopted name, Le Corbusier. He studied at the local art academy and was stimulated by a series of European study trips. He worked first with Auguste Perret, the French pioneer in ferroconcrete construction, and then with Peter Behrens in Berlin. In Paris, with painter Amédée Ozenfant and poet Paul Dermée, he founded the revolutionary design review *L'Esprit Nouveau*. His book *Vers une Architecture* as well as many others had worldwide impact on architectural thinking. Le Corbusier formed an architectural partnership in Paris with his cousin, Pierre Jeanneret, and developed numerous city schemes incorporating his concepts of urban planning; these plans, along with exhibition buildings such as the Pavillon de L'Esprit Nouveau and Pavillon des Temps Nouveaux, contributed to his international fame. He designed a series of houses, including the most influential one, Villa Savoye, in Poissy-sur-Seine, France, which dramatized the rational and aesthetic forms of the new architecture. Le Corbusier's important theories and great works have, in different ways, made him one of the most influential architectural geniuses of our time. Other outstanding works include Houses, Weissenhof Exhibition, Stuttgart; Swiss Pavilion, University City, Paris; Unité d'Habitation, Marseilles; Notre-Dame-du-Haut, Ronchamp, France; Punjab Capitol Buildings, Chandigarh, India; Monastery of Sainte-Marie-de-la-Tourette, Eveux-sur-l'Arbresle, France; Carpenter Center for the Visual Arts, Harvard University, Cambridge, Massachusetts.

KUNIO MAYEKAWA (1905–1986). Born in Niigata, Japan, Mayekawa graduated from Tokyo University and apprenticed to Le Corbusier in France and Antonin Raymond in Tokyo. He then established a private practice, with Kenzo Tange as one of his assistants. His first major building was the boldly modern Kanagawa Prefectural Concert Hall and Library in Yokohama; this was followed by workers apartments at Harumi. Mayekawa's Japanese Pavilion at the 1958 Brussels Exhibition introduced modern Japanese architecture to the world. In a number of significant concrete buildings, Mayekawa continued to explore a distinctive Japanese expression of the International Style. Other outstanding works include Nihon Sōgo Bank Main Office, Tokyo; International House of Japan, with Junzo Sakakura and Junzo Yoshimura; Kyoto Cultural Hall; Tokyo Cultural Hall; Gakushu-in College, Tokyo.

LUDWIG MIES VAN DER ROHE (1886–1969). Born in Aachen, Germany, Mies attended the Cathedral Latin School and learned to respect craftsmanship from his stonemason father. In Berlin he apprenticed with leading cabinetmaker Bruno Paul and later in the office of Peter Behrens. His many professional activities—including his involvement with the Deutsche Werkbund—his sketches and model for a stunning glass office tower on Berlin's Friedrichstrasse, and the De Stijl–influenced plans for country houses established him as a leader of the modern architectural movement in post–World War I Germany. He was director of the Werkbund-sponsored Weissenhof Exhibition in Stuttgart and designed an important apartment building for it. His superb German Pavilion for the 1929 International Exposition in Barcelona and the Tugendhat House in Brno, Czechoslovakia, brought him worldwide recognition. He served as the last director of the Bauhaus in the aggressively antimodern Nazi climate and in 1933 he left Germany for the United States, where he accepted the directorship of what is now the Illinois Institute of Technology. His master plan and structurally explicit buildings for its Chicago campus as well as his Lake Shore Drive apartments rapidly established his presence and prominence in the United States. Mies expanded this series of inspired buildings, expressing his genius in the art of architecture in an age of science and technology. Other outstanding buildings include Seagram Building, New York City; Federal Center, Chicago; Houston Museum of Fine Arts, Texas; Dominion Center, Toronto, Canada; New National Gallery, Berlin.

PIER LUIGI NERVI (1891–1979). Born in Sondrio, Italy, Nervi graduated with a degree in civil engineering from the University of Bologna. He gained experience with a concrete contracting firm and during the First World War served as an officer in the Italian army corps of engineers. In Rome he established his engineering and contracting firm. As designer and builder of the Municipal Stadium in Florence, with its cantilevered roof, Nervi attracted international attention. His prefabricated hangars for the World War II Italian air force in Orvieto and Orbetello led directly to his great Exhibition Hall in Turin and the Sports Palace in Rome. He was the engineer with a number of architects on such buildings as the UNESCO Conference Hall in Paris, the Pirelli Tower in Milan, and Place Victoria Tower in Montreal. For his influential writings, his teachings as professor of technology and construction techniques at the University of Rome, and his extraordinary works, Nervi is recognized as a master builder who added ferroconcrete shell structures to the vocabulary of modern architecture. Other outstanding buildings include his only bridge, in Verona, Italy; a cinema in Naples, Italy; St. Mary's Cathedral, San Francisco, California.

RICHARD NEUTRA (1892–1970). Born in Vienna, Neutra studied architecture at the Technical College there and worked briefly in Switzerland and in Eric Mendelsohn's Berlin office before moving to America. In Los Angeles he designed the Jardinette Apartments; employing reinforced concrete and metal-framed windows, they were one of the first major examples of the International Style in the United States. The light steel-frame Lovell House in Los Angeles, with its concrete, glass, and metal panels assembled from an architect's supply-house catalogue, established his international reputation. In a series of residences, apartments, and acclaimed housing projects, as well as a pioneering school, Neutra was able to demonstrate his artistry with interchangeable, prefabricated parts, as well as his zealous dedication to the rationale of modern architecture. These works include Nesbit House, Los Angeles; Kaufmann Desert House, Palm Springs, California; Tremaine House, Montecito, California; Corona Avenue Elementary School, Los Angeles; Channel Heights Housing, San Pedro, California.

OSCAR NIEMEYER (b. 1907). Born in Rio de Janeiro, Brazil, Niemeyer received his architectural degree there at the National School of Fine Arts. He joined the office of his teacher Lucio Costa and worked as chief architect with him and Le Corbusier on the celebrated Ministry of Education and Health in Rio de Janeiro. His first independent design was a group of recreational buildings and the Church of St. Francis of Assisi in Pampulha, Brazil. When Costa won the competition for the plan of Brasília, the new capital of Brazil, Niemeyer was made responsible for the major buildings. These structures—all the main government buildings, the cathedral, university, theater, and housing complex—are renowned for their plasticity and dramatic use of space. In 1955 he moved in self-imposed exile to France, where he executed his first international projects. In the late sixties he returned to his practice in Rio. Niemeyer's audacious forms, which combine new technology with the freedom of the Brazilian baroque, have made him South America's best-known architect. Other outstanding works include Brazilian Pavilion, 1939 World's Fair, New York City; Pampulha Casino and Yacht Club, Belo Horizonte, Brazil; Niemeyer House, Rio de Janeiro.

ELIOT NOYES (1910–1977). Born in Boston, Noyes graduated with an architectural degree from Harvard University, Cambridge, Massachusetts. After working in the office of Walter Gropius and Marcel Breuer, he was appointed director of the Department of Industrial Design at The Museum of Modern Art, New York. In private practice in New Canaan, Connecticut, he designed numerous houses, schools, exhibitions, office buildings, and products for corporations such as IBM, Westinghouse, and Mobil. Noyes was both an articulate advocate and a talented practitioner of integrating architectural, product, and graphic design in business and industry. Outstanding works include Bubble House, Hobe Sound, Florida; Noyes House, New Canaan, Connecticut.

JUAN O'GORMAN (1905–1982). Born in Mexico City, O'Gorman studied at the Architecture School of the National University of Mexico, Mexico City, and worked in the office of José Villagrán García. He was initially influenced by Le Corbusier, but later became deeply affected by Frank Lloyd Wright. His houses and schools were the first examples of the International Style in Mexico. With Gustavo Saavedra and Juan Martinez de Velasco, he designed the celebrated National Library at the University of Mexico, Mexico City. An important Mexican architect, O'Gorman sought to integrate pre-Columbian elements into modern design to express his country's social, cultural, and environmental heritage. Other outstanding works include O'Gorman House, San Angel Inn, Mexico City; Diego Rivera House and Studio, San Angel Inn, Mexico City; Electricians Union Building, Mexico City.

J.J.P. OUD (1890–1963). Born in Purmerend, the Netherlands, Oud studied at the Quellinus Arts and Crafts School in Amsterdam and the Technical University in Delft. After a brief period in Germany, he moved to Leiden, designing there, with Willem Dudok, the Leiderdorp workers' housing complex. He joined the De Stijl group, which included the painters Theo van Doesburg, Piet Mondrian, Georges Vantongerloo, and Bart van der Leck. Soon afterward, he was appointed architect in charge of housing for the city of Rotterdam. His two-story row housing at Hook of Holland and his row of five terrace houses at the Weissenhof Exhibition, Stuttgart, placed him in the vanguard of the practitioners of the new International Style. In his Shell Office Building in The Hague, and in other commercial projects, he sought to restore monumentality and ornament in architecture. As one of the most influential and articulate pioneers of the modern movement, Oud created some of its finest early buildings. Other outstanding works include Housing at Spangen and Oud-Mathenese, the Netherlands; Kiefhoek Development, Rotterdam.

I.M. PEI (b. 1917). Born in Canton, China, Ieoh Ming Pei was raised in Shanghai, graduated from the Massachusetts Institute of Technology in Cambridge, and studied architecture with Walter Gropius at Harvard, where he was later appointed to the faculty. Working with the New York City real estate developer William Zeckendorf, he designed an unusual number of large-scale projects. In private practice in New York City, he developed urban plans for New York City, Boston, Washington, D.C., and Paris. In these and in his remarkable range of buildings, he has demonstrated the admirable ability to design each project with suitability to its context. Consistently Pei has brought great talent, imagination, and quality to each of his works. Outstanding buildings include Mile High Center, Denver, Colorado; Kips Bay Plaza, New York City; Green Center for Earth Sciences, Massachusetts Institute of Technology; Society Hill Apartments and Town Houses, Philadelphia, Pennsylvania; National Center for Atmospheric Research, Boulder, Colorado; University Plaza, New York University, New York City; John Hancock Tower, Boston.

ENRICO PERESSUTTI (1908–1973). Born in Pinzano al Tagliamento, Italy, Peressutti studied architecture at the Milan Polytechnic School of Architecture. As a member of the architectural and design group BBPR—Banfi, Belgiojoso, Peressutti, and Rogers—in Milan he contributed two post–World War II projects which drew worldwide attention: the Monument to Italian Victims of the Concentration Camps, Milan, which employed the space frame; and the interior redesign of the Sforza Castle Museum in Milan. The group's Torre Velasca, an office unit topped with a wider apartment block, caused widespread architectural controversy, as did their unconventional Italian Pavilion at the 1958 Brussels Exhibition. Peressutti had the ability to work in a team without losing his individual talent for imaginative and forceful design.

GIO PONTI (1891–1979). Born in Milan, Ponti studied at the Polytechnic Institute in Milan. Working independently and with others he designed a number of buildings, including the Pirelli skyscraper in Milan. He was active in the Department of Architecture at Polytechnic Institute of Milan, served as a member of the Higher Council of Fine Arts and for many years on the Board of Managers of the Triennial Exhibition, and worked as an editor of *Domus*. In his writings and works Ponti promoted the postwar renewal of Italian design, and celebrated Italy's contribution to international architecture. Other outstanding works include Banca Unione, Milan; School of Mathematics, University of Rome; Montecatini Office Building, Milan; RAI Offices, Milan.

L.L. RADO (1909–1993). Born in Czechoslovakia, Ladislav L. Rado studied architecture at the Technical University in Prague and at Harvard University in Cambridge, Massachusetts. He formed an architectural firm with Antonin Raymond in New York City; Rado was in charge of the office while Raymond returned to his practice in Tokyo. Together they produced a number of noteworthy buildings molded by a strong sense of design and a bold use of materials. Rado also served as professor of architecture at Florida International University, Miami. Outstanding works include Electrolux Industrial Buildings and Recreational Center, Old Greenwich, Connecticut; Reader's Digest Building, with Antonin Raymond, Tokyo; United States Embassy Apartment Buildings, Tokyo; One Dag Hammarskjold Plaza, New York City; Gunma Music Center, Takasaki, Japan.

RALPH RAPSON (b. 1914). Born in Alma, Michigan, Rapson graduated from the University of Michigan, Ann Arbor. He studied with Eliel Saarinen at Cranbrook and worked in the Saarinen office. He headed the Department of Architecture at the Institute of Design, Chicago, and subsequently was appointed associate professor in the School of Architecture, Massachusetts Institute of Technology, Cambridge. Both his commitment to teaching and his buildings display a strong interest in social goals, new construction technology, and innovative functional design. Outstanding works include schools designed with Eero Saarinen, Willow Run, Michigan; United States Embassy Office Building, Stockholm; Tyrone Guthrie Theater, Minneapolis, Minnesota.

ANTONIN RAYMOND (1888–1976). Born in Kladno, Czechoslovakia, Raymond graduated from the Technical College of Prague. He joined Frank Lloyd Wright's Taliesin Fellowship and went to Tokyo with him to assist in the building of the Imperial Hotel. Raymond opened his own office in Tokyo; with sensitive skill he combined the techniques of modern European architecture with the Japanese spirit and tradition. He then opened an office in India and after the Second World War established a partnership with L.L. Rado in New York City. He subsequently returned to Tokyo to carry on his international practice. Through his offices across the globe—with such assistants as Junzo Yoshimura and Kunio Mayekawa—his writings, exhibitions, and his lean, functional buildings, Raymond contributed significantly to the worldwide spread of the International Style. Outstanding works include Raymond House, Tokyo; Saint Paul's Church, Karuizawa, Japan; Golcond Dormitory, Pondicherry, India; Saint Luke's Medical Center, Tokyo; United States Embassy, Tokyo; Reader's Digest Building, with L. L. Rado, Tokyo; Nanzan Campus, Nanzan University, Nagoya.

AFFONSO EDUARDO REIDY (1909–1964). Born in Paris, Reidy studied at the National School of Fine Arts in Rio de Janeiro, Brazil, where he became a major contributor to modern architecture in South America. He was a member of Brazilian planner Lucio Costa's team of young architects who, with Le Corbusier as consultant, created Rio's celebrated Ministry of Education and Health Building. Appointed to the Department of Public Housing, he designed the huge low-income housing project Pedregulho Estate in Rio. The complex, which included apartments, a school, gymnasium, clinic, laundry, and shops, followed the winding contour of the hill site. Reidy's civic work ranged from the Gávea Communal Theater to the Museum of Modern Art, both in Rio. Reidy sought to achieve high social goals in his influential urban planning schemes and widely admired innovative structures. Other outstanding works include Home of Good Will, Rio de Janeiro; Museum of Visual Arts, São Paulo, Brazil.

MARCELO ROBERTO (1908–1964). Born in Brazil, Roberto graduated from the National School of Fine Arts in Rio de Janeiro. He formed an unusually close-knit office in Rio with his brothers Milton and Mauricio. They won their first architectural competition, the Brazilian Press Association Building, with their design for the first large reinforced-concrete office in Brazil.

Influenced by the work of Le Corbusier, they experimented in a series of structures with various designs to control Brazil's intense sunlight. Inspired by Frank Lloyd Wright, they sought to address each project as a separate and unique problem, and thereby introduced distinctive variety to the International Style. Other outstanding works include Santos Dumont Airport, Rio de Janeiro; Resort Development, Barra da Tijuca, Brazil; Seguradores Office Building, Rio de Janeiro; SOTREQ-Caterpillar Offices and Showroom, Rio de Janeiro.

ERNESTO ROGERS (1909–1969). Born in Trieste, Italy, Rogers studied at the Milan Polytechnic. As a founding and active member of the Milan-based architectural firm BBPR—Banfi, Belgiojoso, Peressutti, and Rogers—he contributed to their award-winning buildings. He was a frequent speaker on architecture and an early and important Italian representative at CIAM (Congrès Internationaux d'Architecture Moderne). As editor of *Domus* and *Casabella* Rogers became the most internationally influential Italian writer on modern architecture and design. Outstanding works include Monument to Italian Victims of the Concentration Camps, Milan; remodeling of the Sforza Castle Museum, Milan; Torre Velasca, Milan; Italian Pavilion, 1958 Brussels Exhibition, Belgium.

ALFRED ROTH (b. 1903). Born in Wangen, Switzerland, Roth studied at the Technical College in Zürich. He worked with his teacher, Karl Moser, then with Le Corbusier on two houses for the Weissenhof Exhibition in Stuttgart. After some years in Sweden, he established his practice in Zürich. In partnership with Emil Roth and Marcel Breuer, he built the well-known Doldertal Apartments for the art historian Sigfried Giedion. Working internationally, he designed buildings in Sweden, the United States, Yugoslavia, and the Middle East. As a prolific author and the editor of the Swiss architectural magazine *Werk,* Roth was an ardent advocate of the contribution of education and architecture to improving people's lives. Other outstanding works include Apartments, Göteborg, Sweden; Roth House, Zürich; Swiss Pavilion, 1957 Triennial Exhibition, Milan.

PAUL RUDOLPH (b. 1918). Born in Elkton, Kentucky, Rudolph received his architectural training at Alabama Polytechnic Institute and with Walter Gropius at Harvard University, Cambridge, Massachusetts. He began his practice in partnership with Ralph Twitchell in Sarasota, Florida, and subsequently worked alone there and in Boston, New York, and New Haven, where he was chairman of the Department of Architecture at Yale University. His buildings, executed in an individual, modern style, are located in many American cities as well as in Asia and the Middle East. His concern for urban problems led him to design a number of important large-scale projects, many of which are unrealized. Through activities as a teacher, lecturer, and critic, his uncompromising work, and distinctive architectural drawings, Rudolph has challenged and advanced the role of the architect in the modern world. Outstanding works include Healy Guest House, Siesta Key, Florida; Riverview High School, Sarasota; Jewett Arts Center, Wellesley College, Wellesley, Massachusetts; Art and Architecture Building, Yale University; Blue Cross-Blue Shield Building, with Anderson, Beckwith, and Haible, Boston; Tuskegee Institute Interdenominational Chapel, Tuskegee, Alabama.

EERO SAARINEN (1910–1961). Born in Kirkkonummi, Finland, Saarinen studied sculpture in Paris and architecture at Yale University, New Haven. He worked with his famous father, Eliel, on projects such as the pioneering Crow Island School in Winnetka, Illinois. He then established his own practice in Bloomfield Hills, Michigan. Unified only by a modern approach to color, form, and materials, Saarinen's buildings are characterized by remarkable diversity. Working with intense vigor, he sought in each project its appropriate form. He attempted not only to satisfy the demands of each project, but with each one to make a new architectural statement. Saarinen died suddenly at the height of his career as one of the most respected and talented architects of his generation. Outstanding works include General Motors Technical Center, Warren, Michigan; Jefferson National Expansion Memorial, St. Louis, Missouri; Chapel and Kresge Auditorium, Massachusetts Institute of Technology, Cambridge, Massachusetts; Ingalls Hockey Rink, Yale University, New Haven, Connecticut; TWA Terminal, Kennedy International Airport, New York City; John Deere Headquarters, Moline, Illinois; Bell Laboratories, Holmdel, New Jersey; Dulles International Airport, Reston, Virginia; CBS Building, New York City.

MARIO SALVADORI (b. 1907). Born in Rome, Salvadori was educated at the University of Rome and University College, London. One of the leading concrete structural engineers in the world, he worked with engineering firms such as Weidlinger Associates, New York City. He is renowned in the field of education: his technical books have been translated into multiple languages; he has lectured at universities throughout the world; he established and taught some seventeen courses in engineering mathematics at Columbia University, New York; and he instituted a pioneering program and educational center on the built environment in elementary, junior high, and high schools in New York City. Outstanding buildings include La Concha Resort Hotel and Nightclub, San Juan, Puerto Rico; St. Louis Priory Church, St. Louis, Missouri.

TOMÁS SANABRIA (b. 1922). Born in Caracas, Venezuela, Sanabria studied at the Institute of Civil Engineering of Venezuela in Caracas and the Harvard Graduate School of Design in Cambridge, Massachusetts. At Harvard he studied with Walter Gropius and Marcel Breuer. Sanabria returned to Caracas, where he became one of his country's most recognized architectural talents. He designed a wide range of hotels, banks, industrial, educational, cultural, and government buildings. He made an important contribution to the development of the profession in his own country and internationally. Outstanding works include C.A. La Electricidad de Caracas, San Bernardino, Venezuela; Hotel Humboldt, Caracas; First National City Bank, Caracas; Laboratorios Abbott, Caracas.

MARC SAUGEY (1908–1971). Born in Vésenaz, Switzerland, and based in Geneva, Saugey combined a sharp intellectual approach with a strong appreciation of technology and design. His numerous buildings established him as a modern architectural leader in Switzerland. Outstanding works include Malagnou-Parc Apartments, Geneva; Gare-Centre, Geneva.

PAUL SCHWEIKHER (b. 1903). Born in Denver, Colorado, Schweikher studied at Yale University School of Architecture, New Haven, and practiced with several firms in Chicago. A dedicated educator, he served as professor and chairman of the Yale School of Architecture, and later in the same position at Carnegie-Mellon University, Pittsburgh. He designed with integrity in a forthright manner, selecting simple forms and durable, natural materials. Outstanding works include Stone House, Topeka, Kansas; Unitarian Church, Evanston, Illinois; Women's Dormitory, Maryville College, Tennessee; Chicago Hall Language Center, Vassar College, Poughkeepsie, New York; Trinity United Presbyterian Church, East Liverpool, Ohio; Knoxville Branch, Carnegie Library, Pittsburgh.

JOSÉ LUIS SERT (1902–1983). Born in Barcelona, Sert studied at the School of Architecture there. He worked briefly in the office of Le Corbusier and Pierre Jeanneret in Paris, and upon returning to Barcelona he opened his own office. Later he went back to Paris, where for the 1937 World's Fair he designed the Spanish Republican Pavilion made famous by Picasso's *Guernica*, Joan Miró's painting *El Segador Catalan,* and Alexander Calder's *Mercury Fountain*. Before the outbreak of World War II, he emigrated to the United States. In New York City he became associated with Paul Lester Wiener and the two worked on a number of important city planning projects in Central and South America. On Walter Gropius's recommendation he was appointed dean of the faculty and professor of architecture at Harvard Graduate School of Design, Cambridge, Massachusetts, where he established the first professional urban-design degree course. He subsequently opened an office in Cambridge in partnership with Huson Jackson and Ronald Gourley and designed a number of houses, offices, and university buildings. As a dedicated internationalist and officer in CIAM (Congrès Internationaux d'Architecture Moderne), a cultural leader integrating modern art and sculpture into architecture, an author and educator, Sert played an important role in the modern movement. Other outstanding works include Studio for Joan Miró, Palma de Mallorca, Spain; Apartment House, Calle Muntaner, Barcelona; United States Embassy, Baghdad, Iraq; Sert House, Cambridge; Health and Administration Building, Harvard University; Fondation Maeght, St.-Paul-de-Vence, France; Peabody Terrace Married Students Housing, Harvard University.

RUDOLF STEIGER (1900–1982). Born in Zürich, Switzerland, Steiger studied at the University of Zürich with the Swiss architect Karl Moser. In partnership with Max Haefeli and Werner Moser in Zürich, he made an important contribution to postwar Swiss housing and most particularly to town planning. Outstanding buildings include Werkbund Neubühl Estate, Zürich; Hochhaus zur Palme, Zürich; Prilly Housing, Lausanne.

EDWARD DURELL STONE (1902–1978). Born in Fayetteville, Arkansas, Stone studied art at the University of Arkansas, entered the School of Architecture at Harvard University, Cambridge, Massachusetts, and transferred to the Massachusetts Institute of Technology, Cambridge, to study modern design with Jacques Carlu. He toured Europe on a Rotch Traveling Fellowship and on returning to the United States assisted in the design of Radio City Music Hall in New York City. Based in that city he worked in the International Style, designing the much-admired Mandel House in Mount Kisco, New York, and, with Philip Goodwin, the original Museum of Modern Art building in New York City. He then departed from the pure principles of the modern style to create a more personal idiom that embraced ornamentation. Examples from this phase of his career include a series of buildings protected by ornamental sun-shielding or grilles, among them the United States Embassy in New Delhi, India. Other outstanding works include El Panama Hotel, Panama City, Panama; Robert Popper House, White Plains, New York; United States Pavilion, 1962 World's Fair, Brussels, Belgium.

KENZO TANGE (b. 1913). Born in Imabari, Japan, Tange studied architecture, city planning, and engineering at the University of Tokyo, where he subsequently became assistant professor of architecture. He worked for Kunio Mayekawa before starting his own Tokyo office. Tange won the architectural competition for the Hiroshima Peace Museum, Hiroshima, Japan, and later the competition for the Tokyo City Hall complex. His graceful Yoyogi Gymnasium for the Tokyo Olympic Games capped this period, which merged Le Corbusier's modernism with the spirit of traditional Japanese architecture. Tange then repudiated regionalism and became an exponent of the abstract International Style, executing designs worldwide. He also created a number of city plans, including the Future Tokyo, which although unrealized remains an influential study in planning. Talented, innovative, and intellectually curious, Tange is recognized as Japan's leading second-generation modern architect. Other outstanding works include Kagawa Prefectural Government Office, Takamatsu, Japan; Imabari City Hall, Ehime, Japan; Kurashiki City Hall, Okayama, Japan.

MARTÍN VEGAS (b. 1926). Born in Caracas, Venezuela, Vegas studied with Ludwig Mies van der Rohe at the Illinois Institute of Technology in Chicago. On returning to Caracas he established a practice with the Argentinian José Miguel Galia; they provided Venezuela with worthy examples of International Style architecture, combining Miesian precision with respect for the South American climate and regional materials. Outstanding works include Polar Building, Caracas; Commerce and Agriculture Bank, Caracas; Eastern Professional Center of Sabara Grande, Caracas; Twin Morochos Apartments, Caracas.

CARLOS RAÚL VILLANUEVA (1900–1975). Born in London, where his father was in the Venezuelan diplomatic service, Villanueva was educated at the Lycée Condorcet in Paris. He obtained a degree in architecture from the Ecole des Beaux-Arts there and then returned to Caracas to begin private practice. The University City project for the City University of Caracas spanned much of his career. For it he executed the master plan and designed its Medical Center, Library, Concert Hall, Botanical Institute, the Humanities, Science, and Physics Building, and School of Dentistry. He also designed the School of Architecture and Urbanism, which he founded and where he served as professor. The culmination of the University City project was the breathtaking concrete Olympic Stadium. Villanueva served as architect to the Ministry of Public Works and founder and director of the National Planning Commission. Many of his architectural aims were realized in an outstanding series of major housing developments, and his concepts and designs for low-cost, low-rent, modern housing remain unsurpassed. He was founding president of the Venezuelan Association of Architects. Villanueva greatly enriched the profession with his dedication to social goals, and he brilliantly established modern architecture in Venezuela. Other outstanding works include Bullring, Maracay, Venezuela; Venezuela Pavilion, 1939 World's Fair, Paris; General Rafael Urdaneta Housing Development, Maracaibo, Venezuela.

PAUL WEIDLINGER (b. 1914). Born in Budapest, Hungary, Weidlinger studied at the Technical Institute in Brno, Czechoslovakia, and the Swiss Polytechnic Institute in Zürich. He worked as a designer with Le Corbusier in Paris and as an engineer with a number of organizations in South America and the United States. His own consulting engineering firm, Weidlinger Associates, New York City, has an international reputation for commercial, institutional, and defense structures. As an educator, author, and engineer, working with many of the world's leading architects, Weidlinger has contributed notably and creatively to the advancement of modern architecture. Outstanding buildings include Reader's Digest Office Building, Tokyo; Banque Lambert, Brussels, Belgium; United States Embassy, Baghdad, Iraq; Beinecke Rare Book and Manuscript Library, Yale University, New Haven, Connecticut; United States Embassy, Athens; Carpenter Center for the Visual Arts, Harvard University, Cambridge, Massachusetts.

PHILIP WILL JR. (1906–1985). Born in Rochester, New York, Will studied at Cornell University School of Architecture, Ithaca, New York. He moved to Chicago to work with General House, Inc., an early manufacturer of prefabricated homes. With Lawrence B. Perkins and E.T. Wheeler, he formed a partnership and collaborated with the Saarinens on the innovative Crow Island School in Winnetka, Illinois. Perkins and Will became one of America's largest architectural firms, with additional offices in New York City and Washington, D.C. With the firm he designed a number of schools, such as Heathcote School in Scarsdale, New York, which had wide influence on modern educational building design. During his career he produced a wide range of buildings in both size and type. Other outstanding works include Steel House, General Houses, Inc., Century of Progress Exposition, Chicago; Philip Will Jr. House, Evanston, Illinois; Rockford Memorial Hospital, Rockford, Illinois; U.S. Gypsum Building, Chicago; Scott Foresman Office Building, Glenview, Illinois.

FRANK LLOYD WRIGHT (1867–1959). Born in Richland Center, Wisconsin, Wright studied engineering at the University of Wisconsin, Madison, and worked in the office of the Chicago residential architect J. Lyman Silsbee and then as assistant to Louis Sullivan in the office of Adler and Sullivan. He designed a series of houses for the latter firm. Then, without Sullivan's knowledge, he executed some houses on his own, which caused an abrupt break in their contractual relationship. From his studio and home in Oak Park, Illinois, Wright created the influential open-plan Prairie Houses. Outstanding examples are his own home; the Willits House, Highland Park, Illinois; the Thomas House, Oak Park, Illinois; the Dana House, Springfield, Illinois; the Martin House, Buffalo, New York; the Robie House, Chicago; and the Coonley House, Riverside, Illinois. During the same period he designed the Larkin Administration and Office Building in Buffalo, New York, and Unity Temple in Oak Park, pioneering the use of monolithic reinforced concrete. Wright journeyed to Europe, where the publication of his early work by Wasmuth in Berlin had a broad impact. He went to Japan during the construction of the Imperial Hotel in Tokyo. Facing difficult times he then returned to Wisconsin. He was commissioned by Aline Barnsdall to design her Los Angeles home; the result was the concrete "Hollyhock" House. A number of textile block residences followed, including the Millard House in Pasadena and the Ennis House in Los Angeles. In the 1930s he formed the Taliesin Fellowship, based in Spring Green, Wisconsin, and Scottsdale, Arizona. During this period he designed the Johnson Wax Company Administration Building and Johnson's house, Wingspread, in Racine, and the Kaufmann house, Fallingwater, in Bear Run, Pennsylvania. One of his last works was among his most celebrated, the Solomon R. Guggenheim Museum in New York City. Wright's professional life spanned seventy years. As a speaker, writer, teacher, and designer of nearly a thousand buildings, some four hundred built, Wright was surely one of the greatest and certainly the best known architectural genius of the twentieth century. Other outstanding works include Thomas H. Gale House and Cheney House, Oak Park; Winslow House and Roberts House, River Forest, Illinois; Broadacre City (unrealized); Usonian houses such as the Herbert Jacobs House, Madison; H.C. Price Tower, Bartlesville, Oklahoma.

WILLIAM WURSTER (1895–1973). Born in Stockton, California, Wurster studied architecture at the University of California, Berkeley. As a principal partner in the firm Wurster, Bernardi, and Emmons, he designed a great number of residences, housing projects, and institutional and commercial buildings. He was a fellow of the Harvard Graduate School of Design, Cambridge, Massachusetts, and dean of the Harvard University School of Architecture and Planning, Massachusetts Institute of Technology, and the College of Architecture at UC–Berkeley. In addition he was founder and dean of the College of Environmental Design at UC–Berkeley. Through architectural education Wurster was determined to expand the scope of the profession to include concern for the total environment. He believed architecture is a social art and that buildings should be a forthright response to regional needs and conditions. Outstanding works include Gregory Farmhouse, Santa Cruz, California; Center for Advanced Studies in Behavioral Sciences, Medical Plaza, Married Students Housing, Stanford University, Palo Alto, California; Golden Gateway Redevelopment Project, San Francisco; Ghirardelli Square, San Francisco; Cowell College, University of California, Santa Cruz.

MINORU YAMASAKI (1912–1986). Born in Seattle, Washington, Yamasaki was educated at the University of Washington, Seattle, and at New York University, New York City. He worked as a designer for prominent firms in New York City and Detroit; throughout his career he preferred to work in teams and did not set up his own private practice. Combining functional and humanistic values, Yamasaki explored ways to bring the enrichment of machine-made ornament to his modern architectural forms. Among his award-winning buildings are the Terminal Building at Lambert Airport, designed with George Hellmuth and Joseph Leinweber, St. Louis, Missouri, and the twin towers of the World Trade Center in New York City. Other outstanding works include McGregor Memorial Community Conference Center, Wayne State University, Detroit, Michigan; Reynolds Metals Regional Sales Office, Southfield, Michigan.

JUNZO YOSHIMURA (b. 1908). Born in Tokyo, Yoshimura graduated from the Tokyo Art Institute. He was exposed to the new International Style when he worked with Antonin Raymond; he then opened his own office in Tokyo. His projects include houses, offices, museums, and college buildings. He made a noteworthy contribution to Japanese professional education as professor of architecture at the Tokyo College of Arts. In his buildings Yoshimura mixed modern international and traditional Japanese elements with widely admired skill. Outstanding works include International House of Japan (with Kunio Mayekawa and Junzo Sakakura), Tokyo; Hotel Kowaku-en, Hakone, Japan; National Cash Register Building, Tokyo; Aichi Prefecture College of Arts, Nagakute, Japan.

Bibliography

Achilles, Rolf, Kevin Harrington, and Charlotte Myhrum, eds. *Mies van der Rohe: Architect as Educator.* Chicago: Illinois Institute of Technology, 1986.

Baker, Geoffrey, and Jacques Gubler. *Le Corbusier: Early Works by Charles-Édouard Jeanneret.* London: Academy Editions/St. Martin's Press, 1987.

Barford, George. *Understanding Modern Architecture. Worcester,* Massachusetts: Davis Publications, 1986.

Bastlund, Knud. *José Luis Sert: Architecture, City Planning, Urban Design.* New York: Frederick A. Praeger, 1967.

Bayley, Stephen, Philippe Garner, and Deyan Sudjic. *Twentieth-Century Style and Design.* New York: Van Nostrand Reinhold Company, 1986.

Bill, Max. *Le Corbusier Oeuvre Complète,* 1934–38. Vol. 2. Erlenbach-Zürich: Les Éditions d'Architecture, 1947.

Blake, Peter. *Marcel Breuer. Architect and Designer.* New York: Architectural Record/The Museum of Modern Art, 1949.

Blake, Peter, ed. *Marcel Breuer. Sun and Shadow, The Philosophy of an Architect.* New York: Dodd, Mead and Company, 1955.

Blake, Peter. *The Master Builders.* New York: Alfred A. Knopf, 1960.

Blaser, Werner. *Mies van der Rohe.* New York: Frederick A. Praeger, 1965.

Boesiger, Willy. *Le Corbusier 1938–1946.* Vol. 1. Erlenbach-Zürich: Les Éditions d'Architecture, 1946.

———. *Le Corbusier et Pierre Jeanneret, Oeuvre Complète, 1929–1934.* Vol. 3. Erlenbach-Zürich: Les Éditions d'Architecture, 1946.

———. *Le Corbusier et son atelier rue Sèvres, 35, Oeuvre Complète, 1952–1957.* New York: George Wittenborn, 1957.

Bolon, Carol R., Robert S. Nelson, and Linda Seidel. *The Nature of Frank Lloyd Wright.* Chicago: The University of Chicago Press, 1988.

Brownlee, David B., and David G. DeLong. *Louis I. Kahn: In the Realm of Architecture.* New York: Rizzoli, 1991.

Canty, Donald, ed. *The New City.* New York: Praeger/Urban America, 1969.

Coulin, Claudius. *Drawings by Architects, from the Ninth Century to the Present Day.* New York: Reinhold, 1962.

Curtis, William J.R. *Modern Architecture Since 1900.* Englewood Cliffs, New Jersey: Prentice-Hall, 1982.

De Witt, Dennis J., and Elizabeth R. De Witt. *Modern Architecture in Europe: A Guide to Buildings Since the Industrial Revolution.* New York: E.P. Dutton, 1987.

Drexler, Arthur. *Ludwig Mies van der Rohe.* New York: George Braziller, 1960.

Drexler, Arthur, and Thomas S. Hines. *The Architecture of Richard Neutra: From International Style to California Modern.* New York: The Museum of Modern Art, 1982.

Emanuel, Muriel, ed. *Contemporary Architects.* New York: St. Martin's Press, 1980.

Fleming, John, Hugh Honour, and Nikolaus Pevsner. *The Penguin Dictionary of Architecture.* 3rd ed. London: Penguin Books, 1980.

Fletcher, Sir Banister. *A History of Architecture.* London: The Royal Institute of British Architects and The University of London, 1987.

Frampton, Kenneth. *Modern Architecture: A Critical History.* London: Thames and Hudson, 1985.

Franck, Klaus. *The Works of Affonso Eduardo Reidy.* New York: Frederick A. Praeger, 1960.

Gage, Richard L. *A Guide to Japanese Architecture with an Appendix on Important Traditional Buildings.* Japan: Shinkenchiku-sha Company, 1971.

Giedeon, Sigfried, ed. *A Decade of New Architecture.* Zürich: Editions Girsberger, 1951.

Giedeon, Sigfried. *Architecture, You, and Me.* Cambridge, Massachusetts: The Harvard University Press, 1958.

Giedeon, Sigfried, ed. *CIAM, Les Congrès Internationaux d'Architecture Moderne: A Decade of New Architecture/Dix Ans d'Architecture Contemporaine.* Zürich and New York: Éditions Girsberger and George Wittenborn, 1951.

Giedeon, Sigfried. *Space, Time, and Architecture.* Cambridge, Massachusetts: The Harvard University Press, 1944.

———. *Walter Gropius: Work and Teamwork.* New York: Reinhold, 1954.

Gill, Brendan. *Many Masks: A Life of Frank Lloyd Wright.* New York: G.P. Putnam's Sons, 1987.

Goody, Joan E. *New Architecture in Boston.* Cambridge, Massachusetts: The MIT Press, 1965.

Gregotti, Vittorio, "Ernesto Rogers," *Casabella,* vol. 53, May 1989, pp. 2–3.

Gropius, Walter. *The New Architecture.* Cambridge, Massachusetts: The MIT Press, 1984.

———. *Scope of Total Architecture.* World Perspectives, vol. 3. New York: Harper & Brothers, 1955.

Gutheim, Frederick. *Alvar Aalto.* New York: George Braziller, 1960.

Gutheim, Frederick, ed. *Frank Lloyd Wright on Architecture: Selected Writings 1894–1940.* New York: Duell, Sloan, and Pearce, 1941.

Halprin, Lawrence. *The RSVP Cycles.* New York: George

Braziller, 1969.
Hammett, Ralph W. *Architecture in the United States: A Survey of Architectural Styles Since 1776.* New York: John Wiley and Sons, 1976.
Heyer, Paul. *Architects on Architecture: New Directions in America.* New York: Walker & Company, 1966.
Hitchcock, Henry-Russell. *Architecture: Nineteenth and Twentieth Centuries.* London: The Pelican History of Art, 1989.
———. *In the Nature of Materials: The Buildings of Frank Lloyd Wright 1887–1941.* New York: Duell, Sloan, and Pearce, 1942.
———. *Latin American Architecture Since 1945.* New York: The Museum of Modern Art, 1955.
Hitchcock, Henry-Russell, and Philip Johnson. *The International Style: Architecture Since 1922.* New York: W.W. Norton, 1932.
Hunt, William Dudley, Jr. *Encyclopedia of American Architecture.* New York: McGraw-Hill, 1980.
Isaacs, Reginald. *Gropius: An Illustrated Biography of the Creator of the Bauhaus.* Berlin: Gebr, Mann Verlag, 1983.
Jacobus, John M., Jr. *Philip Johnson.* Makers of Contemporary Architecture Series. New York: George Braziller, 1962.
Jacobus, John. *Twentieth-Century Architecture: The Middle Years, 1940–1965.* New York: Frederick A. Praeger, 1966.
Jencks, Charles. *Le Corbusier and the Tragic View of Architecture.* Cambridge, Massachusetts: The Harvard University Press, 1973.
———. *Modern Movements in Architecture.* New York: Viking Penguin, 1985.
Johnson, Philip C. *Architecture 1949–1965.* New York: Holt, Rinehart, and Winston, 1966.
———. *Mies van der Rohe.* 2nd rev. ed. New York: The Museum of Modern Art, 1953.
Jones, Cranston. *Architecture Today and Tomorrow.* New York: McGraw-Hill, 1961.
Jordan, Robert Fumeaux. *Le Corbusier.* New York: Lawrence Hill & Co., 1972.
Jordy, William H. *American Buildings and Their Architects: The Impact of European Modernism in the Mid-Twentieth Century.* Vol. 4. New York: Doubleday, 1972.
Kandinsky, Vasily. *Point and Line to Plane.* New York: Solomon R. Guggenheim Foundation, 1947.
Kaufmann, Edgar, Jr. *What Is Modern Design?* New York: The Museum of Modern Art, 1950.
Kaufmann, Edgar, Jr. and Ben Raeburn, eds. *Frank Lloyd Wright, Writings and Buildings.* New York: Horizon Press, 1960.
Kidder Smith, G.E. *Looking at Architecture.* New York: Harry N. Abrams, 1990.
———. *The New Architecture of Europe: An Illustrated Guidebook and Appraisal.* Cleveland: The World Publishing Company, 1961.
Kidder Smith, G.E., with The Museum of Modern Art. *The Architecture of the United States.* Vols. 1-3. New York: Anchor Press/Doubleday, 1981.
Kostof, Spiro. *A History of Architecture.* London: Oxford University Press, 1985.
Krantz, Les. *American Architects: A Survey of Award-Winning Contemporaries and Their Notable Works.* New York: Facts on File, 1989.
Lampugnani, Vittorio Magnago, ed. *Encyclopedia of Twentieth-Century Architecture.* New York: Harry N. Abrams, 1986.
Lao-tse. *The Wisdom of Laotse.* Trans., ed., and introduction by Lin Yutang. New York: Random House, The Modern Library, 1948.
Le Corbusier. *The Decorative Art of Today.* Trans. and introduction by James I. Dunnett. Cambridge, Massachusetts: The MIT Press, 1987.
———. *La Ville Radieuse.* Paris: Éditions de l'Architecture d'Aujourd'hui, 1933.
———. *Towards a New Architecture.* London: The Architectural Press, 1927.
Lloyd, Seton, David Talbot Rice, Norbert Lynton, Andrew Boyd, Andrew Carden, Philip Rawson, and John Jacobus. *World Architecture: An Illustrated History.* New York: McGraw-Hill, 1963.
Lummis, Trevor. *Listening to History.* London: Hutchinson Education, 1987.
Magalhaes, Aloisio, and Eugene Feldman. *Doorway to Brasília.* Philadelphia: Falcon Press, 1959.
Marks, Robert W. *The Dymaxion World of Buckminster Fuller.* New York: Reinhold, 1960.
Meehan, Patrick J., ed. *Truth Against the World: Frank Lloyd Wright Speaks for an Organic Architecture.* New York: John P. Wiley & Sons, 1987.
Morgan, Ann Lee, and Colin Naylor, eds. *Contemporary Architects.* 2nd ed. Chicago and London: St. James Press, 1987.
Moss, William. *An Oral History Program Manual.* New York: Frederick A. Praeger, 1974.
Mumford, Lewis. *The Culture of Our Cities.* New York: Harcourt, Brace, and Company, 1942.
Murphy, Wendy Buehur. *Frank Lloyd Wright.* Englewood Cliffs, New Jersey: Silver Burdett Press, 1990.
Neutra, Richard J. *Life and Human Habitat.* New York: George Wittenborn, 1956.
Oud, J.J.P. *Mein Weg in De Stijl.* The Hague and Rotterdam: Nijgh en Van Ditmar, 1958.

Papadaki, Stamo. *Oscar Niemeyer.* Masters of World Architecture Series. New York: George Braziller, 1960.
Pehnt, Wolfgang, ed. *Encyclopedia of Modern Architecture.* New York: Harry N. Abrams, 1964.
Peter, John. *Aluminum in Modern Architecture.* Vol. 1. Louisville: Reynolds Metals Company, 1956.
———. *Masters of Modern Architecture.* New York: George Braziller, 1958.
Pevsner, Nikolaus. *An Outline of European Architecture.* Middlesex, England: Penguin Books, 1972.
———. *Pioneers of Modern Design, from William Morris to Walter Gropius.* New York: Viking Penguin Books, 1986.
Pile, John, ed. *Drawings of Architectural Interiors.* New York: Whitney Library of Design, 1967.
Placzek, Adolf K., ed. in chief. *Macmillan Encyclopedia of Architects.* Vols. 1–4. New York: The Free Press/Macmillan, 1982.
Quantrill, Malcolm. *Alvar Aalto: A Critical Study.* New York: Schocken Books, 1983.
Robertson, Bryan. *Philip Johnson, Johnson House.* Global Architecture Series. Tokyo: A.D.A. Edita, Tokyo Co., 1972.
Roth, Alfred. *The New Architecture.* Erlenbach-Zürich: Les Éditions d'Architecture, 1946.
Saarinen, Aline B., ed. *Eero Saarinen on His Work.* New Haven and London: Yale University Press, 1962.
Saarinen, Eliel. *The City, Its Growth, Its Decay, Its Future.* New York: Reinhold, 1943.
Sanchis, Frank E. *American Architecture: Westchester County, New York—Colonial to Contemporary.* Croton-on-Hudson, New York: North River Press, 1977.
Sartoris, Alberto, "Joseph Marc Saugey o l'architettura ritrovata," *Domus,* no. 667, December 1985, p. 30.
Scully, Vincent, Jr. *Frank Lloyd Wright.* New York: George Braziller, 1960.
———. *Louis I. Kahn.* Makers of Contemporary Architecture Series. New York: George Braziller, 1962.
———. *Modern Architecture: The Architecture of Democracy.* New York: George Braziller, 1986.
Secrest, Meryle. *Frank Lloyd Wright: A Biography.* New York: Alfred A. Knopf, 1992.
Sert, José Luis. *Can Our Cities Survive?* Cambridge, Massachusetts: The Harvard University Press, 1942.
Sharp, Dennis. *Sources of Modern Architecture: A Critical Biography.* St. Albans and London, England: Granada Publishing Ltd./Technical Books Division, 1981.
Sharp, Dennis, ed. *The Illustrated Encyclopedia of Architects and Architecture.* London: Quarto Publishing, 1991.
———. *Twentieth-Century Architecture: A Visual History.* New York: Facts on File, 1991.
Stimpson, Miriam F. *A Field Guide to Landmarks of Modern Architecture in Europe.* Englewood Cliffs, New Jersey: Prentice-Hall, 1985.
Storrer, William Allin. *The Architecture of Frank Lloyd Wright: A Complete Catalog.* Cambridge, Massachusetts: The MIT Press, 1978.
———. *The Frank Lloyd Wright Companion.* Chicago: The University of Chicago Press, 1993.
Sullivan, Louis H. *Kindergarten Chats and Other Writings.* New York: Wittenborn, Schultz, 1947.
Tafel, Edgar. *Apprentice to Genius: Years with Frank Lloyd Wright.* New York: McGraw-Hill, 1979.
Tafuri, Manfredo, and Francesco Dal Co. *Modern Architecture.* History of World Architecture Series. Pier Luigi Nervi, gen. ed. New York: Harry N. Abrams, 1979.
Trevor, Dannatt, ed. *Architects Yearbook 5.* London: Elek Books Limited, 1953.
Venturi, Robert. *Complexity and Contradiction in Architecture.* New York: The Museum of Modern Art, 1966.
Venturi, Robert, Denise Scott Brown, and Steven Izenour. *Learning from Las Vegas.* Cambridge, Massachusetts: The MIT Press, 1977.
Watkins, David. *Morality and Architecture: The Development of a Theme in Architectural History and Theory from the Gothic Revival to the Modern Movement.* Oxford, England: Clarendon Press, 1977.
Wingler, Hans M. *The Bauhaus.* Cambridge, Massachusetts: The MIT Press, 1969.
Wiseman, Carter. *I.M. Pei: A Profile in American Architecture.* New York: Harry N. Abrams, 1990.
Wolfe, Gerard R. *New York: A Guide to the Metropolis—Walking Tours of Architecture and History.* New York: McGraw-Hill, 1975.
Wolfe, Tom. *From Bauhaus to Our House.* New York: Washington Square Press, 1981.
Wright, Frank Lloyd. *An Autobiography.* New York: Duell, Sloan, and Pearce, 1943.
———. *The Future of Architecture.* New York: Horizon Press, 1953.
———. *Genius and the Mobocracy.* New York: Duell, Sloan, and Pearce, 1949.
———. *The Living City.* New York: Horizon Press, 1958.
———. *The Natural House.* New York: Horizon Press, 1954.
Wright, Sylvia Hart. *Highlights of Recent American Architecture: A Guide to Contemporary Architects and Their Leading Works Completed 1945–1978.* Metuchen, New Jersey, and London: The Scarecrow Press, 1982.

Everson Museum of Art

Washington, D.C. 20041

Time Chart

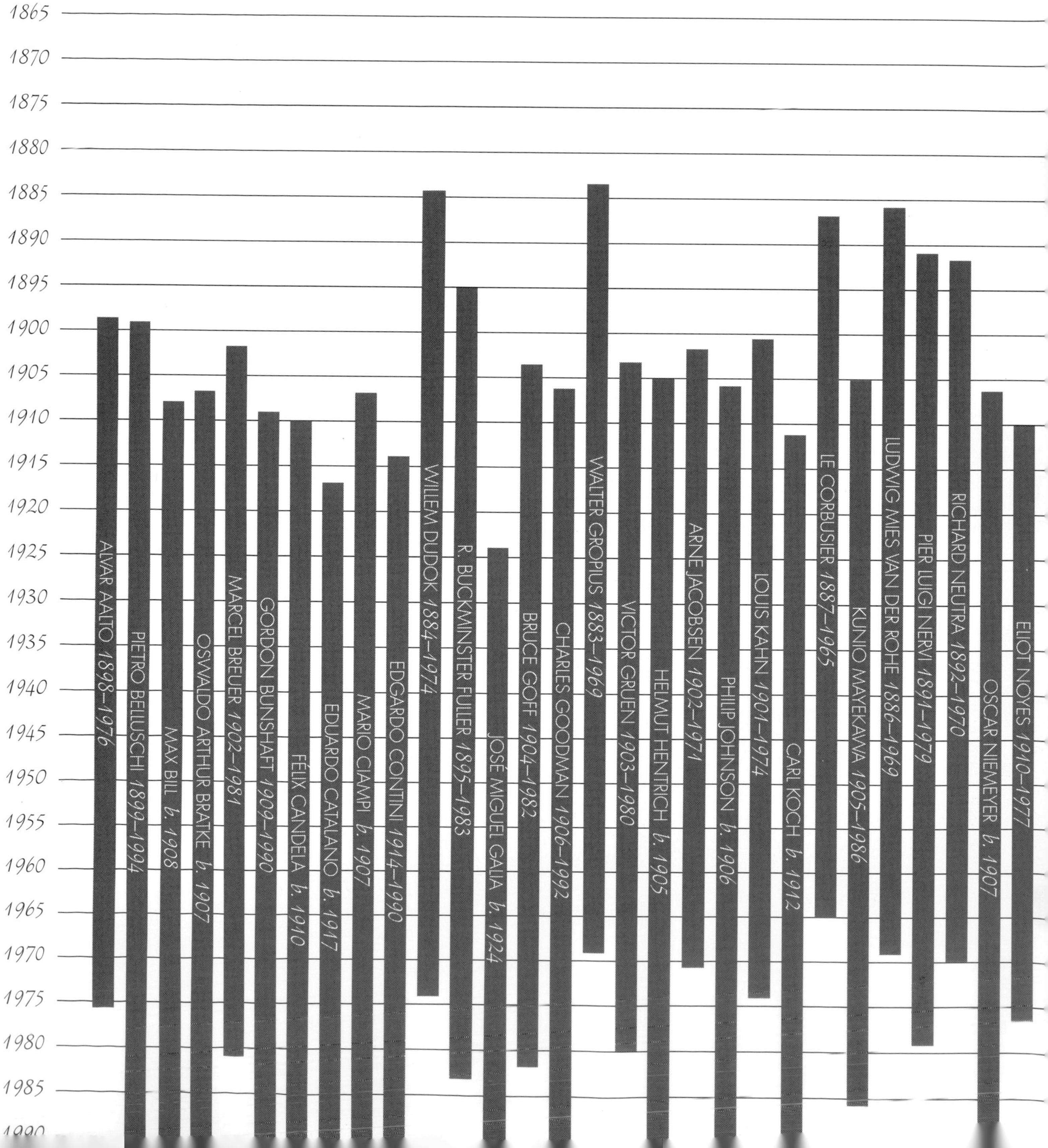

1865
1870
1875
1880
1885
1890
1895
1900
1905
1910
1915
1920
1925
1930
1935
1940
1945
1950
1955
1960
1965
1970
1975
1980
1985
1990
ALVAR AALTO 1898–1976
PIETRO BELLUSCHI 1899–1994
MAX BILL b. 1908
OSWALDO ARTHUR BRATKE b. 1907
MARCEL BREUER 1902–1981
GORDON BUNSHAFT 1909–1990
FÉLIX CANDELA b. 1910
EDUARDO CATALANO b. 1917
MARIO CIAMPI b. 1907
EDGARDO CONTINI 1914–1990
WILLEM DUDOK 1884–1974
R. BUCKMINSTER FULLER 1895–1983
JOSÉ MIGUEL GALIA b. 1924
BRUCE GOFF 1904–1982
CHARLES GOODMAN 1906–1992
WALTER GROPIUS 1883–1969
VICTOR GRUEN 1903–1980
HELMUT HENTRICH b. 1905
ARNE JACOBSEN 1902–1971
PHILIP JOHNSON b. 1906
LOUIS KAHN 1901–1974
CARL KOCH b. 1912
LE CORBUSIER 1887–1965
KUNIO MAYEKAWA 1905–1986
LUDWIG MIES VAN DER ROHE 1886–1969
PIER LUIGI NERVI 1891–1979
RICHARD NEUTRA 1892–1970
OSCAR NIEMEYER b. 1907
ELIOT NOYES 1910–1977

JUNZO YOSHIMURA b. 1908
MINORU YAMASAKI 1912–1986
WILLIAM WURSTER 1895–1973
FRANK LLOYD WRIGHT 1867–1959
PHILIP WILL JR. 1906–1985
PAUL WEIDLINGER b. 1914
CARLOS RAÚL VILLANUEVA 1900–1975
MARTÍN VEGAS b. 1926
KENZO TANGE b. 1913
EDWARD DURELL STONE 1902–1978
RUDOLF STEIGER 1900–1982
JOSÉ LUIS SERT 1902–1983
PAUL SCHWEIKHER b. 1903
MARC SAUGEY 1908–1971
TOMÁS SANABRIA b. 1922
MARIO SALVADORI b. 1907
EERO SAARINEN 1910–1961
PAUL RUDOLPH b. 1918
ALFRED ROTH b. 1903
ERNESTO ROGERS 1909–1969
MARCELO ROBERTO 1908–1964
AFFONSO EDUARDO-REIDY 1909–1964
ANTONIN RAYMOND 1888–1976
RALPH RAPSON b. 1914
L.L. RADO 1909–1993
GIO PONTI 1891–1979
ENRICO PERESSUTTI 1908–1973
I.M. PEI b. 1917
J.J.P. OUD 1890–1963
JUAN O'GORMAN 1905–1982

Koch:

600 Forbes Avenue, Pittsburgh, Pennsylvania 15282

Visitor's Guide

The way to appreciate a work of architecture is to experience it. As Frank Lloyd Wright warned me, "Architecture is what photography leaves out." Simply to view a great building is worth the trip. To walk through it is to enjoy the superb pleasure of interior space that architecture alone provides.

Arranged by architect, this list features more than one hundred fifty important buildings that may be visited. It includes only the work of the modern architects in this book, and only their work within the period covered in the book. Like the Oral History, it does not include the many outstanding Post-Modern architects or buildings.

Some of these buildings may be viewed only from the exterior, but a good number are open to the public. Many offer special tours. It is advisable to secure up-to-date information in advance.

Aalto:

Aalborg Art Museum (Nordjyllands Kunstmuseum)
Kong Christians Allé 50, DK 9000, Aalborg, Denmark
Baker House, Massachusetts Institute of Technology
362 Memorial Drive, Cambridge, Massachussetts 02139
House of Culture (Kulttuuritalo)
Sturenkatu 4, 00510 Helsinki, Finland
National Pensions Institute (Kansaneläkelaitos)
Nordenskoldinkatu 12, 00250 Helsinki, Finland
Säynätsalo Town Hall (Säynätsalon Kunnantalo)
40900 Säynätsalo, Finland

Belluschi:

Chapel, Portsmouth Abbey School
285 Cory's Lane, Portsmouth, Rhode Island 02871
First Presbyterian Church
216 South Third Street, Cottage Grove, Oregon 97424
Portland Art Museum
1219 South West Park Avenue, Portland, Oregon 97205
Unitarian Church
4848 Turner Street, Rockford, Illinois 61107

Bill:

School of Design (Fachhochschule Ulm, Fachberelch Gestaltung)
Prittwitzstrasse 10, W-7900 Ulm, Germany

Bratke:

Legislative Assembly (Assembleía Legislativa do Estado de São Paulo)
Palácio 9 de Julho, 04097-São Paulo-SP-Brazil
Town Hall (Prefeitura de Santo André)
Praça IV Centenário, s/no 09015-080 Santo André-SP-Brazil

Breuer:

Annunciation Priory
7520 University Drive, Bismarck, North Dakota 58504
Arts Center, Sarah Lawrence College
1 Meadway, Bronxville, New York 10708
Engineering Building, Yale University
15 Prospect Street, New Haven, Connecticut 06520
St. Francis de Sales Church
2929 McCracken Avenue, Muskegon, Michigan 49441
St. Johns University Church
Collegeville, Minnesota 56321
Whitney Museum of American Art
945 Madison Avenue, New York, New York 10021

Bunshaft (Skidmore, Owings, and Merrill):

Beinecke Rare Book and Manuscript Library, Yale University
121 Wall Street, New Haven, Connecticut 06520
Lever House
390 Park Avenue, New York, New York 10022
Manufacturers Hanover Trust Building
510 Fifth Avenue, New York, New York 10036

Candela:

Chapel at Lomas de Cuernavaca
Dead end of Paseo de la Reforma, Lomas de Cuernavaca, Temixco, Morelos, Mexico
Church of the Miraculous Virgin (Iglesia de la Virgen de la Medalla Milagrosa)
Ixcateopan y Matías Romero, Col. Vertiz Narvarte, Mexico, D.F.
Las Chalupas Restaurant
Jardines Flotantes, Xochimilco, Mexico, D.F.

Catalano:

Julius Adams Stratton Student Center, Massachusetts Institute of Technology
84 Massachusetts Avenue, Cambridge, Massachusetts 02139

Ciampi:

Corpus Christi Roman Catholic Church
62 Santa Rose Avenue, San Francisco, California 94112

Contini:

Midtown Plaza
Broad and Clinton Streets, Rochester, New York 14604

Dudok:

Town Hall
Dudokpark 1, 1217 JE Hilversum, the Netherlands

Fuller:

Geodesic Dome
Flushing Meadow, Corona Park, Flushing, New York 11368

Goff:

Boston Avenue United Methodist Church
1301 South Boston Avenue, Tulsa, Oklahoma 74119
Ford House
404 South Edgelawn, Aurora, Illinois 60506

Gropius:

Academic Quadrangle, Brandeis University
415 South Street, Waltham, Massachusetts 02254
Arts and Communications Building, Phillips Academy
Main Street, Andover, Massachusetts 01810
Bauhaus
Thälmannallee 38, 0-4500, Dessau, Germany
Gropius House (Society for the Preservation of New England Antiquities)
68 Baker Bridge Road, Lincoln, Massachusetts 01773
Pan American (Met Life) Building
200 Park Avenue, New York, New York 10166
Putterham Branch Library
959 West Roxbury Parkway, Brookline, Massachusetts 02167
Residential Complex, Children's Hospital
300 Longwood Avenue, Boston, Massachusetts 02115
United States Embassy
Queen Sofia Street, Athens, Greece

Gruen:

Northland Shopping Center
21500 North Western Highway, BC2, Southfield (Detroit), Michigan 48075
Southdale Shopping Center
6601 France Avenue South, Edina (Minneapolis), Minnesota 55435

Hentrich:

BASF Tower
Carl-Bosch-Strasse, W-6700 Ludwigshafen, Germany

Jacobsen:

Town Hall
Rødovre Parkvej 150, DK 2610 Rødovre, Denmark

Johnson:

Amon Carter Museum
3501 Camp Bowie Boulevard, Fort Worth, Texas 76107
Congregation Kneses Tifereth Israel Synagogue
1575 King Street, Port Chester, New York 10573
Kline Biology Tower, Yale University
219 Prospect Street, New Haven, Connecticut 06520
Kline Geology Tower, Yale University
210 Whitney Avenue, New Haven, Connecticut 06520
Lab of Epidemiology and Public Health, Yale University
60 College Street, New Haven, Connecticut 06520
Munson-Williams-Proctor Institute
310 Genesee Street, Utica, New York 13502
New York State Theater, Lincoln Center for the Performing Arts
20 Lincoln Center Plaza, New York, New York 10023
New Harmony Shrine
420 North Street, New Harmony, Indiana 47631
Sheldon Memorial Art Gallery, University of Nebraska
12th and R Streets, Lincoln, Nebraska 68588

Kahn:

Dining Hall and Library, Phillips Exeter Academy
Exeter, New Hampshire 03833
First Unitarian Church
220 Winton Road South, Rochester, New York 14610
Goddard Laboratories, University of Pennsylvania
Hamilton Walk at 37th Street, Philadelphia, Pennsylvania 19104
Jewish Community Center Bath House
999 Lower Ferry Road, Trenton, New Jersey 08628
Kimbell Art Museum
3333 Camp Bowie Boulevard, Fort Worth, Texas 76107
Richards Medical Research Building, University of Pennsylvania
Hamilton Walk at 37th Street, Philadelphia, Pennsylvania 19104
Salk Institute
10010 North Torrey Pines Road, La Jolla, California 92037
Yale Art Gallery, Yale University
1111 Chapel Street, New Haven, Connecticut 06520
Yale Center for British Art, Yale University
1080 Chapel Street, New Haven, Connecticut 06520

32 Atlantic Avenue, Boston, Massachusetts 02110

Public Library

610 Main Street, Fitchburg, Massachusetts 01420

Wellesley Free Library

530 Washington Street, Wellesley, Massachusetts 02181

Le Corbusier:

Carpenter Center for the Visual Arts, Harvard University

24 Quincy Street, Cambridge, Massachusetts 02138

High Court Building

Capitol Complex, Uttar Marg (Sector 1), Chandigarh, India

Le Couvent Sainte-Marie-de-la-Tourette

Eveux-sur-l'Arbresle, 69210 (Rhône), France

Notre-Dame-du-Haut

70250 Ronchamp (Haute-Saône), France

Swiss Pavilion, University City (Pavillon Suisse, Cité Universitaire)

7, boulevard Jourdan, 75014 Paris, France

Unité d'Habitation

280, boulevard Michelet, 13000 Marseilles (Bouches-du-Rhône), France

Villa Savoye

82, avenue Blanche de Castille, Beauregard, 78300 Poissy, France

Mayekawa:

Kanagawa Prefectural Concert Hall and Public Library

9–2, Koyogaoka, Nishi-ku, Yokohama-shi, Kanagawa-ken, Japan

Tokyo Cultural Hall

5–45, Ueno Koen, Taito-ku, Tokyo, Japan

Mies van der Rohe:

860–880 Lake Shore Drive Apartments

860–880 Lake Shore Drive, Chicago, Illinois 60611

Federal Center

South Dearborn between Jackson Boulevard and Adams Street, Chicago, Illinois

Highfield House

4000 North Charles Street, Baltimore, Maryland 21218

S.R. Crown Hall, Perlstein Hall, Robert F. Carr Memorial Chapel of St. Savior, Main Campus, Illinois Institute of Technology

33rd and State Streets, Chicago, Illinois 60616

Lafayette Park

Lafayette Avenue between Rivard and Orleans Streets, Detroit, Michigan

Mellon Hall Science Center, Duquesne University

Altes Museum, Bodestrasse 1-3, 0-1020, Berlin, Germany

Seagram Building

375 Park Avenue, New York, New York 10152

Tugendhat House

Černopolnf 45, 613 00 Brno, Czech Republic

Nervi:

Exhibition Hall (Palazzo delle Espozioni)

Corso Massimo D'Azeglio, Turin, Italy

Sports Palace (Palazzetto dello Sport)

Quartiere E.U.R., via C. Columbo, Rome, Italy

Neutra:

Community Church

12141 Lewis Street, Garden Grove, California 92640

Corona Avenue Elementary School

3825 Bell Avenue, Los Angeles, California 90001

Niemeyer:

Brasília Cathedral

Eixo Monumental, 70000-Brasília DF-Brazil

Church of St. Francis of Assisi (Igreja de São Francisco de Assis)

Pampulha, 30000 Belo Horizonte-MG-Brazil

Plaza of Three Powers (Praca dos Três Poderes)

Congresso Nacional, 70000-Brasília DF-Brazil

O'Gorman:

National Library, University of Mexico

Ciudad Universitana, Delegación, Coyoacán, Mexico, D.F. 04510

Oud:

Row Houses

2e Scheepvaartstraat, Hook of Holland, the Netherlands

Pei:

Cecil and Ida Green Building, Massachusetts Institute of Technology

21 Ames Street, Cambridge, Massachusetts 02139

Chancellory for United States Embassy

Abadie Santos, 808 Montevideo, Uruguay

Denver Hilton Hotel

7801 East Orchard Road, Englewood, Colorado 80111

East-West Center, University of Hawaii

Manoa Campus, 2444 Dole Street, Honolulu, Hawaii 96822

H. Leslie Hoffman Hall, University of Southern California
701 Exposition Boulevard, Los Angeles, California 90089
National Center for Atmospheric Research
1850 Table Mesa Drive, Boulder, Colorado 80303
Roosevelt Field Shopping Center
Old Country Road, Meadowbrook Parkway, Garden City, New York 11530
S.I. Newhouse School of Public Communications, Syracuse University
215 University Place, Syracuse, New York 13244
University Plaza, New York University
100 and 110 Bleecker Street, New York, New York 10012
505 West Broadway (Mitchell-Lama Apartments), New York, New York 10012

Ponti:

Pirelli Tower
Piazza Duca D'Austa, Milan, Italy

Rapson:

Tyrone Guthrie Theater
725 Vineland Place, Minneapolis, Minnesota
United States Embassy
Dag Hammarskjölds Allé 24, DK 2100, Copenhagen Ø, Denmark
United States Embassy Office Building
Stockholm, Sweden

Rudolph:

Art and Architecture Building, Yale University
180 York Street, New Haven, Connecticut 06520
Jewett Arts Center, Wellesley College
106 Central Street, Wellesley, Massachusetts 02181
Married Students Housing, Yale University
292–311 Mansfield Street, New Haven, Connecticut 06520
Southeastern Massachusetts University
Old Westport Road, North Dartmouth, Massachusetts 02747

Saarinen

CBS Building
51 West 52nd Street, New York, New York 10019
Chapel, Massachusetts Institute of Technology
48 Massachusetts Avenue, Cambridge, Massachusetts 02139
Concordia Theological Seminary
6600 North Clinton Street, Fort Wayne, Indiana 46825
Dulles International Airport
73 Sachem Street, New Haven, Connecticut 06520
Jefferson National Expansion Memorial
Information available from National Park Service, Jefferson National Expansion Memorial, 11 North 4th Street, St. Louis, Missouri 63102
John Deere and Company Administrative Center
John Deere Road, Moline, Illinois 61265
Kresge Auditorium, Massachusetts Institute of Technology
48 Massachusetts Avenue, Cambridge, Massachusetts 02139
Milwaukee County War Memorial Center
750 North Lincoln Memorial Drive, Milwaukee, Wisconsin 53202
Stiles and Morse Colleges, Yale University
302–304 York Street, New Haven, Connecticut 06520
Thomas J. Watson IBM Research Center
Route 134 East, Yorktown, New York 10598
TWA Terminal, Kennedy International Airport
Building 60, Jamaica, New York 11430
United States Embassy
24 Grosvenor Square, W1A 1AE, London, England
United States Embassy
Drammensveien 18, 0255 Oslo, Norway
Yale Cooperative Building, Yale University
66 Broadway, New Haven, Connecticut 06520

Schweikher:

Fine Arts Center, Maryville College
502 E. Lamar Alexander Parkway, Maryville, Tenne
First Methodist Church
404 Second Street, Plainfield, Iowa 50666

Sert:

Fondation Maeght
06570 St.-Paul-de-Vence, France
Holyoke Center, Harvard Universit
1350 Massachusetts Avenue, C
02138
Martin Luther King Elemen
100 Putnam Avenue
New England Gas
130 Austin Stre
Schools of
765 Co

Stone:

The Museum of Modern Art
11 West 53rd Street, New York, New York 10019
State Legislative Building
16 West Jones Street, Raleigh, North Carolina 27603
Stuhr Museum of the Prairie Pioneer
3133 West Highway 34, Grand Island, Nebraska 68801
United States Embassy
Shantipath, Chanaryapuri, New Delhi, India 110021

Tange:

Hiroshima Peace Museum
1–2 Nakajimacho, Naka-ku, Hiroshima, Japan 733

Wright:

Annie Pfeiffer Chapel, Esplanades, Ordway Building, Polk County Science Building, and Roux Library, Florida Southern College
111 Lake Hollingsworth Drive, Lakeland, Florida 33801
Annunciation Greek Orthodox Church
9400 West Congress Street, Milwaukee, Wisconsin 53225
Barnsdall "Hollyhock" House
…00 Hollywood Boulevard, Los Angeles, California 90027
… Synagogue
…k Road, Elkins Park, Pennsylvania 19117
…se
…venue, Springfield, Illinois 62703

… Los Angeles, California 90027

…r Run, Pennsylvania 15464

… 60302

Rosenbaum House
601 Riverview Drive, Florence, Alabama 35630
Robie House
University of Chicago, 5757 Woodlawn Avenue, Chicago, Illinois 60637
Solomon R. Guggenheim Museum
1071 Fifth Avenue, New York, New York 10128
Taliesin West
Cactus Road and 108th Street, Scottsdale, Arizona 85261
Unity Temple
875 Lake Street, Oak Park, Illinois 60301

Yamasaki:

Lambert Airport
10701 Lambert International Boulevard, St. Louis, Missouri 63145
McGregor Memorial Community Conference Center, Wayne State University
495 West Ferry Mall, Detroit, Michigan 48202

Yoshimura:

International House of Japan
11–16, Roppongi 5-chome, Minato-ku, Tokyo, Japan

Acknowledgments

Special thanks are due to Patricia Del Grosso, Curator of The Oral History of Modern Architecture project, Rachel Paul, Edward Hamilton, Robert Riley, The Ford Foundation, Reynolds Metals Company, and The Graham Foundation.

I am indebted to the team at Abrams: Paul Gottlieb, Publisher; in far more than the usual sense to my insightful editor, Diana Murphy; to Bob McKee, who created the design of the book and accompanying CD; Sam Antupit, Director, Art and Design; Barbara Lyons, Director, Rights and Reproductions; and Gertrud Brehme, Production Manager.

I would also like to acknowledge the valued help and expertise of Paul Goodrich, digital editor and engineer, Carolyn Fabricant, Sidney Liebowitz, William Murphy, Louis Muller, Patricia Goldstein, Meg Wormley, Stephanie Jackson, Neil Perlman, Paul Weidlinger; Jacques Barsac and Christian Archambeau of Ciné Service Technique, Paris; Fondation Le Corbusier, Paris; Mary Daniels of the Harvard University Graduate School of Design, Cambridge, Massachusetts; Marie-Josiane Rouchon, Institut National de l'Audio Visuel, Paris; Trevor Lummis and the Oral History Association; The Museum of Modern Art, New York City; The New York Public Library, New York City; the library of the American Institute of Architects, Washington, D.C.; The Art Institute of Chicago; Bodleian Library, Oxford University, England; Bibliothèque Nationale, Paris.

Finally, I would like to express my gratitude to the architects and engineers, many of them friends, without whose help, patience, and encouragement The Oral History of Modern Architecture would not exist: Alvar Aalto, Pietro Belluschi, Max Bill, Oswaldo Bratke, Marcel Breuer, Gordon Bunshaft, Félix Candela, Eduardo Catalano, Mario Ciampi, Edgardo Contini, Willem Dudok, Buckminster Fuller, José Miguel Galia, Bruce Goff, Charles Goodman, Walter Gropius, Victor Gruen, Helmut Hentrich, Arne Jacobsen, Philip Johnson, Louis Kahn, Carl Koch, Le Corbusier, Kunio Mayekawa, Ludwig Mies van der Rohe, Pier Luigi Nervi, Richard Neutra, Oscar Niemeyer, Eliot Noyes, Juan O'Gorman, J.J.P. Oud, I.M.Pei, Enrico Peressutti, Gio Ponti, L.L. Rado, Ralph Rapson, Antonin Raymond, Affonso Reidy, Marcelo Roberto, Ernesto Rogers, Alfred Roth, Paul Rudolph, Eero Saarinen, Mario Salvadori, Tomás Sanabria, Marc Saugey, Paul Schwiekher, José Luis Sert, Rudolf Steiger, Edward Durell Stone, Kenzo Tange, Martín Vegas, Carlos Villanueva, Paul Weidlinger, Philip Will Jr., Frank Lloyd Wright, William Wurster, Minoru Yamasaki, and Junzo Yoshimura.

Credits

b = bottom, c = center, l = left, r = right, t = top

Wayne Andrews, p. 123 r; Wayne Andrews, © ESTO, p. 93; The Architects' Collaborative, p. 177; Architectural Publishers Artemis Source, reproduced from p. 164, Kenneth Frampton, *Modern Architecture, A Critical History*, Thames and Hudson, London, 1980, p. 159; *Architectural Review*, p. 55; courtesy The Art Institute of Chicago, p. 98 c; Arteaga Photos, p. 200 t; Bauhaus Archive, p. 189; reproduced from p. 171, Willy Boesiger, *Le Corbusier, Oeuvre Complète, 1938–1946*, Les Éditions d'Architecture, Erlenbach-Zürich, Switzerland, 1946, p. 147; courtesy Oswaldo Bratke, pp. 46 bl, 47 t; Buffalo and Erie County Historical Society, p. 117 r; courtesy Félix Candela, pp. 74, 75 t; collection Centre Canadien d'Architecture/Canadian Centre for Architecture, Montreal, pp. 51, 115, 141t, 184, 226 t, 254; Chicago Architectural Photographing Company, p. 133; The Chicago Historical Society, p. 36 b; Condit Studio, p. 40l; George Cserna Photographer, courtesy Pei Cobb Freed and Partners, p. 261; C. A. Dehl, p. 24; Dell and Wainwright Photographers, courtesy *Architectural Review*, p. 190; © John Ebstel, pp. 215, 216; Erben Photographer, courtesy Harvard University, p. 247; Fondation Maeght, p. 259; reproduced from p. 159, Kenneth Frampton, *Modern Architecture, A Critical History*, Thames and Hudson, London, 1980, p. 143 t; Lionel Freedman, p. 220; Marcel Gautherot, p. 241; Marcel Gautherot Photographer, reproduced from p. 130, John Peter, *Masters of Modern Architecture*, Bonanza Books, New York, 1958, p. 245; Marcel Gautherot Photographer, reproduced from illus. 132, Stamo Papadaki, *Oscar Niemeyer*, Masters of World Architecture Series, George Braziller, Inc., New York, 1960, p. 242 t; Alexandre Georges, p. 225; Helga Schmidt Glassner, p. 142 bl; courtesy Gruen Associates, p. 79; courtesy Harvard University, pp. 149, 185, 252, 253, 255, 258 b; Robert D. Harvey Studio, Otto Hassenberg, p. 180; Hedrich-Blessing, pp. 82–83, 86, 89, 90 t, 91, 170; Hedrich-Blessing Photographers, courtesy Lohan Associates, Chicago, pp. 88, 90 b,

duced from p. 202, Dennis Sharp, *A Visual History of Twentieth-Century Architecture*, New York Graphic Society, Ltd./William Heinemann, Ltd., 1972, p. 38; Chuji Hirayama Photographer, reproduced from p. 178, illus. 7.17, David B. Stewart, *The Making of A Modern Japanese Architecture, 1868 to the Present*, Kodan-sha, Ltd., Japan, 1987, p. 32 lt; David Hirsch, pp. 161, 272–73; courtesy HPP, Hentrich-Petschnigg and Partner KG, p. 75 r; Ingervo Photographer, courtesy The Museum of Finnish Architecture, pp. 44–45, 46 c; reproduced from p. 249, Reginald Isaacs, *Walter Gropius, An Illustrated Biography of the Creator of the Bauhaus*, Bulfinch Press, Little, Brown and Co., Boston, 1983, p. 181; courtesy Johnson Wax, pp. 123 b, 124; © Clemens Kalischer, p. 37; Phokion Karas Photographer, courtesy Harvard University, p. 256; Phokion Karas Photographer, courtesy Sert, Jackson and Associates, p. 257; G.E. Kidder Smith, pp.54 t, 81, 84, 85, 150, 213, 237; G.E. Kidder Smith Photographer, courtesy SANDAK, An Imprint of Macmillan Publishing Company, p. 58, 92 t; Kolmio Photographer, courtesy The Museum of Finnish Architecture, pp. 3, 68 t; Balthazar Korab, pp. 71, 155, 172, 173, 198, 200 b, 210; F.S. Lincoln Photographer, reproduced from illus. 57, Stamo Papadaki, *Oscar Niemeyer*, Masters of World Architecture Series, George Braziller, Inc., New York, 1960, p. 239; Massachusetts Institute of Technology Historical Collections, p. 107; © Rollie McKenna, pp. 22–23, 34, 36 t, 52 t, 95; courtesy Metlife Archives, p. 54 b; Joseph Molitor Photographer, courtesy Pei Cobb Freed and Partners, p. 265; Munson-Williams-Proctor Institute, p. 230; The Museum of Modern Art, pp. 4–5, 28, 62, 166, 182; Oscar Niemeyer, reproduced from p. 46, Claudius Coulin, *Drawings by Architects, from the Ninth Century to the Present Day*, Reinhold Publishing, New York, 1962, p. 238 t; reproduced from illus. 113, Stamo Papadaki, *Oscar Niemeyer*, Masters of World Architecture Series, George Braziller, Inc., New York, 1960, p. 242 b; Rondal Partridge, p. 68 b; courtesy Pei Cobb Freed and Partners, p. 267 b and t; Pei Cobb Freed and Partners Source, reproduced from p. 60, Carter Wiseman, *I.M. Pei: A Profile in American Architecture*, Harry N. Abrams, Inc., New York, 1990, p. 271; John Peter, pp. 2 bl, br, and l, 3 br and c, 27, 29, 33, 35, 40 t, 42 l, 49, 52 l, 53 r, 63, 66, 67 r, 73, 76, 78, 87 r, 98 l, 101, 106, 157, 178, 197, 214, 229, 243, 244, 248, 263; Roy E. Petersen Photographer, reproduced from p.95, Frank Lloyd Wright, *The Living City*, Horizon Press, New York, 1958, p. 53 c; courtesy Philadelphia City Planning Commission, p. 266; courtesy Pirelli Company, p. 47 r; Louis Reens Photographer, courtesy The Architects' Collaborative, p. 191; Louis Reens Photographer, courtesy Weidlinger Associates, p. 258 t; Steve Rosenthal, p. 269; courtesy Alfred Roth, pp. 56, 57; Jan C. Rowan, p. 70; reproduced from Imprint of Macmillan Publishing Company, p. 196; courtesy Skidmore, Owings, and Merrill, p. 30; Ezra Stoller, © ESTO, pp. 26, 42 t, 43, 72, 100 t, 167, 175, 193, 194, 204, 205, 206, 226 b, 231, 232, 234, 264; © William Allin Storrer, pp. 112, 116, 117 t, 121, 122, 128; Struwing, p. 102; Masami Tanigawa Photographer, courtesy William Allin Storrer, p. 126 t; Marvin Trachtenberg, pp. 60–61, 64, 87 b, 146; courtesy United States Embassy, Brazil, p. 94; University of Pennsylvania, Louis I. Kahn Collection, Architectural Archives of the University of Pennsylvania, Gift of Richard Saul Wurman, pp. 222, 223; University of Pennsylvania and Pennsylvania Historical and Museum Commission, Louis I. Kahn Collection, pp. 219, 221; Tony Vaccaro, pp. 3 r, 118–19, 139; courtesy Weidlinger Associates, p. 67 b; courtesy The Frank Lloyd Wright Archives, The Frank Lloyd Wright Foundation, pp. 97 b, © 1957, 126 b, © 1957, 127, © 1958, 130.

Berlage quotation on p. 159 is taken from Sergio Polano, *Hendrik Petrus Berlage, Complete Works*, New York, Rizzoli, 1988, p. 98. Lao-tse quotation on p. 120 is taken from Lao-tse, *The Wisdom of Laotse*, trans., ed., and introduction by Lin Yutang, New York, Random House, The Modern Library, 1948, p. 87. Le Corbusier quotation on p. 106 is taken from Le Corbusier, *Towards a New Architecture*, London, The Architectural Press, 1946, p. 210. Loos quotation on p. 94 is taken from Benedetto Gravagnuolo, *Adolf Loos*, New York, Rizzoli, 1982, p. 20. Maillart quotation on p. 30 is taken from Max Bill, *Robert Maillart*, Verlag für Architektur A.G., Erlenbach-Zürich, 1949, p. 15. Mies van der Rohe quotation on p. 181 is taken from Hans M. Wingler, *The Bauhaus*, Cambridge, Massachusetts, The MIT Press, 1969, p. vii. Sullivan quotation on p. 125 is taken from Louis Sullivan, *Autobiography of an Idea*, New York, Dover Publications, Inc., 1956, pp. 257–58. Venturi quotation on p. 274 is taken from Robert Venturi, *Complexity and Contradiction in Architecture*, The Museum of Modern Art Papers on Architecture, New York, The Museum of Modern Art, 1966, p. 22. Viollet-le-Duc quotation on p. 109 is taken from Eugène-Emanuel Viollet-le-Duc, *Lectures on Architecture*, London, Sampson, Low, Marston, Searle, and Rivington, 1877, p. 283. Wagner quotation on p. 93 is taken from Frank Borsi and Ezio Godoli, *Vienna 1900: Architecture and Design*, New York, Rizzoli, 1986, p. 160.

Numbers in *italics* refer to pages bearing illustrations.